Continental Britons
German-Jewish Refugees from Nazi Germany

MARION BERGHAHN

Continental Britons
German-Jewish Refugees from
Nazi Germany

BERG
Oxford / Hamburg / New York
Distributed exclusively in the US and Canada by
St. Martin's Press, New York

Berg Publishers Limited
Market House, Deddington, Oxford OX5 4SW, UK
175 Fifth Avenue/Room 400, New York, NY 10010, USA
Schenefelder Landstr. 14K, 2000 Hamburg 55, FRG

First published by the Macmillan Press Ltd 1984
This edition published by Berg Publishers Limited 1988
© Marion Berghahn 1984, 1988

All rights reserved.
No part of this publication may be reproduced in any form or by any means
without the written permission of Berg Publishers Limited

British Library Cataloguing in Publication Data

Berghahn, Marion
　Continental Britons: German-Jewish
　refugees from Nazi Germany. —— 2nd ed.
　1. Refugees, Jewish —— Great Britain
　2. Jews —— Great Britain —— Social conditions
　I. Title　　II. Berghahn, Marion. German-
　Jewish refugees in England
　305.6'96'041　　DS135.E5

ISBN 0-85496-212-3

Library of Congress CIP Data applied for

Printed in Great Britain by Billings of Worcester

To Barbara, Harry and Volker
with affection and gratitude

Contents

	Acknowledgements	ix
	Introduction	1
1	Concepts of Assimilation and Ethnic Identity	9
2	The Process of Jewish Assimilation in Germany	21
	The Debate on German–Jewish Assimilation	22
	Towards a Re-Definition of German–Jewish Ethnic Identity	30
3	Life Under the Threat of Nazism	47
	The Crisis of the German–Jewish Identity	47
	A Period of Re-Orientation	50
	The Significance of the Eastern European Jewish Immigrants	53
	Aspects of Jewish–Gentile Relationships in the 1930s	57
	Effects of the Nazi Policies on the German–Jewish Community	71
4	Emigration	75
	Academics	77
	The Medical Profession	83
	The Legal Profession	87
	Artists	92
	Business People	106
	November 1938	113
5	Search for New Roots	121
	The Burden of the Past	121
	German–Jewish Institutions	150

6	The Ambiguities of Ethnic Identification	173
	England – a New Haven?	173
	Germany – a Winter's Tale	189
7	'Continental' Britons	216
	Problems of Identity	216
	Elements of 'Continental' Ethnicity	223
	Encounters with Anglo-Jewry	231
	The Third Generation	234
	Conclusions	250
	Notes	254
	Bibliography	274
	Index	290

Acknowledgments

I wish to express my gratitude to all my respondents and to the representatives of various refugee organizations who kindly offered information and assistance. Without their willingness to collaborate, I would have been unable to carry out my research. Special thanks are due to Ruth and Francis Carsten for their generous hospitality and friendship during my extended visits to London. I am particularly indebted to Margaret Stacey, who guided this study through its various stages, for her never-failing support and most helpful suggestions. I would like to thank Lionel Kochan for his comments on several chapters and the staff of the Wiener Library for their friendly and competent assistance. My thanks are also due to the Social Science Research Council which provided the financial support for my study. Special feelings of gratitude go to Tami and Jay Winter, Barbara and Harry Weinberger for their friendship; always prepared to listen patiently and comment on my research, they offered invaluable moral and practical support. Finally, my warmest thanks are due to my husband, Volker Berghahn, for his constructive criticism and continual encouragement.

M.B.

Introduction

This study is concerned with the experience of German and Austrian Jews who came to Britain as refugees from Nazism. This means that at the most general level it involves the study of forms of group contact between ethnic minorities and the majority society. Compared with North America, where this type of research has proliferated for several decades, relatively little work of a substantial kind has been done in this field in this country. This would certainly appear to be true of work on Jews from Central Europe who settled in Britain.[1] The apparent lack of interest in this group seems amazing in view of the economic, cultural and academic impact which the German–Jewish refugees have had on British society. Evidently, here lies a wide field of research still open for historical and sociological exploration. This study can merely scratch the surface, although an attempt will be made to raise a number of more fundamental questions.

These latter theoretical and conceptual problems which a study of ethnicity and assimilation involves are discussed in the first chapter. In the second chapter the general notion of German–Jewish assimilation will be examined in greater detail. Of course, this notion developed into one of the crucial concepts of German–Jewish history at large. But we shall see that many of the underlying assumptions of the debate may require reconsideration in the light of recent sociological and anthropological data. The empirical material will be presented in the subsequent chapters and discussed in the context of the theoretical framework previously elaborated. The material is ordered in a chronological way, i.e. it is basically structured so that we can follow the refugees through the various phases of their life in Germany, departure and re-settlement in Britain. Yet this chronological principle has not strictly been adhered to. A thematic approach will be adopted when this seems more helpful to gaining a better understanding of certain situations and behaviour patterns.

The fieldwork for this study and consequently the evaluation of the collected material presented a number of difficulties. Given the fact that Jews are not officially registered as such in Britain, any hope of obtaining a representative sample had to be abandoned from the start. I had to rely instead on the 'snowball system' in order to find respondents. This meant building up a list of interviewees through some initial contacts leading to an ever widening circle of potential respondents. I approached official bodies, such as the Association of Jewish Refugees from Germany and Austria and various other communal organizations, such as Synagogues and the Leo Baeck Lodge. Through personal contacts, I was also able to reach refugees not involved in German–Jewish group life.

The 'snowball system' proved to be highly successful: within a short time many more refugees responded than could be interviewed in the end. But this was fortunate insofar as it offered me the opportunity to select respondents to some degree according to certain principles. One of my concerns was to achieve a fairly even distribution among members of the older and younger generations. Moreover, I was able to contact representatives from various walks of life, though not from different classes, for German Jews overwhelmingly belong to the middle class. I deliberately neglected academics, although some have been included, since they tend to be over-represented in general studies of Jewish life and history, and I was concerned also to interview people whom one would probably never hear of as prominent individuals.

I would like to stress, however, that sociological representativeness was not my main concern. Apart from the fact that this would have been impossible to achieve under circumstances which did not allow me to set up a random sample, it never was my intention to present a generalized picture of German Jews in this country. My research interest focused on the ethnic group itself: the aim was to explore attitudes and feelings of those who still identify with this community, but to stress diversity at least as much as typicality. Statistical evaluation of the data has therefore been undertaken only occasionally. Like Ferdynand Zweig, 'I often neglected the average for the individual, stressing the point that average behaviour does not exist, as the average man does not exist. But the understanding of an individual caught up in a specific situation is often the key to the better understanding of the generic.'[2]

More importantly, a number of social scientists have expressed serious doubts not only as to the desirability but also as to the possibility of achieving absolute scientific reliability in the social 'sciences'. Indeed, other sciences have not escaped similar scepticism. Even natural scientists have admitted 'that there is no "scientific method", and that what is called by that name can be outlined for only quite simple problems'.[3] The personal involvement of the researcher of whatever science he or she is pursuing makes it impossible to control 'all the factors under investigation'.[4]

The foregoing reflections had an important bearing on the methods chosen for the present investigation. Although I attempted to proceed with the fieldwork in a systematic way, I avoided methodological rigidity. Rather a flexible approach was adopted in order to gain an insight into German–Jewish attitudes from various angles. Important information was gleaned from memoirs,[5] fiction and publications of various German–Jewish organizations, apart from the relevant secondary literature. Yet the open-ended interview formed the major tool, supplemented by less formal conversations with a wider circle of respondents. Included here are also 'group sessions' which some respondents arranged in order to allow me to discuss some of my questions with a larger number of people. All in all about 250 people were approached. About 180 of these were interviewed in the stricter sense. These respondents were divided into three main categories: representing the first (80 respondents), second (68 respondents) and third (32 respondents) generation. As first generation were considered those who were born up to 1920, as second generation those born between 1920 and 1945 and third generation those born after the war. The main consideration in establishing these categories was the stage within the life cycle the respondents had reached at the time of emigration. It was assumed that it would make a significant difference to the attitudes of individuals whether they had left Germany and settled in Britain as an adult or as a child or whether they were born in Britain after the war and brought up in a changed political climate and within a primarily British environment.

As mentioned above, the interviews were informal: they were not based on firmly structured questionnaires. Instead, a catalogue of questions was used as a guideline to give the conversations some direction. However, interviews often took on the form of dialogues during which the respondents and I jointly explored the questions I was interested in (and as it turned out so were the respondents themselves). The areas covered were not the same in all cases. They varied according to respondents' life histories, to the locality where the interview was conducted and to the time available. Moreover, tact sometimes demanded that certain questions should be dropped when it became apparent that they would be too upsetting for the respondent.

The interviews lasted two to three hours on average, ranging from about one hour to about five hours. In a few cases they stretched over several days. Often they blended into what constituted the second major tool of study, that of participant observation. This meant taking part in various social activities. In fact, my 'participation' became so intense finally that I stopped 'observing'. That was the signal for me to end the empirical part of this study and to begin with the evaluation of the collected material.

It has already been pointed out that field workers inevitably become personally involved in the studies they are undertaking. Being in constant and often close contact with the individuals of one's group, it is only natural that the researcher steps out of his or her role as the objective observer and subjectively responds to the individuals with whom she or he interacts. This was even more true in my particular case in which a non-Jewish German met German Jews to discuss their attitudes towards Germany with them. Such a situation was bound to create complicated emotions on both sides which have no doubt influenced this study. And since most respondents were just as curious about my motives as I was about their feelings, it is perhaps not inappropriate to end this introduction on a more personal note.

I would like to stress that it was *not* guilt feelings and an attempt at *Vergangenheitsbewältigung*, as a number of individuals interested in my research have argued, rather it was a purely scholarly interest which had originally motivated me to undertake this study. To be sure, I was well aware of recent German history; there had been numerous intensive and upsetting discussions among my contemporaries at school and university, as we tried to come to terms with the past of a society into which we happened to be born. Yet, growing up in post-war Germany meant having hardly any personal contact with Jews. Our parents and grandparents, for obvious reasons, were unable or unwilling to discuss these matters with us openly. The issue of the persecution of the Jews under the Nazis therefore remained a disturbing, yet primarily 'theoretical' problem. This relative detachment probably explains why, when starting out, I held the naïve belief that in spite of what had happened in the past, this would neither interfere with my objectivity nor significantly hamper my efforts to establish contacts with 'my community'.

However, I quickly realized that the past was still fully alive in the victims of the Nazi period, that nothing was forgotten or forgiven. And I, as a German, well-meaning as I may have been, could not place myself outside history. Whether I wished to or not, I was identified with Germany, although most respondents clearly distinguished between the pre- and post-war generations. Nevertheless, I could not dissociate myself from German society as a whole; I began to feel some kind of moral responsibility for that past. It was an uncomfortable discovery; it hurt when people flatly refused to talk to me because of my German background or made inquiries, as I learnt afterwards, about my person. Yet I soon learned not to take these expressions of hostility personally, particularly not, after it had dawned on me that being judged, even condemned, on these impersonal grounds reflects a common experience of many Jews, or of members of other minorities for that matter.

Even so, I was unable to suppress a certain rebelliousness at times when confronted with a hatred of Germany which knew no bounds, understandable psychologically as it may have been. My own critical attitude towards German society and especially the older generation notwithstanding, I was appalled by the sweeping generalizations about 'the Germans'. As a result, my own previously harsh criticism of the older Germans softened, and I began to take a more differentiated view of German society in the 1930s, which is confirmed by recent historical research.

However, on a different level all this hatred and bitterness did affect me deeply, as did the sadness pervading the lives of so many respondents. Even though I find the notion of 'collective guilt' difficult to accept, I felt shame and embarrassment at belonging to a society which had brought about all the misery and suffering I was witnessing in my interviewees. Thus this study which initially had been motivated by purely scholarly interests in the problems of assimilation and ethnicity, had turned into a confrontation with my own German identity.

My feelings were so overwhelming at one stage that I thought I would be unable to carry on with my research. I feared that it would be impossible for me to disentangle my own emotions from those of my respondents. But I decided to carry on. My curiosity to find some answers to the questions which intrigued me was too strong. Yet more importantly it was the intensive contact with my respondents, our long discussions of the problems concerning them just as much as myself, the kindness they showed towards me as an individual and, not least, their interest in and understanding of my own situation, in some ways the reverse of theirs, which enabled me to regain a degree of detachment necessary for the continuation of my work. What is more, I felt that my personal involvement might have a positive effect after all. I feel it helped me gain a deeper understanding of the refugees' attitudes than an 'objective' outsider might have brought to the subject. There is a related aspect: if my being German occasionally proved problematical, at the same time it also formed a link. It often established a spontaneous familiarity because of the common cultural background which facilitated the mutual understanding.

Finally, a word about the wider context in which this study has to be seen. It will become clear from the following pages that it was strongly influenced by the *Zeitgeist* which dominated the 1960s and 1970s. During these years ethnicity developed into a significant social phenomenon. Although unconscious of this influence at the time, I became aware of it when talking to older respondents. My stress on and interest in ethnic peculiarities of the German Jews obviously made quite a number of them feel uncomfortable. Group solidarity was readily asserted. Yet to talk about the same issue in terms of non-assimilation, often evoked slightly defensive reactions. Younger respondents were quite unperturbed in this respect. It became apparent that their – like my own – positive evaluation of ethnicity reflected differences in experience compared with those of the older respondents. Evidently, these were still marked by the racialist attitudes of the 1930s when, in L. D. Nachman's words, cultural differences were 'put to ugly use', in that they were made to serve as 'the basis for massive denials of elementary rights, including the right to life itself'.[6] The open proclamation of non-assimilation is therefore still felt as a threat by those who experienced cultural differentiation in the form of racist segregation and witnessed its deadly consequences.

However, since the 1960s a new awareness of the significance of ethnic groups within plural societies has emerged. It led to a revitalization of ethnic group consciousness and a new appreciation of cultural differences among ethnic groups. It became recognized that the richness of social life was not to be found in homogeneity but in heterogeneity, in the diversity of social life forms rather than in their similarity. These perceptions – in contrast to the hierarchical and discriminatory tendencies of racialist attitudes – were shaped by an anti-authoritarian and egalitarian impulse. This study records facets of ethnic relations existing within those perceptions.

1 Concepts of Assimilation and Ethnic Identity

Before we can talk about the Jews as a group, we have to ask the more general question: What is a Jew? This is by no means clear. Although innumerable studies have been written on various aspects of Jewish life, it has become a sort of ritual to introduce a work with the statement that it is impossible to fit the Jews into any known category of people.[1] One writer, impelled to offer a positive description of the Jews, re-introduced a biblical term and called them just 'peculiar' – clearly not a satisfactory term for a sociological or historical study.[2]

Among the general public as among the Jews themselves it has, to this day, been common usage to talk about 'the Jewish race' and regard what are considered typical Jewish traits as conditioned by 'racial genes'. This view is also shared by a number of historians or sociologists, although some express a certain amount of ambivalence. Thus one author admits to not being too sure 'whether the Jews correspond to a religion, or a race, or a combination of both'.[3] To introduce the category 'race' actually means in this context to ask two questions at once: can human populations be divided into races at all and, if so, can 'race' sufficiently explain human behaviour. The position taken here is that both questions have to be answered in the negative. It thus follows in this regard the 'Proposals on the Biological Aspects of Race' which resulted from a conference held by UNESCO in Moscow in 1964. The first statement says that 'all men living today belong to a single species, *Homo sapiens*, and are derived from a common stock'.[4] From this species sub-populations have developed which most anthropologists divide into three major groups: Negroid, Caucasoid and Mongoloid. These groups are generally called 'races', but more for convenience sake, because biologically speaking this term is a misnomer. For in contrast to animals and plants human 'races' can and do interbreed. It is therefore not only the common descent of all human populations which should prohibit the use of the term 'race', let alone 'pure race'. It is also the fact that repeated interbreeding has occurred among the subgroups of the human species as a result of constant migration, this being one crucial element of human history.

It is the combination of these two factors which explains why there are more elements which human beings share than those which separate them. There certainly are hereditary physical differences between human populations, but striking as they may appear, they do not form exclusive groups or 'species'. On the contrary, 'it has been estimated that 90-95 per cent of genes are common to all men'. The difference does not lie in the kind of genes various groups possess, but in the 'greater or lesser frequency' with which each gene occurs in certain populations.[5] This accumulation of genes in specific populations is, of course, the result of the opposite of interbreeding, namely, 'inbreeding', or endogamy. This has led to the differentiation of the human species into distinct, but not 'pure' types of human beings. But it should be added that the distinctions made by anthropologists are purely physical; they do not concern mental, let alone cultural characteristics which, so far, cannot be explained genetically. This point seems particularly important in a study like the present one, since it is so often the alleged Jewish 'racial' characteristics which, as was mentioned earlier, are made to serve as an explanation for Anti- and Philosemites alike of what are considered to be Jewish achievements or shortcomings. Such an argument is based on the common assumption that because certain physically distinct groups show similar cultural traits, these are genetically linked with each other. But this is a fallacy; the reverse is true, as is stated in the UNESCO proposals. For 'human beings who speak the same language and share the same culture have a tendency to intermarry, and often there is as a result a certain degree of coincidence between physical traits on the one hand, and linguistic and cultural traits on the other. But there is no known causal nexus between these and therefore it is not justifiable to attribute cultural characteristics to the influence of the genetic inheritance'.[6]

The conclusion from this and similar statements can only be that 'race' should be deleted from any discussion of cultural or social activities not only because it is so easily abused in the form of racist discrimination, but because, as a biological concept, it is unsuitable for sociological and historical analysis. This is particularly true in the case of this study which is not concerned with *the* Jews, but with a specific group, namely the Jews of Germany who, as will be shown below, differ in many ways from Jews in other countries.

Since it is not race but culture that distinguishes Jews from and also unites them with other Jews, or non-Jews for that matter, one has to look for a sociological concept to interpret 'peculiarities'. The most commonly used concept to denote groups who differ culturally from each other is that of 'ethnic groups', defined as 'a distinct category of the population in a larger society whose culture is usually different from its own. The members of such a group are, or feel themselves, or are thought to be, bound together by common ties of race (!) or nationality or culture'.[7]

As plausible as this definition seems at first glance, it is not unproblematic. Apart from the questionable inclusion of 'race', the juxtaposition of 'race', 'nationality', 'culture' seems to indicate that ethnic groups are seen here as clearly distinct from each other. This definition reflects the widespread and – as Barth puts it – 'simplistic view . . . that geographical and social isolation have been the critical factors in sustaining cultural diversity'.[8] From which it is only logical to conclude that where there are no geographical boundaries, separate cultures cannot survive, and some sort of fusion is to be expected.

And this indeed is the view which dominated sociological analysis of ethnic stratification until recently. The relationship was seen as one of assimilation, of an inevitable convergence of cultural groups. This was particularly true for the United States where it was generally believed, by common people and social scientists alike, that the 'future of American ethnic groups seems to be limited; it is likely that they will be quickly absorbed'.[9] This notion has become more popularly known as that of the 'melting pot', the functional aspect of which seems obvious; fostering the belief that the various immigrant groups would 'melt' into a new American culture helped to sustain the myth of equal, democratic participation within that new American society which was to be seen as a creation of all. In the multi-cultural context of America the 'melting pot' concept thus served as a useful ideology to integrate the heterogeneous ethnic groups.

The conviction of the desirability and inevitability of the ultimate complete cultural fusion was so deeply ingrained in American sociology that it came as quite a surprise, even as a shock, when this creed came under violent attack from the Black Nationalist movement in the 1960s and, in its wake, from other American minority groups. 'Assimilation' suddenly became a term of invective. A new key word was created: 'ethnicity'. Thus social scientists were faced with the unexpected fact, as Epstein puts it, that 'ethnic groups have taken on a new lease of life when in theory they were supposed to be disappearing'.[10] Even Glazer and Moynihan who, after all, were among the first social scientists to dispel the myth of the melting pot,[11] 'have been surprised by the persistence and salience of ethnic-based forms of social identification and conflict'.[12] Some of this amazement pervades their definition of this 'recent phenomenon' which they describe as a 'sudden increase in tendencies by people ... to insist on the significance of their groups' distinctiveness and identity and on new rights that derive from this group character'. They admit that social scientists were mistaken in looking on ethnic groups as representing a transitional phase in the assimilation process; they now agreed that they have to be understood, instead, 'as *forms* of social life that are capable of renewing and transforming themselves'.[13]

This latter idea has by now become so firmly established that the question must be asked how could it possibly have been ignored for so long. Thus Epstein, in his discussion of the emergence of 'ethnicity', blames the neglect of ethnic cultural characteristics. One reason has been, as just mentioned, the emphasis in the study of ethnic groups until recently more or less exclusively on the process of acculturation and assimilation which was seen as inevitably leading to a blending of the different cultures. Those elements which became 'similar' were therefore seen as decisive, whereas those which remained 'dissimilar' were neglected. They were regarded as 'survivals from an earlier age'[14] – doomed to extinction in the course of time. But more is involved. Since geographical isolation was considered an important prerequisite of the survival of cultures,[15] their extinction was automatically assumed after these boundaries had ceased to exist. Social scientists therefore failed to develop tools of analysis which were refined enough to cope with the different situation of the 'poly-ethnic' society which is marked, as Epstein puts it, 'by a high degree of cultural erosion'.[16] This means that traditional practices have been largely abandoned by most members of the ethnic groups, and those institutions or customs which were retained have often been adjusted to similar institutions in the wider society.

Yet, despite the diminishing significance of customs, individuals have shown a remarkable 'emotional attachment to the ethnic group'.[17] And this affective tie 'is all the more powerful', Epstein adds, 'because it is rooted in the unconscious'.[18] He introduces the term 'intimate' culture for this very personal relationship with the ethnic group and its expressions, which he contrasts with 'public' culture, pertaining to the more concrete cultural forms of customs and institutions. Nothing is said, however, about the relationship between these two manifestations of ethnic culture, or about its link with the majority culture. Frederick Barth, one of the few social scientists to tackle systematically the problem of ethnicity in a multi-ethnic setting, makes a similar distinction. But he goes further than Epstein and assigns the crucial role in the constitution and continuation of ethnic groups to the 'intimate' culture. Overt cultural traits serve mainly to define the boundaries among groups; but they may change, just as 'the organizational form of the group may change'. It is the ethnic identity of a group which is decisive for its persistence. And this identity is based, according to Barth, on 'overt signals and signs' such as 'dress, language, house-form, or general style of life' and on 'basic value orientations: the standards of morality and excellence by which performance is judged'.[19]

In other words, if one intends to determine a group's or an individual's cultural identity, one has to go beyond the analysis of certain customs or institutions, and look at modes of behaviour, attitudes and at value systems, for 'perception lies at the heart of the matter'.[20] It is a person's perceptions which give coherence to events in the outer world and shape reactions to them. Since perceptions are formed practically from birth onwards, they become so deeply ingrained in an individual's personality that they become subconscious and hence move largely out of one's control.[21] It is true that they can be raised to the conscious level, but it seems highly unlikely that spontaneous reactions are not influenced to a considerable extent by one's cultural outlook. In this sense perception takes effect on three levels: on the personal level it helps to order an otherwise chaotic universe; on the second level it binds people of similar perceptions to each other, thus creating social groups or categories within the larger society; on the third level it also shapes an individual's relationship with the majority society, i. e. his or her relations or adjustments to its institutions and cultural life in general.

In other words, if we accept that perception, i.e. viewing reality through a culturally specific value system is the ultimately unifying factor, the organizing system of the individual, then we must assume also that it is at work at all levels of identity formation. Ethnicity is not to be regarded as a residual category which only comes into force to explain an otherwise inexplicable residue of social behaviour. To put it differently though rather crudely: there are no given, 'objective' situations; a person will always interpret a situation on the basis of his or her evaluation of it and react to it accordingly.[22] This applies to the immediate environment just as much as to the level of cultural contact between a minority and a majority group.

Although this point is crucial for an understanding of the process of acculturation, it is curiously neglected in the literature on ethnicity. The prevailing view seems to be that ethnic culture and majority culture are overlapping, but basically distinct, as if individuals move culturally in completely different worlds. Although mostly implicit in studies of ethnicity, this view is made explicit by Frederic Barth when he says: 'Members of ethnic groups may accept a 'minority' status, accommodate to and seek to reduce their minority disabilities by encapsulating all cultural differentiae in sectors of non-articulation, while participating in the larger system of the industrialized group in the other sectors of activity'.[23]

This division of the world into 'ethnic' and 'non-ethnic' strata echoes the more familiar notion of the 'dichotomy of private and public spheres' which Peter Berger characterizes as the 'fundamental aspect' of the 'pluralization of social life-worlds',[24] generally regarded as a phenomenon of modern society. Yet, it has often been pointed out that every individual is born and brought up as a member of a particular society which penetrates all, even the most intimate, relationships between its members in the form of attitudes and values. Consequently, all spheres of life have to be located within the social domain; a 'private sphere' as such does not exist. It is true, however, that a 'pluralization' of modern society did take place. But this is the result of the variety and relative openness of the 'different social worlds'[25] for the members of modern society and not of an opposition of social and non-social spheres.

Thus one can similarly argue that people do not have split cultural identities, reacting, 'ethnically' in one context and 'non-ethnically' in another. On the contrary; 'Socialization' means nothing but the acquisition of a specific ethnic culture. We normally talk about these processes within the context of homogeneous cultures. The ethnic element therefore is less significant than the social character of these processes as such. It is only in a multi-ethnic setting that the ethnic peculiarities of the socialization process come into play and these primarily manifest themselves in specific attitudes and value systems. Of course perceptions are also influenced by factors other than ethnicity, but again these elements are usually integrated into the overall personality which is basically shaped by specific cultural elements.

This is shown for instance in the varying rates of social mobility in the different ethnic groups in the United States which seem to indicate that it is not class background as such, but specific attitudes towards achievement and education which help to explain why some groups have been more successful than others in moving upwards.[26] A good example in a wider context is provided if one looks at the influence of the process of industrialization on the countries of Europe and the United States. The homogenizing effect of technology and expanding industrialization is beyond dispute. However, one cannot deny that each country has met industrialization in its own way and integrated it into the existing social and political system differently. As a result, the various countries show considerable cultural differences – seen as a whole. Even though a similar class structure developed, behaviour patterns of members of the same class are not identical as has, for instance, been shown in analyses of conflict situations in industry,[27] but shaped by culturally conditioned norms.

In the context of the acculturation process in poly-ethnic societies this means that it is unlikely that members of a minority will incorporate total cultural elements into their own culture, but will rather re-interpret them in the light of their own ethnic background and then assimilate them to the body of the existing culture. It follows, of course, that through this process of re-interpretation of other cultural elements, the original ethnic culture is also changing, even if, at times, the changes may barely be noticeable.

Still, this kind of 'assimilation' has to be seen as something quite different from what is normally meant by the term: a one-dimensional process of a cultural move from the original ethnic culture towards the majority culture.[28] To speak of assimilation as a process of re-interpretation means rather the reverse, namely an adjustment of the new to the old. However, since through this process the 'old' culture is changing one should not think in terms of 'direction' at all. Rather, the traditional culture of an ethnic group will develop into something new which is shaped by both the original culture and that of the larger society, but it is not identical with either.

It should be obvious by now that stressing the persistence of ethnicity in a multi-cultural society does not mean that separate entities are being considered. Not only does one find a high degree 'of mobility, contact and information'[29] among groups: the very formation of the ethnic culture itself reflects this interaction which also affects the majority culture. It may be useful to think in terms of an ethnic 'core culture' which is defined through the basic direction given by the perceptions or value systems of the individual members of the group and which may or may not find expression in specific customs and institutions. To what extent and in what way this 'core culture' interacts with the culture of the majority, probably depends on the social, economic and psychological situation of the individuals and on the type of the larger society. Jews, for instance, have lived among many different societies or cultures, but did not feel attracted to all of them in the same way and therefore did not always incorporate non-Jewish elements into their own core culture to the same degree. There is no fixed boundary between cultures in a poly-ethnic context: they may be seen as being in a state of unstable equilibrium.

So far, the focus has been primarily on the acculturation process of the minority group as a whole. It is even more important to look at the behaviour patterns of the individual members who constitute the group, as the transmitters of culture. The situation is still more complex here. Individuals do not reproduce their culture automatically – especially not in a multi-ethnic setting: living in a continuous confrontation with 'them', they have to adapt their culture, reflect upon it, perhaps give up some ethnic traits, or possibly stress all the more those which they have retained. On the other hand, they may not be aware of their ethnic culture at all. This is likely to happen in those cases where the practice of certain customs has been given up and where the ethnic background manifests itself only in the subtle form of perceptions. In this context the well-known phenomenon has to be mentioned that in social life the actors are rarely aware of the roots of their attitudes and behaviour which constitute their, in Scheler's words, *'relativnatürliche Weltanschauung'*.[30] It therefore seems important to distinguish between ethnic *culture* or ethnicity and ethnic identity, because there is no necessary correlation between the two. Whereas *ethnicity* represents cultural continuity at a conscious, but more often at a subconscious level, *ethnic identity* is delegated to the battle at the front, so to speak, where it shapes and re-shapes itself through confrontation with other ethnic identities and also with other identities of the self. For, 'identity . . . is essentially a concept of synthesis. It represents the process by which the person seeks to integrate his various statuses and roles, as well as his diverse experiences, into a coherent image of the self'. Epstein then continues to point out the great importance of the ethnic identity, sometimes called 'terminal identity', because it is 'one that embraces and integrates a whole series of statuses, roles, and lesser identities'.[31]

This might seem to be the case in a period when ethnicity has become one of the key issues of contemporary social life. Here it is argued somewhat differently that it is *ethnicity* which is 'terminal', since the culturally conditioned perceptions and value systems influence individual behaviour, yet the image people have of themselves may only be loosely connected with their ethnic background. Their ethnic identity may be strongly developed and reflect a great attachment to their group, or it may be considered relatively unimportant compared with other identities of the self. Another combination is also possible, namely that the ethnic identity figures prominently in a person's self-image, but largely as a negative force reflecting 'the internalized (negative) evaluations of others',[32] which may lead one to deny one's ethnic background. And last but not least, there are cases, such as those of converts, where the ethnic background is non-existent, but the identity is held on to all the more fervently to make up for the missing background.[33]

The ethnic identity – be it strong or weak, positive or negative – may be fairly constant throughout a person's life, but it may also undergo rapid change. This could be observed in the 1960s, when, especially in the United States, the emergence of various nationalist or cultural movements suddenly caused many people to think of their ethnic identity in more positive terms. Usually, it is negative factors such as acute racism and persecution which force people to confront the question of their ethnic identity. Often enough, as the history of the Jews under Nazism shows, it was only under pressure from a hostile environment that people became at all aware of their ethnic background. They rejected, of course, the distorted and offensive image of the Jews forced upon them by the Anti-semites. Many, however, took a renewed interest in genuine Judaism and not few of them developed a more pronounced Jewish consciousness as a result, as I will show below.

It is obvious that form and development of the ethnic identity are to a considerable degree influenced by forces and pressures from within as well as without. This last point especially has given rise to the assumption, quite commonly encountered, that its openness to conscious manipulation makes the ethnic identity less 'genuine', less autonomous than for instance cultural traits. Thus Isaac Deutscher writes in his famous article on the 'Non-Jewish Jew': 'Auschwitz was the terrible cradle of the new Jewish consciousness and of the new Jewish nation. We, who have rejected the religious tradition, now belong to the negative community of those, who have, so many times in history, been singled out for persecution and extermination. . . . It was from the ashes of six million Jews that the phoenix of Jewry has risen. What a resurrection!'[34]

One can easily see why Deutscher defines modern Jewry in a purely negative way. Following older traditions, he identifies culture with institutions, Judaism with religion (which is not surprising considering the fact that he came from an orthodox home). Seen from this angle, the non-religious Jew finds himself in a cultural vacuum. He is not a Jew proper anymore, but purely defined as such by his enemies. Yet Deutscher ignores the fact that cultural movements and identities are generally defined or influenced through confrontation with the outside world. What comes to mind in this context are the various nationalisms and movements of cultural renewal in Central and Eastern Europe throughout the 19th century. Thus, German nationalism is not less 'genuine', because it was largely stimulated by the Napoleonic wars.

Another example is provided by some of my empirical material. I became aware of a renewed interest in traditional Judaism in quite a number of the younger Jews of German extraction. This is quite a common phenomenon, also to be found among other young Jews, especially in the United States. In most of the cases that I encountered, this re-orientation reflected influences from outside, but not necessarily of a hostile kind. Even small differences in attitudes and behaviour suffice to make one aware of one's peculiar ethnic background. But what is more, this awareness often resulted in a decision to become more observant or orthodox in everyday life. In cases such as these it is not only the ethnic identity which is affected, but the ethnic culture in itself; part of a new, what Martin Buber called 'autonomous (Jewish) reality' has been created.[35] Ethnic identity and ethnic culture are closely linked, as we can see, but their relationship is not compelling.

Before we turn to the problems of ethnicity and ethnic identity among German Jews in particular, the main points of the foregoing theoretical explanations should be recapitulated: it has been argued that in order to find a suitable category for the Jews as a group one has to discard the notion of 'race'. As a biological concept it is not applicable within a social and cultural analytical framework. However, the sociological concept of ethnic group also turns out to be problematical. More often than not it is based on a static notion of culture, correlated with geographical isolation. This is reflected in the theory of assimilation which until recently dominated the analysis of cultural contact with multi-ethnic societies. It was taken for granted that because of the lack of geographical isolation, minority cultures would inevitably gravitate to the majority culture. Whatever traditional cultural traits survived were regarded as archaic, doomed to extinction in the long run and were therefore neglected in sociological analysis.

This theory of assimilation was influenced by the prevailing concept of culture. Whenever one looked for manifestations of culture, attention was primarily paid to clearly observable customs and institutions. Since these were indeed declining in the United States (and the same was true for other multi-ethnic societies), it was taken as a sign of the slow extinction of ethnic cultures. After the resurgence of ethnicity a couple of decades ago, this approach to culture had to be revised. It became obvious that the ties which link people to their ethnic background were much more subtle than cultural practices as such and at the same time more deeply embedded, since they are intimately woven into the fabric of the personality. Ethnicity is first and foremost expressed in perceptions and values which are not inborn, but normally affect a person from birth onwards, through close interaction with members, normally the family, of the particular society into which the individual is born. Because ethnicity is so deeply rooted and largely subconscious, it was emphasised that it permeates an individual's total system of attitudes and behaviour and therefore also colours his or her interaction with the wider environment. This approach seems helpful in explaining cultural change within the ethnic group. It was further pointed out that it is advisable to differentiate between ethnicity and ethnic identity, although both concepts are normally used interchangeably.[36] Without doubt, these two elements very often overlap, but one should at least be aware of the fact that whereas ethnicity, although not stable, is largely beyond the individual's immediate control, ethnic identity implies an evaluation of that heritage, a perception of the self which might not correspond directly with the cultural background.

So far, I have discussed some of the important theoretical aspects of assimilation and ethnicity in general. The next step will be to examine more specifically the situation of the Jews within German society from the perspective of more recent sociological findings concerning the process of assimilation and of ethnicity. It is hoped that this will throw fresh light on this controversial issue.

2 The Process of Jewish Assimilation in Germany

Few other Jewish communities have attracted more attention and critical evaluation than those of Germany. This is in large part due to the prominent position German Jews achieved among world Jewry from the late eighteenth century onwards, when the Jewish communities in Germany took on a new lease of life. There were several reasons for this. Not the least important was the process of secularization which accelerated after emancipation. It led to the lowering of barriers between Jews and non-Jews and made the former more receptive to ideas from outside. Since at that time many ideas prevalent in German philosophy and cultural life generally were highly congenial to certain elements in Judaism, the ground for intellectual and spiritual re-awakening thus created proved particularly fertile. Very rarely in Jewish history had such intellectual forces been unleashed as in the decades following the emancipation, stimulating Jewish thought and opening up new horizons to Judaism as a whole.[1]

However, German Jewry owed its significance not only to its prominence in spiritual and cultural matters. Emancipation also meant that German Jews became more intimately involved with the Gentile world than almost any other Jewish group in early modern times. Indeed, German Jews are seen as having been instrumental in paving the way for the 'return of Jewry to Society'.[2] Accordingly, Germany has been considered as the 'classic land of assimilation'.[3] To be sure, in other countries of Western Europe such as France or Italy assimilation had set in earlier, but in Germany it was given more weight because of the cultural prominence of the German Jews. The latter also represented the largest Jewish group in Western Europe at that time.[4] Even more important was the fact that Germany was one of the first countries which introduced the principle – if not the reality – of legal equality for Jews. Finally, 'in no other country did (assimilation) assume the character of a social program'.[5] What happened in Germany with regard to the process of Jewish emancipation gained a special, paradigmatic significance. German Jews were considered the leaders of Jewry on the path to modernity and especially to assimilation.[6] On the following pages the notion of assimilation, as it appears in German-Jewish historiography, will be briefly examined in order to establish what is understood by it, how this term is used and what are its implications for the assessment of the group character of the German-Jewish minority.

THE DEBATE OF GERMAN-JEWISH ASSIMILATION

Most students of the process of German-Jewish assimilation seem to have been guided by the common view previously described that the cultural characteristics of a group find their expression in concrete institutions and clearly observable traditions serving as boundaries between two different cultures. Once traditions are eroded, the boundaries disappear and the groups as culturally distinct minorities are doomed to extinction. Thus, it is generally believed that once Jews deviate from traditional Judaism in any way, nothing can stop the ensuing process of assimilation, commonly understood as leading to submersion in the Gentile environment. Since the German Jews initiated secularist and reformist movements, their full and complete 'assimilation' came to be accepted as a self-evident truth. In fact, up to this day, 'assimilation' has been used in this sense as one of the key concepts throughout German-Jewish historiography. We read that as a result of 'total assimilation' the Jews in Germany did not have any other wish than that of becoming 'completely absorbed by the German nation'.[7]

Another author claims in a similar vein that the Jews in Germany had completely adopted German culture; the language was the same, so were the 'loyalties, values, and goals'. From this 'fact' he draws the conclusion that the attitudes of German Jews 'may more easily be understood, if (the latter) are studied not as Jews, but as Germans'.[8]

However, these arguments are usually not presented as calmly as the above quotations may suggest. To this day, German-Jewish assimilation has remained a highly controversial issue. For it is believed that even if emancipation brought the Jews of Germany economic and perhaps social gains, they had to pay a high price –

some would say, too high a price – for their advancement. In other words, German Jews are considered to be pioneers of modernization, but the course they took in order to achieve this goal is not necessarily judged as exemplary. On the contrary – it is a widely held view that it should not uncritically be followed by Jewry in general.

After all, did not the pull of the non-Jewish world lead to the 'internal disintegration of Judaism'?[9] And did it not tempt many Jews to marry out and to convert? Given such an absolutist notion of assimilation it is not surprising that baptism is usually seen as the logical conclusion of this process: 'Most (German Jews) looked upon conversion as the ultimate expression of commitment to being German.'[10] It is for the same reason that at least one analyst found converts of particular interest to the scholar of Jewish history, because 'they represent a phenomenon of conscious complete assimilation through their rejection of everything Jewish'.[11]

Assimilation, it is claimed, badly affected the allegedly homogeneous structure of the traditional religious organization, resulting in serious upheavals within the community which sometimes even threatened to tear it apart. Thus one writer maintained that German Jewry 'got caught in an evolutionary process . . . which is completely un-Jewish (!) . . . The idea of the nation cannot be separated from that of religion in the case of Judaism'; Judaism, it is added, had been 'degraded' to a mere denomination.[12]

We touch here on what can be regarded as the core question of the whole debate on Jewish assimilation. It turns largely on the role which religion plays in the continuity of Judaism and with it in the survival of Jewry as a group. This point will be discussed in greater detail below. What is important here is the fact that religion has been traditionally regarded as crucial for the transmission of cultural values. This was thought to be particularly true of Judaism because, until recently, the Jews did not possess a state which, through its institutions, guaranteed the perpetuation of the nation as a cultural group. In the case of the Jews, religion had to take on the vital role of creating group cohesion, and most scholars agree that it fulfilled this function admirably. It is not surprising therefore that the effects of assimilation on Judaism – given its generally understood meaning – have been watched with great apprehension. It was feared that any weakening of traditional observance would ultimately lead to the destruction of Jewry as such.[13]

Yet, assimilation is seen not only as a danger to communal life as a whole. Equally disastrous, it is often said, were the effects of assimilation on the Jew as an individual. 'Assimilation made the Jews deeply insecure. Having renounced the old, protective ghetto community – the comforts of Jewish peoplehood – Jews fell into an "emotional confusion".'[14] Their condition was made worse by a hostile environment which constantly frustrated their efforts at integration into the wider society. The image of the Jew emerging from many studies on the era of Jewish emancipation and afterwards bears a strong resemblance with the well-known concept of the 'marginal man'. The Jew appears as highly neurotic, unsure of himself, driven by insatiable social ambition and a yearning for acceptance and, finally, as an individual tortured by self-hatred.[15]

Usually, these traits are attributed to the Jews' position in Germany. Other authors, however, focus on the allegedly widespread self-hatred which they see as having resulted from the cultural identification with Germany. A good example of this view is offered by Hannah Arendt who stated: 'One cannot choose what one wishes oneself to assimilate to, whether one likes it or not; one cannot leave out Christianity, just as little as the contemporary hatred of Jews. . . . There is no assimilation, if one gives up only one's own past, but ignores that of the surrounding society. . . . Assimilation is only possible, if one assimilates oneself to Antisemitism.'[16]

To be sure, self-hatred is quite a common phenomenon among members of an oppressed minority whose striving for recognition and equality is constantly frustrated. The racialist stereotypes they encounter in their relationship with the majority society are finally internalized and expressed in self-rejection. To call this 'assimilation' is justified only in a very limited sense. It is by no means clear, though, how representative were the chosen examples such as Rahel Varnhagen. Heine, Rathenau, Weininger and a few others, who appear in the relevant literature with conspicuous regularity. Hannah Arendt's sweeping statement is interesting for yet another reason: it is remarkable not only for the at best dubious identification of antisemitism with German, even European, culture in its entirety, but also for the assumption that assimilation means the total loss of one's own culture. It appears that 'Judaism' and 'assimilation' are perceived as mutually exclusive. They are also evaluated accordingly. Whereas 'Judaism' is generally presented in a positive light, the connotations of 'assimilation' tend to be negative. Thus a 'traditional', i.e. 'religious' Jew appears to be a 'good' Jew, an 'assimilated' Jew, on the other hand, a 'bad' Jew. As we shall see later, this evaluation has also filtered through to the level of the common understanding and self-perception of many Jews. Assimilation is generally seen 'as a kind of submission ... suggesting that the Jews undervalued their own tradition and gave way too easily'.[17]

However, in numerous works the negative image of assimilation is even more glaring. The attitudes of the Jews as regards their own situation in Germany are overwhelmingly described as 'ironical', 'paradoxical', 'contradictory', 'singularly shortsighted', even totally 'blind'. Furthermore, we are told that the Jews had a 'tragic misconception' and that they harboured nothing but 'illusions' about their position within German society; that emancipation was 'wrong' or achieved 'too rapidly'.[18] These condemnations have to be understood as expressions of the deep disappointment with, even despair of, the failure of emancipation and of assimilation to secure complete integration for the Jews in Germany and, even worse, the final destruction of German Jewry. Thus the already negative connotations of assimilation are further reinforced so that, in the end, it appears as a contemptible process altogether.

It is remarkable that nearly all these arguments are to be found in the writings of Jewish authors, some of them very eminent. We encounter a tradition here which goes a long way back in Jewish history, namely that of laying the blame for the growth of antisemitism – ultimately even for the persecutions – at the feet of the Jews themselves. The victims are declared guilty of the oppression they suffer.[19] This is well illustrated by no less a scholar than Gershom Scholem who says: 'The self-surrender of the Jews, although welcome and even demanded, was often also seen as evidence of their lack of moral substance and thereby contributed to the disdain in which they were held by so many Germans.'[20] We shall encounter a similar attitude in the empirical part of this study which shows that, to this day, many Jews feel that antisemitism and Jewish behaviour are somehow interrelated and therefore try anxiously to avoid 'sticking their necks out', lest the monster of antisemitism be provoked.[21]

Most students of the history of the Jewish–Gentile relationship would agree, however, that antisemitism has very little to do with the 'Semites', and is in effect a problem of the Antisemites: 'All attempts to discover the sources of Anti-Semitism at the points of contact between the two peoples, or in possible friction between them in commerce, society, politics and culture, have yielded no satisfactory results'.[22] Or to put it differently: although Jews were the victims of the social conflicts erupting in certain parts of German society and the targets of feelings of frustration and aggression, as they still are in many other societies, the behaviour of the Jews in such a situation, either as a group or as individuals, is unimportant. It is well-known that racialist stereotypes primarily represent a projection of the fears on the part of the racist person who will interpret, whatever the chosen victim does or fails to do, in such a way as to fit the stereotype.[23] Efforts to explain the presence or absence of oppression or racism in a given society in terms of the relationship between the various groups therefore seem to be misguided.[24]

Behind the predominantly critical evaluation of German–Jewish emancipation and the process of assimilation is hidden another, even more controversial issue. It is obvious that harsh judgments such as those mentioned so far can only be passed by the observer who enjoys the benefit of hindsight; they illustrate what E. P. Thompson in a different context called 'the enormous condescension of posterity'. This position has had serious implications for the evaluation of modern German history in general and of German–Jewish history in particular. It has led to a strangely distorted view of recent historical processes.

Only few historians of German Jewry could resist the temptation of looking at historical developments in Germany with the catastrophic end in mind which the National Socialists brought about. From this perspective it becomes understandable why H. Arendt is able to look upon antisemitism as the crucial element of German culture. Other authors condemn the tendency of German Jews during the process of assimilation to identify with liberal, enlightened and humanistic representatives of Germany as found in the classical tradition of German philosophy and literature, maintaining that this was not the 'real' Germany, but an idealized one. The 'real' Germany, one reads, was that of the reactionaries, of the Antisemites; in other words, many historians share the view that 'German history since 1871, or even an earlier date, has tended inevitably and with some kind of inner purpose towards National Socialism.'[25] But, one may ask, does not every society contain diverse potentialities; is it really justified to maintain that the winning party in the struggle for power is typical of the whole? One could further ask whether it is fair to dismiss as irrelevant all those groups who represent different traditions and, as we shall see later, actually put up courageous resistance against Nazism. Clearly, all these groups represented 'Germany' which, like any other society, was composed of a multitude of diverse groups and factions. As Peter Gay put it: 'There was significant continuity between the Germany of the 19th and that of the 20th centuries, but there was equally significant discontinuity. . . . To say that the Third Reich was grounded in the German past is true enough; to say that it was the inescapable result of that past, the only fruit that the German tree would grow, is false.'[26]

If many historians were unable to escape the effects of the 'modern German trauma' (Gay) in their analysis of German history, even fewer managed to do so in the field of German–Jewish history in particular. A considerable proportion of post-war writings on the history of the Jews in Germany have been overshadowed by the horrifying end of German Jewry under the Nazi regime. The ground must have been well prepared, one is easily led to think, for a persecution on the Nazi scale. And, indeed, those historians who look for signs which point towards the end as we know it, find them in rising waves of antisemitism throughout German history. Since the course of events seems to have been so clear, these historians say, it could only have been an extraordinary blindness on the part of the Jews to ignore the writing on the wall; they should have realized that there was no future for Jews in Germany. One student of German–Jewish history even put forward mass neuroticism as an explanation for the German Jews' failure to do so.[27]

This whole complex of questions has hardly lost any of its actuality. Time and again Jews of German extraction are confronted with the question of why they did not leave earlier, why they did not realize what was coming. A number of historians forcefully reject this approach to German–Jewish history and the evaluation of assimilation in particular. Thus the protagonist of Walter Laqueur's documentary novel gives the drastic answer: 'Every fool knows what happened yesterday, but even the greatest genius cannot tell you what will occur tomorrow. Looking backwards, everything usually seems inevitable: it happened, because it was bound to happen.'[28]

Another historian, Eva Reichmann, arguing in a similar vein, observes that to declare emancipation a 'myth' or 'failure' is unjustified because such an assessment is 'based on a confusion of sequence with consequence, on the fallacy: . . . Events follow each other, events also give rise to each other'.[29] Clearly, if continuities are shown to exist, they should be evaluated in the light of previous and not future events.[30] One might go even further and say, value judgments such as 'good' or 'bad', 'right' or 'wrong' seem irrelevant in a historical context altogether, for 'seen as a whole, the social life of Germans and Jews developed neither in a negative nor in a positive way. It entered different phases over the centuries which were dependent on the respective historical events and changes'.[31]

Those authors who condemn the acceptance of assimilation among German Jews tend to give the impression that the rejection of the Jews in Germany was absolute, that, in the words of one author, the 'Jewish masses [were] completely terrorized' by anti-Jewish hostility;[32] they seem to assume that the Antisemites constituted a homogeneous block and more or less dominated the whole of German life. But societies are not total systems to be classified neatly as 'racist' or 'pluralist'.[33] To be sure, antisemitism was firmly planted in German culture, but so it was in Western culture generally. Its strength as a political force, however, varied with changing socio-economic developments within the wider society. Furthermore, anti-semitism did not pervade all social classes or groups to the same degree. Although Hitler and his followers succeeded fairly easily in activating the latent or open antisemitism of large parts of the population, historians have shown that the Social Democratic, Progressive and Catholic parties as well as the aristocracy were relatively immune to antisemitism, as they were to fascism in general.[34] Even in the 1930s, as will be shown in greater detail later on, Jews encountered less militant antisemitism than one would expect under a racist dictatorship. Experiences varied greatly from individual to individual and from region to region. The picture must have been even more diffuse before the emergence of organized antisemitism. 'Every Jew had non-Jewish friends, and they would defend him against criticism and attack', Laqueur's protagonist says, 'but Jews in general had few friends.'[35]

This was certainly true of Germany. But was the situation better in other countries? If this had been the case, it might have given the German Jews a clue that they were heading for disaster. Rather the opposite was true: compared with the events in France which had led to the Dreyfus affair and with the pogroms in Russia and Poland, Germany seemed relatively 'safe', even a haven of freedom for thousands of Jewish refugees from Eastern Europe who fled to Germany at the beginning of this century.[36] In short, 'antisemitism did raise its head on occasion, Jews were discriminated against, but on the whole there was good reason to believe that such prejudice would gradually disappear. Thus the assimilation of Jews seemed a perfectly natural process; to reject it made no more sense than rejecting rain or snow or wind or any other natural phenomenon'.[37] Another well-known historian, Peter Gay, would agree with this view for he writes similarly that 'Jews felt as Germans', and rightly so; 'the Germanness of Jewish high culture in these decades (before 1914) was not an effort at disguise. It was not craven self-denial, but a proprietary feeling for a civilization that had produced decent cosmopolitans like Schiller and Kant, ornaments to modern humanism like Goethe.' Jews had not only whole-heartedly identified with this culture, but also 'made distinct contributions' to it.[38] They were therefore fully justified in claiming it as their own. George Mosse likewise emphasizes the similarity between Jews and Germans which, according to him, became apparent in the development of identical institutions and ideas. Finally, he comes to the same conclusion as Gay: 'Rejecting the Jewish past as it had evolved during the centuries, Jews partook in a culture which in a very real sense was theirs as much as it was the Germans'.[39]

This takes us back to the beginning of this brief survey of representative attitudes towards assimilation in German–Jewish historiography. It is obvious from the various statements given above that opinions differ radically as to how the process of Jewish assimilation in Germany is to be evaluated. At the same time, however, assimilation as such is hardly ever questioned; it is taken as a fact by most scholars of German–Jewish history that the Jews of Germany had more or less become Germans. There are some notable exceptions as we will see further below, but the overwhelming view has been that the general trend of Jewish assimilation in Germany ultimately meant to exchange 'Jewishness' for 'Germanness'.

Yet, a closer look at the various studies of German Jews reveals that this is not the only conclusion one can draw from German–Jewish history. A somewhat different picture emerges if one puts German–Jewish assimilation in the wider context of ethnic groups and their relationship with the majority society as outlined in the previous chapter. This will now be attempted in the second half of this chapter.

TOWARDS A RE-DEFINITION OF GERMAN–JEWISH ETHNIC IDENTITY

The question of how to define the Jewishness of the German Jews has been asked many times. For in spite of the often repeated 'assimilationist' tendencies of the German Jews, nearly all observers agree that an element of foreignness', however elusive, still adhered to them.[40] Yet opinions differ considerably as to how to interpret this 'foreignness'.

The main distinction between Jews and non-Jews – apart from 'race' – is often attributed to religion. Yet again, views are divided as to what significance the Jewish religion has for the whole of the Jewish group and how Judaism affects the relationship of the Jews with the wider society.

By far the majority of the German Jews would have defined their situation as that of 'German Citizens of the Jewish Faith', as indicated by the name of the largest defence organization of German Jewry which was founded in 1893. The popularity of this organization suggests that this title apparently expressed fairly adequately how most German Jews felt about their Jewish origin: that of being born into a group which they considered to be mainly denominational. They felt attached to it, even though the strength of the link varied from individual to individual; but Judaism as such had ceased to occupy a central place in their lives which were otherwise governed by non-religious factors, resulting from the contact with the wider society. It has frequently been pointed out by spokesmen of this part of German Jewry that their situation matched exactly that of the Catholics and Protestants; their bonds with Germany were in no way less strong and sincere than those of the members of the other two major denominations in Germany. This argument was primarily put forward in reaction to antisemitic propaganda, coupled with the demand for social equality.[41] Although this interpretation pointed in the right direction, as we shall see later on, it cannot be called an exhaustive definition of what constituted the Jewishness of the German Jew.

Other observers – a significant minority – severely criticized this attitude towards Judaism which the majority of Jews in Germany took and which they shared, by the way, with most Jews in France and England. The 'National identification with the Germans, the French etc.' led to the 'confessionalization of Judaism' which amounted to more than a mere deviation from Judaism; it was as

Heinz Moshe Graupe maintained 'a falsification of its character'. 'Judaism becomes a confession', he continued, 'when it is seen through the glasses of the Christian view of religion, where religion is the relation of the redemptive need of the individual, or of a collection of individuals, the Church, to God'.[42] This means that Graupe sees the relationship of the Jews with Judaism as being qualitatively different from that of the Christians with Christianity. For a Christian it is the state and its institutions which form the principal frame of reference. These institutions may be permeated by Christian values but they are not identical. A Christian remains a member of this cultural group, whatever his/her beliefs about Christian dogmas.[43] The Jewish situation is said to be quite different. Due to the peculiar character of Judaism, Jewish social institutions receive their essential values and their legitimation through Jewish religion. Seen from this perspective, the survival of the one element depends on the preservation of the other. There is no room for a form of Jewishness outside the national–religious sphere of Judaism. Any attempt to break out of it and to form other national allegiances are considered as 'un-Jewish', as a 'betrayal' of Judaism.

Hardly any writer has expressed his contempt for the liberal stratum of German Jewry which in the main represented the 'confessional' approach towards Judaism, as openly as Gershom Scholem, himself a product of it. His criticism of the religious observance of his parents' generation is scathing. In his eyes, their superficiality in religious matters is proof of their depravation as regards Judaism generally. But the observations which accompany his critical remarks are extremely revealing. They show that in spite of the apparent shallowness of his parents' Judaism, something more was involved. Even Scholem cannot fail to realize this without being able, however, to find a satisfying explanation. Thus we read: 'An astonishing phenomenon within wide circles of the Jewish middle class was their uncompromisingly negative attitude towards conversion which, despite their eagerness for assimilation, they condemned . . . [as] superfluous, undignified and humiliating. (Within my own large family circle there was not a single case of baptism between 1870 and 1933). This is the reason for the strikingly ambivalent attitude of so many Jews towards Heinrich Heine, who in the eyes of the majority of Gentiles appeared as so typical a representative of Jewish assimilation. The evaluation of Heine ranged from admiration, as I frequently encountered in my youth, especially in Jewish families, to definite condemnation, not so much of his writings as of his lack of character.' Equally puzzling to Scholem are the predominantly negative attitudes towards mixed marriages; attitudes which he calls 'very ambivalent and often quite irrational'. 'My father', he continues, 'a pronounced protagonist of assimilation, was against mixed marriages within his own family and circle of acquaintances. According to his theory he should have welcomed them; yet when my brother married a Gentile girl he never spoke to her after their first short encounter'. Scholem also notices with amazement that non-Jews and Jews mixed much less socially than one would expect and, what is more, that the Jews seemed 'quite happy' with the situation as it was. For Scholem this is just another example of German–Jewish 'irrationality': 'So great was the discrepancy between the ideology of submersion into everything German and the widespread instinctive tendency to remain among one's own kind'.[44]

But who is 'irrational' here, the reader of these 'paradoxes' cannot help to ask. Is it not perhaps the author who imposes an image of what constitutes 'genuine' Judaism on German–Jewish attitudes? As a consequence, he is led to expect extreme assimilationism although this obviously conflicts with the actual behaviour he is describing. So strong is his conviction of the complete absorption of German Jews by the majority society because of the abandonment of traditional orthodox Judaism that he considers whatever Jewish elements he may find as being no more than mere remnants of a dying culture.

Another well-known scholar of Jewish history, Simon Dubnow, arrives at exactly the opposite conclusion. In his eyes these Jewish remnants do not signify the loss of Judaism but rather its persistence. In an original analogy he calls the 'assimilationist' or anti-nationalist Jews of Germany 'national Marranos' who, similar to the Jews of medieval Spain, adhered to their Jewish culture in secret only: 'Following such a long process of assimilation in Germany, they had become so accustomed to the national mask that they often considered it as their true face.' Their 'true face', however, was that of the Jewish nationality, of a 'Jewish self-consciousness'. For Dubnow even German–Jewish forms of religious Judaism were part of the disguise, for he believes that what many Jews regarded 'as a *religious* association was in reality a national one'.[45]

Dubnow's notion of Jewishness thus differs markedly from that mentioned earlier. He does not define it in religious, but in 'national' terms. 'The Jewish national idea and the national feeling connected with it', he explains, 'have their origin primarily in the historical consciousness, in a certain complex of ideas and psychic predispositions. These ideas and predispositions, the deposit left by the aggregate of historical impressions, are of necessity the common property of the whole nation, and they can be developed and quickened to a considerable degree by a renewal of the impressions through the study of history. Upon the knowledge of history, then, depends the strength of the national consciousness.'[46] To be sure, all concepts of Jewishness contain a historical–national dimension. But Dubnow's approach was much more radical: he ignored the religious element completely and 'regarded (the national aspect) as the sole valid factor' of Judaism.[47]

Although Dubnow's concept of Jewishness contrasts with that of those who consider religion the primary force in Jewish life, both views overlap to the extent that they perceive 'Jewishness' and 'Germanness' or any other non-Jewish nationality of the Diaspora as opposing principles. Time and again in German–Jewish historiography, the reader is told that 'Germanness' and 'Jewishness' were experienced as a 'contradiction' by the German Jews which forced 'each German Jew . . . to resolve his own inner conflict between the equally compelling ideological concepts of *Deutschtum* and *Judentum*; accordingly, each was forced to examine his loyalties to German nationality and culture on the one hand and to Jewishness on the other'.[48] Even those observers who do not necessarily accept this 'conflict model' of the German–Jewish situation, nevertheless tend to perceive the German and the Jewish sphere as basically distinct. Yet, is this dichotomization justified? What, for instance, does 'Jewishness' mean in the context of Diaspora Jewry? Unfortunately, apart from occasional references to 'tradition' or 'religion' we are hardly ever told.

As is well-known, Judaism has undergone many changes not only over time but also from region to region. Which of the many forms that have developed should be considered 'genuine'? Moreover, it seems doubtful whether 'Jewishness' can be considered in isolation from the total social and cultural environment in which each Jewish community exists. Not all developments within Jewish communities are due to outside influence, but it cannot be denied that, since emancipation at least, various 'Judaisms' took shape in the different countries of the Diaspora which reflect the socio-economic position of the Jewish minority and the adjustments made to the wider society. In other words: the 'Jewishness' of a German Jew, even that of the most orthodox members, differs significantly from that of an Italian or Russian Jew.[49]

However, to stress the interrelationship with the majority should not be confused with the assimilationist 'absorption' approach described above. What is meant here is perhaps most clearly expressed by the social historian Jacob Katz who, in his numerous studies on the process of assimilation in Germany, has analysed the development of German Jewry since emancipation in great detail.[50] He pointed out that, up to the era of emancipation, world Jewry did form a nation; a nation, though, whose members were dispersed.[51] Even so they were endowed with a national culture, including a language of their own which made them easily distinguishable from the non-Jewish societies in which they resided. Thenceforth, however, national Jewry changed its character: a 'novel and singular social entity' developed. This new 'entity', as Katz stressed, has to be seen as a transformation of the Jewish community, rather than as its disintegration. This process is reflected in the fact that, since the middle of the 19th century, 'a new type of the German, French, or English Jew' emerged who identified more closely with the main society in which he/she lived than the Jew of the 'national' era.[52]

This rapprochement between Jews and non-Jews was not dictated by an 'assimilationist craving', as so many students of German–Jewish history would want us to believe. Katz shows convincingly that it was a combination of socio-economic and political factors which led to changes in the traditional Jewish social system. These factors were part of the process of the 'modernization' of Western European societies. The Jews living in the West adapted themselves primarily to this general 'modernization' rather than to the non-Jews as such.[53] Needless to say (but often forgotten), Jews of other Western countries were affected by this process just as much as German Jews.[54]

It was said earlier, however, that the changes, far-reaching as they might have been, did not lead to the destruction of Western or German Jewry for that matter as a distinct cultural group. Although assimilation did take place, most Jews preserved an attachment to their community which even Katz who perhaps more than any other scholar has stressed the retention of the Jewish element found 'difficult to account for'.[55] How, then, can one interpret this 'novel and singular social entity' which emerged in the 19th century and which combined Jewish and non-Jewish elements in a new and peculiar fashion?

Any explanation of this phenomenon turns on the definition of Jewish assimilation. Only too often we find, it is used in the sense of becoming 'the same', even though the literal meaning is nothing more than to become 'similar' – a significant difference. To be sure, sometimes different groups become so similar as to be indistinguishable, but these cases of complete absorption seem to be the exception rather than the rule.[56] Assimilation, or 'acculturation', occurs wherever different cultural groups live together and in this sense it can be regarded as a 'natural process'.[57] From this it follows that there is no state of 'non-assimilation', even though the degree of cultural change may vary from group to group. Strictly speaking, therefore, the opposition 'non-Jewish' vs. 'Jewish', or 'Deutschtum' vs. 'Judentum', is false. For if 'non-Jewish' stands for the total social, economic and political environment in which the Jews lived and to which they had to respond, their Judaism must have been affected by this; traditional Judaism was not, as one observer put it, 'something apart, immaculate, and mysteriously self-sufficient, adapted to all the exigencies of life'.[58] It follows that 'Germanness' and 'Jewishness' did not constitute alternatives; only complementary elements.[59]

Before German–Jewish assimilation is examined from this angle, a brief remark seems desirable concerning its 'naturalness'. 'Natural' does not mean here that the process of cultural adaptation was painless and smooth. This was certainly not the case. But it suggests that assimilation resulted from socio-economic and political changes which were not brought about by the individuals themselves and on which they had no or very little direct influence. What is important here is that assimilation primarily affected the Jews themselves. Quite a different matter, however, is the relationship with the main society, the reaction of the non-Jews; in other words: the integration of the Jewish minority into the majority society. These two processes should be distinguished more clearly than is usually the case.[60] Instead, numerous authors treat them as identical. Thus, assimilation is commonly judged by the degree, or rather by the failure, of integration and, with a view to the ultimate fate of the German Jews, accordingly condemned. That these two processes are linked to some extent, cannot be denied, but the interrelation is rather diffuse and certainly not as simple and straightforward as the critics of German–Jewish 'assimilationism' seem to believe.

But to come back to the process of assimilation itself: it was suggested that the Jewish and the non-Jewish, in this case the German, element do not stand in opposition to each other but are complementary. This, however, does not mean that Germany's Jews just became Germans, with a few random Jewish elements attached. Nor is it permissible to classify them purely as members of a Jewish nation who have only made certain adaptations to the majority society. In both cases, assimilation is regarded as nothing more than an addition of Jewish to the German elements or vice versa.

If we remind ourselves of the remarks on assimilation and ethnicity made in the previous chapter, it should become clear that the process of acculturation is much more complex than is usually assumed. It was argued that assimilation does not consist in the addition of one cultural element to the other; it has to be understood, instead, as a fusion of the 'old' and the 'new'. This process is a dialectical one; it is characterized by the interpretation of 'foreign' elements pertaining to the wider society, i.e. social, political, economic factors and cultural elements in the narrower sense, in the light of indigenous traditions and perceptions. The resultant adaptations to the re-interpreted environment will further shift the sense and meaning of the old traditions which are then in their turn adjusted to the new situation. It follows that – applied to the position of Jews *vis-à-vis* German society since emancipation and possibly before – a form of ethnicity had developed which integrated Jewish and German elements in a specific, unique way; an ethnicity which was not identical with either culture, but possessed a character entirely of its own.

To be sure, the Jews of Germany were not unique in developing a new identity; similar changes of Jewish ethnicity can be observed in other countries. A brief visit to Israel will offer ample proof of the ethnic diversification of Jewry which has taken place over the centuries. Yet, it is probably true to say that the Jews in Germany were among the first to attempt – both consciously and unconsciously – the transition from a national to an ethnic minority within a plural society. They thus represented an early case of ethnic consciousness as reflected in the 'hyphenated' identity more commonly associated with ethnic groups in the 20th century. As with these, their main characteristics were on the one hand the transference of the national identity from one's own group on to that of the wider society. Yet, strong ties of ethnic solidarity persisted within the group and across national boundaries.[61]

Whereas these two aspects of identity – the national and the ethnic – do not normally pose conflicts for their bearers, the situation of the German Jews was more problematic in this respect. Or, more correctly, it was *made* problematic by large parts of the non-Jewish population who continuously questioned the national loyalty of the Jews and their claim to equal citizenship. These were thus driven to assert forcefully their commitment to the German nation over and over again. 'Whoever disputes my claim to the German fatherland', said Gabriel Riesser, one of the earliest and most prominent spokesmen, 'disputes my right to my thoughts and feelings, to the language that I speak, the air that I breathe. He deprives me of my very right to existence and therefore I must defend myself against him as I would against a murderer'.[62]

Statements such as these, of which we find many in German–Jewish history, might easily be mistaken for an overwhelmingly assimilationist stance of German Jewry. Such a view, however, disregards the existence of a strong group life fed by continued adherence to Jewish traditions. 'Assimilationist' expectations, but also 'male-centered, élite-centered, and Berlin-centered histories of German Jewry have tended to neglect the attachments of culture, religion, and tradition felt by the "silent majority" of German Jews'.[63] This majority preferred a relatively traditional life-style, as one American Reform Rabbi stated with surprise: 'Judging by American standards of Reform the German Reform service was distinctly Conservative, if not Orthodox'.[64] Especially women, as Kaplan has shown in her study of the *Jüdischer Frauenbund* (Jewish Women's League) possessed a 'strong sense of Jewish identity (which) indicates the strength and the continuity of tradition and community in the face of rapid social change in late nineteenth century Germany'.[65]

The relatively conservative Reform congregations, called 'liberal' in Germany, represented what one might call modern, secularized Judaism, since considerable adjustments had been made by it to the 'modern' social and economic situation, although German Orthodox, in contrast to Eastern European, Judaism had also fully accepted secularism. Yet, interestingly enough, those few congregations which went further than appeared necessary and became hardly distinguishable from Christian congregations, as did the *Reformgemeinden* were ridiculed by the 'Liberals' as 'assimilationists' (*Assimilanten*). This again casts doubt upon the widespread assumption that a straight line of progression leads from emancipation to Reform Judaism and finally to conversion.

Outside Synagogue life there existed a host of organizations such as charities, Lodges, defence organizations and cultural associations which fostered a Jewish consciousness and group life.[66] With the creation of these institutions which were, in fact, based to a large extent on traditional associations, Jews had thus established a Jewish (middle class) society alongside the non-Jewish society.[67] This can be read as a further indication that assimilation and integration are two different processes. But what is more: separation should not be confused with segregation. With the tendency to equate the recent history of Germany with the history of antisemitism as such, especially with regard to the situation of the Jews, any signs of social dissociation are often interpreted as results of exclusion on the side of the non-Jews.[68] In many instances, this was certainly the case. But remembering the conditions under which ethnic groups persist, it seems clear that German–Jewish associations also express genuine feelings of group attachment.[69]

Yet ethnic ties transcended those of the religious community. They were felt by many who had become indifferent to religion, not least by baptized Jews who tended to form sub-groups within the ethnic community,[70] although many will have disappeared among the non-Jews without leaving a trace. As with 'modern' ethnic groups we also find here that the attachment to one's ethnic group is nurtured by more than purely religious elements. For the majority, common perceptions and similar 'temperament', born out of a common culture and history, weigh much more heavily. Seen in this light, it becomes understandable why, in spite of increasing religious indifference, most German Jews during the 19th century and early 20th century continued to feel loyal to their group, as Scholem's description so well illustrated.[71]

It is nevertheless interesting that most Jews continued to define their ethnic ties in terms of religion and reacted strongly against conversion; that, indeed, the rate of conversion was not much higher, considering that German Jews were under tremendous pressure to become baptized. This seems to indicate that although for most Jews Judaism had ceased to be the principal force in their lives, it had preserved some of its centrality in that it still fulfilled its function as a symbolic representation of group values, on the one hand, and of marking the boundary between Jews and non-Jews, on the other.

Yet, boundaries between ethnic groups should not be confused with barriers. Whereas many German Gentiles had difficulties in realizing this vital difference, most German Jews did not, as is made clear in the words of a prominent member of the *Centralverein*: 'I do not find it necessary to segregate myself from the society around me in order to continue functioning as a Jew and I do not have to argue myself out of my Jewishness in order to continue living as a man among other men. . . . In the German fatherland, on German soil, we were born, and that entitles us to call ourselves German without baptism and so-called assimilation. We want to belong to the German nation and shall belong to it; at the same time we can and must remain true to our religious community and ethnic heritage'.[72]

The interdependence of religion and the wider social system is, of course, not a uniquely Jewish phenomenon.[73] It was after all the differences in attitudes and achievements between Catholics and Protestants in Germany, observed by Max Weber, which stimulated his study of the 'Protestant Ethic'.[74]

It has often been pointed out that the identification of the Jews in Germany with German culture was of special intensity, perhaps more so than is the case with most other Jewish communities. The reason for this is usually seen in the striking affinity between certain Jewish and German cultural elements in the 18th and 19th centuries. Enlightenment, Humanism and later the stirrings of Liberalism had created a spiritual and intellectual climate in Germany with which the Jews could easily identify: 'As never before Jewry found that the ideas governing society in general were related and familiar to its own creed.' It was 'reason and knowledge' in particular which 'were held in higher esteem than ever before'. Thus a 'spiritual environment was created which seemed to them hospitable and sympathetic and no longer strange and hostile'.[75] One author pointed out that 'the Central European Jewish intellectual, alienated from a Judaism which (he) regarded as parochial, (was) greatly attracted by the single-mindedness and relentless moral seriousness of a German cultural tradition which had profound affinities with that of the Jews themselves'.[76] And we read in Gustav Mayer's *Memoirs* that it was through the works of Lessing, Schiller and Goethe that he, who had grown up in a strictly orthodox home, found 'the way out of the narrowness of my former world into the world of the German spirit'.[77] A highly developed work ethic and a propensity to legal positivism and abstract thinking have likewise been stressed, as has the significance of German classic literature.

But perhaps most important of all was the affinity with philosophical idealism as represented by Kant to whom Germany owed, as Max Horkheimer put it, the 'deliverance of the idea, of the spirit'. Horkheimer sees the similarity between Judaism and idealism 'in its basic structure which combines the sense of reality with the unerring adherence to the idea, the opposite of reality'.[78]

The similarity went even further and extended to the socio-economic and psychological situation. Fritz Stern, for instance, has pointed out that both Germans and Jews were peoples without a nation. They therefore shared the same characteristics stemming from this lack, namely a basic insecurity, the vulgarity of the *nouveaux riches* and a craving for recognition, to which Goldschmidt added *Parteisucht* (factious spirit), lack of civil courage and a leaning towards self-hatred.[79]

More importantly, the identification with Germany on a national as well as on a cultural level affected the entire Jewish community. Its most orthodox members embraced it just as enthusiastically as its most unreligious. 'If we want to know how pure humanity finds its necessary culmination in Judaism, all we have to do is to study Kant', said the leader of the *Agudat Israel*, the association of the orthodox congregations. And Max Wiener said of S. R. Hirsch, the founder of the neo-orthodox movement: 'Hirsch in no way lagged behind the most radical liberalism; [he was] modern . . . and an intellectual, no less than any of his opponents'.[80]

This, again, seriously calls into question the widespread tendency to measure the degree of assimilation in terms of religious observance. The same applies to Zionism: not only was Zionism strongly influenced by German nationalism – German was originally the *lingua franca* of Zionists. One student of Zionism has expressed his amazement at 'how very German' Zionists from Germany were.[81] Their reluctance to leave Germany for 'Zion' has become a common quip among German Jews: a German Zionist is someone who pays a second Zionist to send a third to Palestine. Zionists differed from non-Zionists in their assessment of integration; less so as regards the question of identity. It was only among members of the younger generation of Zionists that it was 'decided

The Process of Jewish Assimilation in Germany

to abandon the fervor of their elders for German nationalism and chauvinism in favor of a total commitment to *Judentum*.[82] But culturally, there was no difference. If 'assimilation' is meant to designate the appropriation of the culture of the wider society, then all German Jews clearly belonged to the same category. Characterizations as 'more' or 'less assimilated' are highly misleading.

This is the point at which we might usefully take a brief look at the other side of acculturation. Since we are primarily examining the situation of the *Jews* here, the impression might arise that their acculturation was a one-way process. But clearly this was not so. Without doubt, cultural cross-fertilization took place to a considerable extent, although it would be difficult to determine this process in detail. It has been well documented, however, that German Jews greatly stimulated and enriched German cultural, academic and intellectual life. They also played leading roles in German politics; in fact, all German parties, apart from the Catholic *Zentrum*, were founded by Jews.[83] Yet, to follow this aspect of culture contact between the groups, would lead us too far from the objectives of this particular study.

Interesting as the affinity between two originally different groups may be, it has to be asked: what were the consequences for the character of German–Jewish assimilation. Most students of German–Jewish history refer to it in their efforts to explain why assimilation in Germany was so much more thorough-going than elsewhere; why the Jews had become so 'German'.

However, at least one eminent scholar, Jacob Katz, has disputed this. He claims that the affinity was more a myth than reality. It had existed to some degree, but its significance had been vastly exaggerated; the cultural differences between Germans and Jews were greater than is usually assumed. What from the 18th century onwards appeared as an affinity was hardly more than the reflection of socio-economic adjustments which had anticipated cultural adjustments.[84]

One must agree with Katz that assimilation also occurred where there was no affinity; that affinity is not a pre-condition of assimilation. Yet it is well-known that German culture was greatly admired by Jews outside Germany. Many Eastern European Jews, untouched by socio-economic developments in Germany, grew up with the German language and the German classics whose ideas, as we are often told, were so close to their own feelings: 'Schiller's poetry came like a breath of spring into the oppressive and stale atmosphere of the ghetto. When Jewish youth began to read foreign works, they took up Schiller first; he excited them and formed their knowledge of German.'[85] What is more: their own language – Yiddish – was closely related to German.[86] It is also significant that where Jews were free to choose which of two cultures to adopt, as in the Polish, Czech or Hungarian areas bordering on the German-speaking lands, the Jews opted largely for the German culture.[87] Such a far-reaching identification seems to prove that the affinity was to a considerable degree 'genuine' and not simply the expression of a secondary 'sameness', as Katz believed.

It is important to stress this point. For what makes the formation of the German–Jewish ethnic identity so striking is the fact that in spite of this high degree of affinity, Germans and Jews did *not*, in the end, become the '*same*', although they did become '*similar*'. The case in question therefore illustrates well the survival of ethnic groups even in circumstances which are extremely favourable to absorption. It is probably true to say that the affinity between Germans and Jews facilitated the process of 're-interpretation',[88] and created a fusion of the different ethnic elements of a rare intimacy, but – and this is crucial – the identification was not total.

On the contrary; there existed significant areas of *dissociation*. Thus it has often been pointed out that the Jews remained relatively (certainly not completely) untouched by irrationalism, certainly a striking element of German culture and political life; that they remained the 'guardians' (Peter Gay) of Humanism and Kantianism when these had ceased to be the focus of German intellectual life.[89] It is often judged to have been a 'failure' on the part of the Jews to recognize the 'real' developments within German society in the 19th century.[90] It has already been explained why this view is untenable. It would seem more fruitful to interpret this divergence as an expression of German–Jewish ethnic peculiarity which led them to identify with certain German characteristics but to reject others.[91]

Yet, it is interesting to note that even in those areas where identification was closest, a Jewish perspective emerged none the less, incorporating the German elements. Thus Graupe has shown how deeply affected *Wissenschaft des Judentums* was by secularist, rationalist and historicist currents within German intellectual life of the early 19th century. It was then that a new approach to history developed in Germany which was 'to see history as a process, as

The Process of Jewish Assimilation in Germany

development. This process leads into and culminates in the present. But for the actual present, for the reflecting historian, the previous ages are past and gone. They have fulfilled their task of bringing about the present and now a new relation exists between them – that of *distance*'. What is missing here, Graupe continues, 'is the inclusion of the past in the present, whereby the Jewish scholars of the old school held past and present actively together. *Development and distance* came to be criteria in the modern historian's view of history and method of working'; whereas in traditional Judaism 'the present in the plane of projection. It finds its confirmation in the events of the past and its goal in the messianic concept of the future. The accent is always on the present'. The new concepts of historiography greatly stimulated Jewish scholarship; yet an essential element of Judaism was preserved: 'At one point the process of development is limited: the Wissenschaft of Judaism abides by the concept of a *goal of history* for the Jews and for all mankind. By setting a goal to historical development, which is geàred to the future, the Wissenschaft of Judaism approached again the old Jewish doctrine of history regarding the "days of the Messiah". It thereby took over a pronounced theological motif into its basic concepts. Messianism links the new discipline with traditional Jewish scholarship. And as with the latter so the Wissenschaft of Judaism remains linked also with the Enlightenment's and Kant's doctrine of history. Their messianism is messianism in "cosmopolitan perspective" '.[92]

Graupe's study contains further fascinating examples of the attempts made in this period to integrate the Jewish perspective with the German one. Moritz Lazarus, for instance, the founder of *Völkerpsychologie* whom his 'contemporaries regarded . . . as the most distinguished and illustrious representative of Judaism', tried in his popular *Ethics of Judaism* 'to apply Kant's concept of autonomy to the ethics of Judaism'. Similar efforts were made by the greatest Kantian, Hermann Cohen – 'the recognized representative of German Jewry and Judaism . . . during the first quarter of this century' – of whom Graupe says: 'The detour via Kant brought Cohen back into a new relation with religion and to an awareness of his Judaism. Yet this detour also set the perspectives of his portrayal of Judaism, fixing its methodical boundaries'. It is significant that Cohen, too, finally 'arrives at the Jewish concept of God as the principle of ethics'.[93]

What these examples show is how significant was the merging of two different perspectives. It is not so much the Kantianism of the

Jews as such which is important; there were, of course, also non-Jewish Kantians, although, interestingly enough, Kant was more popular among Jews. The decisive factor here is the Jewish perception of Kant's philosophy and its re-interpretation in (German–) Jewish terms. This would seem to support what has been stressed above, namely that it is *perception* rather than cultural *institutions* which characterize ethnic differentiation in plural societies. Any definition of the 'ethnic' element therefore has to focus on mental structures rather than on content.[94]

An analysis of German–Jewish culture along these lines has only rarely been undertaken. Instead, the focus is on the content with the predictable result that a German–Jewish culture is mostly declared non-existent. Thus, one author complains that 'the German Jew of the last few generations had a unique opportunity to create a new Jewish culture'. He should have combined 'Hebraic learning' with 'the complete command of the content of Western culture. But the amalgamation failed to take place. . . . No distinctive Germano–Jewish culture' emerged.[95] The shortcomings of a content analysis is also obvious in Norbert Altenhofer's article on Gustav Landauer's Judaism. In this study of Landauer's intellectual development the rather questionable claim is made that because no mention is made in Landauer's memoirs of Jewish traditions or of Jewish thinkers, his philosophical and sociological thinking which had been formulated previously, can not have been influenced by his Judaism![96] Peter Gay likewise dismisses a German–Jewish culture out of hand and maintains point-blank that 'most Jewish cultural activity was German in form and in substance, alike in manner and matter'. Though a few pages later he makes the revealing remark that the 'general mediocrity [of Jewish contributions to German art in the 19th century] partly reflected the ancient Jewish aversion to making images. Receptive as Jews have always shown themselves to the cultures in which they were embedded, much as they have always learned even from their persecutors, some of their cultural traits have been a response to internal impulses'. He adds elsewhere: 'While Jews have not been traditionally associated with the arts, they have for many centuries been enjoined to pay devout attention to words. Clearly, this concern with language has critical psychological consequences'.[97]

Unfortunately, Gay was not aware of the implications of his observations and stopped his analysis where it should really have begun. Consequently, he is unable to make sense of a famous statement by Else Lasker-Schüler. After her emigration to Palestine, the poet refused to have her poems translated into Hebrew, giving what to Gay was an 'astonishing, almost mystical' answer: 'But they are written in Hebrew.'[98] There is nothing 'mystical' about this admission. Intuitively, the poet had grasped the essence of 'genetic structuralism' which helps us to gain a more subtle understanding of the problems of ethnicity and culture raised in this chapter and to be illustrated in the empirical part of this study.

To summarize the crucial aspects of the foregoing discussion: it was pointed out that German Jews are traditionally considered as the 'most assimilated' Jews. We have seen that not only the assumptions, but also the evaluations underlying the notion of assimilation are questionable. Assimilation did take place; it usually happens where groups are in contact with each other, especially if their members are dispersed among the main society. However, Germany's Jews did not become Germans, did not simply exchange Jewishness for Germanness. Instead, Jewish and German elements were integrated in such a way that a form of German–Jewish ethnicity emerged which was not identical with either culture. This 'new' culture is often not immediately apparent because of the lack of overt cultural elements. Religion had lost its central significance for Jewish life in the age of secularization, even though many Jews continued to define their 'peculiarity' in terms of religion. Judaism had developed into an ethical system of values and in this way had contributed to the shaping of an ethnic identity which comprised also the indifferent and even many baptized Jews. To become aware of this ethnic culture one has to focus on mental structures, i.e. on perceptions, rather than content.

A peculiar characteristic of German–Jewish ethnicity was said to lie in the high degree of affinity between certain Jewish and German cultural traditions in the 18th and 19th centuries. This may explain, it was suggested, that the identification of the Jews in Germany with German culture was, if not total, nevertheless particularly intense.

One might add that other – non-German – Jews often have great difficulties to understand how deeply rooted German Jews were in Germany which most of them, in spite of fierce hostility at times, regarded as their natural and only home, even as the 'Promised Land' (Hermann Cohen); a feeling which was further strengthened by the fact that the Jews as a group had been established in Germany for well over 1500 years. In contrast to Jews in all other countries they were the only Jews – until Hitler – never to have been expelled completely from their territory.[99]

The German Antisemites, of course, disputed this affinity and declared the Jews an alien and hostile 'race'. Their temporary victory, however, has not legitimated their claim. Other minorities, such as the Social Democrats, Catholics, Communists, even modern artists, were similarly stigmatized at various stages in modern German history. The German Jews constituted just as much an integral part of German society as these groups. 'Jewishness' and 'Germanness' were not, by most of them, experienced as conflicting concepts, let alone conflicting forms of life, but as an organic and indestructible whole.

3 Life Under the Threat of Nazism

THE CRISIS OF THE GERMAN–JEWISH IDENTITY

Anti-Jewish hostility – always present in German social and political life in varying degrees – finally broke through to the surface in the 1920s and 1930s when it developed into the major political force. After the deceptive 'Golden Age of Security'[1] which German Jews had enjoyed during the period before World War I, they were rudely shaken out of their dream of progressive integration and, ultimately, full acceptance by the majority society.

The anti-semitism experienced previously, nostalgically called the "good old antisemitism",* appeared to them as "something we were used to", "something we could live with". Its main characteristic was 'the paradox of simultaneous nearness and distance' which is, as Reichmann pointed out,[2] typical of Jewish–Gentile relations and – one might add – of the relationship between an ethnic minority and the majority society generally. For some Jews this distance, often perceived as hostility, was a source of pain and bitterness.[3] Others, such as Max Born, the physicist, felt that their Jewish extraction 'did not constitute a greater deviation from the norm than to be a Catholic in a Protestant region'.[4] Most of my older interviewees would certainly agree with him here.

However, once the Nazis had seized power, the German–Jewish identity of Germany's Jews came under heavy attack. Their spiritual and later physical existence was threatened as never before. Considering how deeply rooted the Jews were in Germany, it is easy to imagine what a shattering experience the increasingly violent persecution and gradual expulsion from all spheres of German life must have been. And indeed, many memoirs written in

---

* Respondents' comments appear in double inverted commas throughout the following chapters. Quotations from other sources appear in single inverted commas.

exile, tell us the sad story of the trauma suffered in the early years of the Nazi-regime.[5]

Persecution and expulsion from one's home are, of course, always painful. But for the German Jews the blow was particularly crushing, for 'we were Germans, otherwise all that happened later would not have been so horrifying, so shattering. We spoke the German language, so dear to us, our mother tongue in the truest sense of the world, through which we received all words and values of our lives, and language means almost more than blood. We did not know any fatherland other than Germany and we loved the country as one loves one's fatherland, a love which was to become fateful later on'.[6]

The Nazis' rise to power, the growing threat of anti-semitism, threw German Jews into deep confusion; it led to a fundamental identity crisis.[7] German culture, as we have seen, had become an integral part of their own cultural and spiritual existence. In this they differed from the 'Jewish Jews' of Eastern Europe, as Wassermann called them,[8] who had preserved some more distinct Jewish cultural elements which they took wherever they went, and which offered some emotional protection in times of persecution. It was impossible for the German Jews simply to extract the 'Jewish' part of their culture, to respond to the exclusion from German life with a retreat into a Jewish shell, without seriously upsetting the fabric of their total existence. In this sense, German Jews were more vulnerable than 'Jewish Jews' and expulsion cut deeper. For many, in fact, it meant a death blow. Thus it was repeatedly mentioned by interviewees that their parents never recovered from the shock of the persecution and forced emigration. They reported that their fathers had often literally died of a broken heart soon after emigration. Even today, after 40 years in exile, many members of the older generation are still filled with bitterness and indignation at the impertinence of the Nazis declaring them aliens in their own country. "It was all so senseless", Mrs C. remembered, sadly, "I was only young, and we were just in the process of laboriously building up our lives. The Jews were very highly educated (*gebildet*), weren't they? And they have done such a lot of good. Not all of them were bad. We were totally normal people, after all, I cannot get over the senselessness of it all." To be sure, the problems of sheer survival, of securing a livelihood before and after emigration aggravated the strain. Yet it seems that, for most, the psychological traumas of the upheaval, the humiliation were even harder to bear.

Under the impact of the "catastrophe", the "earthquake"[9] of 1933 leading members of the community undertook strenuous efforts to cushion the effects of mental dislocation and to search for a new point of reference for German Jewry. 'Urgent appeals for the preservation of dignity in the face of unending humiliation'[10] alternated with self-accusation for having gone too far astray as Jews. This is well reflected in one of Eva Reichmann's articles written in 1934:

> The age of Emancipation has come to an end. Our inner security (*seelische Sicherheit*) is shattered. Perhaps it made us dull, only too self-confident and satisfied. Admittedly, there always were anti-Jewish attacks, but we hardly let them penetrate our consciousness. We saw the historical development too one-sidedly to be able to believe in serious upheavals. . . . In this state of inner uprootedness . . . there is only one support: our Judaism. We have, during the period of our social rise, neglected our Judaism too much. . . . Who knew Jewish history, who still observed our precious (*innigen*) customs? Who regarded his Jewishness, even if he was conscious of it, as something other than his unalterable, tired fate; who was still aware of it as a creative force, to be shaped lovingly?

But she nevertheless warned her readers not to condemn the process of emancipation as a failure, for German Jews had every reason to be proud of their achievements during that period. She continues:

> The awareness remains as a result: the opening of the gates of the ghetto, the gift of freedom which was offered to the German Jews through the Emancipation, was fate, was danger and was hope. . . . Jewish and German energies grew together to form a human and mental–spiritual attitude which need not fear the judgment of history. Of all emancipated countries and for many reasons, only Germany has created this genuinely fruitful synthesis.

She finished her article on the encouraging note that 'we as Jews have always been used to the most difficult living conditions, and if we understand to learn from our history we will find that we have stood the test all the better the rougher the storm of the struggle for survival which was raging around us'.[11] This time, however, the storm was to develop into a hurricane and the German Jews would have to muster all the skills, experience and intelligence at their disposal to weather it.

A PERIOD OF RE-ORIENTATION

This is not the place to examine the activities of the German–Jewish community, its successes and shortcomings, in those dark years of the Nazi regime.[12] However, it is interesting in this context to note that a return to Judaism did take place to some extent. Even if it was initially often brought about by outside pressure, many German Jews developed a genuine interest in Jewish traditions and history, resulting in a stronger sense of Jewishness which has persisted to this day.

Nor was this trend a new phenomenon in the 1930s. On the contrary, it linked up with a movement which had started during World War I, when antisemitism reared its head again after a period of relative calm, and gained momentum in the 1920s and 1930s. It was supported by a number of German Jews who had been particularly sensitive to the rising waves of antisemitism. Critical of the 'assimilationism' – as they saw it – of the German Jews, they turned towards Judaism to counter the hostility they met in the wider society.[13] Through strengthening the Jewish dimension of the German–Jewish ethnic identity, they hoped to be effectively armed spiritually against the offensive 'racialist image' disseminated by the Antisemites.[14]

The most determined and consistent attempts were made by Zionist groups which particularly attracted younger Jews. They were 'the only happy and well-adjusted people' in Germany in the 1930s, one observer recalled during his British exile. He also mentioned that, as in his own case, frequent conversions to Jewish Orthodoxy took place at the same time. 'To experience the atmosphere, to hear the familiar tunes . . . gave me a feeling of security and shelter in those days'.[15] A fellow-refugee stated likewise that his interest in Zionism was kindled by the persecution: 'Without the gift (of Zionism) life under the Nazis would have been unbearable for me. Yet, from now on it became not only bearable, but thanks to my studies of Jewish history and philosophy in which I immersed myself, I continuously gained a better and a new understanding of, and insight into, the position of the Jews in the Christian world and with it of my own'.[16]

The interest in Judaism was also fostered by other organizations such as the *Lehrhaus*, founded in the 1920s by the influential philosopher Franz Rosenzweig and led successfully by Martin Buber in the 1930s. It was an institute of Jewish adult education which was given the task of educating the German Jews 'for a community linked by memory, for the immediacy of life together in order to found a new Jewish community, and a new community of labour. That hardship, hitherto known to German Jewry as essentially an intellectual problem only, "has seized us with both hands and turned the eyes of all those to Judaism, where this was still necessary. What we must now know is whether we are walking the path to Judaism in truth. In our history, hardship has always had a reviving power. It is not the worst thing that our starting point is hardship and compulsion. What we must do is make of it freedom and a blessing"'. Interestingly enough, the courses of the Institute, according to Simon, 'were also attended by some Frankfurt non-Jews who in their own circle, except for the *Freies Deutsches Hochstift*, could hardly enjoy any longer such intellectual freedom'.[17]

The B'nai B'rith Lodges with a membership of some 120 000, mainly from the more prosperous strata of German Jewry, represented another institution encouraging German Jews 'to walk the path to Judaism'. It had changed from a social club into an association consciously cultivating Jewish traditions. This happened as early as 1924, under the influence of Leo Baeck who, as *Grosspräsident*, assumed the spiritual leadership of German Jewry in the years to come, and was to do so beyond the expulsion and dispersion of Germany's Jews.[18]

The efforts were intensified after 1933 when the segregation between German Jews and non-Jews became more pronounced. After the first shock, caused by the Nazi seizure of power, was over, the Jews started to re-organize their community life. This also applied to their cultural life. Thus the main body, the *Reichsvertretung* advocated the 'creation and cultivation of our Jewish sphere of feeling and education. We avoid the word "culture" intentionally, for a Jewish secular culture does not exist in Germany and will only exist in a very limited sense in times to come. We German Jews must and will continue to live within the German cultural realm. We believe nevertheless that a positive Jewish world of education has to be built and that it is in this field that greatest efforts will have to be made by us in future. This all the more so since, over the last hundred years, we have neglected this area and did not know anything about Judaism when we awoke in 1933'.[19]

One of the fruits of these efforts was the *Jüdische Kulturbund* which enabled Jewish artists to continue working after their dismissal by the Nazis from their former positions in the arts. Although founded by the Nazis as part of their policies of segregation, the *Kulturbund* soon became a major force in Jewish cultural life in the 1930s with a rapidly growing membership of up to 180000.[20] The works performed, however, had to be restricted to those created by Jewish artists which, in the eyes of some, made the *Kulturbund* rather "provincial". Yet, for many others it offered one of the 'main sources of amusement, distraction and edification',[21] since many Jews now avoided theatres, concert halls and other public places and, from 1935 onwards, were not permitted to enter them at all in most parts of Germany.[22] Knowing, as we shall see again later, how much *Kultur* – music, theatre, literature and the arts – meant to German Jews, it is not surprising that the *Kulturbund* formed the 'largest voluntary association of Jews in Germany'.[23] *Kultur* became the expression of their human dignity, after their political, economic and social rights had been taken away from them.[24]

To this list must be added further institutions which offered the comfort of group solidarity and strengthened the Jewish identity, such as Jewish sports and youth clubs, the latter with a membership of 55000, or the League of Jewish Women with a membership of 50000.[25] This is a high proportion considering that the Jews in Germany numbered only a little over half a million in the 1930s.

The Synagogue, traditionally the focus of Jewish community life, continued to play an important role. This is also borne out by the experiences of individuals interviewed for this study. Of 66 respondents of the first generation, 38 belonged to liberal, 8 to orthodox Synagogues, 18 kept a kosher household, 16 were agnostic or indifferent. Out of a total of 70 informants of the second generation 30 described their families as 'liberal', 9 as 'orthodox' and 10 as 'non-religious'. Thus, out of a total of 136 nearly two-thirds, namely 85, belonged to a Synagogue. To be sure, membership of a Synagogue did not necessarily express a deep religiosity. Among the Liberals in particular attitudes varied widely. We find 'very observant' or 'traditional' Jews among them, or, much more commonly, the *3-Tage-Juden* who went to Synagogue only on the three most holy of Jewish Holy Days; some started to go more often

Life Under the Threat of Nazism

after 1933; others even went for the first time in their life "to see what it's like". Some kept a kosher household, others again preferred "Matzah with ham". Yet whatever the degree of observance, the main fact is that the Synagogue represented an active link with the Jewish community.

Last but not least the Jewish schools must be mentioned which, although not very popular before 1933, played a vital role for the community later, when Jewish children were dismissed from state schools. This happened to quite a number of refugees interviewed. A few resented the heavy dose of Judaism which was provided all of a sudden. Most seem to have welcomed it; what is more, in a Jewish school they were sheltered from some of the effects of anti-Jewish hostility. The Jewish school, Hans Gaertner said, was 'a safe island, which . . . enabled the children not only to lead their own life but to grow mentally'. It offered protection from "humiliation and loss of their self-confidence".[26]

THE SIGNIFICANCE OF THE EASTERN EUROPEAN JEWISH IMMIGRANTS

It has been pointed out that Zionist and non-Zionist movements of *Selbstbesinnung* were greatly stimulated by the influx of largely orthodox Eastern Jews before and after World War I. Whereas many of these continued their journey to France, Britain and the United States, a large number settled in Germany – permanently, as they thought, not suspecting that they or their children would have to resume their move westwards a few decades later. A considerable number of refugees interviewed for this study belong to this group.

The encounter between German and Eastern European Jews was fraught with problems. Most of the immigrants from the East were destitute and "uncultured" in the eyes of the mainly middle and upper-middle class German Jews. There were 'important class and temperamental differences'.[27] These gave rise to tensions to be felt even today. The German Jews have been accused of arrogance and 'antisemitism' in their dealings with the *Ostjuden*. Still, hostility of this kind was nothing new in Jewish history. On the contrary: 'In no country and at no period – with the exception of Palestine – did the settled Jews welcome large numbers of immigrant Jews or were prepared to accept them with open arms in their midst'.[28] As in the case of Jews in other countries, the German Jews made generous donations to enable the majority of the refugees – not only to stay but, hopefully, to move on.[29] This should not necessarily be interpreted as hard-heartedness, as Wertheimer stressed; it was 'the fear of protected but insecure Jews forced to confront their own vulnerability when they were exposed to Eastern immigrants'.[30] They were afraid that these often strange-looking and poor Jews from the East would fuel the antisemitic propaganda that Jews constituted an alien and unassimilable 'race'. Plausible as they are, these Jewish–Jewish tensions reflected an ironic situation: the roles of the 'native' Jews and the 'foreign' Jews would soon be reversed, the 'native' Jews of today were to be the 'foreign' and despised Jews of tomorrow. For in the 1930s, the German Jews themselves would have to seek assistance from the by then 'native' Jews of Eastern European origin in the countries of refuge, such as Britain and the United States.

Although hostility may have been widespread, its extent should not be exaggerated, however. Thus Wertheimer stressed that 'while . . . individuals often treated Eastern Jews contemptuously . . . German Jewry acted responsibly as a group. . . . Even as they scorned their Eastern co-religionists, German Jews also displayed genuine concern for the needs of Eastern Jews. Native Jews lent support, advice, and comfort to the newcomers'.[31]

More than that: a significant minority of German Jews was deeply impressed by the encounter with the largely orthodox Jews from Eastern Europe. They seemed to represent 'pure Judaism' which many Jews in Germany were longing to regain. Especially among Zionists a veritable cult sprang up with the Eastern Jew being given the role of something like the Noble Savage.[32] It was during World War I that many young German Jews had come into contact with the Judaism of the Eastern Jews for the first time. Quite a number of them were deeply moved by this experience.[33] However, the subsequent idealization of the *Ostjudentum*, on the one hand, just as the hostility of others on the other, demonstrated how difficult it was for German Jews 'to gain a realistic attitude towards Judaism'[34] – and one should add, towards non-German Judaism. For it was undeniably the ethnic differentiation between German and non-German Jewishness which expressed itself here. It is not surprising therefore that, except for the small circle of dedicated Zionists, attempts to revive a general interest in Yiddish and Hebrew and to foster a Jewish culture based on *Yiddischkeit* largely failed.[35]

Instead, Eastern Jews who joined the *Gemeinden* of the native Jews as 'full-fledged members . . . quickly became Germanized' (Wertheimer). But it was precisely through their 'rapid absorption', he continues, that 'the immigrants had a profound impact on their native co-religionists'.[36] Not only did they strengthen the orthodox elements of the community, being a strong group numerically. They also made their influence felt as teachers and Rabbis, thus, in a way, resuming traditions of the 18th and 19th centuries.[37] It has therefore been argued that the Jews from Eastern Europe 'exercised a Judaising influence on their more assimilated fellow-Jews; they strengthened the Jewish ethos', in Eva Reichmann's words.[38]

But was this generally true? Or put differently: was it only due to the Eastern European influence that German Jews took renewed interest in Judaism? The main impression one gets when listening to German Jews is that direct association with Eastern Jews seems to have played only a minor role in their relationship with Judaism before emigration. In fact, many Jews who lived in Western and Southern Germany may not have had any contact with them at all or at least but very little, since the majority of the immigrants from the East tended to settle in Eastern Germany, more particularly in certain towns such as Berlin, Leipzig or Chemnitz.[39] Even in these places social contact between native and immigrant Jews seems to have been limited. Because of class differences the groups lived in different parts of the town. If they met, at school for instance, as some respondents did, it was the ethnic difference which often divided them, namely the particular brand of eastern Orthodoxy which German Jews found bewildering and outlandish.[40]

This degree of alienation, as expressed by a number of respondents, is remarkable, because many German Jews are themselves descendants of Eastern Jews who had moved to the West not more than one or two generations previously. In fact, out of 143 respondents 41 said that one or two parents or grandparents had originally come from Poland, some 28 gave Prussia and Silesia and another 22 Berlin as places of origin of their families. We know that many Jews from those areas had also been immigrants from provinces further to the East so that the number with Eastern ancestors must have been even greater. It is reflected in the popular definition of a Berlin Jew which I heard on several occasions: "A Jew from Berlin is a Jew whose parents come from Posen and whose grandparents from Poland." This was fully borne out by my sample: by far the majority of Eastern European descent had lived in Berlin in the 1930s, only a minority in Breslau, Leipzig and some other towns in the Eastern Provinces of the German Reich. This also seems to answer the question: when does an Eastern Jew cease to be one, namely once he has settled in Berlin, with Posen with its formerly large German-speaking Jewish community forming an important link in the process of 'Germanization'.

It became obvious during our conversations that a close link with Eastern Jewry made many people feel slightly uncomfortable when asked about their families' background. One person described it as a "family joke". In others it sometimes turned into embarrassment, when the 'Eastern connection' was coupled with a father's or grandfather's occupation of low status as that of peddler or rag dealer. Jews from Western or Southern Germany of equally humble background showed less self-consciousness. It seems that the embarrassment about the link with it was caused by what Eastern Jewry stood for, in the eyes of the German Jews, namely the backwardness and poverty of life in the ghetto, from which their parents or grandparents had managed to escape. There were exceptions. Thus Mr. E. who had come from Danzig never felt part of German Jewry, although his mother had come from Prussia, but identified closely with the *Ostjudentum* to which his father's family belonged. Mr. E. in fact became more orthodox than his father. And he added that the 'mixed' marriage of his parents had never caused any problems in his family.

Admittedly, the information collected by me on this point is sketchy, since it was of only marginal importance for this study. Yet the impression remains that the pull towards German–Jewishness was on the whole stronger than it was in the Eastern European direction.

Mixed or even hostile feelings towards a 'Jewish Jewishness' could also be detected among Jews from other parts of Germany. Thus interviewees reported that noisiness, conspicuous behaviour of any kind were considered 'Jewish' and forbidden in many families, exactly as Charles Hannam describes it in his autobiography: 'Anything that resembled Jewish or Yiddish culture had more or less been eliminated from speech and custom.' Exceptions were made when one was within the family circle with no outsider around. 'Hair had to be short', and no garlic was permitted because of its association with Polish Jews.[41] Hannam mentions another expression of the rejection of the 'Jewish Jewishness' which I also encountered, namely an admiration for the blond and blue-eyed 'Hans' and 'Inge', immortalized by Thomas Mann in his *Tonio*

Kröger. It emerged unconsciously in most cases, as when a woman repeatedly described her daughter as "pretty" because of her blond curly hair and her blue eyes, "not like me, dark hair and so", or when a brother was said to have been a very attractive child because of his fair hair and blue eyes. Or similarly Mr. M. who liked the non-Jewish boys in his class better than the Jewish ones. "I found them prettier. Boys should be blond, blue-eyed and strong, I felt."

These elements of rejection of a certain kind of Jewishness, while clearly expressing some degree of self-hatred, should nevertheless not be mistaken for a flight from Judaism altogether. Notwithstanding some exceptions, the older interviewees left no doubt that in Germany there had never been any question about their Jewishness in a positive sense; but theirs was a 'German Jewishness' and not a 'Jewish Jewishness'. It could be found in a community life of a specific German–Jewish character, and as such it has flourished to the end. But even all those who had neglected the Jewish dimension of their lives in the sense of an active involvement in Jewish affairs had stored enough of it in their subconscious to reactivate it within a short time, creating a sense of solidarity whose strength took some by surprise: 'At the moment of mortal danger the tie among us non-believers, alienated brothers proved stronger than one would ever had thought possible.'[42] A group spirit emerged – or was re-inforced – which would last well into the period of resettlement in the countries of refuge.

Yet in spite of this – qualified – 'return to Judaism', German Jews did not become more nationalistic than before, or aspire to 'Zion' as their new haven; to most of them emigration appealed just as little in the early 1930s as before. 'Even Zionism', stated Robert Weltsch, himself a well-known Zionist, 'as strange as it may sound today, was an emigration movement in a restricted sense only; it was essentially the affiliated youth groups which planned their emigration. Zionists considered themselves to be an ideological group which advocated a national centre to give the Jews an identity and free them from their "shadow existence".'[43]

ASPECTS OF JEWISH–GENTILE RELATIONSHIPS IN THE 1930s

Only a small minority was convinced that there was no future for Jews in Germany. The majority believed – and so did the majority of the respondents – that the "madness" of the Nazi regime would not last or that, after the dust of the take-over had settled, a new form of German–Jewish synthesis might develop allowing a co-existence on the basis of complete segregation.[44] The Nürnberg racial laws of 1935 seemed to point in this direction. In the eyes of many Jews they created, within strictly defined legal limits, a 'mental and spiritual living space for us'.[45] Before 1933 German Jews had continuously stressed that they were just as much part of German society as non-Jewish Germans. They made their point even more forcefully after 1933, the more discrimination and socio-political ostracism increased: 'No paragraph can rupture our tie with German culture: it has developed through us, around us and within us German Jews living in the realm of German culture. We can claim it as our 'own' culture, insofar as it has been felt and practised by Jews – thus we can be German in our own sphere, while it has become inadmissable in the *general* sphere'.[46] To be sure, life would have been anything but pleasant under these circumstances, but it might have been bearable. After all, 'hardly ever is Jewish life a life without danger, the individual Jewish life rarely, and the collective Jewish life never'.[47]

After events had taken their fateful course in the 1940s, German Jews have been repeatedly taken to task for the 'illusions' they harboured about their situation in the 1930s. Some of the severest critics came, not least, from their own ranks. Thus Karl Stern found only harsh words for 'the masses of Jews (who) were, in spite of years of gathering clouds, psychologically and ideologically utterly unprepared. Most people think of us as cunning, foxy, with a great amount of practical foresight. The years after 1933 proved us to be as sentimental in our attachments, as emotional and stupid in our practical decisions, as much given to wishful thinking and self-deception as any other people'.[48]

Yet again, as in the case of our earlier evaluation of assimilation, one may argue that the political developments in the 1930s and the seriousness of the threat to the Jews can be discerned much more clearly today than was possible at the time. It seems odd indeed that a whole population of largely highly-educated and, one would think, on the whole fairly enlightened individuals should have been so 'stupid'.

A more satisfactory answer may be found if one tries to understand how the situation presented itself to the German Jews at the time. Only then will it be possible to do justice to their reactions to the 1930s. Of course, one would have to question eye-witnesses on a large scale to obtain a full assessment. Nevertheless, the picture which emerges from the information given by the relatively small sample interviewed for this study, seems illuminating enough to be of wider significance.

Some of the questions which immediately come to mind in this context are as to whether the situation changed dramatically after 1933 and whether there was a conspicuous deterioration in Jewish-non-Jewish relations in everyday life. Friendship patterns can be considered as a reliable indicator; accordingly the interviewees were asked about the proportion of Jews and non-Jews in their circle of friends and in that of their parents. Out of a total of 36 individuals of the first generation who remembered their parents' friends, 24 or two-thirds described them as "mixed" which meant in 11 cases "completely mixed", i.e. roughly half and half, in further 11 cases "mainly Jewish", and in another 2 cases "mainly non-Jewish". It seems interesting that among the remaining 12 parents with a "purely Jewish" circle of friends, 7 had an East European background, with six of these coming from Posen. Among the "purely Jewish" or "mainly Jewish" friends were also included "assimilated Jews" or, in the words of the interviewees: "My parents were highly assimilated", "very German", "good Prussians", but nevertheless "consciously Jewish". However, we also find cases among the parents with "mainly" or "purely" Jewish friends who considered their own Jewishness and that of their friends as accidental; some were baptized or had their children baptized. Their friends tended to show a similar degree of detachment from institutionalized Judaism, just as orthodox Jews tended to recruit their friends from similarly observant Jews. They thus offer an example of the fact, mentioned in the previous chapter, that Jews tend to form subgroups within the Jewish community according to the degree of detachment from or closeness to institutionalized Judaism. Mention should also be made of the fact that in quite a number of cases of "mainly Jewish" friends, the non-Jewish friends were the closest and that the friendships with them generally withstood well politically difficult times; often these bonds even survived the years of emigration and wartime when contact was interrupted.

If we now turn to the first and second generation respondents themselves, we find that out of a total of 57 individuals 46 had a mixed circle of friends of which 26 were "completely mixed", 16 "mainly Jewish" and 4 "mainly German (non-Jewish)"; 4 had "purely German" friends and 7 "purely Jewish" friends. These figures reveal some changes. For the first time, "purely German" friends appear; there is only a slight increase in "mainly non-Jewish" friends, but a stronger increase in the "completely mixed" category. Furthermore, the distribution of the "closest friends" is remarkable: out of a total of 41 individuals 22 mentioned non-Jews, 18 indicated Jews and one spoke of "mixed", i.e. she could not decide who was closer, her Jewish or her non-Jewish friend.

Similar trends can be observed in the following generation, i.e. among those interviewees who were born during the 1920s and 1930s. Of course, not all could remember who their friends in Germany were, because they had left when they were still very young. The total of the answers therefore is relatively small. 20 individuals out of 44 said their friends were "completely mixed", 15 replied "mixed, but mainly Jewish". This adds up to about three quarters of all "mixed" friends (no answers for "mixed, but mainly German" in this group), and 3 each for "only Jewish", "only non-Jewish" and "no friends". Of no statistical value, but nevertheless of some interest may be the fact that 8 interviewees had non-Jews as "closest friends" and 3 had Jewish ones. .The others could not remember who their closest friends were or whether they had any at all. More significant appear to be the comments made on their parents' friends. Out of a total of 24 who remembered these friends, 8 stated "mainly Jewish", 12 "completely mixed" and another 4 "only Jewish".

These figures seem to suggest that a high proportion of German Jews mixed freely – and at an increasing rate – with non-Jews, with a correspondingly small number of Jews who moved in exclusively Jewish or non-Jewish circles. This trend was only partly to be reversed in the second half of the 1930s, after complete segregation between Jews and non-Jews had been decreed, particularly through the introduction of a compulsory Jewish school education for Jewish children. Up to that point, social contact between Jews and non-Jews had increased throughout the 1920s and 1930s, in spite of rising waves of antisemitism. This is in marked contrast to the Wilhelmine period, the so-called Golden Age of German Jewry.[49]

To be sure, the intensity of the relationships in the 1920s and 1930s varied. Often the non-Jews belonged to the wider circle of friends only; but the fairly high number of non-Jews among the close friends indicate that even intimate relationships were not uncommon.

Because of the limited size of the sample, one may hesitate to accept these figures as representing more general trends. They are confirmed, however, by the incidence of mixed marriages, even though the statistics on this subject vary considerably. Arthur Ruppin gives 22.2 % as the mean rate of mixed marriages for the years 1904 to 1908, with wide regional variations, such as 9.6 % for Bavaria, 43.8 % for Berlin and 49.5 % for Hamburg.[50] According to other investigations an even more dramatic increase took place in the years between 1920 and 1930. At that time, the general rate was 48.6 %, with 73 % for Berlin and 75 % for Hamburg.[51] However, these figures have been dismissed by various scholars as unrealistic. Their computations arrived at much lower figures: the average rate of mixed marriages is estimated to be 17.5 % for the 1920s with 24 % for Hamburg and 27 % for Berlin. These figures, even if considerably lower than the earlier ones, must still be regarded as fairly high.[52] This is certainly true when compared with some figures from the United States. They were 2 % for New York City between 1908 and 1912, 3.6 % for Cincinnati between 1916 and 1919, 3 % for New Haven in 1930 and 7.2 % for Stamford, Connecticut, in 1938. Even the figures for the 1950s did not exceed 7 to 10 %.[53] This is not to say that the German situation was unique. An increase of the intermarriage rate could be observed throughout Europe from 'the latter part of the 19th century until the advent of Hitler'.[54] This seems to corroborate the trend in Jewish–Gentile friendship relations which, according to our samples, show a very high degree of mixing. It is to be expected that the circle of friends out of which the non-Jewish marriage partner was chosen must have been considerably bigger than the actual number of Jewish–Gentile marriages.

It is not only the relatively high degree of social integration, at least at the level of friendship, which seems significant, but also the fact that the trend continued practically uninterrupted by the rise of the Nazi party. However, there were some exceptions among our respondents: 4 individuals of each of the first and second generations said that they did not have any non-Jewish friends any more after 1933 because they changed from a state school to a Jewish school. We shall also see that antisemitism poisoned some relationships, even close ones.

If the picture looks too rosy against the background of upheavals in the early part of this century, we should remind ourselves that so far we have been talking only about friendships, not about Jewish–Gentile relationships in general. Let us take a brief look therefore at how other spheres of Jewish life in Germany were affected by antisemitism. Again it seems advisable to distinguish between the first and second generation, i.e. between those who consciously experienced the pre- and post-1933 periods and those who had mainly childhood memories of those years.

Out of a total of 74 of the older generation, 24 had personally suffered from antisemitism. 8 of these experienced it only after 1933; out of 50, 35 had no personal and 15 very little experience of antisemitism. The high proportion of the latter group seems striking, and indeed, some of the interviewees themselves expressed their amazement when they looked back on their life in Germany. One found it "remarkable how little affected we were by the political situation as such"; inflation was felt much more strongly, he added. Mr G. said that he had hardly noticed anything, "or I did not want to. I cannot understand it today. Perhaps someone called me a Jew, but I did not take any notice". "To some extent I was very naive, not sufficiently conscious of the danger", Mr W. explained. Mrs S. who had made no secret of her anti-German hostility in fact admitted: "I feel sort of rather guilty about not having encountered any antisemitism in Germany; the terrible thing is they were all so nice to me, especially when I emigrated."

It also seems significant that my question about personal encounters with antisemitism in Germany was considered somewhat ridiculous by some and countered with remarks such as: "Of course, I did", "I should, shouldn't I?" – followed by astonishment when the search in their memories brought forth relatively little evidence. Clearly as refugees they certainly did not have any motivation to idealize their experiences in Germany. We can therefore assume that the answers give an accurate representation of their past experiences. Here are some examples of how many respondents felt in the 1920s and 1930s: "We were not conscious of who was Jewish or who was not"; "I did not feel at all different at school." Several, in fact, stressed that "all had been very fair at school", "I was absolutely happy at school." Teachers and heads of schools were more often than not described as "decent".

It should perhaps be added that it would be wrong to assume that those who have not had any personal experience of antisemitism were not aware of its existence. "Of course, we have always known about antisemitism, but Berlin was an oasis where we felt secure." One interviewee had "the feeling to suffocate because of the political atmosphere" and therefore left Germany as early as possible, but he had not suffered from antisemitism directly. Mrs St., her happy life in Düsseldorf notwithstanding, found the "atmosphere terrible". But so did non-Jews: "My greengrocer", Mrs St. added, "would have loved to emigrate together with me."

Those who had encountered antisemitism remembered some occasional anti-Jewish remarks. One woman was aghast at the blatant ignorance betrayed by her classmates with respect to Judaism and Jewish people. Someone else who had heard other people saying that all Jews "were sitting on a fat sack of money", was actually wondering whether his father possessed such large amounts of money and, if so, where he might have hidden it! Another respondent found out about anti-Jewish attitudes only indirectly when, being dispensed from religious instruction at school, he heard his teacher from behind the classroom door indulging in Nazi propaganda. His outpourings were spiced with antisemitic remarks, yet emphasizing in the same breath: "But our Hans is completely different. He is a nice boy." A similarly schizophrenic attitude was displayed by another teacher who said: "What a great shame it is that a person like you who has such an excellent feeling for German literature, is not a German." Mr G. found this combination of flattery and anti-Jewish feeling comical rather than offensive. In another case, the remark of a teacher had more serious consequences. When Bohemia had become part of the newly created Czechoslovak Republic after the end of World War I, Mr M. was asked by his teacher what he thought about it. His reply was that he did not consider it all that important. He hoped "that the world after the war would be organized in such a way that it should not matter all that much on which side of the frontier one lived". Whereupon the teacher answered: "As a Jew, of course you have cosmopolitan ideals and lack the same feeling for the nation and for the fatherland that we non-Jews have." The boy never forgot this lesson and later on decided for this reason not to become a solicitor as he had originally intended. "I was not upset. I thought it might have been true."

The forms of antisemitism which emerge from these experiences were generally considered as relatively mild. They were expressions of the "good old antisemitism" which "one was used to". After all, "the relationship between Catholics and Protestants was not all that fantastic either".

However, other respondents related much more unpleasant memories. Thus Mr H. from the Ruhr area was still filled with bitterness about his youth in Germany: "Antisemitism in our area was very strong. Rathenau's assassin, after all, came from our town. It made my life a perfect hell; it poisoned my youth. My own teachers were decent; in fact, I maintained contact with them and visited them in Germany after the war. They had tried to stem antisemitism; it was the children mainly: they called me names. It was much better later on at the Universities (Bonn, Berlin, Freiburg)."

Like most of Mr H.'s generation, he went to school in the 1920s. In some respects those years seem to have been much worse than later years. There were four other individuals who, out of the 24 who had experienced serious antisemitism, specifically mentioned the year 1923 – the height of the inflation – as having been particularly violent. It was in that year that *Völkisch* extremism was very noticeable. To be sure, the fights among the schoolboys or students at some universities, especially in Austria, were basically fights of Nazis against anti-Nazis, and many Jews involved in them primarily fought for political reasons. Nevertheless anti-Jewish hostility often enough added extra fuel to the flames.

Regional variations became apparent: 4 of the 5 Austrian refugees of this group had suffered badly from antisemitism. And they all agreed that it was much worse there than in Germany. Long before the *Anschluss* in March 1938, the official occupation of Austria by the Nazis, there were violent clashes between Nazis and Antinazis. Public abuse of the Jews was widespread. There was also a large measure of agreement that anti-Jewish hostility within Germany was strongest in eastern parts of the Reich, with Leipzig and Breslau standing out as particularly virulent.

Out of this group of 24 representatives of the first generation there were 8 who did not remember antisemitism before 1933, but clearly afterwards. For 6 it had meant painful personal experiences: close friends, sometimes even the best friend, did not come to visit any more; some even refused to know them. In one case, it was the fiancé who broke off the engagement after he had been put under pressure from his colleagues at the hospital where he worked as a doctor. He later on had the good taste of sending his former fiancée a photo of himself donning as SS uniform. The husband of another couple, married this time, was pressed by 'friends' in 1933 to divorce his Jewish wife, but he refused. In fact, 40 years afterwards, when telling his story, his voice was still betraying the anger he had felt about the fact that someone could ever have conceived such a vicious idea. He and his wife emigrated together. The 'Aryan' partner in another mixed marriage did not have the strength to resist the pressure. The respondent, apparently noticing my dismay, quickly assured me that the pressure had been tremendous. It was in 1942 that his wife divorced him which – as she must have realized – meant immediate deportation and death for most, although the respondent luckily survived.[55]

It was to be expected that antisemitism – overt or hidden – created barriers, "invisible dividing lines", between Jews and non-Jews. The point is that these barriers were not impenetrable. On the contrary, close ties of friendship existed – and persisted – to a surprising degree. Even those who suffered badly at the hands of Antisemites, on the one hand, spoke warmly about the 'loyalty" and "integrity" of the non-Jews in their circle, on the other. Some even went so far as to maintain that Nazism was "something from outside"; most Germans were said to be basically "conservative" but "decent"; although some of them were "*aufgehetzt*" (subverted) later on by Hitler. Still, many friends and acquaintances continued to visit secretly after 1933: "We had a good name, after all." It is difficult to imagine today what these visits meant, the awkward problems they could cause under the Nazi dictatorship. An unsensational, but touching scene conveys it perhaps better than many words: "Do you remember, Karl", Mrs L. asked her husband during our conversation [in German] when we visited our friend? She only came secretly [to me], you know. And we visited here after dark only. And do you remember, Karl? On one occasion you took a rubber plant which you held in front of your face so that people would not recognize you. And then you fell into a ditch, because you could not see, and it was so dark. Your shoes were terribly messy, all muddy, but you still had them in England for quite a while. Yes, you kept them, do you remember?'

Not only friends but also maids, nannies and cooks were remembered with deep affection. Most of them remained loyal and continued visiting their former employers, even after it had become dangerous for them to do so. In a number of cases – the same also applied to non-Jewish friends – they kept contact with the parents long after the children had emigrated, until the former were deported. Some then took charge of the flat and furniture of the family and returned them to the children as soon as contact was reestablished after the war.

With the notable exceptions in the legal and medical professions, similar loyalty was reported to have been shown by business partners, workers, customers or patients and colleagues at work. A number of these helped Jews to escape. This happened either in the form enabling the Jewish business partner to take over an overseas office or by opening a branch of the firm abroad. In some cases the Jewish partner was not even aware of the urgency of the situation: "My father had to be pushed out of Germany by his firm to save him." If the emigration occurred early enough, a business partner was enabled to take his share of the capital with him. There are also many cases of non-Jews warning their Jewish employers, customers, friends or their relatives before a wave of arrests. This happened mostly in November 1938, a day or two before the *Kristallnacht*. In one case it was a policeman; in another it was the milkman who offered a family his van to enable them to escape. Last but not least there remains the fact that some 20 000 Jews inside Germany survived Nazi persecutions and likely death owing to an evidently fairly large number of non-Jews who hid them and provided them with food.[56]

Some of those who helped and gave a discreet warning, also included a number of Nazis. Some even were – and remained – friends, such as Mr G.'s best friend who even was to join the SS during the war. But this did not impair the friendship: "He stood by me absolutely, although it was dangerous for him. And after the war we helped each other again. He was in prison and I vouched for him that he had not had anything to do with the persecution of the Jews. He later on helped me to get a nice pension (restitution). He also helped my mother to get her restitution money. Our families are very close. Also the younger generations."

Up to now we have described the experiences of the first generation, i.e. those German Jews who were grown up by the time the Nazis rose to power. We will now turn to the second generation, i.e. to those whose childhood was overshadowed by the Nazi regime. Surprisingly, in spite of the worsening political situation, the pattern of their experiences closely reflects those of their parents' generation. ('Parents' should not be taken literally here since, in fact, only two respondents were the children of representatives of the first generation). Out of a total of 56, 25 had never encountered antisemitism personally and 10 very little, 64% in all. Nine had suffered badly, a further 11 only from about 1935 onwards. This adds up to 36%, as compared with 68% and 32% respectively for the older generation and shows no significant increase in the personal experiences of antisemitism over the generations. There are other consistencies: several of those who did not suffer personal attacks were nevertheless aware of antisemitism. "The whole atmosphere was depressing", Mrs S. remembered. "There was general suspicion in the society. And the Jews were suspicious of each other in another way: one never knew who would emigrate next." This was felt as a sort of desertion and had an unsettling effect on the relationships.

Although primarily felt as an "undertone", antisemitism could still be most disturbing emotionally for children or young people, especially when experienced at school. Thus Mrs F who was allowed to continue at the state school – a privilege temporarily granted to children of World War I veterans – thought that it was a "big mistake" not to have sent her to a Jewish school. Neither her teachers nor the children in her class were antisemitic, but the general atmosphere was so poisoned that she felt extremely unhappy. There was "nothing really nasty, but I just felt so out of it". This feeling of being a "misfit" has never completely left her since then. To this day, she has not quite forgiven her father for having been too "blind" to realize how she suffered.

Quite a number of this generation did switch to a Jewish school in the course of the 1930s which eliminated one important source of potential anti-Jewish hostility. If their friends had been purely or mainly non-Jewish in the early 1930s, the emphasis shifted more to the Jewish side; so much so that a number of respondents moved in a purely Jewish environment from the middle of the 1930s onwards.

On the other hand, we have those for whom life continued much as before. Again, the teachers do not fare too badly: overt or outspoken Nazis seem to have been the exception rather than the rule; as Mrs J. remembered, "one teacher appeared in uniform in 1933, he was just a sadist who got worse". Mr F. recently read that his grammar school was regarded as one of the most reactionary schools in Berlin. "I am staggered", he exclaimed, "I don't remember any antisemitism at school at all." In fact, the majority of the teachers were described as *"korrekt"* and some even as sympathetic and "unhappy" about incidents of antisemitism among the pupils. Mrs S. still fondly recalled her teacher who wrote into her *Poesie-Album* (autograph book): "*Nicht zu hassen, mit zu lieben sind wir da*" (We live not to hate but to love one another).

However, about a third suffered badly from anti-Jewish hostility. Children were the main villains either at school or in the street or both. The attacks occurred mainly after 1935, the year of the Nürnberg Laws were introduced. It was from that date onwards that children more than ever before, spat on, threw stones at or beat up Jewish children or called them names. Thus Mr T. was actually threatened by schoolmates with knives on a school outing. Life in Germany for these children was made very miserable: "I was always scared", said Mrs M., "because children spat on me when I went home (from the Jewish school). And then there was the *Stürmer* (antisemitic paper) displayed in a glass-cage at the corner of our road. I still have some horrible memories of seeing members of the community displayed in the paper, another one every day. That person then committed suicide. And I remember signs of *Juden unerwünscht* (Jews unwanted) at the entrance of villages . . . I was always worried when father was not at home." Mr E. remembers likewise: "I was not happy at school. There was a lot of anti-semitism." "I was always depressed", said Mr C. who saw antisemitic demonstrations in 1936 during which blood-thirsty anti-Jewish slogans were sung. It also happened about that time that a bigger boy beat him up because "I had killed 'our Jesus'. Thenceforth it got worse all the time".

Not less painful were personal disappointments. For example other children refused to play with them from one day to the next, or – worse – friends turned away. There is the case of Mr D.'s previous form teacher "whom I had really loved. When I met him in the street (after Mr D.'s transfer to a Jewish school) he turned away. That shocked me deeply. But I sensed that the situation was unpleasant for him as well. I felt more sorry for him than for myself".

Some remember to have been upset when being turned out of their swimming or gymnastics club. Yet others did not mind these discriminations all that much: "That were just a bit annoying", one respondent said. If possible, the regulations were ignored, that is if one's 'Aryan' looks – or those of an accompanying cousin – permitted it. Other effects of the ever harsher anti-Jewish policies of the Nazi regime had much deeper repercussions on the life of the children. Thus they saw their parents suffer, especially their fathers whose struggle for economic survival became ever more desperate.

In some cases, even their parents' life was at stake. In 1938, Mr E.G.'s parents, living in Vienna, were denounced by a waiter in a restaurant after making some anti-Nazi remarks. Both were imprisoned by the Gestapo. His mother was released a year later, but his father was so badly beaten up during the interrogation that Mr G. did not recognize him when he was brought home on a stretcher; he soon died.

Yet, as with the previous generation, we also find a few cases of active support by non-Jews; under what circumstances this took place is indicated by the fact that the business partners of Mrs St.'s father had to go to prison because they had helped him and other Jewish partners. Other non-Jews showed a more passive loyalty: customers who came to the backdoor after 1933 because they were too scared to enter the shop by the frontdoor; private patients who did not desert their Jewish doctors, thus enabling these to carry on practising. Small acts of solidarity are again reported by interviewees before the *Kristallnacht* in the form of warnings or shelter given to the families. There were also expressions of sympathy or horror at the events of the 9 and 10 November.[57]

As we have seen, there were also many who were indifferent or who betrayed their Jewish spouses, friends or colleagues. Yet, the reports by the refugees show that this was not necessarily true for the majority of the non-Jews with whom they were in contact: most passed the test relatively well, especially when judged against the violently anti-Jewish hostility of an extremely racialist regime.

But what about the Germans in general? It might appear reasonable to assume that these friends, let alone the "nice Nazis" among them, were just a small minority. However, there is some evidence that the balance was different. It has already been mentioned that certain groups within German society had proven less immune to Nazism and antisemitism than others. But it has also been shown that the attraction Nazism exercised on other parts of the German population had 'relatively little to do with Antisemitism'. Anti-Marxism, authoritarian attitudes, economic crisis, anti-Versailles nationalism and other factors played a role at least equally important in the relative success of the Nazi party.[58] Certainly the extent to which latent antisemitism existed within German society and which the Nazis were able to exploit to a considerable degree, should not be underestimated. And yet, they never succeeded in mobilizing and radicalizing the majority of the population.[59] Thus they failed to instigate mass pogroms against the

Jews in spite of strenuous efforts in this direction on various occasions. If the Germans 'had been moved by outright hatred of the Jews', Reichmann consequently remarked, 'their practical aggression against them would have been excessive after the Jews had been openly abandoned to the people's fury. Violence would not then have been limited to the organised activities of Nazi gangs, but would have become endemic in the whole people and seriously endangered the life of every Jew in Germany. This, however, did not happen. Even during the years in which the party increased by leaps and bounds, spontaneous terrorist assaults on Jews were extremely rare."[60]

It should be clear that what has been said so far is not meant to whitewash the Germans or to offer a discussion of German antisemitism as such, let alone of the controversial question of resistance during the Third Reich. Rather the intention has been to put the answers given by the respondents into a wider perspective. It is hoped that the points made will lend credibility to the experiences as related by the refugees which might easily be dismissed as 'illusionary' or 'selective' by those with more simplistic notions of Nazism and antisemitism, their causes and effects. The starting point of this section was how the events in the 1930s presented themselves to the German Jews. Many – even their children – have expressed astonishment at the fact that most Jews in Germany felt relatively safe until the late 1930s. But going by their experiences with non-Jews as described, is it surprising if so many thought "Hitlers come and Hitlers go?" Many non-Jews thought the same. As long as the majority of the non-Jews around them remained "decent", the Jews felt secure, "only too secure", as is now admitted remorsefully. "My colleagues in Hamburg were all so nice", Mrs C. remembered. She added: "Even in 1938 we still did not believe how serious the situation was." And similarly Mrs T., actively involved in Jewish community work throughout the 1930s: "We believed for a long time that Hitler would not last. We were always encouraged in this by the Social Democrats and other parties. All believed we would succeed. We were asked to stay because we would be needed for the reconstruction of Germany [after Hitler's fall]. Today, I often feel guilty for having persuaded people to stay on. But how could we know? . . . The years under Hitler were not particularly unhappy because we had the feeling to be able to help [through community work]. No, these years were not necessarily years of despair. They were interspersed with hope and also help from allies, from sides from which we had never expected it. All this contributed to our reassurance and encouragement."

EFFECTS OF THE NAZI POLICIES ON THE GERMAN–JEWISH COMMUNITY

But it was not only at the level of human relations that the Jews were led not to expect the worst for their community. Other factors reinforced this feeling. To begin with, in the early years of the regime, its full wrath was directed against all political enemies, whether Jewish or not. This was confirmed by some respondents who do not remember any antisemitism but anti-Communism from the early 1930s. A number of other respondents pointed out that the deterioration of their situation was so slow that it was difficult to become aware of the direction it took. Only those who had been abroad for some time were appalled how "terrible" the atmosphere had become: "If one grows up with it, one doesn't realize what is going on."

To this must be added that different groups of the Jewish population were affected differently by the various anti-Jewish regulations which were introduced in the course of the 1930s. The first to suffer were the Jewish civil servants. Being employed by the state, they were dismissed after the Nazi take-over and the promulgation of the law for the Restitution of the Professional Civil Service in April 1933. Employees also often suffered badly from discrimination; self-employed businessmen, on the other hand, were not hampered until the dismissal of Hjalmar Schacht in 1937 who, up to that point, had prevented serious interference by the Nazi Antisemites in economic policy-making. According to the respondents' account of their own or their father's experiences, Jewish doctors suffered because they were struck off the register of the national *Krankenkassen* scheme with the effect that their practice shrank to private patients. But most of these patients remained with their doctors, thus enabling them to live in some material security.[61].

The picture which the developments in the 1930s presented to the Jews, was confused and confusing not only because the impact of antisemitism varied considerably. It played a much more significant role as a political factor than as a social factor, i.e. on the level of Jewish–non-Jewish relationships. Yet, even on the political level anti-Jewish regulations were not implemented systematically, but often in contradictory ways: periods of violence and draconian measures were followed by periods of relative calm which gave rise to fresh hope "that the madness would stop". Thus, several thousand Jews who had emigrated in 1933, actually returned to Germany in 1934 because it looked as if the regime had adopted a more "legal" course after the initial turmoil of 1933 when arbitrariness ruled.[62]

Last but not least there was a socio-psychological factor which influenced the perceptions of a number of Jews and hence their reaction to the events in the 1930s: not all of them found Nazism totally unacceptable. Considering that Jews were subjected to the same pressures and stresses as Germans in general, it is not surprising to hear several respondents admit: "If we had not been Jews, who knows – we may have been Nazis, too."[63] Mr I. went even further and frankly confessed: "My father once said to me: 'Thank God, you were born Jewish, because you would have made a vicious Antisemite.' I am one of the Jewish Antisemites, I tell you. I find what is a typical Jew repulsive. ... I know, it is unforgiveable."

Whatever hopes or uncertainties the German Jews had about their situation in the 1930s, the attacks on Jews, and Jewish property and community institutions during the 9 November and 10 November 1938, more savage than ever before, made it brutally obvious to all that there was no future for Jews in Germany. Jewish men and women were beaten up, tens of thousands of Jewish men were rounded up and thrown into concentration camps. The beating, torture, humiliations and shootings they suffered or witnessed made it abundantly clear to them that this was only a prelude to what was in store for all Jews. Some, much to their surprise, met relatives or acquaintances in the camps who had been imprisoned earlier on. Only now did they realize that these had been just as innocent as they themselves were. Needless to say that the encounter in the camps with organized brutality on a large scale, even if experienced for a few weeks only, shook the victims deeply. Not only the men themselves, but their families, too, were shocked when they saw the state their men were in after their return from the camps. There is the case of Mr C. who said that he will never forget the sight of his father, thin and with his head shaven, sitting in the living-room, trying to talk about his experiences, but "he only cried and cried and could not stop crying. Never in my life have I seen a man cry like that".

Outside the camps, shops and synagogues were looted and burnt down, flats were smashed up. To this day, respondents who were still in Germany at the time (and this was the majority) have preserved the most vivid memories of the horrors and fears of that time. It was then that efforts to emigrate were made more strenuously than ever before.

However, there were some, especially among the older ones, who, even at this point, felt so much part of Germany that they could not believe the threat of Nazism had become lethal. Some respondents who had already left Germany, tried hard to persuade their parents to leave; but often in vain. This feeling of being too deeply rooted in Germany to leave, was commonly mixed with the fear of being too old to start a new life in a strange country. Among other motives for the reluctance to leave, the refusal to part with one's possessions, having preserved them at great sacrifice during the hard years of the economic depression was already mentioned. Paradoxically, prosperity facilitated emigration in many cases, but it also proved to be an obstacle.[64] It was similarly reported that relatives had found it impossible to accept the lowly jobs for which their family members in exile had secured work permits. Many others, although they had a comfortable life with servants of their own, overcame their reluctance and accepted positions as domestic helps or butlers. However, there were some who preferred hardship and likely death in Germany to a life in misery and poverty abroad. This gives an impression of the inner struggle involved in the decision to leave under any circumstances which most of them must have experienced.

The majority of Jews frantically explored various ways of getting out of Germany. Thousands failed in their efforts because they were without contacts abroad or simply without luck. Thousands more, although in the possession of friends and visas, were trapped when war broke out. Again there were a number of women who stayed behind, not because they were reluctant or unable to leave, but because, as respondents pointed out, many Jews were under the illusion that the Nazis would spare women and children. This hope was apparently nourished by the fact that only men were imprisoned in November 1938; what is more: the myth of the brave German soldier, evoking images of heroism and chivalry, may have contributed to the idea that defenseless women and children would have nothing serious to fear. Whatever the roots of this belief, the result of it was that in a number of cases the fathers left on their own to search for a new home abroad for their family. However, war broke out before many succeeded, and their families perished. Other respondents lost their parents who had been unwilling to leave their own ageing parents, the respondents' grandparents, behind.

In a way, the shock of the so-called November pogroms of 1938, as well as Austria's *Anschluss* earlier that year, proved to be a blessing, because it forced the Jewish community of "Greater Germany" to speed up emigration before the outbreak of the war put an end to it altogether. It is true that time ran out only too quickly for the Jews. After the outbreak of war, thousands were trapped because foreign countries closed their frontiers and from the end of 1941 emigration was prohibited altogether by the Nazi regime. As a result, about 135,000 German Jews were deported during the war years. Most of them perished. A considerable number committed suicide. Thus in 1942/43 a quarter of all deaths among Jews in Berlin alone were suicides. A similarly high rate was reported by the Vienna correspondent of the *Daily Telegraph* in 1938.[65]

Nevertheless, the majority of German and Austrian Jews succeeded in escaping in time; the larger part in 1938/39. During the one year preceding the war, 'nearly as many Jews left Germany as during the previous 5½ years'.[66] In terms of numbers this meant an exodus from Germany of about 150 000 between 1933 and the first half of 1938 and of about 120 000 in 1938/39 alone. To this number, another 140 000 or so refugees from Austria and Bohemia must be added. In other words: out of a total population of about 680 000 German and Austrian Jews, about 400 000 had been able to leave by October 1939.[67] Sadly enough, for most of those who had sought refuge in countries on the Western European Continent, the escape was only temporary. After the invasion by the German army the Jews in these areas were hopelessly trapped; only a few managed to flee or hide. Among the luckier ones were those who concern us here, namely the refugees who had emigrated to Britain. It is their fate in this country that will occupy us in the second part of this study.

4 Emigration

The exodus of refugees from Germany took place in several stages. The first major wave was released immediately after Hitler had seized power; for as soon as the regime was installed, the Nazis started ruthlessly to persecute whoever was considered an enemy of the Nazi movement. The majority of the emigrants took refuge in West Europe favouring the countries bordering on Germany such as France, Czechoslovakia and the Netherlands. There were several reasons for this. Werner Rosenstock has pointed to the greater familiarity of the refugees with these countries; the wish to be close to family and friends left behind in Germany and, last but not least, the relative ease with which it was possible to *enter* these countries.[1]

By comparison the emigration across the channel was much less significant; only a trickle of between 2000 and 3000 refugees had reached Britain by April 1934. Similarly, during the following years the influx of refugees stayed at a fairly low level compared with the number of immigrants to Palestine or the Americas. It was only after November 1938 that these numbers were drastically pushed up, following strong pressure from various groups within Britain to facilitate immigration. Some 40 000 of the 100–150 000 who left Germany at that stage were allowed to enter the country. Many of these, however, were admitted as transmigrants only and on the condition that they would leave Britain as soon as they had received visas for their original country of destination.[2] The outbreak of the war prevented these transmigrants moving on. Consequently Britain quite unexpectedly sheltered some 80 000 refugees from Germany, Austria and Czechoslovakia during the war. A number of these resumed their migration as planned or returned to the Continent as soon as the circumstances allowed them to do so. As a result some 50 000 refugees from Central Europe were believed to be still residing in Britain in the early 1950s.[3]

There are several explanations for the relatively slow increase of refugees in Britain. One was the greater geographical distance between Britain and Germany which made her less attractive than countries on the Continent, as has been mentioned above. This view is also supported by our sample: out of 95 respondents who left Germany between 1933 and 1938 only about half (49) named Britain as their first choice. The others had either unsuccessfully tried to emigrate to a different country or had in fact arrived in Britain via France, Italy, Switzerland or Czechoslovakia (in order of frequency). It seems that Britain originally was not very popular as a country of settlement with many of the émigrés. To be sure, several refugees described themselves as Anglophiles from early on and gave this as a reason for choosing Britain. There were also other attitudes. "It was the last country I wanted to go to", Mrs Sch. said, "English was my worst subject at school." Or there is the case of Mr T.'s father who went to Britain in the early 1930s to see what it was like. "He came back terribly depressed. He found England so sordid", his son remembered. His parents went to Switzerland instead. Similar motives might have been behind the curious fact, mentioned by Sherman, that 'a total of 79 271 visas had been granted since May 1 (1938) and that some 50 000 of these had not been used. It was apparent to the Passport Control Officers', Sherman continued, 'that many refugees had obtained British visas as a hallmark of respectability and a form of insurance, without any present intention of using them'.[4]

However hesitation on the part of the refugees is only one aspect of the answer to the question why the number of immigrants was so low up to 1938. Probably more significant was the fact that the British government pursued a highly restrictive immigration policy throughout the 1930s. It is true, 'as the exodus from Germany increased, . . . practically every European country tightened its immigration regulations and its frontier security'.[5] The British government, however, adopted a rigorously selective admissions policy right from the beginning. As early as 12 April 1933, it was decided at a Cabinet meeting to

> try and secure for this country prominent Jews who were being expelled from Germany and who had achieved distinction whether in pure science, applied science, such as medicine or technical industry, music or art. This would not only obtain for this country the advantage of their knowledge and experience, but would also create a very favourable impression in the world, particularly if our hospitality were offered with some warmth.[6]

Even if no firm resolution followed this proposal, it was nevertheless relatively easy for individuals who had achieved some reputation in their field to be granted a permit to live and work in Britain. Permission to enter, if not to work, was furthermore given 'to persons coming to the UK on business, for visits to friends, or for purposes of study'.[7]

Most German Jews succeeded in converting their visitor's permit into a resident's permit after a few years. The same applied to many of those who had come over to Britain as students. To be granted permission to stay was not easy though; often some string-pulling was necessary. However, it posed much less of a problem to enter the country during the early years of emigration.

In 1938 a visa system for German and Austrian nationals was introduced which drastically reduced the chances to immigrate. 'More stringent regulations accompanied the visa requirement, and required the intending migrant to demonstrate either possession of financial resources or definite guarantees of maintenance until such time as he might leave the United Kingdom for permanent settlement elsewhere.'[8] Yet exactly these requirements were particularly difficult for the refugees to fulfil, as we shall see below. The situation was alleviated somewhat when, after November 1938, the British Government responded to the pressure of various groups within Britain: visa requirements for unaccompanied children up to the age of 17 were waived and admission granted to domestic servants, nurses, transmigrants and trainees of the age of 16 to 18 years.

Nevertheless, the more generous interpretation of the admissions policy in certain areas of employment did not basically alter Britain's official attitude that it was a 'country of transit, not of settlement for the purpose of work, except in individual selected cases. . . . But the limitations [of employment] have been very strict'.[9] We shall see in a moment in what ways the German–Jewish refugees were affected by these regulations.

ACADEMICS

The first group forced to leave Germany was in a fortunate position. It largely consisted of distinguished academics, well-connected businessmen and famous artists. What is more, in the early years of the regime, the refugees could still bring out some money and other possessions. Thus, this group on the whole had a relatively easy start compared with later arrivals.

This was particularly true for the large number of scholars and scientists. Those who were without private means were helped by the Academic Assistance Council (AAC), later called the Society for the Protection of Science and Learning (SPSL). It later joined forces with the *Notgemeinschaft Deutscher Wissenschaftler im Ausland*.[10] The SPSL was founded shortly after Hitler's seizure of power in order to assist German scholars who had been dismissed for 'racial' or political reasons to find jobs abroad. It was largely privately funded with a 'substantial part' coming from British university teachers who contributed a certain percentage of their salary.[11] However, not every scholar who asked for employment in Britain was offered a place. The SPSL had its own panel of advisors who assessed the candidates. In order to be sure the money would be well invested, only the likely winners were backed, i.e. only the best were given grants.[12] Moreover, the Society tried to find a place at a university for the scholar – or, if that failed, at least to persuade the university 'to give hospitality of their laboratories, their libraries'.[13] Those who were not selected by the Society's panel were given advice on employment elsewhere.

However, the number of British universities was fairly limited in the 1930s and their capacity to accommodate refugee scholars was soon exhausted. Those scholars who could not be placed in Britain were helped by the Society in a different way. It organized a lecture tour to the United States for them, provided them with a six-month's grant and the return fare. By the time of their return to Britain all of them had succeeded in finding jobs.[14] They could now prepare their re-emigration to the United States.

As a result of the rigorous principle of selection and the restricted number of university places available, only a relatively small part of all these scholars registered with the SPSL was admitted to or stayed in Britain. Thus it was stated in a report by the Society that 601 out of 2541 registered scholars were living in Britain in 1946, 307 of these being German.[15] The 'great majority' of the registered scholars had gone to the United States.[16] It is very likely that most of those who had to re-emigrate were quite happy with this outcome, since the United States had, by this time, become one of the most favoured countries of emigration.

The main concern of the SPSL were university teachers. However advice and help, if not financial assistance, was also given to 'several thousand displaced scholars who were not university teachers'.[17] This rescue operation of scholars by scholars, especially if compared with the performance of other professional bodies, was very remarkable notwithstanding its limitations. It was the result of the basically international spirit of the "republic of science". Scholars had long before exchanged their knowledge with colleagues abroad, worked in each other's laboratories and libraries and met at conferences in various countries. Thus a network of human contacts had emerged which proved its importance in this hour of danger not only to academic but also to physical survival. A few examples may illustrate how this network operated in individual cases. Thus Professor C., a biochemist from Berlin, had gone to Britain in 1926 as a young man to visit some relatives. It was on this occasion that he made the first contact with important British scientists. In 1929 he again went, this time to do some research at University College London. Both visits had an "enormous effect on me", he remembered, "they were a liberating experience for me". For, at that time, the atmosphere at British scientific institutions was much more liberal than in Germany. This experience was "very important" because it was an eye-opener for him. But perhaps even more significant was the fact that during his stay he was able to make further contacts. As a consequence he was invited by a colleague, a leading British scientist, when Hitler came to power and offered a job at UCL Hospital.

Or there is the case of Professor H., also a scientist, who made his first contact with Britain on a short visit in 1931. He liked the country immediately. What decided the issue for him was a policeman whom he saw playing with a cat. "Can you imagine a German policeman doing that? I said to myself that is a civilized country. I have seen what matters." There were elections in Germany on that day, he added, with the Nazis showing large increases for the first time. He would have liked to stay in London, because he had misgivings about the future of Germany. But nobody in England would have believed him. Also he thought it better to finish his studies in Germany. He therefore returned temporarily. He continued his research, published widely, thus establishing himself in his field. Through various contacts his case was brought to the attention of an influential British scientist who invited the young scholar to join UCL where he stayed until his retirement. He never regretted having left Germany. "There are few places which I would have liked better than this college."

Even in law, not exactly a particularly outward-looking discipline, it was possible to establish contacts which alleviated the problem of emigration. Thus Professor Tr., as the previous scholars, had been to Britain before; in his case it was in 1926 when he came on a 3-month visit to London. He liked it very much and decided there and then to come back. He returned to Germany because of his girlfriend, his future wife. The early contacts, made during his short stay, and the fact that by the time he was forced to leave Germany he had already published three books, helped him to receive introductions from various academics. He settled in Britain in 1934 and, having done another Ph.D., started on a distinguished career in International Law.

Further examples could be added. They all show that the contacts were achieved through hard work and international reputations resulting from it. It is not all that surprising therefore that so many from their ranks would later become British scholars of the highest distinction.

This is not to say, however, that the refugee scholars were always received with open arms by their British colleagues. One of the main principles of the highly selective admissions policy of the SPSL had been to avoid friction with the latter.[18] But even after having overcome this barrier, the foreign scholar was often faced with xenophobia or antisemitism. This was particularly true of Britain whose universities were 'less receptive to foreign-born scholars than those of America'.[19] The large influx of eminent scholars evoked jealousy and fear of competition, if not simply anti-German feelings on the part of native academics.

On the other hand, not all refugees found it easy to adjust to a new, sometimes even hostile environment. They felt insecure and resentful, often hiding these feelings behind arrogance and aggressiveness which led to further tensions with their colleagues.[20] After all, the difference in the style of teaching and doing research was considerable. It was particularly strong in the contrast between the German preference for theory and the English leaning towards empiricism. Thus Karl Popper wrote in his autobiography:

> In Oxford I met Schrödinger, and had long conversations with him. He was very unhappy in Oxford. He had come there from Berlin where he had presided over a seminar for theoretical physics which was probably unique in the history of science: Einstein, von Laue, Planck, and Nernst had been among its

regular members. In Oxford he had been very hospitably received. He could not of course expect a seminar of giants; but what he did miss was the passionate interest in theoretical physics, among students and teachers alike.[21]

Over the years however that opposition often led to a fruitful integration of both elements. A famous example of this process is offered by Karl Mannheim who enriched British Sociology but was in his turn positively influenced by the English academic environment:

> Academic life was far less Olympian and less inbred in England than in Germany. And within academic life, sociology was far less self-contained and self-assured. To Mannheim, transplantation into such a more fluid, more humane and less status-bound world was by no means a loss. . . . The English responded to him in spite of the language barrier which he overcame only with difficulty. But he in turn was also profoundly influenced by the Anglo-Saxon mind. . . . He saw the merits of a more concrete, more peripheral, less systematic and more pragmatic approach.[22]

This influence was particularly strongly felt in language. To quote Popper again:

> My main trouble was to write (*The Poverty of Historicism*) in acceptable English. I had written a few things before, but they were linguistically very bad. My German style in *Logik der Forschung* had been reasonably light – for German readers; but I discovered that English standards of writing were utterly different, and far higher than German standards. For example, no German reader minds polysyllables. In English, one has to learn to be repelled by them. But if one is still fighting to avoid the simplest mistakes, such higher aims are far more distant, however much one may approve of them.[23]

Similar experiences were made in quite different fields of scholarship. Thus Erwin Panofsky, the art historian, remembered that every art historian

> had to make up his own dictionary. In doing so he realized that his native terminology was often either unnecessarily recondite or downright imprecise; the German language unfortunately permits a fairly trivial thought to declaim from behind a woolen

curtain of apparent profundity and, conversely, a multitude of meanings to lurk behind the term. . . . In short, when speaking or writing English, even an art historian must more or less know what he means and mean what he says, and this compulsion was exceedingly wholesome for all of us. Forced to express ourselves both understandably and precisely, (we realized), not without surprise, that it could be done.[24]

Even so, the result was not always successful and probably the majority of the refugee scholars had to rely on the 'editors at the publishing houses (who) did what they could to turn Teutonic English into a passable imitation of the literary language'.[25]

These scholars appear to have welcomed the switch to English as their new idiom. Yet there were others who were much less happy about this transition and who remained ambivalent. Thus Max Born wrote that it was 'his ineradicable longing (*unüberwindliches Heimweh*) for the German language' which made him return to Germany after the war. He may have felt the same as Moritz Bonn whose case is particularly interesting since he has always had close family and professional ties with Britain, even long before his emigration. He considered England his 'second home' and was completely bilingual: 'I spoke and wrote English as fluently as my native tongue. Yet I was always under a heavy handicap when I had to express my innermost thoughts in English. . . . I rarely ever again experienced the creative joy that is the reward of a writer who has succeeded in saying what he meant to say in words that perfectly render his thoughts.'[26]

The remarks made by the scholars quoted above reflect experiences which are also common among German–Jewish refugees outside the academic world, as will be seen below. The two languages have generally been contrasted in the same way and the concreteness and directness of the English weighed heavier than the 'darker' German. In this context Hughes made an interesting observation in his study of refugee scholars in the United States. But the same may be said of the refugees in Britain. He pointed out that

> in spheres in which nuance of expression was not crucial – where the major terms employed were conventional or international, and meanings direct and unambiguous – exposure to Anglo-American intellectual life brought almost pure gain. For the natural sciences or for disciplines that approached them in

precision of method, it is appropriate to speak of a fusion or symbiosis of thought. . . . In the speculative type of thinking, however, which the Germans had always considered their peculiar province, the fusion remained incomplete or aborted.

It is not accidental therefore, Hughes remarked, that 'the more concrete and empirical styles of thought' – generally speaking – were most influential in Britain and the United States, whereas metaphysical elements as represented by the works of Heidegger, Hegel and Husserl, were primarily adopted by French thinkers[27] – an interesting example, incidentally, of the process of assimilation as outlined in the first chapter of this study.

It is probably due to this self-selective mechanism within the different spheres of the academic world that the integration of scholars into British society seems to have proceeded fairly smoothly. But what is more: unlike the majority of refugees, their professional activities continued much as before. They might have had to adjust to a different style of university life. But most of them did not have to suffer serious disruptions in their work or even to discontinue it.

THE MEDICAL PROFESSION

Members of other professional groups such as lawyers and doctors had far bigger hurdles to overcome. To begin with, access to medicine and law was legally restricted.[28] As regards the former, the British government was ready to accept 500 doctors from Germany. But 'the British Medical Association brought all its guns to bear and succeeded in reducing the number to fifty.'[29] This meant that originally by far the majority of doctors coming to Britain had no hope of ever finding employment in their field, let alone being given the permission to practice. Their German qualifications were not recognized in Britain. After their emigration to this country, many therefore tried to find jobs in countries, anywhere in the world, which would accept them as doctors. But many were too depressed at first to try. Often it was their wives who seized the initiative; they ran from place to place to find out about any, even unpaid, job possibilities for their husbands or sifted the advertisement pages in medical journals. These efforts were not always fully appreciated though. Thus Mrs S., after having taken a lot of trouble of this kind, at long last succeeded in finding a place at a hospital for her husband, a well-known German (non-Jewish) surgeon. Their married life had come under severe strain because the enforced inactivity had made him very depressed. But to her great disappointment, Mrs S.'s husband refused to accept the position offered to him because 'it was not good enough for him . . . he did not belong to the persecuted community of Jews. He did not know how important this job was. He had no idea what you have to do in the world, what you have to accept". Whether her husband's reaction was indeed typical of non-Jewish refugees is difficult to judge. But his case illustrates well some of the problems of adjustment the refugee doctors were facing.

In spite of the bleak prospects several hundred doctors registered with medical schools in Britain to obtain British qualifications. A major obstacle for them was to secure enough financial support in order to be able to pay for the fees and their livelihood at the same time. They had to take up loans, try to get a scholarship or scrape together whatever money they and their wives were able to earn at a time when, officially, refugees were not given work permits in most cases. Thus a surgeon secretly washed corpses in a morgue, a radiologist repaired radios and a bacteriologist peddled baking powder.[30]

Once started on a course, the refugee doctors had to overcome considerable language difficulties and had to get used to a different teaching style. Finally, they had to face the examination situation which many found difficult to cope with after having practised for a long time. A number of them failed therefore; others dropped out before the final examination because they had been unable to overcome their anxiety.[31] However strenuous the course may have been, there also were advantages: 'rusty knowledge' had to be brushed up and the chance was provided to learn about recent methods in medicine.[32]

Those who passed the final examinations got permits to practice or work in medical institutions. Yet later in the 1930s the BMA succeeded in restricting further the number of permits granted. The Association also intervened, again successfully, when plans were made in 1938 to transfer whole medical schools of international reputation to Britain. Only 'after persistent struggle' was the resistance of the BMA 'partly broken'.[33] Refugee doctors were admitted on a temporary Register of the Medical Council and allowed to work in hospitals, clinics and as assistants to British practitioners who, as individuals, were generally described by respondents as "fair" and "kind" towards the foreign doctors.[34] In September 1939 there were some 1000 doctors on the Temporary Register (as compared with some 10 000 doctors out of work in Germany at the same time) to which another 400 dentists have to be added.[35] In spite of a shortage of doctors in some parts of Britain, 'only 460 foreign practitioners of *all nationalities* had Home Office permits to practice' in July 1940. All of them had been living in Britain since long before 1938.[36] It was only after the war, when the refugees acquired British citizenship, that restrictions were lifted. Ultimately, most of those who had been on the Temporary Register remained in the medical profession.

Once in practice, however, this still did not mean the end to all their problems. There remained the task of getting used to English customs. One such peculiarity was that, as Westman put it, patients were generally treated 'like idiots'. They were given too little information about their illness or about the medicine prescribed.[37] Of course, these difficulties were of minor importance compared with those encountered by refugee doctors at the time of their arrival and could be overcome over the years.

Following this brief section on the situation of doctors the individual case of a dentist recorded for this study is of interest. Although it does not completely correspond to the pattern outlined above, it illustrates some of the points made.

Mr S. had interrupted his studies of mathematics in Germany in 1933 because he knew he would be unable to find any job in his field under the Hitler regime. Urged by his father to emigrate, he went to study at Cambridge, but found that the fees were too high. He could not study in London, because his German A-levels were not recognized there. But he learned that he would be accepted at Manchester University. So he resumed his studies there, but found it very difficult because of language problems and because of the different teaching system. He decided that mathematics was not for him and returned to London. By chance, he met a relative who was a dentist. Through him he was introduced to another refugee dentist who had settled in Manchester and was doing some research at the University. This gave him the idea of doing the same. "Besides I was always good at work with my hands." Another refugee friend gave him the advice to go back to Germany to study dentistry because he would get a better training there. Since he was half-Jewish, it was still possible for him during the early years of the regime to be readmitted to the University. So he went and stayed until 1937 when he should have taken his *Physikum*, an important examination the studies for which, he felt, had given him a solid grounding, and which at the time he had been able to supplement as a learner in some privately-owned dental laboratories. Because of his Jewish father he was however not permitted to sit for this intermediate or any further examinations, and he left to return to Britain where he worked as a technician with a refugee dentist. "This was not a happy time", he remembered. "I was left more or less to my own devices, not always with good results but I worked as well as I could." Fortunately his study course in Germany had given him a foundation which proved to be useful now.

He might have remained a technician for the rest of his life if it had not been for an old schoolfriend of his whom he ran into one day. This friend had become a successful solicitor. When told about Mr S.'s experiences he remarked: "Well, it is time you did a bit more". Mr S. took the point and immediately decided to look around to improve his qualifications. He started evening classes in science subjects with a view to studying dentistry again. He even went to the United States for a brief period to improve his knowledge. He changed employers and found more productive work with another refugee friend back in Manchester.

His wife joined him as his apprentice. She had had some training as a window-dresser in Germany, after she was forced to leave her school shortly before her A-levels examinations, but was unable to find employment in her field in Britain. During their first year on the new job they bought equipment by instalments and opened a laboratory in the basement of the house where they lived while they were still working for the dentist. In 1941, after the first year, they started a business of their own. They worked mainly for refugee dentists and did jobs which English technicians were unable to do. The German techniques were known in Britain, Mr S. remarked, but they were not so widely used. Yet there apparently was a great demand for them for "all the German dentists did extremely well in Manchester".

Three months after starting the laboratory, Mr S. went back to University to resume his studies in dentistry and "did the whole lot again". His wife took over the laboratory with her husband assisting in some of the difficult cases at first. Under her management it developed into a flourishing business from which she semi-retired only recently. Her husband successfully graduated in dentistry in

1946 and it was also at about that time that the long-awaited naturalization came through. "Up to then we had great fear of what would happen, (and) whether he would get a work permit." Not long after graduation, in 1948, he was offered a lectureship at a College in London, where he was soon promoted to a Readership. He is now looking forward to his retirement – with no intention to stop working. "I always had a hankering after maths, you know; I went to lectures occasionally." He had started to take evening classes in mathematics and was, at the time of the interview, waiting for some examination results.

Mr S.'s career is not only interesting because it illuminated some of the experiences and difficulties of a member of the medical profession. It also pinpoints some of the aspects of German–Jewish life in Britain as a whole, such as the crucial role of the wife as breadwinner or contributor to the family income, especially during the first years of emigration; moreover the case illustrates a high degree of perseverance and dedication to work and the importance of the ethnic group as providing contacts and support, both moral and practical. It finally shows how the refugee dentists found – and filled – gaps in the British market. If this may have been true of dentists in more than one sense, it certainly applied to refugee businesses generally, as will be shown in a moment.

THE LEGAL PROFESSION

If emigration had been difficult for doctors and dentists, the situation was even more desperate for members of the legal profession. They were subjected to the same restrictions of access as alien doctors. Above all their knowledge of German law was more or less useless in a British context. Those who had come in the early years and had the chance to study English law or had qualifications in International Law were in a better position. The refugee lawyers who were able to carry on with their profession came mostly from their ranks. Even though they were luckier than most of their refugee colleagues life was not necessarily easier. Thus Ernst J. Cohn who was driven from his chair of Civil Law at Breslau University emigrated to Britain in 1933. As the editors of his *Festschrift* wrote: 'With a perseverance and tenacity which are so typical of the man, Cohn managed to maintain himself by giving advice on German law, mainly to other German refugees, while at the same time he – already a Professor of Law – studied English law. At the end of his studies he was called to the Bar by Lincoln's Inn. But the outbreak of war prevented him from engaging seriously in legal practice'.[38]

Considering the fundamental differences in character of German and English law however, to study English law was not as easy as it may sound or rather, as Professor T. put it: English law in itself was not difficult; it was a question of adopting the right attitude.[39] Professor T. was unable to study English law as long as he approached it with German law in mind. He had to approach it like an English undergraduate and adopt an historical point of view. Such a transition required a considerable flexibility of mind.

In fact, flexibility was also needed by the great majority of refugee lawyers who were not able for some reason to establish themselves in practice. They had to find different occupations. Looking at the careers of respondents who had a legal training in Germany, a clear pattern emerges: some went back to University in Britain and studied a different academic subject. Some went into banking or commerce, where they became involved either in management or accountancy. Others again took to journalism or publishing. For some, the transition may have been fairly smooth. It seems however that the majority had quite a chequered career before they finally found their niche in British society and economic life. What is more, the upheavals often started even earlier than from the date of emigration. As many of them were either civil servants or through their work in the courts closely connected with the state bureaucracy from which they were barred immediately after April 1933, they belonged to those who were the first to be affected by the anti-Jewish policies of the Nazi-regime. For this group of refugees the period of disruption and stress was particularly prolonged therefore. This clearly emerged from various life histories told by respondents. Thus Mr K. left Germany for Switzerland in 1933. He soon moved on to Paris where he studied political economy. After graduation he worked for a news agency until his internment by the French and deportation to the notorious camp at Gurs. After a dangerous escape from Gurs into the Free Zone of Southern France; across the Pyrenees on foot into Spain; from Spanish imprisonment finally to Britain – he resumed work as a journalist and soon became the editor of the organ of an industrial federation. In a sense, one may even regard this occupation as representing some continuity in his career.

Another lawyer, Mr I., managed to stay even closer to his original professional leanings. Already as a student of law he had been interested in wine and the relevant legislation which led him to write a thesis on German wine law. After his eviction from his position in 1933, he and his family went to Britain on the invitation of English relatives. They decided to stay and Mr I. had to think of earning a livelihood for himself and his family. He started by selling wine which his father-in-law (himself a lawyer) bought and sent over from Germany to Britain until he, too, emigrated. But even without this source and in spite of the fact that a considerable portion of the wine holdings were lost during the bombings in the 1940s Mr I. succeeded in building up from modest beginnings an enterprise which became one of the leading wine businesses in Britain. And yet, to this day, he has always had a hankering after his legal firm in Germany. So, after 40 years in business, he returned to law. He does not practise officially but clients come to him for legal advice. More significantly, he now acts as consultant on German and Common Market wine law and goes to Germany to lecture on English wine law.

Mr Tr. also found his way back to law, albeit in a less spectacular way. Faced with an uncertain future as a lawyer in 1933, he thought of abandoning his legal practice. Instead he planned to become a watchmaker. But he failed to find a firm which would offer him an apprenticeship. Reluctantly, he resumed his legal practice and carried on until 1938 when he managed to emigrate to Britain: an English family whom he had once met on a holiday, got a visa for him and invited him to stay with them as their guest for a year. In 1940, he found a job as a manual worker in a hat factory. And although this work severely damaged his hands, he continued in this job until 1957. In that year, he was able to return to his original profession following the introduction by the West German government of restitution regulations which led to a great demand of legal advisors. Refugee lawyers with their training in German law and their knowledge of the refugee situation, were ideally suited for this work. Thus many of them seized the chance to return to law. Mr Tr. furthermore took on divorce cases of German women married to foreigners in Britian.

How important the restitution work was, not only for those seeking compensation but also for the refugee lawyers themselves, is shown by at least one case in which it acted as nothing less than a life-line: Mrs R.'s father gave up law in the 1930s and joined his brother who had a leather business in Germany. This uncle then emigrated to Britain and carried on with his leather firm. After Mrs R.'s family had in vain tried to emigrate to Latin America, they joined her father's brother early in 1939. However, the two brothers had never got on well. And it had been with great reluctance and after persistent requests that Mrs R.'s uncle could bring himself to sponsor his brother and his family. When the two families met again in Britain, the relationship deteriorated even further. Mrs R.'s father was offered neither help, nor a job, by his brother. He now took on a job as a welder. Because of the heavy physical work this job involved he developed serious heart trouble. Having always been a shy person, he had by now also lost all the friends of his old circle and, given his background, found it impossible to make new ones among his work mates. He became very depressed; his self-esteem vanished and, for a while, he completely lost interest in himself. His daughter recalled that he went around like a tramp, picking up cigarette butts. Fortunately, all was not lost; he gathered enough energy to take a correspondence course in book-keeping which enabled him to give up the job as welder. In the end he, too, found employment in his original profession with one of the restitution organizations. Soon afterwards he returned to Germany and decided to stay. His wife refused to follow him. They separated, but without much heart-break on either side since, according to Mrs R., her parents' marriage was never happy.

Finally, there is Mr G.'s case which may stand for many of those who had to adjust to a different occupation. After his *Abitur* (A-levels) Mr G. served an apprenticeship with a bank with a view to joining his father's private banking firm. However he decided to study law later on; he passed the obligatory examinations and, thanks to a sympathetic supervisor at his university was still able to receive his doctorate in 1934. Since it was not possible anymore at this stage to find employment in his field, he went back into banking and joined a Jewish firm. However, soon afterwards the leading members of his firm decided to emigrate, whereupon Mr G. worked as secretary for a Zionist association concerned with emigration. He hoped that through this work he, too, would ultimately be able to leave. In November 1938 he was imprisoned in a concentration camp and released after he had succeeded in obtaining a visa for Britain. He was admitted to Kitchener Camp, the camp set up by the British government for transmigrant men.[40] There he resumed his activity as a co-ordinator for the emigration to Palestine. His parents whom he had to leave behind managed to smuggle out some money for him with the help of friends. To his great disappointment some of these embezzled the money entrusted to them; but others returned it. As soon as the Pioneer Corps was created, Mr G. joined it, since he had lost all hope of obtaining a certificate for Palestine. Later on he became a member of the Intelligence Corps where he worked as a pay clerk. It was then that he started seriously to think about his future. It was clear to him that he had no hope of being able to practice law. He therefore took a correspondence course in book-keeping. After his demobilization in 1945 he nevertheless tried his luck with the Law and Solicitors Societies as well as Chartered Accountants Societies. The Law Society was most unhelpful, Mr G. remembered. They would not take an enemy alien, as he was still classified at that time. The Chartered Accountants Society was more sympathetic. They were prepared to drop some of their conditions. But there still remained the problem of finding a firm which was prepared to article him. He finally found an English–Scottish firm which waived the fee normally payable for the "honour of being articled"; instead he was offered remuneration of £2 per week. But he needed an additional grant to make ends meet. He found the final examinations extremely difficult because he was not familiar with the English system. He failed twice, but tried again and passed the third time. After that he was offered a minor job in the taxation department of his old firm. His training in law now proved to be of great advantage to him. He quickly moved upwards and was soon promoted to be head of his department. He brought his firm many German–Jewish clients. How much his services were appreciated is perhaps best shown by the fact that an antisemitic colleague who called him 'stinking Jew' was dismissed without further notice. In the end, Mr G. was the highest paid employee of his firm where he stayed for 27 years until his retirement; so-called retirement, one should add, for Mr G. is now working privately from his home. Significantly enough, his clients are mostly refugees.

These few examples may suffice to give some impression of the difficulties which lawyers in particular faced after emigration. Most seem to have achieved success in whatever occupation they had ultimately found. But we do not know how many failed and despaired as Mrs R.'s father did. It is not surprising therefore that many of them seized the chance to apply for re-admission to legal practice when the German government introduced regulations to this effect. As a result the number of those returning to Germany was much higher among members of the legal profession than among most other groups of refugees.[41]

ARTISTS

There is yet another group of refugees which stands out as having been at least as severely affected by the upheavals and dispersion of the 1930s as the lawyers: artists and writers. They, too, were dismissed for 'racial' or political reasons immediately after the take-over by the Nazis. As in the case of the legal and medical professions, their colleagues abroad were not particularly forthcoming in their assistance which led Bentwich to make the resigned remark in 1936: 'If the lawyers, the doctors, the teachers, and the artists, would co-operate for the aid of members of their professions in the same way as the academic bodies have co-operated, more could be done.'[42] Little did he know that this situation was to become the rule rather than the exception.

Again the famous ones among the artists were warmly received in Britain.[43] Those less well-known abroad had a much harder time. To enter the country, though, was not the biggest problem before 1938. Thus Mr and Mrs O., both sculptors, were able to leave for Britain in 1937, with the help of a Christian friend in Berlin and a cousin in London. They were initially given visitors' permits which were eventually converted into residents' permits, but only because Mr O. was a wood-carver. At that time, wood-carving was practically unknown among British sculptors and Mr O. therefore did not compete with native sculptors. Even so – or perhaps because of it – "it was extremely difficult for us to establish ourselves as artists in this country". At the beginning, there were language problems which were impeding contacts with British fellow-artists. Yet, later on, after Mr O. had been elected Fellow of the Royal Society of Sculptors, friendships with British artists were as scarce as before. And with that, the world of art and all the important networks necessary to gain a reputation in one's country remained closed to them. The O.'s think it had to do with a difference in life-styles as well. "In Berlin we had a beautiful studio where we lived. Visitors and friends came at all times, also late at night. But not so in London. People always go to bed early here. What is more, most artists here live in the country." Nevertheless the O.'s creativity was not diminished. They had a number of exhibitions each; they also sold some of their work. But for a living they – as artists usually do – had to rely on private pupils. Furthermore they taught pottery at a London college for 22 years.

Emigration was a fairly smooth transition for Miss N., another sculptor. In 1934 she left Germany for Paris where she worked with a famous sculptor. She even had an exhibition there. She returned to Germany a year later or so, but decided to leave for good in 1937. She went as a visitor to Britain where she had English relatives: a brother of her father, a banker who, together with a third brother, had settled in Britain as a young man at the end of the 19th century. This is quite a common pattern, as subsequent cases will confirm. Thanks to the help of a friend of her uncle's who was a member of Parliament, she was granted permission to stay and to work professionally which she has done to this day without interruption. Her livelihood is secured through letting three houses which she acquired over the years.

However, Miss N.'s case seems to have been the exception rather than the rule. The majority probably had to struggle with the sort of problems the O.'s had to face or those described by Mrs I. She is a painter by training and her late (non-Jewish) husband was a sculptor. In the 1920s, both had lived and worked in Worpswede, a famous artists' colony in Northern Germany. With the deepening of the depression however they were unable to make a living in this "idyllic place". They moved to Berlin where Mr I. modelled dummies which were painted by his wife. During that time they met Harold Nicolson who showed considerable enthusiasm for Mr I.'s busts. Mr I. had developed a special material to produce masks which were exact replicas of the original. Nicolson advised them to go to Britain where, he was sure, these busts would be a great success. He also helped them generously and offered them a studio in Kensington. And, indeed, soon enough the visitors who wanted their portraits made turned up at their doorstep in great numbers. Mrs I. worked as her husband's assistant. Yet in spite of this positive response, they were not happy. "The atmosphere was rather strange. We were invited to many cocktail parties with aristocrats. It was a much more mundane life-style than we had been used to before." They felt uncomfortable also for another reason: "Our portraits caused a sensation, but there was not much interest in sculpture generally in Britain at that time." So they returned to Berlin after four months. In 1933, having escaped a round-up by the SS of artists who were suspected of subversive activities, they left

Germany again. This time they went to Paris, where Mrs I. had studied with Fernand Leger for a while in 1924, since when they had often been back to visit friends. One of them found them a studio. It was a difficult but "wonderful time". However they felt they were not safe from the Germans in France. They renewed the contact with Nicolson who again helped them and secured them visas which had become obligatory by now. The fashion of portrait busts was over, however. Instead, Mrs I. started to paint tiles for a factory manufacturing tables. By and by she became interested in pottery which was taught at a nearby art college. She first joined classes as a student, but soon started to teach herself. It is not without irony that, in 1946, a German prisoner of war built her her first wheel. She did not stop teaching pottery before she was 75 years and has since specialized in enamelling.

Her husband was less happy, Mrs I. reported. Like the O.'s, he found it very difficult to put down roots in Britain. To make a living he taught life classes, pottery and painting. Yet he was not successful in his own field. He therefore never felt at home in Britain. When he went back to Germany for the first time in 1953, where he was received with open arms, he wanted to return. But Mrs I. refused to leave Britain. "He was non-Jewish and still had family and friends in Germany, whereas I lost some of my relatives in the camps." The couple did not separate; Mr I. regularly travelled to Germany instead. This raised the question whether Mr I. was thus deprived of a successful career as a sculptor which he was denied in Britain and which he might have achieved had the couple returned to Germany. Mrs I. disagreed, but this was what her husband had felt. She thought, however, he was deluded about his prospects. During the years in exile he had lost touch with cultural developments in Germany. Had they returned, he would have been an outsider and it was questionable whether he would have found the response he had been hoping for. The sad thing was that, although living in Britain, he had no roots in British cultural and artistic life. His art was considered alien and struck no chord in the British public.

It is interesting that this feeling of alienation was also expressed by a member of the next generation, Mr V., who had left Germany when still an adolescent. "As much as I have an accent in my language I have an accent in my painting." And he added, "In German art of our century, expression and feeling comes into it a lot. Whereas mainstream art in Britain is more good taste and playing down feelings. The majority of English people find my paintings too emotive, too direct. English art is refined understatement." The effects of his greater affinity with German than with English art were felt by him at art school already. His paintings did not fit in; they were considered strange and he was continuously asked to tone down his colours. On the other hand, his experience throughout the years has been that the German public has responded much more positively to his work than the English.

That Mr V.'s basic experience was also shared by other artists is shown in a note on another painter, Martin Bloch. What was perceived by Mr V. as a clash of cultures, has apparently been accepted by Bloch and possibly other artists as a challenge to bridge the gap. Thus a reviewer pointed out on the occasion of an exhibition of Bloch's work, that

> he imported, so to speak, to this country the German Expressionism which he conveyed to his numerous English pupils, and thus contributed to diminish the British animosity against a style so alien to the British character. But having been resident in England for many years, he added to the German Expressionism not only his innate Jewishness, felt even stronger after his transplantation to a foreign soil, but also some English qualities which were to be a complementary element to his Jewish passionate temperament. The clear and calm English landscape forced him to enrich his palette with cool and matter of fact colours without lessening their intensity. His forms became clearer and stronger. And through this unique fusion of opposite elements he became a powerful artistic personality of a very high order so that one might consider him as the most important Jewish exponent of Expressionism.[44]

It is true, the differences between the various national forms of art have ceased to be so obvious today; art has become largely international in character. Still, Mr V. insists, "the flavour of German art is different; it is more open to visual elements. English society is more literary. There has been a longer tradition in Germany to encourage art." Mr V. felt that, generally speaking, German people "take greater pride and have a greater awareness of their homes than their equivalent in England". Since artistically he feels more at home in Germany than in Britain this respondent would have liked to go back but, so far, it was impossible for him to take this step because of what happened in the 1930s and 1940s.

Another artist came to the opposite conclusion although his assessment of the situation was basically the same, even if mixed with a good deal of sarcasm: "The beauty of England is there is no cultural snobbery outside a small circle. They got the real thing, they got the queen, they got the horses, they got the county life. That's why I live in England. Nobody is interested in art. There is much less phoney art than there is in Germany. In France it is even worse.... That's the thing which exasperates you. That's what makes it human."

As in these statements we shall encounter, throughout this study, a tendency to contrast German and English culture, to weigh one against the other. This has already emerged in the comparison of the two languages described above. If the opposition of the two cultures has been felt by sculptors and painters, how much more strongly must writers have been affected by the transplantation into a different cultural setting. After all, their medium is more culture-specific than that of all other artists or professionals: 'There is no more terrible fate for a writer than to lose his readers, his natural and indigenous audience. Most of the exiles have their newspapers and magazines, a few publishing houses and other outlets, but it is hardly necessary to explain how different this is compared to reaching out to your public in your own country. Very few of them are able to achieve regular translation into the great languages of the West.'[45]

Yet not all writers are even translatable, be it that the linguistic peculiarities of their work cannot be conveyed in any other language, be it that their material is of no or little interest to a non-German readership.[46] Thus a refugee wrote in 1946 that 'to be a writer is not easy; to be a Jew is very difficult; to be a Jewish writer almost amounts to a minor tragedy. But what about the Jewish writer who, on top of that, comes from Germany?' Not only, the author continued, does he find himself without a 'homogeneous reading public', but whatever potential public there is, the refugee author is not part of it. He cannot write about English people, because he does not know them well enough. He could write about Jews but this again would be of only minor interest to a largely Gentile readership.[47]

Perhaps the fact that Continental literary traditions did not find much favour with the English public weighs even more heavily than the problem of the writer's lack of familiarity with the society in which he was living. Thus the writer and playwright Berstl remembered that in the 1930s and 1940s the 'average London theatre-goer' was not keen on 'phantasy'; 'they only wanted to see what reflected their own experiences'. There was no interest in experiments; it was relaxation that the audience wanted.[48]

The same applied to contemporary German literature as a whole which was widely ignored in Britain, by the general public as well as the specialists, the Germanists. Even worse: 'Insofar as the academics themselves took an interest in it their judgments coincided far too often with those prevalent inside the Third Reich. . . . Emigrés in those days were treated as cut off from the German tradition and the periodicals in which their new work appeared were not bought for our libraries.'[49] It is only since the war that this negative attitude has been changing. Although this does not necessarily mean that Continental traditions are actively promoted but rather, to quote Willett: 'The novelty, in our insular society, is that [the English] were no longer actually unaware of such foreign matters, or positively prejudiced against them.'[50] This is still far from a positive recognition.

A striking example in this respect is Arthur Koestler, one of the few refugee writers whose writings have become fairly well-known in Britain. What is more: he himself has closely identified with English culture and adopted its language. Initially, though, it seems to have been primarily the attraction of opposites: 'I was intrigued by a civilization whose social norms were a reversal of mine which admired "character" instead of "brains", stoicism instead of temperament, nonchalance instead of diligence, the tongue-tied stammer instead of the art of eloquence." In course of time, with increasing proficiency in the English language, Koestler adjusted to the English environment which he now finds 'particularly congenial and soothing', in spite of 'moods of impatience and fits of exasperations'. Nevertheless his overall attitude is one of positive identification with English society. He regards it as an irony therefore that 'the sales figures of my books, . . . are proportionately lower for England than for any other country including Iceland'. This fact results from the dislike of the political and ideological novel in Britain, Koestler explained, adding: 'I realise that the reason why the English find my books unlikeable are to be found in precisely that lotus-eating disposition which attracts me to them.'[51]

Apparently, English as a language came quite easy to Koestler. For most refugees, however, the problem to switch from their native language to a foreign one proved to be an insurmountable obstacle. It was not the question of acquiring a basic knowledge of English. As a writer the refugee had to develop the most intimate relationship with the language. Thus Karl Stern wrote: 'All, even the oldest among us, learned the language. However, the city gave us only the hand-me-down, the second-rate words, instruments of practicality as useful and comfortable for the life of strangers as the underground, the bus, the park and the public bath. The infinite in language is something quite beyond public convenience. We used, with great dexterity and cunning, inexhaustible variations of nouns, adjectives, verbs, sentences, while all the time Language gazed upon us remotely.'[52]

Only a few succeeded in overcoming this barrier,[53] and many of these merely temporarily. For if one compares early lists of publications by exiled writers, it is noticeable that apparently many of those who had started to write in English during the first years of emigration returned to German in the 1950s.[53]

Interestingly enough, this predominance of the Continental background is not only characteristic of older writers. As in the cases of some artists, it can also be found among members of the younger generation of writers. Here it makes itself felt in a more subtle way than among the older generation; it is expressed in a certain degree of detachment from English society, notwithstanding the fact that these younger writers appear much more 'English' than their parents; that their education was largely influenced by English institutions and, most important of all, that they had mastered the English language to such an extent that it is impossible for most English people around them to detect their Continental background. Yet it has left its traces. Judith Kerr, in an article significantly entitled: 'Writing with borrowed words', vividly described her own experience. After her arrival at the age of 12 with her family she learnt English easily. Moreover, with a fervour typical of her generation she had, within a relatively short period, 'become so anglicized that most people simply assumed that I was English'. Later on, having finished her formal education, having worked and having married a Briton, she, too, 'took it for granted that I was English', after all 'by this time I had lived most of my life in England'. But then, 'I started trying to write, and it all went to pieces'. She continued:

> Straightaway, a terrible sense of insecurity set in. Had I really

known English words long enough to push them about in this familiar fashion? I had only learnt them at the age of twelve. If I had spoken them from the beginning, like real English people, would they not have a different weight, a special kind of patina acquired as a result of my having heard and used them during those early years? I used to see them in my mind – a row of uncertain figures, drawn in pencil, and all the feet had been rubbed out. Surely an attempt to write in this deliberately learnt language was a kind of impertinence? . . . When, about the same time, I had a miscarriage followed by the usual depression and loss of confidence, I was obsessed by an extra fear: suppose I suddenly forgot all my English – then I would not be able to speak to my husband any more. It only lasted a few days, but afterwards I was amazed. It had never occurred to me before that changing languages as a child had had such a profound effect on me. . . . Nowadays I don't worry so much about my English, except for the use of capitals, which my husband says I can never get right. All the same, on a recent visit to Germany a strange thing happened to me. I was on a bus, idly reading the signs above the shops in the street we were passing through, when I saw the word *Blumenladen*. Suddenly I was in a different world. I was conscious of being very close to the floor, surrounded by the legs and feet of people who towered above me. There were plants everywhere, as big as bushes and trees. . . . and then I was back on the bus, a middle-aged woman on a visit from England. I had found a bit of my childhood, pickled in a word that had lain unused for forty years until I happened to come across it. I don't know if it matters, and anyway there is nothing I can do about it. But I regret the fact that never in my life can I be so affected by the word 'florist'.[55]

A similar ambivalence is reflected by a respondent when talking about the same problem: "(Britain) is my country; it's my language", adding abruptly: "I am always deeply touched by the German language and love to hear it. It stirs up all sorts of – difficult emotions."

With other writers of the middle generation the feeling of alienation went even deeper as shown in an article by Eva Figes which led to considerable controversy among its readers. In it she stated: 'I remain essentially stateless. Even though I grew up here, had all my schooling in England, my gut reactions are often very un-

English.' She saw the main reason for this difference in attitudes in the fact that 'England does not share the European experience.' It is not only her day-to-day contact with the English that is affected by this contrast. For she continued:

> It is perhaps as a writer that I feel least English, even though I write my books in the English language and could use no other. It was Kafka who first blew my mind open to the potentialities of prose in a way that three years reading English at university had failed to do. When I began writing prose myself it was the discovery that a novel could take any form, and did not have to be like most of the English novels I had read, which first excited me. If my novels have more in common with post-war writing in Europe than with anything being produced in England, I think this probably goes deeper than a purely intellectual decision. The English still write in the style of Arnold Bennett because they still inhabit his world. England was never invaded, never touched by the cataclysm that shook Europe. After the Second World War life, as far as European writers were concerned, could never be the same again, and prose had to reflect that convulsive change. Only England, locked in her dream of past greatness, believed that everything would go on as before. But I am a European survivor, wrestling with a different reality. A piece of shrapnel lodges in my flesh, and when it moves, I write.[56]

In this respect at least, Figes and other writers of her generation of German–Jewish origin have a clear advantage over the older generation, in spite of some ambivalence towards the English language. They nevertheless have full command over it. As mentioned earlier, the same was true for only a minority of writers of the older generation. Those who failed or did not want to switch to the English language faced considerable problems, yet also found some gratification. Part of the price they had to pay was the fact that they were more or less excluded from the English world of art and literature; for some this was a painful experience, as in the case of H. Sinzheimer who had found work in the warehouse of Cambridge University Press. It made him feel extremely bitter that 'he had to handle books without having found an inner relationship with English authors and artists'.[57]

Yet not all refugee writers regretted this lack of contact. One respondent, a poet, said that he has always kept his distance and refused to "assimilate to the English environment": "I do not belong to the world of English literature, I am only a recipient." He is in contact with a few individual English writers, but this is due more to their joint activities in marxist groups. "English culture, in contrast to American, is not assimilatory. It is different in the natural sciences, for instance, but in cultural life, ethnic groups are not assimilated; what we get is the integration of individuals." This is why there developed no specific English–Jewish culture in the same way as it did in Germany or, more recently, in the United States. To this day, Mr G. has exclusively written in German and it is Germany with which he feels his closest cultural ties. He is much better known over there than in Britain. If he did not return after the war it was for political and personal reasons. The price he has had to pay is a permanent longing to live among people who speak the same language, to be close to his many friends there. But he has accepted his homelessness and regards it as a positive gain in that it enabled him to take on what he considers his most important role which is that of a literary mediator between both countries. Thus he regularly translates works from the English into German on the one hand, and informs an English audience about developments within modern German literature, on the other.

Many examples could be added for German-speaking writers who had preferred exile to a return to Germany and who, to this day, acted as mediators in different ways, be it as novelists who, through their autobiographical writings, helped their German, sometimes also their English readers better to understand the fate of the refugees; or who adapt English plays for the German stage or, vice versa, German plays for an English audience. Equally important are their roles as translators or as journalists who report about Britain for German papers. Mention also has to be made of the German section of the BBC where quite a number of them found work, especially during the war years.[58]

Of course, this mediating role would be fully realized only after the war, when the normalization of life in Germany allowed the refugees to resume contact with old friends and to establish new ties of friendship or professional relationships. In the early years of emigration, feelings of loss and despair prevailed. But some succeeded in seeing some gain even in these experiences, such as Alfred Kerr, the famous theatre critic and writer from Berlin. He is lovingly described by his daughter Judith in her writings, most of them autobiographical in character. Thus she wrote in one of her novels: 'In her mind she saw (Papa) in his poky room with his typewriter that kept going wrong and his writings that no one wanted to publish, in a country whose language he did not speak. How did it feel to be Papa?' And his reply:

> The chief point about these last, admittedly wretched years ... is that it is infinitely better to be alive than dead. Another is that if I had not lived through them I would never have known what it felt like ... to be poor, even desperate, in a cold, foggy country where the natives, though friendly, gargle some kind of Anglo-Saxon dialect ... I'm a writer. ... A writer has to know. ... There is a piece of me, he said carefully, quite separate from the rest, like a little man sitting in my forehead. And whatever happens, he just watches ... – and he says, how interesting! How interesting to know that this is what it feels like. ... It's a great safeguard against despair.[59]

However, a writer does not only observe; he also needs communication with his readers. It has already been pointed out that for the German-speaking writers this readership had ceased to exist. It is true, there was a 'great literary activity' within the German–Jewish communities in the various countries of refuge; exiled or newly set-up publishing houses continued to publish in German. However, none of them were based in Britain; nor were 'any of the major anti-Nazi magazines' published here, as Willett pointed out. That may have been a reason why, in spite of a few cultural associations and clubs, and 'some active and efficient émigré booksellers ... generally the exiled writers were left without either a local outlet or a spiritual home'. As a result, 'in England, unlike France or Russia or America, there was never a coherent nucleus of German literature in exile'.[60]

There was yet another aspect: through emigration the writer's relationship with his very medium, the German language and even culture, became ambiguous. Without contact with the spoken word writers feared to find themselves in a linguistic no man's land; feared they would lose touch with their own language before they acquired the new language of their country of exile.[61] Similarly, there was the danger of ending up in a cultural vacuum. As refugees they could not possibly identify with and cultivate contemporary German culture which, furthermore, was not considered to be the 'true' German culture as it had developed up to the 1930s. As we have seen above, the irony was that their efforts were hardly appreciated by people outside their circles, which only reinforced their isolation. At the same time, the – literally – conservative attitude guiding these efforts, especially if coupled with the writer's insulation against the new cultural environment, could easily threaten their own artistic development. In fact, the works of many writers in exile have been said to show signs of 'formal stagnation'.[62] To the intellectual hazards have to be added the problems of everyday life; the struggle to earn a living, the crowded living conditions – all these obviously impaired creative writing.

These latter problems were, of course, not restricted to writers. The same is true for the ambiguity towards German culture and language generally. Writers may have experienced it more sharply because language and literature occupied a central position in their lives. Yet it will be seen later on that, to some extent, every refugee was faced with the same conflict resulting from the fact that their language and culture had become that of the enemy.

Finally, a few words are necessary about the situation of the performing artists. The musicians, one would have thought, should have had it easier than other artists. Perhaps no other group has made, over time, such an impact on British cultural life as musicians from Germany and Austria. Yet the early years were just as difficult for them as for any other group of refugees. Again, the famous ones were at an advantage, such as Fritz Busch, the conductor, who was invited, together with other refugee artists, to set up Glyndebourne Opera under the management of yet another refugee, Rudolf Bing who also was the creator of the Edinburgh Festival.[63] Younger and less well-known artists were normally not allowed to accept engagements; often it was only after the war, after naturalization, that they were able to take up music as a profession again.[64] But even then, it was not easy to get a place in an orchestra, for instance, since anti-alienism pervaded the world of music just as strongly as other British institutions.[65] "It is completely different now", a respondent commented, "a foreign name nearly is a must." However, she continued, "the main handicap for foreigners was the lack of connections, since they had not studied in this country. There were no influential teachers at their side who could launch them. For that is how one usually first gets into the profession. There was also the lack of knowledge of the whole scene of the music world, who is who and where. My son who plays the same instrument is in a much better position because he was born here and studied here".

This was confirmed indirectly by another respondent who, although not born here, arrived in Britain as a young girl with the Children's Transports. She was a cellist and since she was too little at the time of the emigration someone else, fortunately, brought her cello over for her. She always had help from various people in Britain. When she was still at boarding school it was her headmistress who enabled her to carry on with her lessons. Thus she always had a music teacher. She left school at the age of 16 and studied music in London, but she does not remember who paid for her lessons. Later on, she won a scholarship for the Royal Academy of Music and for the Guildhall School of Music where she formed a quartet with fellow-students. After some years, they joined a London orchestra.

However, for refugees classified as 'aliens' it was still difficult years after the war to be granted a work permit. Thus one respondent, a conductor, who had survived the Nazi era in concentration camps and was recuperating in Scandinavia, was invited as guest conductor to work with a provincial orchestra in Britain. However, he was not given a visa by the Home Office. The members of the orchestra were angered by this refusal and put pressure on the immigration officials. They succeeded and the respondent caught the last boat to be in time for the concert. A few weeks later he was offered the job as chief conductor of this orchestra. Again, the Home Office refused a permit which was only granted after the personal intervention of the Home Secretary. The orchestra soon developed into one of Britain's leading orchestras. The respondent later on worked with other orchestras in the provinces before he finally took over one of the large London orchestras.

It seems that, over the years, refugee musicians succeeded well on the whole to become integrated into and accepted by the British world of music. Continental names abound in music life. This is, of course, due to the medium as such which easily transcends national boundaries. Actors, by contrast, were initially, at least, at a much greater disadvantage, because of the language barrier. Some well-known personalities in theatre and film such as Fritz Lang, Peter Lorre or Lili Palmer had a relatively easy start; Elisabeth Bergner 'was enthusiastically received in the 1930s'.[66] Others were faced with the same problem as artists generally in that 'they had to start all over again to make their gifts and talents known to directors, agents, and publishers'.[67] However, even if actors succeeded in being offered a role, they were not necessarily able to accept it because quite often the work permit was refused. A few were able to perform for the couple of émigré theatres which were founded shortly before the war.[68] But internment and military service for the younger men meant further disruptions. Some worked for the BBC as news readers or translators.

Others, however, found their way onto the stage of British theatre. Yet it was not always easy to be offered interesting parts. Refugees "were mostly given the parts of foreigners, especially in war films", Mrs N., an actress, explained. On the other hand, older character roles were also preferably given to refugees. "My (late) husband's first role was that of a refugee in the United States. His English was not very good at that time, he still had a strong accent, but it was just right for the piece. Afterwards, when his English had improved, he was given leading parts in films and on the stage." A number of refugee actors seemed to have succeeded like him, even if a report in the *AJR Information* on 'Theatre in London' in 1948 which spoke of 'a lot of Continental actors' seems somewhat exaggerated.[69] The majority of refugee actors and actresses probably did not gain a foot-hold in the English theatre,[70] a number left for the United States and many returned, after the war, to Germany.

One such case was the famous Viennese actor and director Fritz Kortner who despaired because of language problems and differences in theatrical traditions of the kind mentioned above. 'My reputation as an actor was sufficient', he wrote in his memoirs, 'to bring me my first film part (but) between my profession and me stood the English language.' He often forgot his text during the shooting of the film. But there was also the problem that English actors 'underplay. . . . Me, always striving to achieve the utmost in expressiveness was expected to renounce it'. He had found the 'overacting often encountered on the German stage just as "enervating". . . . But the anaemia of expression, so it seemed to me, had diminished, and was in turn influenced by, the actual power of imagination of the English. Thus the theatre became paler and paler. And me, the thick-blooded Jew out of a German stable, tried hard to do as they did. I had to be casual – with linguisitic crutches, nonchalant – with a heavy tongue'. Gradually his English improved, though, and he became fascinated by the English language. He learnt to appreciate 'the precision of the language' which consequently benefitted his German. But he could not free himself of his accent and made the discovery that, contrary to a common assumption, neither the linguistic sensitivity of an actor nor musicality, as the examples of Klemperer and Walter show, facilitate the learning of a foreign language. In the end, Kortner returned home.[71]

This outline of the situation of the refugee artists was necessarily incomplete. Its main purpose was to highlight some of the major problems they encountered after their emigration. Although they shared some of these with other groups of émigrés, artists suffered particularly badly notwithstanding a few exceptions. Because of language problems and of the incompatibility of the German and English artistic 'temperament' they largely failed to find a niche in British cultural life.

BUSINESS PEOPLE

The situation was quite different in the case of business people, one of the largest occupational groups of refugees. However they, too, met with hostility when they arrived in Britain not on a temporary business trip but with the intention to make Britain their home.[72] On the other hand, it did not take long for certain circles within the British government to recognize that among this group of refugees there were many with considerable skills and expertise which might be put to productive use in support of the ailing British economy. It was in Wales, the North-East of England and Scotland, the so-called Depressed Areas, where the recession was particularly acute that the British government tried to attract industrialists. British industrialists had been rather reluctant to take up the opportunities the government offered. This made it 'relatively easy' for a refugee intending to set up a factory to be allowed to come to Britain 'if he was prepared to go to these regions'.[73] Quite a number of them did so in the 1930s and set up 163 factories, about a third of all factories founded by refugees up to 1940.[74] They were prominent in the labour-intensive secondary industries geared to the manufacture of consumer goods. They also introduced a considerable number of 'new lines of industrial enterprise' into these regions. It was therefore largely thanks to their efforts that the high unemployment figures in these areas were reduced.[75]

Informative as it is to outline the general developments,[76] it is no less interesting to see what they meant in individual terms. The case of Mrs E.'s father is probably not unrepresentative in this respect.

Mrs E.'s family on both her father's and her mother's side came from the Rhine–Main area where her father, typically, was engaged in the manufacture of leather goods until 1933. He then established himself and immediately started to put out his feelers to Britain. He had known Britain beforehand because he had visited the country regularly for his former employer. This man also helped him now to set up business in Britain. Mrs E.'s father opened an office in London and started a leather factory in Wales. In 1936 she left Germany with her father for a "trial run" in Britain which proved promising and a year later, in 1937, the family decided to emigrate permanently. Only her brother stayed on at the factory in Germany where "life was very difficult for him", until he joined his father at the Wales factory in 1939. The father had in the meantime joined forces with a non-Jewish German partner with whom Mrs. E.'s brother carried on business after their father's death.

In this case the transition from German to British economic life was fairly smooth. Other respondents mentioned serious disruptions and frustrations either suffered by themselves or by their parents when they tried to build up a business after emigration. An example is offered by Mrs N.'s family. The families on both her mother's as on her father's side had been in the hop business for generations. Her father had taken over the business from his father, but in 1934 he considered emigration and left for Britain soon afterwards. He had two uncles in this country who had settled in Britain around the turn of the century and started a leather business. Mrs N.'s father decided to retrain and to become a manufacturer of leather goods. With the help of his uncles he was given a permit and soon afterwards moved to Wales to establish himself. With him came his family, 20 people in all, including two friends from Germany, one of them non-Jewish. Not only that: Mrs N. remembered a constant flux of visitors to the house because her parents were instrumental in helping other refugees to come and establish themselves in business in the Depressed Areas. Interestingly enough, cousins of Mrs N.'s mother who, like her father's cousins, had also settled in Britain before the First World War, helped German refugees in a similar way. Mrs N.'s father himself did not fare too well: 'He found it difficult to settle down and to get used to business life here." On top of that, his factory was taken over by the war ministry during the war and the whole family had to move to a different part of the country. For three years, from 1943 to 1946, her father took over an agency for shirts and blouses. After that he represented four large

British Agencies on the Continent, especially in Germany. He established very good relations with the German buyers but was also successful in other European countries. He had travelled widely before his emigration and his knowledge of languages was of great advantage to him now. But it was with Germany that his contacts became closest. This was also due to the fact that his old business (and friendship) ties with Germany were never completely severed. In his capacity as hop merchant, he had been on the board of a large brewery firm in Germany. After his emigration, his seat was taken over by his company secretary who returned it to him straight after the war. Soon, his German clients also came back. Mrs N.'s father was thus able, to some extent, to carry on as a hop merchant. He continued to travel to Germany regularly, even after he had to retire from his British agencies for health reasons. When he died, his wife took over as an agent and it still provides her income.

Even if this case cannot be strictly called a success story since Mrs N.'s father did not achieve his original objective which was to set up a leather factory in Wales, it is nevertheless a remarkable one. It shows how Mrs N.'s father was able to make the best of very difficult circumstances, and this was largely due to a mixture of business skills, flexibility and perseverance.

These qualities were said to be typical of the German–(Austrain–) Jewish refugees. Complemented by 'reliability, conscientiousness and hard work',[77] such qualities are generally considered to lie at the root of the remarkable success of refugee businesses in Britain in general. The larger part of these firms were set up in regions outside the Depressed Areas. Here, working conditions were just as difficult because of the restrictions imposed by the British government. Permits to establish new firms were only given for goods which had previously been imported. Even so, over 400 factories or major enterprises were established by refugees by 1939; the number increased to about 1000 after the war, providing 250 000 jobs for British workers.[78] The refugees' enterprises were mainly represented in the secondary industries and in particular in the areas of textiles, chemicals, pharmaceuticals, toys and jewellery.[79] Refugees were often instrumental in developing new methods of production and to open up new export markets for Britain thanks to their existing contacts with customers abroad.[80]

Success did not come easily. Often it took many years until the hard labour was finally rewarded. And sometimes it came too late, as in the case of Mrs T.'s family. Her mother and father had originally migrated from Galicia to a small town in eastern Germany. They later moved on to Leipzig for religious reasons, because it was there that a Polish–Jewish orthodox community had established itself. The children would thus be able to get a proper Jewish education. The families on her mother's as well as on her father's side had been engaged in the manufacture of knitwear. On marrying her mother, her father had joined her mother's family business. In 1939, her parents emigrated to Britain. Her mother continued work as before. She travelled as a textile agent until her 80th year when a stroke put an end to her business life. Her father was unable to continue in the knitwear business. Instead he worked as a supplier of silk material to furriers, but only sporadically. The experience of the emigration with all its worries had been too upsetting for him; he was chronically ill in Britain and soon died of heart trouble.

Interestingly enough, he had owed his contacts with furriers to refugee friends from Leipzig. This is not accidental, for Leipzig had been the centre of the fur trade on the Continent before the war. More particularly, this trade was largely dominated by Jews. As a result of emigration, it shifted from the Continent to Britain.[81] Mrs T.'s own case is a good example of trade migration. Her husband was a furrier, a former neighbour in Leipzig and also of Polish origin. In 1933, Mrs T. and her husband emigrated to Paris but found it impossible to gain a foot-hold in the French fur trade. They left for London where Mr T. had some business connections. Every year, since 1927, he had gone to auctions in London to buy furs for his customers on the Continent. From 1933 onwards, he gradually transferred his business to London and supplied his customers from here. The T.'s first entered Britain on a visitor's permit but, in 1936, they were granted the permission to stay permanently. Slowly, the firm grew. When the children were old enough, Mrs T. joined the firm. In 1959 though, "just when the worst years were over and we were getting on", Mr T. died of heart trouble because, Mrs T. believes, "of all we had been through, all our worries". She carried on with the business, until ill-health forced her to retire. In the meantime however two of her sons and two nephews had joined the firm and developed it – as before in Germany – into a prospering family business. One of her brothers, she added, is also in the fur trade; his office is just around the corner from theirs and he drops in every day.

Nearly all the refugees had to start from modest beginnings since they were not allowed to take any larger sums of capital out of Germany. In spite of this handicap, quite a number of refugee firms rose to large concerns. One such remarkable story is that of Mr N. He had emigrated to Britain with his family in 1936. His father had been a butcher in a small German town. Originally, the family had planned to emigrate to South Africa. But since they were not allowed to take more than the legendary 10 *Reichsmark* out of the country, they were unable to maintain themselves and thus could not fulfil the necessary pre-condition for receiving a permit. Thereupon they started to search for relations abroad who might be able to help them; they found some in Britain of whom they had never heard before. They approached these relatives who promised to take Mr N.'s father as a partner into their business. Nothing came of it, however. Nevertheless the N.s decided to stay in Britain where Mr N. sen. took up work as a sausage maker. Mrs N. supplemented the family budget by taking in refugee lodgers – quite a common source of income for refugees in the 1930s. Mr N. sen. soon became manager of a kosher butcher shop but also produced his own sausages in their kitchen at home. The sausages were sold directly to shops by refugees on their bicycles. In 1947 a small butcher business was bought in Hackney which had belonged to an Englishman and a German Jew who wanted to re-emigrate to the United States. At first German recipes and ingredients were used, but the N.s realized that it would be more advisable to cater for the much larger British market than for the restricted circle of refugees whose "palates we would never have been able to satisfy anyway". Thus they adapted their meat products to the English taste and re-introduced Continental recipes when more meat was available in the late 1950s. As in previous cases, Mr N.'s mother was also active in the business during the early stages; for four to five years she worked as the book-keeper of the firm. From the beginning of the 1950s the business continually expanded and moved to ever larger premises. In the 1960s, after having become too big to be run as a family business, it was sold to a concern and is now, under the directorship of Mr N. jun., the largest meat processor in Britain.

Most of the refugees had to pull themselves up by their own boot straps. Only those who went to the Depressed Areas could expect some aid from the British government. Yet British officials went to considerable trouble to persuade German Jews to come to Britain if they were involved in work which was considered important. This was the experience of Mr H., an engineer and leading industrialist from Frankfurt. Back in Germany, during a golf match with the British Consul in 1935, the latter delivered his Government's invitation to come to Britain and set up business there. But Mr H. refused to leave then: "I thought I could fight; I did not want to give in to the Nazis." He also had a large family to support. But in 1936 he changed his mind because he realized "that things would go wrong in Germany". When the invitation was repeated, he decided to accept it because "I felt I had a lot to offer to England." This seems to have been the British government's feelings as well. Mr H. was asked to become a partner in a big manufacturing firm. Although he was unable to contribute much in the way of finance because of having lost 94% of his capital in Germany, he soon made up for it. After a difficult start ("British engineers were very conservative"), he soon succeeded in establishing 'a brilliantly progressive firm destined to play an essential part in the Midlands car industry' which received a 'Queen's award for industry . . . for technical brilliance and international success'.[82]

Mr H.'s case may have been an outstanding achievement but it was not atypical for a large part of German–Jewish industrialists in Britain, who were thus confirming what has been said of them generally: 'In industry and business, the German Jews have been the most enterprising, progressive, and adaptable class of people in Europe.'[83] Yet this is only one side of the picture. On the other, we find many who never regained in Britain what they had achieved in Germany or Austria. Success or failure were not related to the age of the interviewees. Thus Mr G.'s father had built up a successful textile factory in Germany. A considerable portion of the products were exported, including Britain where Mr G. sen. had set up a branch as early as 1924. In the early 1930s it was decided to shift the manufacturing process to this branch and by 1936 the family had settled in London. However the market situation was not as good in Britain as it had been in Germany and Mr. G. sen. did not succeed in re-establishing himself in the same way as before. "It was very difficult. He did not know the English situation well enough."

But this was not the only problem: the troubled political situation, the threatening and later actual beginning of the war, internment and service in the Pioneer Corps were quite formidable obstacles in the way of the refugees trying to build up a business or, for that matter, any other career.

Mr M.'s case offers a good illustration in this respect. He was a banker, who had left Germany in 1937, after the 'Aryzation' of his bank. He had had two years' training as a young man at a bank in London which made the emigration a sort of "home-coming" for him. He had a number of industrial projects in his briefcase which he planned to use as a starting point for a new career. Thus he was given a mandate to set up in Britain a chemical factory for a German friend. Contacts with a friend of his father's, a member of the House of Lords, opened him many doors. But his projects needed time to develop and the outbreak of the war and his subsequent internment put an end to his enterprise. As an 'enemy alien' he also lost his job as a salesman which he had taken on at the same time. He then helped his wife who worked for a refugee firm to make belts and artificial flowers at home. From 1941, when the restrictions of work permits for refugees were partly lifted, Mr M. worked as a statistician for a large concern until 1945 when the original occupant of this post, an Englishman, came back from the war. After a brief and disappointing spell in an office, Mr M. decided to work independently again. He took on a job as a textile agent "of which I did not know anything of course but, thank God, the customers knew more about it and I also learned in the course of time". He never seriously considered returning to banking, since he did not possess the necessary capital to build up a "proper" bank. "I could only have worked as an agent but that would have gone too much against my grain. An agent advises his clients how to buy and sell, but this is not what I have learnt which was: 'Der Bankier schreitet an der Spitze der Kaufmannsschaft' (the banker walks at the head of the merchants)."

It was not easy for many respondents to talk about their own or their parents' lack of achievement in business life. Some were obviously distressed about their "failure"; others were more apologetic about not being able to offer the interviewer a 'success story'. It was not a question of poverty, however: in all cases German restitution or compensation money and/or the often substantial income from whatever occupation they had achieved, provided them with a decent living standard. Often enough it was just a matter of having to be content with a small business rather than a big one such as they had had in Germany. However, German–Jewish refugees possess a considerable degree of group pride based on past and present achievements of the community as a whole and on the examples of many outstanding individuals among them. Expectations therefore are high and to fall short of them causes acute embarrassment.

It was interesting therefore to find that the loss of status was by no means always experienced as hardship. Some respondents felt it had a liberating effect because it meant less social pressure on them to keep up appearances. The fact that nobody in the new environment, it was said, knew of one's social background and previous level of income contributed to this feeling of freedom from the pressure to adhere to the status symbols of one's original social class.

Of course, one had to have a fairly respectable living standard in order to experience a decline in status as 'liberating'. For the majority of the refugees emigration meant deprivation and a hard struggle to make a living under often humiliating conditions. This was particularly true for many of those who came with the last and biggest wave of refugees in 1938/39.

NOVEMBER 1938

It has already been mentioned that the more strongly Jews felt the pressure to leave Germany, the more reluctant became the potential countries of refuge to accept them. Britain introduced a visa system in order to achieve a better control of the influx of refugees, but lifted the restrictions for certain categories such as transmigrants, trainees, domestics and those refugees whose maintenance in Britain was guaranteed.

Among the latter we find the large group of children under 17 years who arrived in Britain from Germany under the auspices of the Movement for the Care of Children, briefly known as the Children's Transports.[84] The Movement was founded on private initiative in November 1938, after the Nazi pogrom, and in December 1938 the first transport with some 300 children arrived at Harwich. During subsequent months a total of nearly 10 000 children, three quarters of them Jewish, were thus rescued. Either friends, relatives or refugee organizations acted as their guarantors. 'From April 1939, however, individual guarantors had to deposit £50 per head to cover the expenses of future emigration; also, it became difficult to find hospitality for the older boys. The rate at which children could be brought to England therefore decreased'.[85] Attempts to channel similar transports to the United States were blocked by Congress.[86]

It is not necessary here to describe the experiences of these children in greater detail. No account could be more telling than the *Collective*

Autobiography edited by Karen Gershon some years ago.[87] We will furthermore meet some of these children as adults in the next chapter when their postwar situation will be examined. Inevitably, traces of the early traumatic period will be found in their later lives. However, it is perhaps worth noting at this point that after listening to the respondents' accounts, one is left with the impression that the misery of the first years in this country with foster parents or at boarding schools was far greater than one might have expected. Only two respondents out of 16 said to have been "very happy" and to have had a "very good relationship" with their foster family. The others were less fortunate. Their experiences ranged from the relatively untroubled situation in which Mrs T. found herself: she was sent to a boarding school for which English–Jewish friends of her mother's were paying. "They were very nice to me. But I felt a bit awkward; I felt I was under an obligation and did not quite know how to handle it.' Her mother had managed to get out of Germany at the last minute and found employment as matron at her daughter's school. "I was very embarrassed about it and about her accent. But the girls were nice about it and about her accent; they teased her in a nice way; they liked my mother very much.' The headmistress was rather insensitive, though. She expected the refugee girl to be grateful and admonished her: " 'You should not behave so badly, especially you'. I found that a bit hard".

The majority of the respondents, however, were rather unhappy. They remember having been "home-sick": "I never felt close with my family"; they had "disastrous" experiences with foster parents; "it was a difficult and lonely time". They admit having been not exactly easy to handle which is not surprising considering all the upheavals they had been through. But they thought the foster parents could have tried a bit harder to understand their problems and emotional needs. Mr I. is a case in point, although the separation from his parents itself had not been particularly traumatic: "I was actually quite glad to get rid of my very strict mother. I looked forward to the adventure of going to a foreign country. I was not consciously home-sick. But I wrote letters home which got longer and longer. In this way I sublimated my home-sickness, I suppose." He was first housed in a camp but soon fostered by a childless couple. "They were business people and terribly mean. They were totally unemotional and did not know what an adolescent felt or needed." They were particularly angered by the naturally good appetite of the 16-year-old boy. His parents already had made fun of it, "but it is quite different if strangers make these remarks. But what was worse: they were serious about it. They feared I would eat them poor. I became chronically hungry; it was purely psychological. I was a mixture of servant and poor relation in their house without the rights of either of them". He got pocket money for helping them in their small shop, but "they were upset that I spent most of my money on sweets and taking a girl to the cinema. They expected me to buy my own clothes. They therefore gave me less and saved the rest for me. I don't mind that; it was probably wiser. I should have saved more money". As soon as possible he left the family and went to live in a hostel for refugee adolescents.

Mrs U. was also callously treated: she and her twin sister were fostered by an English family. But the couple had marriage problems and the two girls were probably too much for them. Thus, after two years, they sent one of them, Mrs U., away. "It was very traumatic for me", the respondent remembered. She was subsequently sent to a boarding school where she was also "very unhappy".

Often, it was refugees who fostered these children or who ran hostels for the older ones. But, sadly enough, they did not necessarily show more understanding or more affection for the children. Hostels were said to be "run with an iron rod" and the older children or adolescents sometimes to have been exploited, even by their own relatives in a couple of cases.

I do not wish to imply that the proportion of good and bad experiences among the respondents is representative for the children who came with the transports as a whole. Their experiences do suggest, however, that the picture emerging from Gershon's book tends perhaps to be too rosy. This applies even more to Bentwich who talks about the 'deep attachment' between the children and their foster families, presenting it as the rule rather than the exception.[88]

Just as these children who came with the transports were guaranteed by people in Britain, so were many of the older refugees. In fact, together with those who arrived on a domestic's permit, they probably represented the majority of the refugees who entered Britain in 1938/39. At any rate, three quarters of the respondents had arrived via these two avenues. It is interesting that among the sponsors were a noticeably high number of Quakers and Methodists. Some refugees had been able to persuade English friends to act as guarantors for them. Most, however, had to rely on their own community, i.e. either on friends from Germany or, more commonly, on relatives who had emigrated before them. It was not easy, though, for the latter to come to the rescue of their families on the Continent. Most of the refugees lived in bedsitters in fairly cramped conditions.[89] But worse: a sponsor had to deposit between £50 and £100 for each immigrant, which was a fortune for people with hardly any income at all. This meant that often refugees frantically searched for people who were able to lend them the necessary sum for a deposit or tried to persuade English acquaintances to guarantee for or take on their relatives, often their parents, as domestics.

One respondent was particularly ingenious: then a young man, he stole taps, lead pipes and other metal from empty houses; sold them and paid Irish working class families with the money who had to sign a statement that they would employ refugees as domestics whom, in fact, they never saw. The method was successful: he managed to save 73 people in this way. This must have been one of the most successful rescue actions led by an individual. Some other respondents reported having used tricks or forged passports to get their spouses or themselves out of Germany. But for most, persuasion was the only weapon they had. Many were successful in their attempts to find money or sponsors just in time before the war broke out. For others time ran out too quickly and they have been haunted ever since by guilt feelings that they had not done enough to save their relatives.

Quite an important role in the process of emigration was played by the so-called 'English' relations. We have already come across a number of cases on the previous pages. Even though, more often than not, this role was taken on rather reluctantly, nevertheless about a quarter of the respondents had been able to obtain a permit through them. A lot of persuasion and perseverance was needed indeed on the part of the German side of the family to induce the 'English' family to act. Often it was only at the last minute that help was finally offered. "They had not been aware how serious the situation was", some respondents said. Or it was felt that as destitute refugees one was too much of an embarrassment to English relatives, generally described as "rich" or "prosperous". Another reason, related to the first one, may have been the simple fact that the English and the German branch of the families had become estranged and the English relatives therefore lacked the necessary personal motivation. Many of these 'English' relatives were descendants of or themselves emigrants from Germany who had moved to Britain either in the middle of the 19th century or at the beginning of the 20th century.

In some cases, the ties had remained close, however. Thus two of Miss M.'s great-uncles had left Germany for Britain in 1848. Like many German Jews some 70 years later, they had arrived without money, but after a few years they set up a factory in Birmingham and became prosperous. They frequently returned to Germany to visit their relatives. One of them sent a piano and money for lessons to Miss M.'s mother. They regularly sent money back home also for other purposes, paid for the university course of their nephew, Miss M.'s. uncle, and took another uncle into their factory. Miss M.'s mother had kept in close touch with the 'English' family and had developed a special liking for England which her daughter adopted. In 1912, Miss M. was sent over to improve her English. Her relatives looked after her. Early in 1938 they helped again in providing her and fifteen other members of the family with permits for Britain.

In a similar case it also was the respondent's mother who had kept up contact with a great uncle's family who had emigrated to Britain in the 19th century. Mrs G.'s mother loved England and saw to it that her daughter learned English well. It was through these relatives, well-to-do lawyers, that Mrs G. obtained a work permit for Britain without any trouble when she decided to leave Germany in 1933. She stayed with her English relatives for a while and was well treated. They also helped to get her brothers out of internment and to obtain a visa for his re-emigration to the United States.

Yet these examples of friendly assistance and concern do not seem to have been all that common. The majority of the respondents with English relatives reported that the assistance did not go further than offering to act as guarantor and this often enough only after prolonged and urgent requests from Germany. Even then it happened that the long awaited reply was written by a secretary. Sometimes a female member of the German family was taken in as domestic by the English family; but it also happened that a refugee was too proud to accept help from the English family and rather preferred to support herself through menial jobs. In several cases, the English relatives were described as "not very helpful". Contact between the English and the German families after their arrival of the latter was generally minimal; often it ceased after the first meeting or remained sporadic. The lack of interest was apparently mutual. A number of respondents felt they had nothing in common; or they thought their English relatives "too rich" or "too stupid". It became obvious that the English and the German branches of the families had in many cases grown far apart. The familial link had been briefly activated in a moment of crisis; after it had fulfilled this function, there was little left otherwise to sustain closer bonds.

From what has been said so far it should have become clear that the refugees, especially those who came in 1938/39, had to overcome formidable obstacles if they wanted to enter Britain – or, for that matter, nearly any other country.[90] 'Every twopence ha'penny country', a refugee remarked with bitterness, 'suddenly invented humiliating restrictions making themselves deeply offensive to people who knew themselves to be the heirs of a proud tradition of hard work and civilised behaviour'.[91] Yet once arrived, the problems did not cease. Most frustrating for the refugees was that, in contrast to those who had arrived before 1938, they were not allowed to take up employment. They were given – with the qualifications described above – the permission to set up businesses of their own, thus providing labour for British workers, or if need be, as partners in English firms.[92] Yet it was only in exceptional cases that they were allowed to take up employment themselves. This was a situation difficult to accept for people, dedicated to an active life, who had enjoyed fairly high incomes or good salaries. Now their standard of living was frequently reduced to subsistence level; worse – many were dependant on the various refugee organizations for financial support.[93] This was yet another humiliating experience from which the refugees tried to escape as quickly as possible. Not surprisingly, respondents who completely managed without 'Bloomsbury House', the headquarters of the various refugee organizations, pointed to this fact with considerable satisfaction.

Those among the respondents who were able to support themselves were by far in the majority in spite of the restrictions on most types of employment. To this group belong those who had found jobs as trainees either in factories or in agriculture for which work permits were given. Those who went into agriculture generally intended to use this training as a preparation for the eventual re-emigration to Palestine. Only the war prevented many from leaving Britain.

Another possibility of earning a modest income was to work as a domestic help. This had the added advantage of not having to pay for a room and for food. In a few cases men took on the job of butler.[94] But it was mainly women who swallowed their pride and worked as domestic servants to support themselves and often husband and children as well.[95] Many of the women had had cooks and maids in Germany and lacked experience in housework. Some taught themselves quickly, just before leaving, some rudimentary skills. Even so, they had to make considerable psychological adjustments. Some took on jobs as cooks or matrons in hostels for refugees or in boarding schools to be near their children who had found a place there – occasionally, as we have seen, to the embarrassment of the latter.

The majority of these women probably worked in families. A few had a good relationship with their employers; some even became friends. For most, however, this was an unhappy time. Yet it may not have been bad treatment, but merely the humiliating experience of being treated as a domestic by employers who lacked any clear ideas of their domestics' background. It seems that many employers were unaware of the middle and upper-middle class upbringing and self-esteem of their 'maids'. Thus Mrs T. "had a horrible job. I got the sack because I stayed in bed when I had the flu, as I would have done in Germany". She was luckier with her next job which was with a left-wing English lawyer who had bought a big house in the country and employed several refugees.

Understandably, strong efforts were made to get out of the domestic employment as soon as possible or to avoid it in the first place. Especially women with families found other means of earning a living. There was no other choice for them than to "work their way through illegally". With an astounding degree of imagination and talent for improvization they found themselves a variety of odd jobs. Thus Mrs C. mended the clothes for refugee men whose wives had stayed behind in Germany. Later she made teddybears and gas m ;ks which were sold by her husband, a former journalist who now travelled as her salesman. Another respondent, Mrs B., first sold her valuables and part of her dowry before she started making stuffed toy animals which, according to her, sold very well. Others did secretarial work for refugees. Or there was Mrs A. who had to open the door at a surgery for board and lodging. How precarious this situation could be is shown by Mrs L.'s case. She had come to Britain on a visitor's permit and first stayed with friends from her hometown. But soon she had to leave, since her friends had to accommodate immigrant relatives. She took a room and, through contacts, found a job as a cleaning woman, of course without possessing a permit. Since she did not earn enough to pay her rent she left secretly. Afterwards she worked for a refugee couple. "It was horrible. They were 150% orthodox and I had a lot of work; imagine all the dishes on Sabbath." But at least they helped her to get a work permit. She left once more, took a room with other refugees and through them found a job with a non-Jewish German refugee couple. Mrs L. had to look after and sleep in the same room with their dogs. She was so hungry that she ate the dogs' food. She also did some secretarial work for her employer. But when he made advances she left. After that she lived off various secretarial and cleaning jobs.

The early 1940s brought some relief. Many refugees found employment in the war industries and restrictions on work were generally lifted. Quite a few of the young men joined the Poineer Corps as did a number of the young refugee women. The war years with their upheavals also marked the end of the emigration and the beginning of the settling-in process. In the next chapter we will look at some characteristics of the emergent German–Jewish community in Britain.

5 Search for New Roots

THE BURDEN OF THE PAST

Homelessness

The war years and the post-war period prepared the way for the eventual integration of the German–Jewish refugees into British society as individuals and as a group. The process of integration was, of course, complex and extended over many years. It is certainly not possible to put precise dates to it. Refugee organizations and cultural associations played an important role in this process. Most of them were founded in the 1940s. Thus the structural foundations were laid for the consolidation of the German Jews as an ethnic group. But, as will be seen below, these organizations also helped to create links between the immigrants and the wider society.

At the same time, however, these were highly troubled years for refugees. Emigration may officially have come to an end at the outbreak of the war. Yet its unsettling effects on the refugees' lives subsided only slowly, if at all. These effects will be outlined here first; the crucial role of the refugee organizations will then emerge more clearly.

One of the biggest problems remained employment. The job situation which had been extremely precarious before and during the war, improved only slowly. For many respondents, the drifting in and out of jobs, lasted well into the 1950s.[1] Not only that; the immediate and most striking impression one gets from the respondents' personal histories is one of restlessness during these years. They were marked not only by constant moves in and out of jobs, but also in and out of bedsitters, in and out of London and, last but not least, in and out of Britain.

As to the last point, it has already been mentioned that there was considerable re-emigration among the refugees: about 20 000 left Britain during or shortly after the war. Thus one repeatedly reads in the pages of the *AJR Information* during these years that certain members of the community had left or were about to leave Britain. One also comes across small advertisements such as this one of August 1946: 'Continental featherbeds and suitable bed linen, first class quality, new, for sale owing to departure to U.S.A.'; or, in May 1948, a complete set of furniture and a 'patented process to be sold because of emigration'.[2]

By far the largest number re-emigrated to the United States: some 10 000 between 1939 and 1945 alone. Only some 1200 re-emigrated to Palestine and South America during the same period. And about the same number of refugees, half of them Jewish, had applied for repatriation to Germany by May 1946, although in June 1946 the *AJR Information* spoke of 'many thousand refugees from Germany and Austria' who had by then applied for repatriation.[3]

Motives varied. Some left for political reasons. This applied to many who returned to Germany after the war to help with the reconstruction of political institutions. But it also applied to refugees who re-emigrated before the war, often to the United States, such as Franz Neumann, the well-known political scientist:[4]

> I spent the first three years in England (1933–1936) in order to be close to Germany and not to lose contact with her. I actively participated in refugee politics, besides pursuing post-graduate studies in political science at the London School of Economics. It was precisely in England that I became fully aware that one had to bury the expectation of an overthrow of the regime from within. The appeasement policy of the official ruling groups in Britain, combined with the pacifism of the Labor Party, then in opposition, convinced me and many others that the Nazi regime, far from becoming weaker, would grow stronger, and this with the support of the major European powers. Thus a clean break – psychological, social, and economic – had to be made, and a new life started. But England was not the country in which to do it. Much as I (and all the others) loved England, her society was too homogeneous and too solid, her opportunities (particularly under conditions of unemployment) too narrow, her politics not too agreeable. One could, so I felt, never quite become an Englishman.

In this context the case of a respondent, Mrs S., is illuminating. She had followed her elder sister who had re-emigrated to the United States. She found an interesting job as a teacher for handicapped children and stayed on for seven years. In 1963, she returned to Britain for a visit and discovered that she liked it better over here after all. "In the United States you have to fit labels", Mrs S. explained. "I was labelled as Jewish, female, white, single and expected to behave accordingly. If you become an American citizen, you are American, but if you become a British citizen, you are still a foreigner. You are considered inferior and you could not become English, whereas in America you are supposed to try and be American as much as you possible can", i.e. through remaining or becoming more so what you ethnically are. At first Mrs S. did not mind being labelled; "I laughed it all down, but the pressures are amazing; it really wears you down." After seven years she had enough. In this sense, she has felt freer in Britain, although there are other restrictions, as Mrs S. found out.[5]

As in this case, the principle motivation for re-emigration seemed generally to have been the wish to join other family members in order to re-establish a coherent family life. Thus Mr N. had arrived in Britain with the Children's Transport and found good foster parents. In the meantime, his parents back in Germany had obtained visas for Rhodesia where Mr N. was supposed to follow them as soon as possible. On their way to Africa, they briefly stopped over in London; Mr N. talked to them on the telephone and found it difficult to communicate with them, because he had forgotten half his German. Subsequently, "I wrote to them regularly, but could not quite understand why I was not with them. I was happy in Britain, but wondered why I was not with them. I had a strong sense of divided loyalties: where should my emotional loyalties be? This was something which always worried me very much". As soon as the war was over, he intended to emigrate to South Africa to be near them at least, because there were no job opportunities in his field where they lived. He had relatives in South Africa who had a job waiting for him. So he stayed with his parents for a period during which he was waiting for his permit. He vividly remembers to this day what a "traumatic experience" it had been for him "to meet his parents again who had become strangers" after all those years of separation. When his permit was finally refused, he returned to Britain.

The drifting in and out of Britain continued for some time after the war and undoubtedly reflects the uprootedness of many among at least the first and second generation which will be dealt with more explicitly below. Not untypical is the example of Mrs H. She had married another refugee in the 1940s. Her husband was in the army and sent to Germany "where he had a lot of German women". The marriage broke up after two years. Mrs H. left for Canada, where she had an old schoolfriend from Germany, to escape from a boyfriend who wanted to marry her; "I could not face it", she explained. She got married in Canada all the same, to a refugee again. But this marriage also ended in divorce and she returned to Britain "for a year to find out what it was like". She did not particularly like Britain then. But she found a job in which she was happy and since her colleagues "were very nice", she decided to stay on.

Or there is the case of Mrs G. She had come to Britain with great hesitation. She was a young girl in 1938 and would have dearly loved to go to Palestine. Indeed she had even undergone some agricultural training in preparation for it. But her mother would not have any of it: " 'We are anti-Zionists; it is out of the question' ". She was sent to Britain with the Children's Transports instead and arrived here, not surprisingly, with bitter feelings (*"mit grollendem Herzen"*). "I never wanted to live here; I was very angry with my mother. I was not at all mature enough to leave home and to be on my own." After a number of unhappy years with foster families and in hostels, she finally joined up with a Communist youth group in exile. Soon after the war her group returned to Germany to help with the 'reconstruction' of the country. Mrs G. had to take up German citizenship again: "I never really thought about it; what it meant." Not only in psychological terms; she also had to share the life of a starving population as she was not among those refugees who went to Germany with the occupying army. To make things worse: the relationship with her group deteriorated; Mrs G. was criticized for being "too bourgeois" in her habits. So she decided to return to Britain. Yet this was not so easy because she had given up her British citizenship. Finally, she obtained a domestic permit which allowed her to re-enter Britain, where she started training in a hospital. After her course was finished, she tried to commit suicide. "I do not exactly remember why; I think it was a delayed reaction to all the upheavals and disturbances of the previous years." Particularly distressing had been the fact that her mother and grandparents had disappeared without trace in the death camps. Mrs G. went to work abroad for two years. She met and got married to a Briton "who gave me all I lacked: security, mental balance and cheerfulness". They moved on to the United States. From there she came to Britain on a visit but was not allowed back into the United States because of her former association with the Communist Party. Her marriage broke up; she found herself a job and finally settled in Britain.

Few refugees can have had more serious disruptions and miserable years caused by the enforced emigration than Mrs M. She and her mother should have emigrated to Montevideo in 1938. But four weeks before their departure, their permit was declared invalid because Jews were no longer admitted to Uruguay. Her mother subsequently left for Shanghai and Mrs M. joined her father in one of the Baltic countries where he had settled after he had divorced Mrs M.'s mother. In 1940, this area was overrun by the Russians and she and her father, together with all other Germans living in this area, were interned and sent on a three weeks journey in cattle cars to Siberia. Mrs M. spent the following eleven years in some twenty different labour camps. "Many people died from starvation, but I was young and healthy and therefore survived." In 1952, she was released and returned to her hometown in Germany, where she tried hard to adjust to the completely different life. But it was difficult and she found it impossible to earn a living for herself and her child who was born in one of the camps. She desperately wanted to be with her mother again with whom she had always been very close and whom she had not seen for thirteen years. Her mother, in the meantime, had left Shanghai because of the Chinese Revolution and gone to Israel where she hoped to set up a textile business, similar to the one she had built up in Shanghai. But this time, she was unsuccessful and therefore joined a cousin in London, the only other surviving member of a large family. Mrs M.'s mother started again in Britain, but the firm did not yield enough income to support both of them. So Mrs M. left her child in Germany with relatives and went to Britain on a domestic permit. Here she worked as a domestic help in various families. But she was terribly lonely. Although she and her mother had established a good relationship again, she found it difficult to make friends. Because of her past experiences, she did not fit in with existing Jewish, let alone English circles. Finally, she joined a group of young refugees with whom she felt at home and where she met her future husband. Soon after the marriage she asked for her child to come over. Her husband got on very well with his stepson; but "it was one change too many for him. He had loved it in Germany and would have preferred to stay. The child that I knew and the child that he had become in Germany were two different people". He felt an outsider in Britain and suffered from loneliness. He was teased at school because he was German and he, in his turn, was very unhappy having "foreign parents". After a few years, he suffered a nervous breakdown from which he recovered only slowly.

The severity of the disruptions experienced by Mrs M. may have been extreme, but her case is not untypical for all that. It pinpoints the upheavals many respondents went through and, what is more, the long-term after-effects of this period which can be seen to this day.

Similar movements, only on a smaller scale, took place within Britain. One respondent lived in 16 different bedsitters during the war years. On the one hand, there were the moves in and out of London. In this respect, the refugees shared the fate of many Britons. Like the latter, many were evacuated either privately or with their schools or firms. It seems that most tried to return to London as soon as possible. Thus Mr C. who had been evacuated with his firm to Maidenhead, "disliked it very much; I wanted to move back to London, because I had all my friends there". Another respondent, Mrs. Ch., together with her husband, had been evacuated to a small town where Mrs. Ch.'s sister-in-law had found employment as a domestic help. Her brother-in-law worked in a factory belonging to a German Jew. The latter found a job for Mr Ch. in his factory as well and both families, including Mrs Ch.'s mother-in-law, lived together. "The women got on very well, we shared everything and never quarrelled." But Mr Ch. wanted to start his own business, together with an Austrian–Jewish friend. This, he felt, could best be done in London, so the Ch.'s went back to the capital.

London also had a strong attraction for many who had originally lived in the provinces after their emigration. In some cases it was the mother who, after her husband's death, moved to London in order to be near her children; or the area, where they had lived, was found to be too provincial; they moved to London, "because there was more culture". Others missed their German–Jewish friends, most of whom had settled in London. The pull of London made itself felt quite early. In 1948 the Leicester branch of the AJR, for instance, announced a noticeable decrease of members due to 'emigration and removal to London'.[6] Similar statements by other branches followed in subsequent years. One respondent's remark is interesting in this respect: she had grown up in London, but through her marriage had to move to the provinces, where she is still living. "If I see myself as an exile then as one from London much more than as one from Germany." From the beginning, London obviously exerted a very strong attraction for refugees in this country, and we shall see below that 'home' often does not mean Britain as much as it means London.

The moves within London were primarily dictated by the wish to "better ourselves". A few had enough income to rent or – even less common – to buy a house as soon as they arrived. The majority, however, started out either from hostels or boarding houses, hotel rooms or bedsitters and moved on to better furnished rooms, to rented flats or houses to owner-occupied flats or houses. This also applied to moves from "less good" to "good" areas. These moves took place mainly during the 1940s and early 1950s. From then on, often thanks to the restitution or compensation money, German refugees were able to buy the property they could previously only afford to rent. In fact, the relative stability of the residential pattern, once it had established itself after the first years of instability, is quite remarkable. The majority of the respondents were still living in the house or flat they had acquired some twenty or thirty years ago. In general, only minor changes had occurred in the meantime, as in those cases in which a widow wanted to live closer to her children or in which children moved to an area which was within easier reach of their parents.

However, it is significant that these moves took place primarily in one particular district, namely the northern or north-western parts of London. It is well-known that the German and Austrian refugees moved straight into the middle and upper-middle class districts of London, in contrast to the previous wave of predominantly working class Jewish refugees from East Europe who started out from the East End, before they, with increasing affluence, also moved into the northern areas.[7] The respondents' residential distribution plainly reflects the familiar pattern: 124 of those resident in London lived in the North and North-West, as against 16 who lived in South-West and South-East London.

Their meagre incomes notwithstanding, the German refugees maintained their middle class life-style as far as possible. To live in a "good" neighbourhood, as they had done on the Continent, was an important part of it. In fact, respondents repeatedly pointed out the similarity of, for instance, Hampstead or Hampstead Garden Suburbs to Grunewald or Tiergarten in Berlin and that they had chosen these parts of London because of it. Another respondent mentioned the similarity of her house in London with her former home in Hamburg. Yet the most important reason was that "all lived here: there is always someone who lives round the corner whom one knows", be it friends or relatives. A few emphasized that it was just by accident that they were living in Hampstead and certainly *not*, because it was a Jewish area! A small group of respondents had consciously avoided the north-west for this very reason; they did not want to live in a ghetto, was the explanation most commonly given. As was occasionally pointed out with some pride, one lived in an 'English' area.

There was a price to be paid for this exclusivity, though. At least for some of the older ones it often meant isolation from their friends, most of whom lived in North London and in many cases it proved more or less impossible to establish an intimate relationship with the English people around them.

Several of the examples described above indicate that the restless moving about had its roots in more fundamental problems such as homelessness in a wider sense (*Unbehaustheit*) and the search for a congenial environment in which to strike new roots. It does not need emphasizing that the loss of one's home, especially under such humiliating conditions as the Jewish refugees experienced, is one of the most distressing experiences in life. Not all of the refugees may have immediately been aware of this wider implication of emigration. In fact, not a few among the younger respondents failed to grasp its meaning at first; they found the move to a different country exciting rather than depressing, especially those who had suffered from antisemitic hostilities. And there may have been quite a few refugees who, like the Viennese journalist Frischauer, were 'disgusted by the moral decay' during the 1930s: 'All I wanted was to get away.'[8] But most of the older refugees were deeply upset by the loss of their home, especially after the Nazi government had stripped them of their German or Austrian citizenship, thus brutally finalizing their expulsion from their home.[9] Many of them may have felt like Stefan Zweig when he wrote: 'Often in my cosmopolitan reveries I had imagined how beautiful it would be, how truly in accord with my inmost thoughts, to be stateless, bound to no one country and for that reason undifferentiatedly attached to all.' But he only felt humiliation now. And he continued:

Since the day when I had to depend upon identity papers or

passports that were indeed alien, I ceased to feel as if I quite belonged to myself. A part of the natural identity with my original and essential ego was destroyed for ever. I have developed a reserve that is not consonant with my real disposition and cosmopolite that I once thought myself – I am possessed by the feeling that I ought to express particular gratitude for every breath of air of which I deprive a foreign people. On sober thought I am, of course, aware of the absurdity of such whims, but of what avail is reason, against one's emotion? For all that I had been training my heart for almost half a century to beat as that of a *citoyen du monde* it was useless. On the day I lost my passport I discovered, at the age of fifty-eight, that losing one's native land implies more than parting with a circumscribed area of soil.[10]

Zweig committed suicide not long afterwards. So did many other refugees. The first report, published in 1951, on the mental health of refugees in Britain stated that the male suicide rate was 5.5 per 10 000 per annum, as compared with a rate of 1.08 and 0.61 respectively for the population of England and Wales. The rates for 1951 were even 'slightly higher than those for 1947–49'. These suicide rates correspond with a similar pattern of neurosis among refugees. In 1950/51 2.7 male and 2.3 female cases per thousand were admitted to mental hospitals, as compared with 0.76 and 0.97 respectively for the population of England and Wales. A recent study shows that time, in most cases, has not healed the wounds sustained through persecution and the loss of home. 'Practically all therapeutic attempts made by the different psychiatric schools of thought using the most diverse methods of approach', the author concluded, 'proved futile'. His results furthermore reveal that victims of 'forced emigration' have been nearly as badly affected psychologically as survivors of concentration camps, although the characteristics of their 'psychiatric pathology' have differed in a typical way. Whereas the former mainly developed anxiety neurosis, the latter have predominantly suffered from reactive depression, although this can also be found among a large number of victims of 'forced emigration'.[11]

Studies of mental health among the victims of persecution are probably all based on the cases of those individuals who were so severely disturbed that they had to seek psychiatric help. We therefore do not know how the majority of the refugees were affected. It is significant that among the respondents of this study, who belong to the anonymous majority, there was nobody who has not experienced some form of trauma either personally or among his or her immediate family. It has been mentioned above that a "broken heart" was frequently given as the death cause of a father or spouse. Of course, heart diseases are among the main killers in western societies generally. But considering what the refugees have been through, the lay-diagnosis of a "broken heart" seems plausible. Suicide of a member of the family was repeatedly mentioned as well, as were nervous breakdowns which were also suffered by a number of respondents themselves. The feelings most commonly shared by the respondents were those " of a great sadness", of being "never absolutely happy anymore"; "there is always sadness in me, also when I celebrate"; feelings of loneliness, rootlessness, homesickness and of guilt for having "left my parents in the lurch"; for having survived when so many others died an unjust and cruel death: "there is not a single day when I am not thinking of the gas chambers". Several respondents still suffer from regular depressions. 'The number of the dead is not the sole measure of the Jewish tragedy', as Chaim Bermant put it; 'there is the vast unhappiness which engulfed so many of the living'.[12]

In the cases of male refugees emigration frequently aggravated mental disturbances which they had suffered as a result of their imprisonment in a concentration camp in November 1938, following the *Kristallnacht*. Although most of them had stayed for only a few weeks, the experience of degradation and brutality either suffered personally or witnessed, for which they were completely unprepared, often had a devastating effect psychologically.

Thus one respondent pointed out that his father regularly had nervous breakdowns after having been to Buchenwald for no more than three weeks. "He was a broken man after it." He arrived in Britain with a nurse because he was so ill. In 1950, his old factory in Germany was restored to him, but he could not decide what to do. "None of the family wanted to go back." At this point of the interview the respondent's mother who was also present contradicted her son: "He would have gone back. But I did not want to go; if I had said yes, he would have gone. And then he had a nervous breakdown."

Another respondent was beaten up and nearly killed as he was driven into Buchenwald camp. The humiliation of it was perhaps worse to bear than the actual physical pain, the respondent said. But something curious happened: he felt very distinctly how his personality split into two different individuals – one that was experiencing the life in the camp and one that was watching what happened to the other half. He thought this detachment helped him to survive these weeks of torment. But at a price: after his emigration he could do nothing but walk about London for the first six months in an attempt to overcome his personality split. In the end, he had to undergo psychiatric treatment to reintegrate his two egos.

There were four death camp survivors among the respondents. Since a substantial literature has built up which deals with the traumatic effects of longterm imprisonment in a concentration camp, and since the interviewer found it too problematical to tackle this past, she decided not to cover this aspect in a systematic way. However, with one respondent the question of what it means to survive persecution in its most extreme and evil form arose naturally in the course of a long conversation and it may be illuminating to mention its main points here. When talking about her experiences, Mrs F. was particularly concerned with her feelings of homelessness and guilt and she probably articulated more clearly what so many others expressed more vaguely, who did not suffer what she had been through. Mrs F. still feels an exile in Britain where she moved sometime after the war. This is not a question of time, though. 'I feel I belong with the people who perished, I should be with them. The fact that I remained, that part of me remained. . . . Very often, especially at crisis points of my life, I feel I shouldn't be here anyway; maybe I am being punished for having escaped a sentence which was a collective sentence, of course, for all of us there, and by escaping that sentence I may deserve. . . . People easily accept a sentence, even if they don't accept the authority of the judge. It is a very deep, strange, inbuilt instinct. One accepts even the most unjust sentence passed. . . . Anyhow I feel I ought to have been with the others I was with. One always asks oneself, what was wrong with me that I was condemned to survive. Or what was wrong with oneself that others couldn't take it and oneself obviously could. . . . Was I less sensitive than others, was I less human than others, did I do something that others did not do. One is basically afraid to find out what these things were. . . . Lately I have become more conscious of what I have gone through and therefore of not belonging. I look at people and just wonder what keeps them alive. I don't know what keeps me alive. I just wonder what it is all about'.

Like Mrs F. there were a number of women among the

respondents who had discovered that memories of the past had begun to weigh on them more heavily in recent years. Thus Mrs L. found that many of her friends had breakdowns only now; she herself "panicked" when her children had reached the age when she left Germany with the Children's Transports; she was tortured by the fear that something similar might happen to her children. Another respondent is often haunted, again only in recent years, by the thought of what all the mothers must have felt who sent their children away with the Transports and what it would have been like, if she had been in that situation. This thought is even more painful to those among the respondents who left Germany quite happily, not imagining the agony of their parents who had to stay behind. "I did not quite understand why mother was crying and what it was all about", one respondent remembered. Their parents standing on the platform, crying and waving as the train pulled out – this for many respondents was the last they saw of them. Again, for some it took a long time, until the whole meaning of this last farewell sank in. In Mr I.'s case, for instance, this insight was triggered off by a film which showed how some Jews were herded together in a small room. "They were utterly dejected", he repeated several times. A young man offered his chair to an old woman, who Mr I. immediately associated with his mother. After the film he broke down and "cried for the first time since I was a boy". He was still shaken by this experience at the time of our conversation; he could not get over the fact that he had survived and his mother had not (his father had managed to emigrate at the last minute).

Another aspect of the traumatic effects is hatred. This is usually not counted among the mental disturbances of the victims. Yet quite a few of the respondents had difficulties in coming to terms with their hatred of the Germans. To be sure, some gave free rein to their hatred during the interview and did not seem to be troubled by it. And many respondents, especially those who had gone to Germany with the army at the end of the war, confessed to have been possessed by a "grim thirst for revenge. I wanted to take my machine gun and shoot down every German within reach", as Mr G. put it; "but by the evening of that day my bloodlust had evaporated". For others, however, their intense hatred had been a "very painful feeling. It is a physical reaction". Realizing that they did more harm to themselves than to the Germans who were, of course, far away and ignorant of their feelings, they made deliberate attempts to cure themselves of this hatred. Thus Mr V., for a number of years, invited Germans to his house to overcome his hatred through personal contact. Another respondent went to Germany specifically for therapeutic reasons.

Yet others are still plagued by it such as Mrs R. who exclaimed: "I can't get rid of my hostility; it is too much part of my life. I am still too scarred by the whole experience". Or as the writer Heinrich Fraenkel put it in his memoirs: when he heard about the concentration camps, about the burning of books 'I first felt shame and then a cold murderous hatred. I hated the new potentates of my country with a loathing so intense that, perhaps, it was merely comprehensible as the correlative of an oddly deepened love for the country I was banned from. There lay the roots of that peculiar sort of homesickness which I had come to know so well, an exile's homesickness which could but grow worse from day to day and which could be neither cured nor soothed except by abiding hatred.'[13]

Some respondents again emphasized that it was the humiliation of the experience of persecution which they found difficult to come to terms with, the fact "that people take away your dignity and turn people into cowards and deprive them of their human dignity. That is worse even than killing people and that people allow this to happen to themselves. I blame the Jews who acted badly, I judge them". Quite a few respondents again still feel an acute bitterness and disappointment at having been "betrayed" by Germany: "It feels like being divorced", as one interviewee put it.

However, with the passing of time hostility and bitterness have mellowed in many cases, as will be seen below, when we look at presentday attitudes towards Germany.

So far, no distinction has been made between the first and the second generations, for both were affected by emigration in more or less the same way. Yet the second generation differed significantly in one particular aspect: the feature most commonly mentioned by respondents of this group was a feeling of insecurity and inferiority – hardly ever mentioned by the older ones. It was a feeling which marred their lives and which they regarded as a direct result of emigration. For their lives had been seriously disrupted at a particularly sensitive stage of their development, namely when they were still struggling with the problem of growing up and forming an identity. The older generation was at an advantage in this respect: they were forced to leave after their formative years; i.e. after they had built a solid psychological, cultural and social base. Nearly all respondents met many of their friends from Germany again after emigration. Their company and the contact with various German-Jewish associations, especially the cultural ones, helped to recreate an *Ersatz* of some sort for the lost home, thus providing them with a degree of emotional security.

In contrast, the younger ones lacked their parents' attachment to German culture. What is more, they had left Germany at an age at which circles of friends and acquaintances were not yet firmly established. They had to start from scratch building up friendship networks in Britain. Not surprisingly, quite a few among the respondents said they had difficulties establishing close relationships with other people or to make friends in general. They found it difficult to fit in anywhere. Although they were closest culturally and emotionally to people of their own background, the ambivalence, if not outright hostility, most respondents felt about their German connection, not least about having been a victim, made them want to dissociate themselves from their group and seek identification with the English. At least, up to a certain point in their lives, most respondents of the second generation[14] said to have tried very hard to "assimiliate" and to become as English as possible. It was not only the flight from a hated past, but also the longing for security of which this generation felt deprived particularly strongly. This becomes apparent in an autobiography written in the early 1960s: 'One day [we went] to Oxford, and I fell in love. Oxford seemed everything that I was not: at ease with herself, at one with its own past – upper class English.'[15] Respondents likewise deplored the lack of a "homogeneous background", of a "stable centre in life" which they envied their English friends for.

Perhaps even more important than the various causes of the insecurity complex already mentioned was the fact that, through the upheavals of emigration, their parents' authority had become undermined. Because of the difficult circumstances most refugees found themselves in, they were deprived of the traditional parental role of offering protection and guidance to their children; and this at a time at which their children urgently needed their parents' assistance – above all emotionally. During the first period of exile there was the language problem which threatened to impair the parents' authority. Thus an article in a refugee newspaper discussed the question, whether one should speak German or English with one's children. The correspondent warned not to talk in broken English, marred by a foreign accent at that: 'Imagine you explain something to a child, or you want to admonish it, and suddenly you get stuck and start looking for the right word or you make a mistake which your child might correct. How easily can linguistic uncertainty be mistaken for factual uncertainty! As a rule, parents should be able to talk to their children with complete openness and without inhibition. Moreover, the children often pick up their parents' wrong accent which, later on, they have to unlearn with great difficulty. Consequently, the children should hear English spoken by English people, but German by Germans."[16] Many parents certainly felt the same. Unfortunately, as will be shown in a moment, the war situation was not conducive to the adoption of this sensible advice on education in exile.

However, language was only part of the problems parents faced. What made their situation particularly difficult was the fact that in Germany, persecution had made the German–Jewish community more inward-looking and this also applied to the family. The parental role was thus strengthened by the pressure from outside: 'They were our one and only source of strength', as a young refugee put it. And he continued, contrasting this situation with the one in Britain: 'Their scale of values and their social behaviour are no longer almost automatically adopted by us, for much of it is, or at first sight seems to be, a source of weakness rather than strength in their new environment. Those of us who were lucky enough to come here with their parents find that the answers to many of our daily problems are no longer found at home, but in our English surroundings.'[17]

One can easily imagine the frictions which must have resulted within the family from such a situation. Since systematic studies of the earlier, still unstable, period of emigration do not exist, it is difficult to assess how these problems were worked out by the older and younger generations at the time. Asked today, respondents do, on the whole not remember serious conflicts between them and their parents. On the contrary, most of them speak with understanding, respect, even admiration of their parents. But time may have helped them to forget the difficulties of the past. That things apparently were not always as smooth as they now seem is indicated by a letter which was published in the *AJR Information* in 1959. It was written by an older refugee who was deeply worried about the rift which she felt had developed between young refugees and their parents: 'Is it to be wondered at that our adolescents took a very deep breath to let the air of freedom, of kindliness and unrestricted youthful exuberance fill their minds, without leaving room for their harassed, tormented and nervous parents, the mere sight of whom conjured up disagreeable associations of hostile and dangerous surroundings? A girl may have felt resentful that her mother had ceased to be 'a lady' and was a domestic servant . . . I, for one, have not encountered a single case of charitable understanding and strong attachment that survived the mental turmoil . . . I have seen resentment, hard criticism or indifference.' This was very painful for the parents but, so the author continued, 'let us face the fact that this is part of the price we have to pay for our survival: fate prevented our living out harmoniously our role as the closest friends, guides and counsellors of children in the formative years at the end of their childhood'.[18]

As has been said before, further evidence would be necessary to judge whether this grim picture of the generation conflict was representative for the majority of the refugee families. Even if this were the case, it is likely that these tensions subsided after a time, as is usual with conflicts arising from the 'generation gap'. It is striking that these 'normal' conflicts were completely ignored by the correspondent; on the contrary, the relationship between the generations is highly idealized, revealing a more general insecurity regarding the evaluation of behaviour, a fact which was also mentioned by the younger refugee quoted above.[19] Because of the dislocation, it has become difficult to know what to expect; there is no yardstick anymore against which to measure 'normal' behaviour. The insecurity of the parents in this respect must necessarily have had an unbalancing effect on the children as well.

Turning away from the family situation, there was yet another factor which deserves mention because it greatly contributed to the feeling of insecurity and inferiority. This was the lack of a continuous education, especially of an academic training, in many cases, caused by the upheavals of emigration and by financial problems as a result of it. Considering that academic achievement has traditionally represented one of the major values in German–Jewish life, it is understandable that to have missed out on it, was considered as representing a serious deprivation.

As if all these hardships were not enough, the younger refugees furthermore have had to cope with the effects of emigration on other refugees around them: in most cases they live with, or have to care for, parents, spouses, sisters, brothers, or even children, who have been similarly affected and often were, or still are, severely disturbed by the traumas of the past. A number of respondents who are in charge of such a relative indicated how heavily this burden has weighed on them and how much it has contributed to their own bitterness.

The overall consequence of emigration for the younger refugees was that they were forced to grow up too quickly. "Hitler has deprived us of our youth", as one respondent put it succinctly and many others likewise remarked that by being denied a normal childhood they had lost something very precious which is irretrievable: "That is what I can least forgive the Nazis for."

Total assimilation, as was mentioned above, was seen by many as the only cure for their troubles. Yet most of them came to realize before long that it was impossible to become completely absorbed by the English environment. Apart from cultural distinctions, their experiences had made the young German Jews more mature for their age and had given them a different outlook on life.[20] This made contact with English people of their age group more problematical. Thus the very background which made them long for putting down roots in their new society alienated them from it.

Looking at the psychological effects of forced emigration on the respondents of both generations – and only the more common experiences were described here – it becomes obvious that these effects have been far-reaching and deeply distressing for most. And yet, there was only one respondent, belonging to the second generation, who felt "spiritually broken". To be sure, a number of the respondents had undergone psychiatric treatment at some stage – mostly in the 1950s – and with a few others the severe mental strain of the years of persecution was still noticeable. Even so, they had not been defeated by their fate; but with striking resilience had re-organized their lives and on the whole very successfully. They, too, show, as has been said about refugees in Canada, 'the manificent ability of human beings to rebuild shattered lives, careers and families, as they wrestle with the bitterest of memories'.[21]

Self-pity was remarkably absent among respondents. Instead the advantages of the émigré situation were turned with great vigour into assets, such as the knowledge of languages or other skills underrepresented in the host society; negative elements were given a positive meaning and perceived as enriching qualities of life. Thus the expulsion from Germany was often seen as an opportunity to widen one's horizon, to escape provincialism and to prove oneself under even the most adverse circumstances; homelessness offered the chance of cosmopolitanism, although the example of Zweig showed that this transference was not always achieved.[22]

On being a guest

Loss of home, however, with all its psychological repercussions, was only one aspect of emigration. Equally important was the reception by the host society.[23] Thus an early report on refugees from which I have quoted above stated that psychosis was 'three times as frequent in groups reporting poor mixing and indifferent or hostile neighbours'.[24] It is interesting therefore to look at some experiences the refugees had during their early years of exile among the British. We have seen in the previous chapter that, apart from a minority of outstanding individuals, the refugees were not exactly welcomed as a group. The restrictions which followed from this reluctant acceptance were difficult enough to copy with. But judging by numerous memoirs and respondents' accounts, one of the most frustrating aspects of their situation in the 1930s was the fact that hardly anybody in Britain believed them how serious the Nazi threat was; as a result, very few British people understood why they had left. When he made critical remarks about Germany, Moritz Bonn wrote, 'it was more natural to [my English friends] to assume that I was prejudiced than that they were blind . . . I shut up'.[25] Similarly, Alfred Kerr noted in his diary: 'Spring 1937 is a difficult spring (*schwerer Frühling*). Yet we as ex-Germans, the most deeply affected spectators, have to suffer most. In a foreign country: – seeing . . . and forced to be silent'.[26]

This disbelief was partly due to sheer ignorance about the situation on the Continent, as respondents pointed out time and again. But it was also the result of Hitler's regime enjoying considerable respect, if not admiration, at least up to the war, the persecution of the Jews and other minorities notwithstanding. There was some reactions against the extreme elements in the Nazi movement, but its antisemitism as such did not arouse general criticism. On the contrary, prejudice against, and fears of, the Jews 'was as pronounced in England as in modern German antisemitism', although for political reasons it did not have the same impact on English society.[27]

However, with the worsening of the political climate, culminating in the outbreak of war, admiration for Germany turned into total animosity. Those refugees who had ceaselessly warned the world of the Nazi threat now saw themselves driven to defend the 'other Germany' and 'vehemently campaign(ed) against Vansittart, Morgenthau and others who were not prepared to differentiate between Germany and the Hitler-Reich'.[28] Their efforts were to no avail; they could not prevent all Germans being lumped together – including the refugees themselves. History, for once, was to repeat itself: as during World War I, they were declared 'enemy aliens'[29] and subjected to even more humiliating restrictions than before. 'They could not change their address without previously obtaining permission; even short absences had to be reported. . . . Maps, cameras, radio sets had to be surrendered, and the possession of cycles and motor cars was forbidden.' Furthermore a curfew was ordered on them. In 1940, as is well-known, these regulations culminated in the internment of nearly all refugees.[30] And to add insult to injury: refugees were often accused by English people, as respondents repeatedly pointed out, of disloyalty towards Germany, of having deserted 'their country' in a time of crisis. '"What is a German girl doing in England in the war"', was one of the comments made.

Germanophobia was encountered by the refugees in all spheres of life. How it affected academics has already been shown. Other refugees were faced with discrimination in the labour market: they either lost their jobs because of anti-German hostility or had problems finding employment in the first place. Others again suffered from it at school, not dissimilar to Eva Figes who wrote that 'the fact that I had arrived as a foreign child was never forgotten or forgiven, and with the rise of anti-German feelings after the outbreak of war my nationality was always good for abuse'.[31] English staff and boys, so another refugee remembered, were 'suspicious of these strange boys who had come in from elsewhere and who were reputed to be "clever"'.[32] It could also be found in the neighbourhood. Thus one respondent who had many friends and pupils visiting her was denounced by a neighbour to the police and accused of having organized "secret meetings" in her house. Another respondent, an artist, was likewise denounced as a "spy", this time by his colleagues at the factory where he was doing war work because he was frequently seen drawing. The police confiscated his drawings, thinking they were maps.

More serious was the case described by another respondent, Mrs S. She had come to Britain as a small child and had picked up a good English accent within a short time. Her mother therefore always asked Mrs S. to go shopping with her. Because of her strong accent her mother had greatest difficulties in the shops (they did not live in a 'Jewish' area). "She wouldn't have got anything during the war. Shop owners said, things she wanted were sold out or made comments: 'Bloody foreigner, get out.' Sometimes I was very cruel; I refused to go shopping with my mother and she implored me in tears to go with her."

Often Germanophobia was mixed with antisemitism, as Mr and Mrs T. found out to their dismay when their neighbours called them "dirty Jews", whereas their neighbours' children shouted "Nazis" after them. The situation became so unpleasant that the respondents had to move house. Mrs G. remembered having been appalled by the anti-German and anti-Jewish talk she overheard in the officers' mess when she worked as interpreter for the British army in Germany. "It was bad enough to be German; even worse to be Jewish; but worst of all to be German–Jewish."

That these were not just isolated incidents is made clear by the fact that in 1940 the Trades Advisory Council was founded by Anglo-Jews for the purpose of defending British Jewry against the 'rising tide of hatred and defamation' by establishing 'friendly relations with important persons, trade organisations and public bodies'. Furthermore brochures, leaflets and books were published and distributed under the auspices of the Council 'to combat Jew-baiting'; they included titles such as 'The Jews: Some Plain Facts'; 'Anglo-Jews in Battle and Blitz'; 'Some Jewish Benefactions to the Nation' or 'It Can Happen Here', 'The A.B.C. of Jew-Baiting'. Those titles clearly reflect how alarmed the Jews in Britain were about the rising tide of xenophobia.[33] The refugees who had unwittingly triggered it off were, of course, particularly worried. Thus their main representative body, the Association of Jewish Refugees, declared it as one of their foremost aims to counter the hostility among the 'broad public' through a 'constant endeavour to overcome prejudices and wrong impressions'.

Self-discipline therefore was thought to be most important: 'Our special situation demands that our behaviour should be impeccably correct and beyond reproach. Each individual Jewish refugee bears a heavy responsibility. Whenever he goes wrong, he does not only imperil himself and his own future – he does so to the detriment of the whole refugee community with which his fate and his acts are invariably bound up.' Similar pressure was brought to bear on the refugee community only a few months later in the same paper, the organ of the AJR, with the protestation the German Jews 'are most anxious to see their abilities and skills used to the full in every sphere of the war. They do not wish to sit back and watch their British neighbours give up every spare hour for additional service, an attitude which would be both foolish and immoral'.[34]

However, the various attempts to enlighten the British population about the Jews do not seem to have been effective. A report published by the Trades Advisory Council about 1946/47 stated that 'even the most cynical and pessimistic could not have foreseen that during the past twelve months Britain would have been swept by such a wave of blatant and open anti-Semitism'. And for the years 1947–9 it said that 'anti-Semitism and discrimination are on the increase'.[35]

The same concern is reflected in the pages of the *AJR Information* during these years. Thus in 1946 a demobilized German–Jewish officer expressed great disappointment in a letter about the fact that 10 000 Polish soldiers ('many of them Nazis and Antisemites') were settled in Britain within months, but 100 000 displaced Jews who had just survived the holocaust were still in German camps. Or one reads about 'suggestions how to absorb the refugees', which end self-reassuringly: 'Refugees will always be able to take their proper place within the economic structure of the post-war world and to prove that their work, their skill and their knowledge are an asset to the country.' The fear of another expulsion is only too apparent. With the foundation in 1946 of a council for the 'promotion of better understanding between British people and refugees', further efforts were made to defend themselves against British hostility.[36] Advertisements appeared in several *AJR Information* issues in 1946, reminiscent of the shameful *Judenzählung* during World War I,[37] but this time initiated by the Jews themselves, saying: 'Show that Jewish Refugees did their share in the War Effort! Plant trees in the Forest of Freedom [in Palestine] in the name of any Jewish man or woman who has, in any capacity, participated in the war effort.'

A rather crude, if not outright offensive, attempt to placate British xenophobia was made by the German Jewish Aid Committee, an Anglo-Jewish foundation, which published a brochure, probably at the beginning of the war, entitled *While you are in England: Helpful Information and Guidance for every Refugee*. It contained eight 'commandments' to teach the refugees good behaviour so as not to provoke any animosity. Thus they were asked to 'refrain from speaking German in the streets and in public conveyances and in public places such as restaurants. Talk halting English rather than fluent German. . . . Do not criticize any Government regulations, nor the way things are done over here. Do not speak of "how much better this or that is done in Germany." It may be true in some matters, but it weighs as nothing against the sympathy and freedom and liberty of England which are now given to you. Never forget that point. . . . Do not make yourself conspicuous by speaking loudly, nor by your manner or dress. . . . The Englishman attaches very great importance to modesty, under-statement in speech rather than over-statement, and quietness of dress and manner. He values good manners far more than he values the evidence of wealth. . . . Do not spread the poison of "It's bound to come in your country." The British Jew greatly objects to the planting of this craven thought. . . . *Above all*, please realise that the Jewish Community is relying on you – *on each and every one of you* – to uphold in this country the highest Jewish qualities, to maintain dignity, and to help and serve others.'[38]

The pressure on the refugees by members of their own community, as in the examples given above, to be grateful for having been given asylum in Britain, to show themselves worthy of their survival, were fairly strong generally. The guilt feelings shared by most of them made them particularly susceptible to these appeals. Thus an advertisement by the United Palestine Appeal in the *AJR Information* in 1946 exploits these guilt feelings quite blatantly: 'You have been spared the horrors that *they* went through. Show your gratitude *now* . . . '.[39] And again in 1960, the author of a little piece on 'The Limits on Integration' in the same paper came to the conclusion: '[But] after all, have we not been spared torture and murder? The concentration camps set the standard by which we, the survivors, should measure our frustrations to the end of our life.'[40]

This trait became most conspicuous in the mid-1960s with the foundation by German–Jewish refugees of the 'Thank-you Britain Fund'. The proceeds of the Fund were to be used, under the auspices of the British Academy, for research and lectures 'in the field of human studies', preferably for research which would 'be concerned with the welfare of this country'.[41] Not all members of the community supported the Fund, though. Thus one respondent became quite agitated when this point was raised. She angrily retorted: "I do not feel any gratitude. I feel, England and I are even (*quitt*). I have given so much. I do not feel, they have done me such a fantastic service, that they have let me in at the last minute. . . . Strictly speaking, a refugee should be accepted anywhere. And they have allowed the people in so that they would become domestic servants and do miserable chores. One should not forget that either. They have opened their doors for me, but I have enriched them.' This respondent was not alone with her feelings. The AJR reported that similar criticisms had been expressed by some of their members who 'said that our debt of gratitude had already been amply repaid, because quite a few in our midst had rendered outstanding services to this country as scholars, scientists and artists. . . . It was also put forward that practically all refugees had done their duty during the war, especially as members of the Forces, and that in peace-time they had also contributed to the development of industry and commerce. Therefore, it was claimed, they would overdo the case if they now took additional steps for expressing their gratitude.'[42]

Yet the reaction of the majority was enthusiastic. Many contributed to the Fund with the result that not less than £90 000 were collected within a short period. The address with which the Fund was handed over by Sir Hans Krebs, the famous scientist, to the then President of the British Academy probably expressed what the donors felt; it also illustrates well the point made above. Thus Krebs said: 'No sum of money can adequately and appropriately express our gratefulness to the British people. Perhaps the only proper way for us to try and repay the debt is to make a continuous effort to be useful citizens, doing a job to the best of our abilities, taking an active part in the general life of the community, fully identifying ourselves with the communal life of the country, and offering our services whenever the occasion arises.' He furthermore did not fail to celebrate British 'tolerance', 'generosity', 'fairness', and 'humanity'.[43] This 'gesture of collective gratitude' has rightly been called 'unique' by the editor of the *AJR Information* who could not refrain from adding an admonition to the community: 'We are confident that everyone in our midst will live up to the occasion.'[44]

One of the roots of this feeling of gratitude was mentioned by Krebs himself when he spoke of the 'atmosphere of political oppression and persecution, of hate and violence, of lawlessness, blackmail and of intrigue' which prevailed in Germany in the 1930s. Similarly, in 1941, a letter appeared in *Die Zeitung*, entitled 'Thank you England' which read: 'Everybody is friendly, although I only speak little English. It is my heart-felt desire to state I have found in England the humanity which gradually lets me forget the worries of the past.'⁴⁵ This attitude was echoed by a respondent when he said "that what happened in England seemed a soft option to me. I have heard so many frightening things about persecution. I had accepted by that time [during the war years] that for one reason or another people like myself were in constant danger, that even in friendly countries, we were considered enemy aliens." Auschwitz had become the yardstick against which human behaviour was measured. From such a perspective and with such low expectations of human behaviour it is understandable that the mere fact of being allowed to live and to be met with 'normal' human kindness seemed like a miracle to be gratefully recognized. This attitude is still prevalent today, especially among older refugees.

However this frequent expression of gratitude might also have another origin. At any rate, it seems to reflect a peculiarity of British antisemitism which may have reinforced the refugees' latent guilt complex and feeling of gratitude. In an article on 'Anti-Semitism in Britain' which appeared in the *AJR Information* in 1947 a recent appeal in *The Sunday Times* was mentioned asking British Jews to be 'grateful'. 'Here indeed', the author continued, 'lies the crux of anti-Semitism among the British people: they have bestowed equality upon the Jews, they have equipped them with privileges but they do not expect them to take this for granted like other subjects of the Kingdom. Not in a few Jew-baiter associations and Fascist journals lies the danger of anti-Semitism in Britain but in that unmistakable differentiation between Jewish citizens and British citizens.'⁴⁶ A case in point is a speech delivered in the House of Lords in 1960, also mentioned in the *AJR Information*: 'The half-million aliens in this country had given little trouble and many were a great credit to themselves and to the country and fully justified (!) their admission.'⁴⁷ The 'Thank-you Britain Fund' which, by the way, was also supported by other Jewish refugee organizations, may thus partly be interpreted as an unconscious response to British antisemitism. At any rate, one wonders what the relationship between a minority and its host society is if, even after so many years of residence, such a tremendous feeling of gratitude on the part of the minority is evoked.

More problematical, however, is the urgent call on the German–Jewish community to conform to the norms and habits of the English environment and the eagerness by some to comply, as demonstrated by Krebs. Apparently, not everybody followed suit, though. The stern admonitions by the German Jewish Aid Community, quoted above in parts, are in themselves an indication that quite a number of refugees stubbornly held on to their traditional ways.[48] Nevertheless, the tendency prevailed, as Eva Figes wrote about her family, 'trying to hide, become English, or at least merge into the background and avoid giving any possible offence to English neighbours'.[49] This attitude can again be most easily understood as a reaction to the British situation. Thus M. Pottlitzer, one of the editors of the *AJR Information*, wrote: 'This country has a long tradition of granting asylum to the persecuted, but it has always expected them either to adapt themselves and to conform or *to go back where they came from* when persecution ended. (Refugees over here have all heard this phrase at one time or another, most of the time prompted by a total lack of understanding rather than by unkindness or antagonism).' And comparing the German–Jewish community in Britain with the one in the United States she continued that 'they [in the US] had none of the reticence which prevented refugees in England from trying to influence public opinion on anything not directly connected with their immediate problems. We here felt that we were on probation for the duration of the war, while they were determined to play their part in public life as they had always done. Once they had taken out their first papers, they were on the way to becoming citizens with a citizen's rights and duties – we did not know whether and when we should be naturalised'.[50]

It is understandable that this state of insecurity in an atmosphere of xenophobia weighed heavily on the German–Jewish refugees. But it is doubtful whether the enforced assimilation at the cost of their own culture was in fact 'helpful'; it is more likely that the unofficial ban on the German language which also discredited large areas of German culture, only added to the insecurity, feelings of rootlessness and of shame, already inflicted by the forced emigration. "If you lose your roots through marrying into another country", as one respondent put it, "or because you want to emigrate and start a new life, it is your choice, then, I think it is easier to come to terms with it. But to be told, this is no longer your country, that is bad and it makes you slightly ashamed, if you like reading German literature and listening to German music, particularly because of the war, when there was a lot of propaganda against it. Indians now have their own programmes. When we came we could not speak German, one had to whisper; one was an enemy, one was treated as an enemy. . . . One certainly did not make any demands. One was pleased to be allowed to live here; it makes a lot of difference. Then, later, it made a lot of difference as a grown-up not to feel that there was a place really that fully accepted one for what one was. A lot of people had to pretend to be English, like my brother, but I could not do that".

What is more, in spite of their willingness to make themselves acceptable to the English 'hosts', the chances for the refugees to come into personal contact with the English, to actually mix with them, remained slim. Thus as late as 1943, Tergit wrote, 'many refugees – at least in London – had never been in an English home, didn't know an English soul except the milkman, the postman and the greengrocer'.[51]

The tension between minority status on the one hand and the aspired integration and assimilation on the other was to remain unresolved for many years to come. Thus a talk given at the AJR Friendship Club, an association of mainly older refugees, was entitled: 'Can an alien country become a new Home for us?' (*'Kann uns zum Vaterland die Fremde werden?'*)[52] In an article, which appeared some ten years later in the *AJR Information*, significantly entitled 'Limits of Integration', it was said: 'Surprising as it may seem, this [the fact of incomplete integration] does not only apply to the older generation. It is the lesson of many observations that the comparatively younger ones also belong to "us".'[53] It is not clear, whether the correspondent saw this state of affairs as a blessing, because the survival of the German Jews as an ethnic group was thus guaranteed for at least another generation, or rather, negatively, as a worrying sign of a lack of integration into the wider society.

Most refugees probably had mixed, if not outright contradictory, feelings about this. Thus an editorial in the *AJR Information* a paper, which otherwise, as will be shown in a moment, strongly advocated the preservation of a German–Jewish identity, claimed not without some satisfaction: 'Many professionals, especially as far as they are attached to universities, are culturally and socially fully absorbed into their environment. . . . Most refugees have not fared too badly.'[54] Apparently, absorption was considered the ideal and the lack of 'integration' as a failure. This attitude was even more clearly stated in a reader's contribution at about the same time:

> It is striking how much the problem of 'belonging' of ex-refugees who immigrated in middle age is at present being discussed, in

the Press, in social gatherings and by smaller groups of friends. Ten or even five years ago it had scarcely come over the horizon. We were still fully preoccupied with our struggle to adapt ourselves to the utmost of our ability to the English way of life, but now, after 20 years or more, we seem to have come to the end of our potentialities. So we stop to reflect and take stock. Our often painful efforts have not been unrewarding. Up to a point we have struck some roots. . . . If one ever hoped to become totally absorbed in the British nation, too much was expected. . . . What can we do about it? Nothing but accept the fact that assimilation is not achieved within one generation. It will go more quickly with us than with ethnic groups – which have a strong emotional urge to preserve their origin for generations to come – as for instance, the German settlers in Russia, but it takes more than one generation in any case.[55]

Obviously, it is the shame about the German link, the revulsion against the culture acting as a constant reminder of the painful experiences, which had caused the longing for absorption. Yet the dangers of the abandonment of one's own culture are clear. Some of them were outlined in a letter to the *Information*, written by parents about the same time as the previous remarks, on the problems of 'Immigrant parents versus British-born child'. The authors had found that they did not know enough about the cultural history of Germany to be able to help their child with her homework. This was even more true with respect to British history and culture. And they admit: 'In our eagerness to make roots here we jettisoned, perhaps too deliberately, all that bound us to Germany. Our immediate memories were clouded by grief and anxiety; our links with it broken; there was the pressure of having to make a living here and there was neither time nor inclination – even the practical possibility – of keeping in touch with life and current affairs "at home".'[56]

These parents were not alone with their neglect of German culture. Another reader, also in the early 1960s, conducted a small survey on her own initiative which showed that 'the refugees in the Middle Years [46–68 years at that time] are those who had a professional and business career on the Continent, who helped to found and now "run" the AJR. They speak, read and write English fairly fluently but tend to slip back into German. One of the surprises of my survey was that many of them no longer *wish* to read

German books and although they may be well versed in German literature from school days they show little interest in new German (Jewish) literature and rarely keep up with the development of the German language – such as the new technological vocabulary. Apart from those who still write in German professionally (and there cannot be many of them), their German has become a kind of refugee jargon, with many English idioms and expressions thrown in. Unfortunately, this is not done in order to make the conversation more picturesque but out of a kind of laziness or perhaps out of a lack of concern for the German language. It strikes me, however, as the very opposite of what German Jewish culture was about'.[57]

Furthermore, most of those who went to school in Germany were not firmly grounded in English literature either. Thus, many of them became considerably impoverished culturally. A respondent made exactly the same point when she remarked – very critically – that her mother always refused to speak German with the result that her (mother's) German has become "very bad. But her English is also lousy and gets worse with age. She will end up 'language-less', in a cultural vacuum".

The development of the following generations, in ethnic terms, was seen by the author of the survey just mentioned as a process of increasing Anglocization. Thus she found "that the *Younger Generation* (between 30–45 years in the early 1960s) speaks and especially writes – English more easily than German. Although they may have gone to school on the Continent they had their professional training in this country. They find it difficult to read German books ("the sentences are so involved and long") and although they are able to read German they do not do so. They are often interested in German (Jewish) culture and feel that they partly belong to it. Thus they may read Goethe and Feuchtwanger in an English translation while, at the same time, absorbing English culture and literature. They are in fact trying to assimilate to their English surroundings".

If in this generation assimilation is not achieved, although aspired, the author expected this to happen within the next generation at the latest. Its representatives were 'born in this country' and 'will be fully assimilated to their English, or Anglo-Jewish, surroundings and only when grandparents are easily available will they learn German colloquially. Otherwise German is just another subject for O-level examinations with which the parents can help a little more than with the arithmetic problems, but

German Jewish culture becomes only a matter of hearsay'. And she concluded that these young Jews of German extraction 'will no longer consider themselves as refugees and are unlikely to be bicultural because we fail them in this respect'.[58]

These last words made it clear that the author did not view this development as positive but as a loss. Nevertheless, it is seen as inevitable, since the author was obviously guided by the traditional model of assimilation of a process of increasing absorption. That the striving for assimilation was fairly strong in the German–Jewish community, is undeniable, as we have seen above. But it did not follow any evolutionary law; it had roots which can clearly be identified. Most prominent among these were the flight from a hated past on the one hand and the longing for security on the other, of which the younger generations in particular felt deprived. Such a view allows a different conclusion: once the inner security is found, the possibility emerges that a more relaxed view of one's background and of 'assimilation' might follow. And we will see below that this is exactly what happened in many cases.

To conclude this section, it may be stated that the picture which emerges from the first decade or so of the German and Austrian Jews in Britain and their relationship with their environment is a fairly depressing one. Still struggling to cope with the traumatic experiences of the emigration and the upheavals it had caused, the refugees' efforts to begin a new life were hampered by the hostility and the rising xenophobia of large parts of the British population. To be sure, some individuals and groups showed 'humanity', 'generosity', 'tolerance' and kindness, but these qualities can hardly be claimed to have been characteristic of the British public in general. Ultimately the refugees were hopelessly trapped: they had been forced to leave Germany because of their Jewishness and they were stigmatized in the country of refuge because of their German nationality as well as their Jewishness. Whereas in Germany their Jewish traditions were defamed, in Britain the same happened mainly with reference to their German culture, with antisemitism continuing to play a part. The refugees therefore faced formidable problems when they tried to reorganize their lives. They not only had to fight hostility and discrimination within the wider society; they also had to sustain or re-establish a positive identity without which it would have been difficult to find a base from which to direct their efforts. And this in spite of contempt for their cultural heritage from outside and, at best, considerable ambivalence towards it on their own part because of the humiliation they had suffered at the hands of the people with whom they shared this culture.

GERMAN–JEWISH INSTITUTIONS

Free German League of Culture

In this atmosphere of disorientation and insecurity the institutions created by the German–(Austrian–) Jewish community were of vital significance. Among the first to be established were associations which combined cultural with political elements. This was particularly true of the Free German League of Culture (*Freier Deutscher Kulturbund* [FDKB], which was founded in 1938 in the house of Fred Uhlmann, a lawyer turned painter and writer. Membership quickly rose to 1500 in spring 1940 and a number of branches were founded in provincial towns.[59] One of the attractions of the FDKB probably was the large number of well-known artists and writers among the founding members, such as Stefan Zweig, Anna Seghers and Berthold Viertel. Alfred Kerr presided until 1941 and was succeeded by Oskar Kokoschka. Members of the board included Heinrich and Thomas Mann, Lion Feuchtwanger and Albert Einstein. Furthermore, some leading figures of British public life were won as Honorary Members, such as the Bishop of Chichester, J. B. Priestley, Sean O'Casey, Sybille Thorndike and Gilbert Murray. Their role went well beyond that of just lending their names. Indeed, 'without the generous support of numerous British artists, writers, scientists and antifascists of other professional groups, the work of the FDKB in England would never have been so successful'.[60]

The aims of the league were twofold: on the one hand, it was meant to offer a social and cultural centre to refugees and a platform for refugee artists, for their own benefit as well as for the purpose of rescuing German language and culture from annihilation. Yet equally important was the political factor: Communists had been instrumental in the creation of the FDKB and their primary intention was to use the league 'to win German émigrés for the fight against Fascism'.[61] Members of the Communist Party held leading positions within the FDKB, although they were in a minority. Collaboration between Communist and non-Communist members apparently was relatively smooth, at least for the first few years. However, Uhlmann resigned as chairman early on because of the Communist influence on the league and Kurt Hiller, critical of the 'Stalinist' leanings of the Communist members, also left and founded the Group of Independent German Authors.[62] More significant became the *Club 43*, also founded by estranged members of the FDKB to which we shall return in a moment.

Dissent notwithstanding, the scope of the FDKB's cultural activities is quite impressive. It offered its members a library, a 'Free German University', a school of drama and, last but not least, a Continental restaurant. It also housed a studio in which theatre and music performances or readings from contemporary or past works of literature took place. The FDKB published works of poetry and prose, often speaking out in defence of the 'other Germany', such as the volumes of poetry published in 1941 and 1943 which are filled with homesickness, sadness and disgust with the events happening in Germany.[63] In 1944, a volume was published entirely devoted to 'Schiller and the idea of freedom'.

Cabaret

Geared to the same aim and particularly successful was the cabaret 'Four and Twenty Black Sheep', founded in 1939 by John Heartfield, Egon Larsen and Frederick Gotfurt under the auspices of the FDKB.[64] 'We wanted to revive the heritage of Germany's *Kleinkunst* (Brecht, Mehring, Wedekind, Tucholsky)', Larsen explained, 'we wanted to show that there was another Germany apart from that of the Nazis; and we wanted to render account of the problems and doings of the refugees in England. . . . We were quite aware of the fact that our London refugee theatres were the only ones that were allowed to play in freedom in the German language while Hitler was master on the continent'.[65] The cabaret's first revue was performed in the Arts Theatre in London's Westend and attracted nearly 5000 visitors during the first three weeks. Because of financial difficulties, the revue came to a premature end.[66]

In spite of its apparent success initially, it is questionable whether the typically Continental form of cabaret, as presented by the 'Four and Twenty Black Sheep' would have made a lasting impact on English cultural life. 'It must have struck our English hosts as odd', Larsen commented, 'that one of the first things we did after finding refuge in this country was to start little theatres of the *Kabarett* type, not to be confused with the Anglo-American cabaret, or floor show. For us, however, it was not just a way of amusing ourselves; we were used to employing this branch of the theatrical art as a political weapon, but we were not really aware of the fact that we were introducing something new to England – the topical, satirical, literary revue with a message'.[67] This tradition had 'never really taken hold in England', where 'Cabaret', on the whole, 'still popularly designates an intimate strip club'.[68]

Its main value probably lay in its significance for the refugees themselves, actors as well as spectators, in that it offered them an outlet for their anger and frustration and a platform for political protest in a form familiar to them. Equally important was that it offered 'a good deal of encouragement, humorous and serious, to our fellow refugees in those dark years'.[69]

The same was true for the first exile cabaret, *Das Laterndl*, founded by Austrian actors and actresses as a Viennese Theatre Club. Its sketches and plays represented a 'satirical commentary on Vienna under Nazi rule'.[70] This cabaret was also very successful in its early stages and not only with refugees. It had enthusiastic reviews in the British press. Thus the critic of the *Spectator* wrote: 'Austria's loss has been our gain . . . I hope also that the Lantern will find imitators and create a tradition here before they leave us again (!). We have no form of theatre so intimate, so direct, as this; it has all the charm of amateur theatricals without the amateurishness'.[71]

Yet in spite of this favourable reception, the effect on the British – as in the case of the German cabaret – was minimal; throughout its existence the audience of the *Laterndl* remained overwhelmingly Austrian. This isolation from wider society meant the ultimate death of the political cabaret. The programme tended to become repetitive, as a respondent, a former member of the *Laterndl*, explained: "It was always the same – always Hitler. We also dealt with the situation of the refugees, but that was slight fare. By 1945, it had exhausted itself. But it had not been planned as a permanent institution anyway. If a few actors and writers are together, one naturally sets up a theatre. What else can one do? Most of us knew each other in Vienna already." Some of the actors and writers went onto English stages or joined the BBC. Others, especially the Communists among them, returned to the Continent after the war.

Austrian Centre

Like the 'Four and Twenty Black Sheep' the Viennese cabaret was affiliated to a larger cultural association, in this case the Austrian Centre. This was founded in 1939 and later served as the base of the Free Austrian Movement, inaugurated in 1941. And similar to the FDKB, the Austrian Centre saw it as its main function 'to preserve the best of our cultural life for a new Austria'.[72] German was the language usually spoken and was used in most of the Centre's publications. Britain was regarded as the 'host country' which had offered the Austrians a provisional home. By no means all Austrian refugees, especially not the majority of the Jews among them, as we shall see below, were seriously considering going back, but the Free Austrian Movement, just as the FDKB, certainly saw its role as preparing the way for a return. It propagated the 'emancipation' of Austria from the Nazi usurpation and the abolition of the status of 'enemy aliens' of the Austrians in Britain in order to be given the chance to 'jointly fight the common enemy', just as 'the Austrian masses struggled against the foreign rule of German Nazism' at home.[73]

During the seven years of its existence it developed a lively cultural and intellectual life on its own premises or elsewhere in London, or in its provincial branches. In 1943, the Centre was said to have had 3500 members and a staff over 70 for its restaurants (purely Austrian cooking), various offices and workshops. The members were offered libraries, bookstalls, concerts, lectures, dances and socials. Its main organ was the *Zeitspiegel* with a circulation of 3000.[74]

Both the FDKB and the Free Austrian Movement were foremost organizations of the political immigration, in spite of a predominantly Jewish membership, with a strong Communist component. Because of this, they provoked opposition from refugees who wanted to leave radical politics out of their cultural activities.

Club 43

Thus in 1943, several writers left the FDKB to set up the *Club 43*, called a 'Free Association of anti-Fascist Writers in Exile'.[75] The Club soon increased its membership to about 200. Politics were initially excluded altogether, but later admitted in moderate doses in the form of talks and discussions, but no particular set of views was allowed to dominate. Views also differed as to the evaluation of the refugees' situation: 'Some were and still are or are again orientated towards Germany, others towards England, and again others towards Israel. And yet another group is hoping to find a synthesis.' The 'common experience' of exile weighed more strongly than the differences. The *Club 43* thus became an important centre where the members have found intellectual stimulation and companionship. As in the FDKB and Austrian Centre, German predominated as a language because the refugees did not feel sufficiently at home in the English language at first. And although English was gradually introduced, German has maintained its position to this day.

This is also reflected in the programme of the Club. Originally its main function was seen, as with the other organizations, in the 'preservation of German culture'. Gradually, however, the scope widened and some attention was paid to British society. This is shown, for example, by the topics of the talks regularly given by members of the Club or speakers from outside. Thus out of 268 talks given during the first 20 years of its existence, some 37 dealt with matters concerning Britain. By far the majority of talks were devoted to German culture, but talks on Russia and France were also numerous. Readings from poetry or fiction were held in German only. The Continental bias becomes even clearer when one classifies the talks according to subject. Thus of 46 talks on art and architecture 8 dealt with Britain; out of 6 on education, 2 with English education; or, even more striking, of 53 talks on history, only 8 were devoted to English, but 21 to German history and of 52 talks on politics, 3 dealt with England, but 19 with Germany. The lack of interest in Britain also extended to her Jews: only one out of 21 talks on Jewish questions dealt with Anglo-Jewry and not more than 2 with the situation of the German Jews in Britain. Also during the following years this picture did not change substantially.[76]

Jacob-Ehrlich-Society

The same uneasiness which compelled the founders of the *Club 43* to break away from the FDKB also befell some Austrians who set up the *Jacob-Ehrlich-Society* (JES) as a rival organization to the Free Austrian Movement. However, the principal motivation in this case was not so much the overt influence of the Communists, but rather the question of the nature of the Jewish immigration. The FDKB as well as the FAM were purely political organizations which paid attention to Jews only insofar as they appeared as the victims of Fascism. Since both movements were primarily geared to the 'reconstruction' of the 'new' Germany (and Austria) after the war, the problems of those Jews who did not see themselves as political refugees but were planning to make Britain their new home, were never seriously considered. This was so despite the fact that 95% of the Austrian emigration in Britain was Jewish, as Bienenfeld pointed out in a talk to mark the foundation of the JES.[77] Among the German refugees the proportion of persons of Jewish extraction was high as well. Bienenfeld was particularly concerned with the FAM's tendency to minimize the active role Austria had played with regard to the *Anschluss* and the extent of antisemitism among the population. Instead, the Jews should enlighten the British authorities about the real conditions in Austria. Otherwise they might consider enforced repatriation of Jews to a 'liberated' Austria. The recent internment measures had shown that such an undertaking by the British government was not unthinkable.[78]

Although Bienenfeld himself and many other Jewish refugees were determined not to return (Vienna is dead, he said), his talk which was given in 1942, highlights some of the difficulties they were experiencing at that time. 'Among the refugees a certain disillusionment with England (*Englandmüdigkeit*) has set in, very much in contrast to the jubilant mood with which they had entered the country at one time. It is caused by the sad internment policies, the previous problems of employment, partly also by the disappointment with the war situation. This is forgiveable but not justified.'[79]

Bienenfeld also made some interesting remarks, very rare at that time, on the relationship between the Jewish refugees and the native English Jews. Although the refugees constituted about 20% of Anglo-Jewry, he said, they are 'nowhere represented in English-Jewish associations and organizations'. This was most 'unfortunate', for Bienenfeld fears that because of this lack of contact, misunderstandings could easily arise. Thus English Jews had complained that not enough German and Austrian Jews had joined the Pioneer Corps which was untrue, Bienenfeld commented. Another reproach expressed by English Jews was that the refugees would speak too much German. 'This is true, but pardonable', Bienenfeld retorted; because of the restrictions on jobs the refugees remained isolated from the rest of society and therefore were not offered enough opportunities to learn English properly. Bienenfeld concluded that the main purpose of the JES therefore was to work for a better understanding on both sides: it intended to explain the problems Britain was facing to its members and the situation of the refugees to the English – Jewish and non-Jewish.[80]

Association of Jewish Refugees

Meanwhile, the same concerns which had led to the foundation of the JES had stirred some German–Jewish refugees into action. 'As early as the spring of 1940', Ernst G. Lowenthal pointed out in the *AJR Information*, 'before mass internments occurred, an attempt to create a kind of independent representation had been made – called the "Refugee Liaison Group". Its members, all voluntary workers, if possible in team-work and outside their activities, were to give help and advice, stimulate a firmer personal and intellectual incorporation of the Jewish refugees and thus establish a permanent relation with the Anglo–Jewish community'.[81]

Internment, however, put a temporary end to these plans, but also added greater urgency to the recognition that the refugees needed 'independent representation'.[82] Thus in the summer of 1941, the *Association of Jewish Refugees in Great Britain* (AJR) was founded and soon developed into the biggest and, to this day, most important of the refugee organizations in this country, representing German as well as Austrian Jews.

Up to 1941, the care of the Jewish refugees had mainly been in the hands of the German Jewish Aid Committee with hardly any German–Jewish representatives.[83] It was this Committee which had organized the rescue operation of those Jews who wanted to enter Britain and which had financially supported those who were unable to earn their own living. The foundation of the AJR marked the wish of the refugees 'to take the settlement of their problems into their own hands'. But the tasks they had set themselves reached 'far beyond daily or weekly welfare work'.[84] Together with a number of other refugee organizations which sooner or later became affiliated such as the Theodor-Herzl-Society, the Association of Jewish Refugee Doctors, the Group of Unregistered Dental Surgeons, the Union of formerly German Rabbis, the Jacob-Ehrlich-Society and Self Aid, the AJR, to this day 'represents the overwhelming majority of refugees from these countries in England, protects their rights, endeavours to safeguard their future, and at the same time participates in the relief work for Jews on the Continent'. From its inception the AJR considered itself as representing an ethnic group, for it declared: 'The Association aims at representing all those Jewish refugees from Germany and Austria for whom Judaism is a determining factor in their outlook on life.'[85] With this claim it dissociated itself clearly from 'the propaganda of certain refugee organizations whose members were politically-minded and frequently desirous to go back'. In contrast, the AJR regarded itself as speaking for those refugees who were here to stay. The AJR was therefore not particularly concerned with re-emigration: the tasks it had set itself were orientated towards the future of the German Jews as a minority within British society.

This is shown in its activities which followed a pattern already established in Germany by previous German–Jewish organizations: on the one hand these activities have been directed outwards in order to defend the community against discrimination and anti-Jewish hostility; it wanted to achieve 'full religious, civic and political rights' of the Jews.[86] The AJR has collaborated with various Jewish and non-Jewish bodies, political and non-political, to this end. The call for self-discipline and group responsibility, mentioned above, as well as the repeated stress on the contribution of German Jews to British society must also be seen in this context.

Equally important have been the activities directed inwards. From the beginning, they have been extremely varied. One of the primary aims was to draw the community closer together: 'The position of Jewish refugees in this country now, in the fourth year of the second world war, is unique. They live in towns and in the country sometimes in touch with fellow-refugees only, sometimes entirely isolated and unaware of the general position. It is therefore imperative for them that there should be one central organisation, which has inside knowledge of their special problems and needs and where they may be sure to find understanding for their individual personal problems.'[87] A number of branches were therefore set up in the provinces.

The immediate problems to be tackled by the AJR were of a practical kind: members were given help with finding accommodation and employment. As regards the latter, the AJR had set up an agency which, as stated in an article on the work of the Association in 1952, proved to be very important. Hardly any of the refugees were skilled manual workers but businessmen, professionals or artists. They therefore had no chance of finding jobs through the local labour exchanges. It also offered some retraining courses such as shorthand, typing and accountancy. From 1944 to

1951 the Relief Department 'collected clothing and food, first for Jews in the liberated countries and later Displaced Persons and new immigrants in Palestine'. Soon after the war, the scheme Homes for the Aged was launched which became more and more important with the increasing age of the community's members. Further projects included meals-on-wheels, home visits and legal advice, such as 'how to make an English will' and, more importantly, on German compensation and restitution legislation.[88]

Communication with its members is achieved through its organ, the *AJR Information*. From a modest newssheet, 'describing the aims, tasks and organisations of the AJR', it developed into a flourishing monthly publication, generally praised by readers for its liveliness and the high intellectual standard of its contributions. The circulation has been kept fairly steadily at 4500; natural decrease of membership has been made up by new enrolments.[89]

Significantly enough, English was adopted as the principal language, in spite of the fact that 'German was the mother tongue of its reader and of most of its contributors'. Yet important information on restitution regulations is published in German, as are contributions by German–Jewish refugees writing from Israel or articles on German literature. The reason given for the preference of English over German reflects the perception of the community's position in Britain. 'The AJR', it was argued, 'had constantly proclaimed throughout the war that the Jewish refugees did not consider themselves as political exiles from Germany and Austria, but as prospective citizens of this country. Therefore it would have been a political inconsistency if the paper had not been published in English.'[90]

But does this argument hold? German –Jewish communities in other countries which found themselves in the same situation, chose German rather than the language of their adopted country for their mouthpiece. A case in point is the *Aufbau*, the successful publication of the refugees in the United States which had 'an enormous impact over the years'. Its 'editorial policy (was based) on three premises: loyalty of the refugees to their new country, to their Jewish identity and to their German linguistic and cultural traditions'. The mixture of these diverse elements obviously produced good results, far from the parochial. Thus the paper's editor stated that '*Aufbau* is an American paper, and yet it is written in German and deals in great detail with German topics. *Aufbau* is a New York local paper, and yet it has faithful readers in 45 countries all over the world. *Aufbau* is a Jewish paper, and yet it is read by countless non-Jews and has a great many non-Jewish staff-members and contributors. *Aufbau* is the voice of a group which was torn by force from its German cultural background, and yet it remains faithful to German language, literature, culture and traditions. . . . it might be a reasonable assumption that after 36 years it was the paper of a generation that is slowly dying out, and yet week after week it is eagerly read by innumerable members of the succeeding generation.'[91]

'This could only have happened in America' was the wistful comment by one of the *AJR Information*'s editors, who quoted this passage, 'a country of immigrants where it was considered natural that new citizens should continue to speak their native language, at least among themselves, and retain many of their social and cultural peculiarities. It could certainly not have happened over here. . . . We all knew from the start that we should have to come to terms with the English language, and it would not have occurred to anyone to publish an independent German-language newspaper or to hold public meetings where German was the main language.'[92] This reluctance hence cannot be explained by the minority status as such, for the example of the *Aufbau* shows that ethnic ties and citizenship do not necessarily conflict with each other. More likely, it reflects the peculiar situation of minorities in Britain in general and the effect of the 'internment' or 'enemy alien syndrome' in particular, from which the refugees in Britain suffered, and which as shown above, adversely affected their relationship with their language and culture.

Even so, the links with their culture and their country of origin were not completely cut. I have already described some of the institutions which kept the heritage alive. But one of the most important mediators in this respect has been the *AJR Information* itself. Throughout the years the paper had regularly reported on political and cultural developments in Germany, past and present. In fact, whereas the front page is generally dedicated to German – Jewish affairs, the next page has, more often than not, been reserved for 'News from Germany', followed by 'Home News' as the third column. The 'News from Germany' are supplemented by frequent reviews of books about or of German literature and also historical studies of special interest to German Jews. One of the most popular columns was, until the author's death, 'Old Acquaintances' with reports on stars from the world of theatre and film well-known in

Germany before 1933. If some of them visited Britain, their arrival was warmly greeted.[93]

On the other hand, anniversaries of fateful events in Germany are also regularly recalled such as the Nazi seizure of power or the November pogroms of 1938. Signs of post-war antisemitism are carefully watched, but due recognition is also given to 'encouraging features of a better Germany'.[94] Furthermore, the remaining Jewish communities in Germany have received wide coverage and active support. Thus, in 1946, 'when postal communications with Germany were resumed, the AJR wrote to all Jewish communities they had heard of, telling them how glad the Jewish refugees in Great Britain were to be able to contact them officially'.[95] From then on, information about the situation in these communities, especially their size, has frequently been published. Often travellers who visited Germany in business, restitution or family matters reported back about their impressions. The *Information* has also offered a platform to Jews in Germany; thus some have sent letters describing their life in Germany, others messages to former friends or appeals to emigrated members of their community to contact them, such as the German Jew 'from Bielefeld, formerly Breslau', who asked his friends to get in touch with him: 'Write to or think of H.H.'[96]

The question of a Jewish presence in post-war Germany has, to this day, been a highly sensitive issue among Jews, and not only those of German extraction. Thus it has been pointed out in the *AJR Information*: 'If a Jew from Germany says that he had made a trip to "the Continent", without specifying the country or countries he visited, more often than not it means he has been to Germany. The circumscription serves to disguise his feelings of guilt for having travelled in a country whose inhabitants perpetrated or condoned the destruction of European Jewry.'[97] Consequently, Jews living in Germany have come under strong moral pressure from Jews abroad to leave. This is evident, for example, in a notice in the paper which said that on the occasion of the congress of the World Union of Jewish Students held in Jerusalem, the West German Jewish Students' organization was attacked by the Israelis: they 'should regard their organization as "provisional", recognizing no higher duty than that of persuading their members to leave Germany as soon as possible'.[98] The AJR has, from the beginning, strongly spoken out against such acts of ostracism. Its attitude was first openly formulated in March 1947 in an article: 'Staying or

Leaving?' by stating: 'No doubt, the majority probably have the wish to leave Germany', although some might want to stay, having re-established their businesses. 'Just in spite of this lasting uncertainty as to a Jewish existence in a country where our people were murdered or uprooted, where anti-Semitism is by no means dead (though there are frequent instances of cordial relations between Jews and non-Jews), the courage and zeal in the rebuilding of Jewish institutions is remarkable and demands the highest respect.'[99] And a few years later, this attitude was confirmed, this time also in defence of those Jews who had actually returned to Germany: 'Whether someone is a good Jew or not cannot be measured by his country of residence, and the right of the individual to make his choice is in keeping with the respected Jewish values of the dignity and freedom of man'.[100] Yet five years later, a justification for a choice in favour of Germany was still deemed necessary. Thus in an article, significantly called 'Jews give Germans a Chance', the author, himself a returnee, talked of the advantages of such a step, for the returnees would keep up contact with their friends left behind in Britain. This would enable them to act as mediators between German Jews in Germany and Britain and, generally, between German Jews and Germans.[101] In the next chapter it will be seen, in greater detail, how refugees feel about this issue today.

The paper furthermore stresses the link with Israel and each number contains news about political and cultural events in Israel.

Another field of interest is the situation of the refugees within British society, although it is given less attention than German or German–Jewish affairs. The development of British antisemitism is anxiously followed and the achievements of the community's many successful members or public appreciation of the community's merits are reported with pride. Some information is also given on certain aspects of life in Britain such as the electoral procedure and the work of the members of Parliament, the Public School system, or on taxation.[102]

Significantly enough, it was not before the end of 1947 that the column 'Anglo-Judaica', covering events in Anglo-Jewry, was introduced. Yet in-depth discussions of British Jewry have remained rare. This reflects a lack of interest about, and lack of contact with, English Jews among German Jews in this country generally, as will be shown below. Slightly more attention is paid to the history of those German Jews who settled in Britain in the 19th century.

Although this might be not more than a reflection of C. C. Aronsfeld's personal interest, the author of most articles in this field.

The main function of the *AJR Information* has doubtless been to foster group consciousness and group solidarity. 'Members of our community' is the standard phrase with which activities of the refugees in Britain are referred to. A most forthright statement as to what constitutes this identity of the German–Jewish community after the expulsion from Germany was prompted by a serious conflict which broke out between British and American Jews on the one hand and German Jewry on the other. The bone of contention was the disposal of the so-called Heirless Assets, i.e. of the property of those Jews in Germany who had perished under the Nazis and had left no heirs to claim their assets. These had been handed over to the Jewish Restitution Successor Organization (JRSO) for it to administer the distribution of the property. But German Jews themselves were only given a minority position within the JRSO. The conflict arose out of the question, as formulated by a German–Jewish spokesman: 'Are the surviving Jews from Germany the heirs of the material assets of the former German Jewry or is Jewry as a whole the heir?' And he continued that 'this question has never been clearly decided, and perhaps in the long run this is for the best'.[103]

In the short run, however, this uncertainty led to bitter rows between the different Jewish organizations. It was not that the German Jews had considered themselves to be the sole heirs of this vast fortune. 'The Council [of Jews from Germany] always recognized that necessitous groups within Jewry, especially Israel as a land of sanctury for masses of Nazi victims, had a prior claim. Nevertheless, the Council felt it had the right to demand that it was entitled to an appropriate proportion of the wealth which German Jews had formed.'[104] Their claim, however, was more or less refused; they were practically put into the position of beggars and were given no more than crumbs of what they considered largely their own. Incensed by this disregard for their rights, the German–Jewish representatives withdrew from the JRSO in 1954. Later that year, an agreement was reached, though, and the German Jews, even if not entirely satisfied, re-joined the organization. Nevertheless, as a response to what had practically amounted to a denial of their existence as a group, the AJR felt compelled to state clearly in its organ: 'Although the German Jews are a small minority among World Jewry, they have not lost their identity as a community. As individuals, too, they are clearly distinguishable (except those who came to their countries of refuge as children), and they will remain so to the end of their lives. They are proud of this individuality, without letting it hinder their integration into and their solidarity with the Jewish communities of their countries of adoption. An important part of this individuality is a deeply rooted social conscience as well as a powerful cultural urge.' The claim for a larger share of the heirless property was thus seen to be justified.[105]

But it is not this particular issue which is at stake here. It is the definition of German Jewishness, and especially the 'cultural urge' which is of interest in this context. Was it really as 'powerful' as claimed? There is no doubt about it that this was so in Germany, but we have seen above that the situation in Britain was rather different. Here German culture was an embarrassment more than something to be pursued with pride. To be sure, there were a number of associations and individuals who have kept the cultural heritage alive. Other refugees however, do not seem to have been able to free themselves from the ambiguity of the early period. One indication may be that the *AJR Information* – and here again it has proven its value as a cohesive force within the community – has often reminded its readers of the German–Jewish cultural heritage; appeals have regularly appeared not to betray it in spite of its intimate association with German culture: 'Being aware of what coined our past we feel the obligation of looking back at its significance and of building bridges that connect it with our present lives.'[106]

Thus a number of contributions attempt to put the expulsion from Germany into some perspective by drawing comparisons with previous catastrophes in Jewish history, such as the exodus from Palestine, or, more commonly, from Spain in the Middle Ages. This offers some consolation: 'Time and again when Jewries were stirred up it proved to be not in vain for themselves and for humanity. Nowhere did they come with empty hands, and wherever they had been they left gaps difficult or impossible to fill.'[107]

Considerable space has been given to the ever-haunting question: 'How could it happen?' Numerous articles or reviews of historical and biographical studies and memoirs have appeared in the paper, reflecting the desire of all refugees to find an explanation for the ultimately inexplicable, namely the senseless destruction of so many innocent lives.

At the same time, efforts are made to instil pride in achievements of German Jewry. No one has perhaps been more eloquent on this issue than Leo Baeck who pointed to past 'creative unions with the culture of the respective countries in which [the Jews] had their place' such as in the Hellenistic world, Spain and Germany. 'Again and again, however, does one stand in admiration, in amazement, often almost in awe in face of this powerful, revolutionising force and of all it has accomplished.' The historic achievement of German Jews 'ended on that soil in greatness'. But it should survive in the countries of refuge as 'the striving for the matters of the mind and spirit, for the humane, the messianic, for whatever is great and beautiful and well ordered'.[108] The same spirit is reflected by the address delivered by the prominent Rabbi Maybaum on the occasion of an AJR general meeting a few years later: 'Heritage and Obligation. Our Responsibility for the spiritual values of German Jewry.'[109]

This was not empty rhetoric; action was to follow soon: in 1955, the Leo Baeck Institutes in Jerusalem, New York and London were founded in order 'to preserve the great spiritual values that German Jewry has created'.[110] In the words of Leo Baeck himself: 'Places of research established by the Ashkenazim, the western and eastern ones, were destroyed, just as those of the western and eastern Sephardim in earlier times. But the spirit cannot and will not be destroyed; it is predestined to survive. Books may be burnt, but what they said remains and seeks a place to abide. Thus, a great work of preservation and renewal is being expected from our generation.'[111] This determination to safeguard the cultural heritage is remarkable. But the important implication that a better understanding and appreciation of German–Jewish history would help German Jews to regain their self-confidence, was also clearly seen. It was expressed in the Leo Baeck Institute's 'directives for publication' which said: 'By scientific research and return to the sources, the Leo Baeck Institute intends to convey a picture of [German] Jewry and their work. In demonstrating what the German Jews were and what they achieved, we shall learn to know ourselves: who we are, where we come from – and perhaps where we are going.'[112]

'*The Hyphen*'

The *AJR Information*, in its own way, has played an active part in this effort. Yet, as significant as spiritual continuity has been, it did not immediately contribute to the problems of present-day life in

Britain. This must have been particularly true for the younger generation whose links with the past were rather tenuous. In fact, in 1964, one of them pleaded with the *AJR Information* to orientate the paper more towards the needs of the young refugees. They wanted to hear less about "Heine and the Jews" etc. than about the question: 'To what extent are we integrated into our English environment and to what extent are we still different?'[113]

Of course, for the older ones it had never been a question but a self-evident, if not always welcome, truth that they were different. The younger ones were much less sure about their identity and as the letter just quoted, written in the 1960s, shows for a number of them the situation apparently had not changed much over the years. Nearly two decades previously this issue had been raised in the paper for the first time. An editorial in May 1948 mentioned that 'various letters to and conversations at AJR headquarters have revealed that there are a great number of younger immigrants (between 20 and 35 years) in London who feel themselves [sic] isolated and would like to come into closer contact with people of their own background'.[114] Later that same year a few members of that generation got together and founded 'The Hyphen', a group for younger refugees between 21 and 35 years.[115] This group consisted 'of young people from the Continent who, having settled in Great Britain, found that owing to their similar background and experiences, they had interests and problems in common which justified the formation of a group without a particular religious or political bias, to provide for cultural, social and welfare activities'.[116] Its main aim was 'to form friendships and to provide for themselves a social climate in which they would lose the feeling of belong "Luftmenschen" and "belong" through friendships'.[117]

The name reflects well how this generation perceived its situation, namely as a bridge between the Continental and the English world or in the words of a Hyphen member who analysed their situation thus: '[Parents can] only make a series of external adjustments . . . . Our way is different in nature and not only in degree. We are not as firmly grounded as they are in another culture and most of us could be absorbed almost entirely by our new surroundings. Yet as we grow up we become conscious of the fact that we are not entirely a part of either the old way or the new, but could only be more or less poor imitators of either. So we go out in search of a formula for a successful synthesis of two ways of life.' Such a synthesis is represented by the 'intermediary' position adopted by 'The Hyphen'. Its representatives 'are not ashamed of the older generation and do not artificially dissociate themselves from their past, nor do they turn their back on their new home'. And the author drew encouragement from the fact 'that most human progress in the past has been due to culture contacts'.[118] But theory and practice are two different things, and the author was only too aware of the difficulties of integrating the two cultures in everyday life – particularly in a society, as one may add, which does not openly encourage ethnic pluralism.

Nevertheless, The Hyphen was one of those German–Jewish institutions which made efforts in this direction. Significantly enough, among its first activities was the setting up of a study and discussion group which covered topics such as immigration in general as well as German–Jewish immigration into Britain and German–Jewish history, thus confirming what C. C. Aronsfeld observed with respect to a different German–Jewish institution: 'Even in their earliest and most difficult days the refugees had never forgotten their duty to educate themselves and, as they would put it, assess their place in the world.'[119] The discussion group was 'always well attended', as was the music circle. One series of talks was devoted to 'Know your London' and there was also given an introduction into the 'Parliamentary procedure'. The discussion group, by the way, had been set up with the same purpose in mind of making Hyphen members acquainted with English culture, namely 'to show members how an organized debate should be conducted'.[120]

The most popular – and probably main – functions were the social gatherings, dances, and rambles. One such occasion was a trip by some members to celebrate New Year's Eve together. The description of it in the *Hyphen News* shows in a small and rather amusing way some of the problems of cultural 'synthesis'. The group asked the hotel manager to spare them 'early morning tea' on New Year's Day, but in vain; they had to fulfil this English ritual. Later that morning, the group wanted to make some music but were told 'that the Sunday peace and quietness must not be disturbed'.[121]

The Hyphen never had more than 100 members at any time although there were 400–500 names on its mailing list. Interest was strongest during the first 10 years of its existence; it gradually subsided and the group was wound up in 1967. Compared with other German–Jewish institutions, it was thus rather marginal. Yet for its members themselves it fulfilled an important function. It gave them a sense of belonging at the difficult stage of settling in into British society; 'even the shyest of our members found they could relax in our group and open up'.[122] The dissolution of the group did not mean the end of the network created. On the contrary, as the friendship patterns of a number of respondents – former Hyphen members – showed, contact has persisted to this day in many cases; indeed, 25 marriages have resulted from it.[123]

The equivalent of the Hyphen for the older refugees is the 'AJR Club', founded in 1956 and still flourishing, with a membership of some 400.[124] It is much more deeply rooted in German–Jewish traditions – combining some degree of social care with social, musical and intellectual events and the communal celebration of Jewish holidays – and as such has become 'part and parcel of the Jewish community in this neighbourhood'[125] [Hampstead]. It therefore had a stronger institutional base than The Hyphen which frequently struggled with the problem of finding 'a justification for the existence of our group' going beyond that of a friendship club.[126]

New Liberal Jewish Congregation and the Leo Baeck Lodge

Finding a sense of purpose was no problem for two further major institutions of the German–Jewish community: the so-called Belsize Congregation and the Leo Baeck Lodge.

The New Liberal Jewish Congregation at Belsize Square Synagogue was founded in 1939. Previously, German Jews, looking for a place of worship, had been given hospitality by the English Liberal Synagogue in London, St John's Wood; they even were invited to join either the Liberal or the Reform Congregations. Yet the refugees, many of them having been actively involved in Synagogue life in their communities back in Germany, intended 'to continue the long-established religious tradition of German liberal congregations'.[127] For German–Jewish religious liberalism was quite different from Liberal Jewish traditions in England which were, by German–Jewish standards at least, rather lax, if compared with the relative conservatism of the German Jews, defined by the Synagogue's late Rabbi Kokotek as follows: 'We are progressive in our approach to the ideology of Judaism, traditional in its practice. We are not blind to inevitable changes in Judaism due to time and environment. But we do not accept changes merely for the sake of harmony with a contemporary trend of thought or practice. We are rooted faithfully and sincerely in the traditions of Judaism, not in a blind credulity or mechanical imitation of the past, but with a deep respect for both our heritage and our contemporary life. We are neither narrow-minded traditionalists nor easy-going assimilationists. We are Jews who strive to live a Jewish life which is a meaningful expression of both Jewish tradition and contemporary environment.'[128]

This mixture of religious conservatism and flexibility in the face of changing circumstances has obviously been successful. From a small circle of 400 worshippers in 1940 the Congregation grew to some 1000 after the first decade and has by now nearly doubled its membership from 1950.[129] A considerable proportion of the members are representatives of the second generation. They have taken over important positions within Synagogue life, thus proving that, to quote Rabbi Kokotek again, 'what seemed (at the beginning) to be the attempt of refugees settled in this country to cling to their own distinctive Jewish tradition, has now proved a dynamic religious force'.[130]

The Belsize Congregation has become affiliated to the Union of Liberal and Progressive Synagogues and considers itself fully integrated into the Anglo-Jewish religious community. Yet, at the same time, it has never lost an awareness of its specific ethnic character and even consciously preserved it, as is shown for instance, in the formulation of the aims of the Belsize Women's Society which were defined as 'to promote Jewish knowledge among the members; to aquaint them with welfare work in this country, and to encourage them to work in support of our Congregation. Moreover, we wished to establish close contact between the members themselves. We joined the Federation of Women's Societies in the Union of Progressive and Liberal Synagogues although we do not entirely follow their pattern of work. Our activities reflect the different set-up of our Congregation and in response to the wishes of our members, we have shaped our Society to fit our particular needs. Thus we have, throughout the years, organised regular monthly meetings or entertainment for our members and their friends. These meetings have been extremely well attended . . . '.[131] This specific German Jewishness, as perceived by the Liberal Congregation, has prevented it from becoming absorbed by Anglo-Jewish forms of Judaism and it seems unlikely that this will be happening in the near future.[132]

Some of the elements which set the German Jews apart from

Anglo-Jewry were, most importantly, a peculiar approach to Judaism as outlined in the quotation by Rabbi Kokotek and, in Lionel Kochan's words, 'a far higher standard of Jewish culture and observance than that prevailing at large in Anglo-Jewry'.[133] As with other German–Jewish institutions, there is a strong emphasis on 'culture', in the sense of acquiring knowledge, in religious as well as non-religious matters. More specifically, German–Jewish traditions were preserved in that 'structure, prayers, and songs in (the Belsize Congregation's) services are largely the same as its worshippers had known on the Continent'. Up to the 1950s, German was the language spoken within the Congregation, but it was gradually superseded by English with the growing influx of the second generation.[134] Group consciousness has, of course, also been fostered by the fact that the congregation's members have undergone similar experiences; and this not only with respect to their common fate of being refugees, but also to their community life in Germany to some extent. For it has been pointed out 'that most of the original organisers of the Congregation – or rather Association as it was then called – and its Ministers had been active in the Berlin and Frankfurt-on-Main Liberal Congregations. It can thus be said that the foundations of our Congregation here rested on the spiritual twin pillars of Berlin and Frankfurt.'[135] Thus quite a number of factors concurred which helped to create strong and lasting ties within th Belsize Congregation.

The development of the Leo Baeck Lodge shows striking parallels. It belongs to the Order B'nai B'rith which, interestingly enough, had originally been founded by German Jews in the United States, in 1843. The founder members of B'nai B'rith were well-to-do business people and the Order has preserved this middle and upper-middle class character. Branches of this *Ur*-Lodge were subsequently set up in several European countries, including Germany. It is a fellowship dedicated to humanitarian and cultural activities, apart from offering its members the advantages of a friendship club. B'nai B'rith's concerns are not exclusively Jewish; its main idea was formulated as 'the striving for human perfection' or, at least, to promote the progress of humanity as a whole.[136] Yet 'nobody can live according to this idea, if he betrays his own nature. Thus we as Jews have to develop our distinctive characteristics on the basis of our Jewish heritage'.[137] As such, B'nai B'rith has always played an important role in fostering a positive Jewish consciousness.[138]

This awareness of ethnic divisions extended not only to the Jewish–non-Jewish contrast but to inner Jewish differentiations as well. The relations between German–Jewish and English–Jewish B'nai B'rith members offers a good example. As in the case of the Liberal Congregation, German Jews had, after emigration, first joined the existing Anglo-Jewish Lodge, the so-called First Lodge of England. Although 'none, of course, would have denied the bonds of brotherhood that united native and newcomer, both as Jews and as Lodge members',[139] tensions soon arose. On the part of the Lodge of England it was the fear 'that the accretion of a large number of German brethren, which would swamp its own comparatively small membership, might temporarily impair the standing and reputation that the Lodge had managed to build up over the years. Without disrespect to its German colleagues, it did not wish to convert the Lodge into a "refugee" organization and, at the same time, it could not but feel that the immigrant members needed time to adjust themselves to their new environment'.[140] The Germans, in their turn, felt that, apart from other differences, the Anglo-Jews were "too uneducated", as one respondent, a lodge member, put it. Thus each side was averse to a merger; instead, the 'Section 43', the 'Continental Section', was founded and affiliated to the Lodge of England. It was 'self-governing and both culturally and (so far as possible) financially independent' and had a membership of some 200.[141]

The gap between 'Section 43' and the English Lodge apparently deepened if anything, for in 1945 the institutional links were completely severed. Section 43 became totally independent and reconstituted itself under the name of Leo Baeck Lodge after Leo Baeck's arrival in London from Theresienstadt. Leo Baeck was the former Grand President of B'nai B'rith in Germany. What is more, he also was an admired Rabbi and thinker and has shown great moral strength when he 'had spurned the chance of saving himself as long as any of his flock were at risk'.[142] He had thus become the most revered spiritual leader of German Jewry, a patron saint so-to-speak, symbolizing its essence and unity even after the expulsion from Germany.

This new beginning had an invigorating effect on the Leo Baeck Lodge which 'has become a true power-house, carrying on the traditions of their illustrious past and adding material strength, vigour and enthusiasm to the work of . . . the Order as a whole'.[143] In fact, not only has it developed into the largest and liveliest Jewish lodge in Britain, with a membership of some 800, but also forms 'the largest body in B'nai B'rith outside the USA'.[144]

The activities of the Lodge cover a wide field, ranging from welfare for the elderly, sick, or other people in distress to matters of culture and learning and 'it is, perhaps in this', Aronsfeld pointed out, 'that the Leo Baeck Lodge most clearly reveals its "continental" origin'.[145] It shows 'an avidity for culture', in Bermant's words, 'which is plainly un-English'.[146] The Cultural Activities Committee is 'regarded as the backbone of the Lodge' and the weekly events and lectures on a wide variety of subjects are well attended; they are supplemented by 'study groups on religious and literary subjects, and on Israel'. Typically, music plays an important part as well. The interest in learning is also expressed practically; the Lodge has set up a scholarship fund for Jewish students of all disciplines: it 'provides probably the greatest number of scholarships in Anglo-Jewry. . . . The Lodge is also one of the main sponsoring bodies of Anglo-Jewry's annual *Book Week* as well as the *Wiener Library*'.[147]

The Lodge's field of interest reaches well beyond Britain; links exist with Israel and Soviet Jewry, the USA and the European Continent. Nor are its activities 'confined strictly to Jewish matters'.[148] Social care and funds benefit non-Jewish individuals and organizations as well.

In this context, it is also interesting to note that right from the beginning, the Lodge regarded it as one of its chief tasks to help its members to become acquainted with the wider society, in other words: to facilitate integration. Thus lectures were regularly held dealing with various aspects of English life and institutions, including that of Anglo–Jewry.[149]

Apart from all these activities, time is also devoted to social gatherings, dinners and balls. German was the *lingua franca* until the early 1960s when, similarly to the Belsize Congregation, English was adopted "because we live in an English-speaking country and we also wanted to attract the younger generation".[150] German, however, is still widely spoken among members in private, it seems.

With this, we have reached present-day life of the German–Jewish community in Britain which will be the subject of the next chapter. In this chapter we were mainly concerned with the reorganization of German–Jewish life at individual as well as collective levels during the war and postwar years. On the surface, this process has been successful, in many cases tremendously so. Yet if one probes a bit more deeply, one soon realizes that the outer security has been gained in spite of the painful burden of past experiences the effects of which are not as easily overcome. We will now look at German–Jewish perceptions of the present day situation.

6 The Ambiguities of Ethnic Identification

German–Jewish refugees have by now lived in Britain for well over a generation. For those who came at the beginning of the Nazi regime, it has in fact been nearly 50 years. This means that most of those who were born in Germany have spent a longer period of their life in this country than in their country of origin. This was often pointed out to me by respondents when I asked them whether they felt themselves to be fully-fledged British or English citizens. How could they not, after all those years, was a common reaction. My question was obviously considered absurd by quite a few of them. But further enquiry revealed that their feelings of identity were rather more complex and did not present a picture of simple progression from 'Germanness' to 'Englishness', with 'Jewishness' adjusted somehow along the way. Nor were attitudes towards Britain or Germany straightforward. On the contrary: ambiguous and contradictory feelings frequently predominated. This did not make it easy to unravel the various strands of a respondent's attitudes. Nevertheless, an attempt will be made in this chapter to single out some crucial aspects. It is hoped, that, at the end, we will have a clearer idea what at present constitutes the identity of the British of German–Jewish extraction.

ENGLAND – A NEW HAVEN?

Has Britain come to occupy the position Germany once had for German Jews? Has she become the new 'home'? One might argue that this is an odd question to ask nowadays. Obviously, many of those thousands of refugees who re-emigrated to other countries or returned to Germany did so primarily because they were unable to put down roots in Britain. One would assume therefore that those who stayed on, apparently did feel rooted here. But it is not quite as simple as that. True, the majority of the respondents feel "at home" in Britain, they feel "very happy", "integrated", "we belong". But it soon became clear that Britain has not become a *Heimat*. "You can only have one home and that was Germany, even if it turned out to be an illusion", "home is where one went to school", or in the words of Gustav Mayer who wrote from Britain shortly after the war that in spite of warm feelings for his host country, 'einer Gefühlswelt bleibt trotzdem die Heimat unersetzlich. An den Begriffen Heimat, Vaterland hängt unablösbar die Erinnerung an das Elternhaus, die Stätten der Jugend und die Muttersprache'.[1] And since childhood memories tend to grow stronger and become more precious for many with age, time is likely to reinforce the sense of irreplaceability of *Heimat*.

Yet, being aware of this, the refugees were perfectly content with and "grateful for" – a recurrent term used by the older generation – the second-best: to be made to feel "at home" in Britain: "No, Britain is not a fatherland for me. But I feel a tremendous appreciation for Britain. England has many attractive traits. We have all grown into English culture a little bit, we have all read (its literature), seen theatre performances, encountered many people, have breathed in the atmosphere of the country. And that is something very beautiful. Because the atmosphere is much better than it was in Germany: friendlier, more polite, calmer, more helpful . . . I feel a critical solidarity with England." Quite obviously, the time factor did play an important role in some sense: "I have grown into it", as another respondent put it. It was time that led to a greater familiarity with English life. One interviewee made the interesting observation that English customs are more formalized, "more structured than in Germany". Consequently, they can be "learned" more easily than they could in Germany and this helped one to find one's way into British society.

More important, however, was the raising of a family in this country. Indeed, most respondents who did so, consider this to have been the crucial factor in the process of growing into British society: "My children are my roots", "my home is where my children are"; it was repeatedly pointed out. And some consolation was often drawn from the fact that, if they, the first generation, did not become 'assimilated', their children certainly will have done so.

Last but not least it was the growing contact in the course of everyday life with the people around them that contributed to the sense of feeling at home in Britain. "Friendliness", "kindness", "helpfulness", "tolerance" of the ordinary English person were almost unanimously praised. It clearly was their English neighbours, colleagues and friends who made the refugees feel welcome after all and let them forget – or at least forgive – the hostility encountered during the early years of exile.

However, on the whole, contact with the English cannot be said to be close. Out of a total of 67 respondents, only 28 have regular contact with English people who they would call friends. But only three respondents counted them among their closest friends and two of these were married to English individuals, through whom they had made these contacts. The majority of the English friends were described as "colleagues" and "acquaintances". Not surprisingly, those who had moved to London from other places said that they had more intimate contact with the English there than in London. Another factor is of significance in this context: the stage of the family life cycle. Thus, as long as the children went to school, contacts with English parents were easily and indeed frequently established; sometimes these even led to close friendships. However, these often ceased after the children had left school. The same pattern repeated itself in the younger generations: Most friendships with non-Jews were established during the period of formal education. Some of these friends became very close and contact persisted afterwards; yet mostly contact decreased later in life and friendships focussed on the ethnic group.

This lack of closeness should not necessarily be interpreted as alienation, resulting perhaps in frustration. Most of the respondents seemed quite happy with the kind of relationship which has developed between them and the English. It has created enough familiarity to enable them to be perfectly at ease when mixing with the English.

In fact, many respondents, especially the older ones, expressed a strong sense of belonging in this country. This sense of belonging focusses on a wider unit which comprises both them and the English and that is Britain. Most respondents carefully distinguished between being 'English' and being 'British' and placed themselves among the latter. True, there were some who claimed to be "more English than the English" – an odd statement, which had also been made in connection with the Jews in Germany. They were said to have been more German than the Germans. Yet curiously enough, this statement was mostly made by respondents with hardly any English contacts at all. This corresponds well, as we shall see below, with remarks often made by respondents who mixed intimately with the English, even intermarried, yet who have become keenly aware of their cultural differences. Thus the paradoxical situation may arise that the more tenuous the contact, the stronger the feeling of similarity; conversely the closer the contact, the more pronounced the ethnic differentiation may become.

Yet the view of the majority of the older respondents was that "one cannot become English", or "you have to be born English, but you can become British". Some expressed doubts, whether a Jew in fact, can ever become 'English'. "Is not 'English' closely associated with Anglicanism, cricket, horse racing, pubs, the monarchy – all alien to us?", asked Mr G. The concept of 'Britain', though, leaves room for identities other than English, even if this concept is rather vague. But in this diffuseness also lies its attraction. It allows people "not to feel anything in particular", to have "no affiliation to any country, but if any affinity then with Britain"; to be "cosmopolitan". To this has to be added their Jewishness which will be looked at further below. All these identities are combined in various, and hardly ever stable, ways. Many respondents feel more British abroad than at home, or more British with some people and less so with others. But these identities are generally not perceived as conflicting with "British loyalties". On the contrary, 'Britishness' was protested with more fervour by members of the older generation than by many of the younger respondents. Is it, because the older refugees are still 'trained assimilationists'[2] who transferred the same feelings of loyalty onto Britain which previously they had devoted to Germany? In fact, this is exactly what a respondent declared when he said: "I became a British patriot during the first few weeks; in Germany I had absolutely felt as a German. But today I feel as British here as I felt German in Germany.'

Nevertheless, in an important respect the situation in Germany was rather different. "Had you asked me then what I felt like, I would have said 'German', of course, and then 'Jewish'", was a view often expressed by respondents. Or to quote another: "Jewishness did not play such an important role in Germany. We were unquestioningly and unproblematically Germans. The Jewish part did not make any difference; it fitted in. Today we know that it was an error. In Britain it is different." Only two or three

The Ambiguities of Ethnic Identification

respondents said they felt decidedly 'Jewish' and not German. But the majority of the German Jews would certainly agree with the former view.

This total identification with Germany of which their Jewishness had become an integral part had led to the strong feeling of rootedness in Germany, so characteristic of German Jews. But once they were denied their 'Germanness', there was no concept beyond it to allow them to identify with or ultimately to physically exist. In 'Britain' the situation is different. Here various ethnic groups live together and, as long as they do not challenge the majority position of the English, are left in peace, although this has not always been the case.[3] And for this, the German Jews are grateful after the constant pressure in Germany to 'assimilate'. In Britain they (now) feel they are respected for what they are, namely refugees from the Continent.

In this respect, their situation has been called unique: 'The (German–Jewish) immigrants are the only ones in the world', Reissner pointed out, "who even after their naturalization have voluntarily retained the term of "refugees" in the name of their association. This is an expression of pride of their origin as well as a wise recognition of the sense of tradition characteristic of the English and which makes them hate nothing as much as renegades who deny their origin.'[4] However, often enough this 'recognition' emerged less from natural wisdom than after a painful learning process. It has already been mentioned that most refugees not only tried, at some stage of their life in Britain, to become 'English', but that they also had come under strong pressure by the English–Jewish community during the war years to make every effort in this direction. Yet contact with the English made it clear that this goal was largely unattainable, at least in the near future. Sooner or later, their un-English sounding names and/or their foreign accent, or the fact of not having any accent at all which would have enabled the English to place them locally, gave their origin away; the polite, yet unavoidable question: where do you come from?, still asked today, time and again shattered any pretence of being 'English'. It was hence a mixture of insight and resignation on the part of the refugees which led them to accept their status within British society.

Nevertheless, the question of status remains a controversial issue, as is reflected in the pages of the *AJR Information*. Thus in 1969, a letter was published suggesting that 'Refugees' be dropped from the AJR's name, because 'most of us are integrated'. The issue was discussed among AJR officials and members whose letters to the *Information* show that opinions on this matter were divided within the community. But the majority – of readers as well as officials – preferred to leave the name as it was. Some of the reasons given were: 'I do not think we need be ashamed of having come from Germany; it is the Germans who have to be ashamed of our having become refugees. . . . No doubt we owe our lives to this country, but if we do our duty as refugees there will be no need to change the name – on the contrary, we should show our gratitude as refugees . . . *AJR Information* was a true friend when we were not so much integrated, and I think it is good to be reminded that we were once "Refugees" and had rather a hard struggle. After all, we still read the Pessach Hagadah after a much longer time to remind us that we were slaves once upon a time.'[5]

'Britishness' has thus been adopted by the German–Jewish refugees as a concept which allows them to feel "at home", "to belong" in a society dominated by a majority which does not consider its country to be multi-ethnic, does not support a cultural pluralism and which is, at best, prepared to 'tolerate' its minorities. Yet, however useful this concept of 'Britishness' might prove to be in many ways, it may not be satisfactory as a permanent basis for the relationship with the English majority. The conclusion drawn from a survey among refugees in 1975, conducted under the auspices of the AJR, 'that quite a few people felt more integrated 20 years ago than they do now', seems significant in this context.[6] These feelings might well reflect the refugees' disillusionment with 'Britishness' and express resentment at – what has to be considered as the other side of the coin – exclusion from 'Englishness'.

For distance is an ambiguous notion, with positive as well as negative associations. It means space between majority and minority; leaving room for each other, leaving each other alone. Many respondents were deeply appreciative of this aspect of life in Britain. Yet distance also implies separation and alienation. This ambiguity was clearly reflected in respondents' attitudes towards the English as a people. Admiration was often tempered by certain reservations which sometimes even gave way to harsh criticism. It became obvious, though, a few exceptions apart, that it was not the Jew–Gentile opposition which apparently still exists within large sections of English Jewry.[7] Respondents generally contrasted "the English" with the Continentals, the Germans, the Refugees. True, not all refugees correspond to the stereotypical passionate Central

European. A number of them therefore feel a "temperamental affinity" with the English. Others again, although aware of temperamental differences, are not disturbed by them: "They were nice to me; I mean, in their English way."

But it is exactly this 'Englishness' which irritates, exasperates and alienates the majority of the 'Continentals': "I hate small talk and sherry parties", said one respondent for whom these two forms of English social life symbolized the unbridgeable foreignness between her and the English. The feeling most commonly expressed was: "One does not really get 'warm' with the English." Sometimes, this remark came quite unexpectedly as in the case of Mrs L. who, after a long lecture on the wonderful English, on the one hand, and the nasty, barbarous Germans on the other, paused and suddenly added (to the desperation of the interviewer): "After all is said and done, I think it *is* difficult to establish a warm relationship with English people; I can get 'warmer' more quickly with Germans." Or there was Mr I: "The English are a people with whom it is easy to live. Their democracy is alright, but could be improved. Economically, Britain should be much better organized. They lack the proper work ethic. And they are too insular. But this is better today. During the '30s they were really 'islanders'." The difference in attitudes towards work was repeatedly stressed: "At home (i.e. Germany!) you do the job you have been trained for and you work conscientiously. The English often work in a field they have not been trained for, they often change, because they want more money, but also the English don't do anything 100%. They are less demanding, but more flexible instead, not so heavy-going as we are." Mr G. found that "a tidy person as I am cannot work with the English. There are nice ones among them, I don't want to sound offensive, but they are not intelligent; they lack élan and verve." And he added: "The English don't make any demands on anything, not even on themselves."

Some respondents showed total disillusionment, and basically for the same reasons: "The English greatly disappointed me. I had such high expectations. But they lack discipline, a sense of responsibility . . . I thought they were efficient, had common sense, but they haven't. I hoped they would shake themselves awake, but they are like that; I have discovered that the 'English disease' has lasted for more than a hundred years."

Attitudes among respondents belonging to the second generation were, on the whole, less extreme. They frequently pointed out that their parents "adored" Britain. This can certainly not be said about their children. Admiration, "gratitude" on the one hand, and criticism, dissatisfaction on the other hand did exist, but were more muted. Ambiguity predominated here even more clearly. Thus we also find that "the friendly reserve", "tolerance", "feeling of freedom" are appreciated. But often it was also said that "I cannot feel close with the English", "somehow there is a wall". Or Mr F.: "I am very fond of the English, but they are not all that wonderful." "Impossible people", exclaimed Mrs G., "they have a coldness in them – on the one hand; on the other, it is easy to live with them. Nobody orders you about; you are left in peace and people don't take themselves so seriously as in Israel, for example. I miss real conversations, though, because basically one talks about nothing." Similarly Mrs Y., formerly married to an Englishman: "I am not very close with English people. They are very bad at developing close relationships even with their closest family members; they are cool and reserved also among themselves. But not in the simple way that people normally think they are. They like to talk; they talk a lot, about crosswords, about the weather – what I miss and what I do have when I go to Germany even now, is, of course, a passionate discussion . . . I miss good poetry. I think German poetry is much better than English poetry."

One also comes across more outspoken criticism such as Mr K.'s who finds the English "lackadaisical; people here don't work, they don't apply themselves". "I am abhorred by my colleagues", Mrs I. remarked, "they are in a constant muddle." Or Mrs F., who, when showing me round her office, pointed to her desk; "But that is what I am doing here all the time (instead of her proper tasks): putting everything in order."

The predominant feeling, as evidenced by these and similar remarks, was one of strangeness, of a cultural gap which it is not easy to bridge. This was clearly put by Mr E. who "feels happy here. The English character suits me. I am also introvert, basically quiet, but I have no close friends among the English. We have not enough in common when it comes down to becoming real friends. I think I am integrated, but it does not reach that far. My close friends are all refugees; one feels very relaxed with people of one's own background. I would have to make an effort to feel the same with the English. This does not mean that I don't like or respect them . . . I think food and drink are a barrier. But also that the average English man will never understand how we feel and what we are. They are

The Ambiguities of Ethnic Identification

often surprised that I have not returned (to Germany). That shows their lack of understanding." And similarly Mr N.: "I get on well with my (business) partners, but I have nothing in common with them socially. They are not very interested in culture. In that respect we are poles apart. But also our background, our outlook on life is different; you find that you don't speak the same language."

Yet this lack of closeness at the level of primary relationships should not deflect from the fact that, on the other hand, a high degree of friendly contact with the English in everyday life does exist. This generation, in fact, mixes much more with the English than their parents do, as is revealed if we look at this generation's friendship patterns more closely. Thus it was found that out of a total of 73 respondents, 69 regularly associated with German Jews. However, 50 of them had English friends, more than two thirds. The same was true for less than half of the older respondents. What is more, in 6 cases friends were exclusively or largely English. When the question of 'closest friends' was raised, 65 referred to German Jews, but 14 also counted "English" as equally close and another 4 said that their closest friends were exclusively English. The issue of intermarriage is also pertinent in this context. Thus 49 respondents were married to German Jews, but 19 had chosen non-Jewish partners.[8] The figures suggest that in spite of a general feeling of cultural differentiation, the line between them and the English is not rigid; it easily allows for friendships across the line, even close ones in individual cases. We thus find the pattern repeated which had evolved in Germany: a relatively high degree of mixing with non-Jews involving a not inconsiderable extent of close contact in conjunction with an awareness of ethnic peculiarities of the group as a whole.[9]

These differences between first and second generation as regards friendship relationships with the English were to be expected. The former had arrived in this country after primary relationships had generally been formed. Yet it was found that there was greater ambivalence among respondents belonging to the second generation towards the English despite, or more probably because, of closer contact with them. This is reflected in the answers to the question of identity which revealed a remarkable difference in attitudes. Whereas out of a total of 54 respondents of the older generation, 6 felt "English" and 23 "British", even fewer did so among the second generation. Out of a total of 63 respondents, 8 felt "English" as opposed to "British". But most felt it necessary to add some qualifications such as: "English, but a bloody foreigner at the same time", "English, but only when I am abroad', " . . . but not hundred per cent", " . . . but not culturally", "yes, English, but I am aware of lacking roots in this country when I am in contact with English people". An interesting description of the ambiguities of her "Englishness" was given by Mrs V.: "I just absorbed my Englishness. In some respects I am more English than the English now. I feel completely at home with the English. It never occurs to them that I am not English. At some stage in my life this must have been a conscious effort to adapt myself to the extent that I had this protective covering of utter Englishness; although I know that it isn't actually so, I don't have to make any conscious effort now. I have a chamaeleon-like ability to adapt myself to any sort of English circumstances. I may hate it, but I can adapt myself."

Only 11 respondents felt "British" without reservations. Another 15 answered: "Only a bit", "only conditionally", "in a way", "only technically", "it is sort of my country", or, finally, "not really; and the longer I live in Britain, the less so; I feel like a tourist".

Like Mrs V., several respondents in this generation mentioned that, when younger, they "had tried to be very, very English", they had "made efforts to conform". But as with the older generation, there came the slow realization that the English did not consider them as being one of them. Thus Mr E. still feels "English; I am liberal, even a royalist. I want to say, 'we, the English', and I must always stop myself, because it must sound too ridiculous to someone who knows I am from the Continent. But I have been here far longer than I was in Germany."

It is again name and accent which give the origin away. Quite a number of refugees anglicised their name. The reason generally given by men was that they "had to do it" when they joined the British army during the war in order to protect themselves in case they fell into the hands of the German enemy. Other respondents kept their names because "if I had become a prisoner in Germany, they would have found out about my background quickly enough. And anyway, we did not get anywhere near the Germans". The AJR actually pleaded at one stage that people should not change the family name so that it would be easier to trace friends and relatives. Nevertheless, quite a few did so and supposedly not so much for reasons of safety in Germany as of 'camouflage' in British society. The accent was a different matter. "I hate it", as one respondent said. A few even took the trouble of taking speech lessons to get rid of their German accent, but to no vail. Thus one respondent found her accent "irritating, because I hated being asked, after 30 years, where I came from. But my friends said: "Your accent is the only charm you have got; don't lose it." Or others told me: 'Don't be silly. Your accent makes you superior, because nobody can make out your social standing'. But I do not find it irritating when I am asked by other people who have an accent. I myself ask others about their origin, if they have an accent."

Those respondents who came here as very small children or were born in Britain, did not mention encountering any problems in this respect.[10] Yet, interestingly enough, many among these felt just as little 'English' as the rest of the respondents in this generation. This seems to indicate that the roots of alienation reach beyond the level of accents and language generally.

Correspondingly, hardly any respondents of this generation consider Britain their "real home", in the sense of *Heimat*. Most certainly they prefer to live in Britain rather than in other countries. Yet they are aware of not being rooted here. "Living here you live this life, but my feeling really is more international." This attitude was echoed by most respondents. "I am at home nowhere, I live happily in a vacuum", "I have no roots anywhere, but I don't mind", "I am European in a strange way", "I don't know whether one can completely feel at home anywhere and whether one should at all", "I am against all nationalisms", "I am a little bit of everything, which really means that I am not anything", "I prefer to say I feel like a *Mensch*, like a human being, not terribly adherent to anything. I adjust easily, I keep an open mind."

I would like to emphasize that these statements concern the question of 'Britishness' or 'Englishness' only, the national identity. They do not exhaust the complex problem of German–Jewish identity in Britain. Other aspects will be examined in a moment. First we will briefly look at another angle of German–Jewish contact with the English majority: that of antisemitism. It was shown above that, in Germany, political anti-semitism did not preclude close contact between Jews and non-Jews and a fairly high degree of social mixing generally. In Britain, as we have seen, antisemitism as such has also been widespread at times, particularly during and after the war, and was never completely absent at other periods.[11] The question was therefore discussed with respondents, whether or to what extent they had been affected by it more recently and how they evaluated it.

On the whole, attitudes towards British antisemitism were relatively mild. "Things like anti-semitism just didn't occur to English people", one respondent thought, "I never came across any. Yes, at the Public School where I went, there was a certain amount, but that was just general xenophobia, bullying of new boys. The Catholics were more hated than the Jews. The National Front is ridiculous. In Germany antisemitism is pathological; the Germans are as little immune to antisemitism as Indians to alcohol." Although clothed in somewhat extreme terms, this respondent's view reflects quite a common attitude among refugees. Many felt that Germans were primarily characterized by their racism and British primarily by the lack of it. And this regardless of the personal experiences people had with Germans or with Britons. More than that; it was equally common among respondents to stress that the British are more "anti-foreign than anti-Jewish". It was obvious that, strange as it may seem, considerable consolation was drawn from this form of general xenophobia.

Nevertheless, the existence of anti-Jewish hostility was not ignored. With one exception, all respondents said that they are aware of it, but opinions as to its seriousness varied. About a quarter of first generation respondents had had some personal experiences of it, and so had about half among the second generation. This increase is probably due to this generation's greater contact with non-Jews. Where the contact was closest, antisemitism was often felt strongest. Thus a respondent mentioned that her daughter had an English boyfriend who was put under strong pressure from his parents to break up with her (which he did); or Mrs I. reported that when she was about to marry an Anglican, "his friends were dismayed". She also feels that there is antisemitism in her tennis club, because she is the only Jewish member and was admitted only, she thinks, because she is married to a non-Jew. Other refugees had actually been barred from membership in sports and social clubs. Anti-semitism was also encountered at schools – quite a number of schools still operate a quota system for Jews – "worse than in Germany", three of them said; others had unpleasant encounters at work. One respondent was particularly critical of English racism. She is half-Jewish, has no foreign accent at all and is not easily recognizable as being of Continental origin. She found that people around her made antisemitic remarks not directed at her. "I still get that quite a lot. I think the English on the whole are very anti-semitic and anti-foreigner. Quite nice people come out with quite unbelievable remarks sometimes. It was never anything dreadful – jokes, disparaging remarks – but it always seems dreadful to me." It is not surprising therefore that the harshest verdicts on British antisemitism and racism in general came from English spouses of respondents who were present at the interview.

The refugees themselves, on the whole, take a more lenient view. Antisemitism exists, they said, but most are confident that the "democratic" forces in Britain or the "common sense" of the British will prevent worse from happening. Nevertheless, at a different level of consciousness, quite a number of respondents are worried – "there always is an undercurrent of fear" – or uncomfortable about any signs of antisemitism in Britain, evident in organizations such as the National Front. Yet, again only few regard it as presenting a serious threat. "But that is how it started in Germany. Perhaps we should take more notice of it", respondents often added. Others said they do not feel threatened by antisemitism in Britain; but admitted that they avoid situations which might lead to unpleasant reminders of its existence. Quite a few think that "antisemitism exists everywhere, but it is tolerable here". This attitude is apparently widespread among Jews in Britain generally, at least according to Bermant: 'The amount of overt antisemitism in this country is well within the tolerance limits of most Jews. This tolerance limit will vary with the level of prosperity and this level is not low and is getting higher, and prosperity blinds'.[12]

But the situation is perhaps not quite a simple as that. The difficulties, for Jews in particular, of gaining an adequate picture of the real extent of antisemitism within the majority society have been pointed out above. In fact, degrees of antisemitism as personally experienced by the respondents in Germany do not differ substantially from their experiences in Britain, and this in spite of totally different social systems and official doctrines. The similarity would probably be even more striking if one compared London, where most respondents live, with reports from big cities in Germany, such as Berlin, Hamburg or Munich.

What conclusion is one to draw from this? Is there a 'lesson' for the refugees in it? Since we are in no better position to predict the future course of society than people were in the 1930s, this is difficult to answer. In the face of this uncertainty of future developments, it is only too understandable that people hope – as Jews have done throughout history – that "common sense", that "human decency" will win out against the forces of evil. What else can they do?

"Hatred is everywhere", as a respondent said; the existence of antisemitism as such therefore is not sufficient reason to leave. To refuse to 'tolerate' it, as Bermant seems to suggest, is a resolution difficult to put into practice either. It is true, since ignorance and government policies play an important role in the emergence of racism, that information, education and pressure on official bodies can counteract the spread of racism to some extent. However, it is questionable to what a degree substantial changes can be effected. Jewish communities have developed quite an expertise in establishing defence organizations to combat antisemitism. In Germany the Jews had developed self-defence almost to perfection. Yet all the German Jews' protest, however well presented and convincing for the converted, had little effect. The roots of anti-semitism are well beyond the reach of the "Semites".

There is yet another aspect to this problem. Obviously, it would be difficult to go on living always expecting the worst to happen. It is true that quite a number of respondents did not exclude the possibility that "it might happen here", but this statement sounded rather theoretical in most cases; as if they tried to avoid appearing 'blind' and 'stupid' yet again, as they were said to have been in the past. The energy with which they have thrown themselves into British life, participated in its social, economic and political systems, the eagerness with which they have 'rebuilt their homes' and put down new roots, the feelings of loyalty – again not unlike the Jews in Germany – which they expressed towards their new homeland – all these elements suggest the prevalence of the optimistic belief that their confidence in English "decency" and "tolerance" will not be betrayed.

It was pointed out earlier that admiration for 'the English' was widespread, especially among the older refugees, despite some reservations. It was interesting to find that respondents tended to idealize them in the same way as Jews were said to have done in Germany. Or more correctly, to focus on one set of attitudes rather than on another. "Tolerance", "generosity and liberalism" were frequently named as typical of 'the English'. Rather less pleasant traits, insofar as they were mentioned at all, were regarded as deviations from the norm, not to be taken too seriously. Views of present-day Germany are, as we will see below, the exact opposite of these perceptions. It would be easy to criticize this one-sidedness as 'lack of realism' as some historians have done with regard to the Jews in Germany. However, seen in the context of the constant and real threat to survival and the will to carry on a normal life in spite of it, such an attitude becomes understandable.

There is yet another historical parallel. It emerges from German–Jewish attitudes towards the immigrant *Ostjuden* in Germany and their attitudes towards black immigrants in Britain today. Basically, the same ambivalence predominates. As before, German Jews are torn between identification with the wider society and its hostility towards blacks on the one hand and solidarity with a discriminated minority on the other. Yet since the cultural differences between them and the blacks are much more pronounced than they were between the German and the Eastern Jews, the link provided by their common fate as victims is even weaker than in the latter case. What is more: judging from the comments most respondents made on the situation of the blacks in Britain, it became evident that racism was only criticized and considered serious when it affected Jews: general xenophobia was forgiven as "normal"; only anti-semitism was considered as quite a different matter, as a 'crime against humanity'.

Unreserved moral support for the black and Asian immigrants was therefore rare, at least among the first and second generations. Less rare were defenders of the opposite position. One respondent strongly advocated curbing black immigration, because "they don't want to work". And: "They are genetically inferior". "It is sad", another respondent pondered, "that England is not England anymore. There are too many ghettoes – the blacks don't want to assimilate. We wanted to become English, they don't. They all sit together and eat their West Indian food (the respondent herself has retained her purely German eating habits!). The more blacks are allowed into the country the more difficult it will become." She was particularly bitter about the fact that when "German Jews wanted to enter Britain, sponsors and deposits had to be provided for every single one of them. The black immigrants get social security from the first day without them having paid a single penny in taxes."

That black immigration should be curbed, was a widely held belief and justified as follows: "Britain's social problems will become too big", "there is too much unemployment here"; "a nation is like an organism; it can only absorb a certain number of foreign elements". Another respondent similarly regarded the restrictions on black immigration as "natural resistance"; so did a further respondent who thought the policies of the National Front 'right in principle, for Britain is overpopulated. Racial instincts are involved here. "The difference between the black and the English is greater than between the Jews and the English. That is why no more blacks should be allowed to come to Britain."

It was common among respondents who advocated restrictions on black immigration to stress the differences between their own immigration and more recent waves. Thus it was pointed out that "we were persecuted, but they come for purely materialistic reasons", or "we were highly cultured", "we worked hard and they don't", "they don't fit in; they have a completely different culture". A few respondents in this category took a more moderate approach. They thought that one should not have allowed the blacks to immigrate in the first place. "But now they are here and we have to get along with them. Repatriation would be totally wrong." That these attitudes are not exceptional, was confirmed by a respondent who said angrily: "Many of my Continental friends sound like the National Front. It is disgusting. I have given up discussing immigration with them."

Yet these negative attitudes do not represent the general rule. "Restrictions are rubbish", said one respondent, "they've all got British passports. One has to let them in, of course. And besides: what would become of England without foreigners." Another respondent argued: "German Jews cannot afford to support the government's racialist policies"; "the Ugandan Asians were in exactly the same position as we were, apart from the fact that all of them, blacks included, have British passports".

Quite a number of respondents were obviously torn between these two poles. Thus Mrs J. began by arguing strongly against black immigration; "We don't like the high number of immigrants." Suddenly she exclaimed: "Oh my God, I sound like the National Front!"; "how awful!" She paused and then markedly toned down her comments about blacks whom she had previously called "lazy and dirty". There were others who were conscious of their inner conflict which they described as follows: "I find it difficult to combine theory and practice in this respect. On a theoretical level, I know one should not discriminate against anybody; but in practice, or on an emotional level I feel that blacks are so different. They don't work hard enough. They cause so many problems for this country."

This last view was voiced time and again in various ways and it became clear that this was one key to the unexpectedly high degree of hostility against the black immigrants. Most of the respondents were only too aware that "today it is the blacks, tomorrow it may be us" to be chosen as targets for an overt racism in Britain. It seems the German Jews are quite relieved that, not being immediately recognizable as an immigrant group, they are able to hide, for once, behind another minority; from this perspective, the general xenophobia, more diffuse as it is, may indeed be considered as being relatively harmless for them.

On the other hand, the violence with which blacks (and Asians) are frequently attacked, not to mention the less overt forms of anti-semitism, is a frightening sign of a dangerous potential of racism in Britain. But by a strange twist of logic, the German Jews fear that it is the blacks who cause the eruption of this racism which might seriously disrupt the social fabric of Britain. The resulting upheavals would ultimately endanger not only the blacks, but the Jews as well. It is this fear which seems to be the major cause of the racism of some German Jews – over and above the general prejudices they share with non-Jews of their class: *in nuce*, it is the fear of a relatively well-established, but still insecure minority. Similar fears, so vividly described by Wertheimer, befell the German Jews when large numbers of Eastern Jews arrived in Germany after 1918.[13] It is possible that the Anglo-Jews harboured similar feelings of anxiety at the arrival of the German Jews.

GERMANY – A WINTER'S TALE

To raise the issue of Germany, as perceived today by respondents, meant evoking a whole range of painful, complex, and also contradictory feelings; they are not easily unravelled. Only indifference was barely encountered, and where it existed, it seemed to have been put on, as in the case of Mr N.: "I am not very interested in my background. This is probably due to what happened; one doesn't like digging out the past." It did not take long to discover that, in this respect, the German–Jewish immigrants of the 1930s differ significantly from the first wave of German–Jewish immigrants of whom C. C. Aronsfeld has said: 'While they cherished their British citizenship, they took pride in their native land'.[14] Whereas the first half of the sentence certainly applies, the material of this study points to a striking change with regard to the second part of this statement. Although both groups of German–Jewish immigrants suffered in the same way because of their

German background during each of the two World Wars, the circumstances of their emigration differed sharply; and so did the Germany they had left behind. Those who arrived in the 19th century were either political exiles or they had left Germany for economic reasons or because of antisemitism which had become stronger since the middle of the century. But with a few exceptions they had left voluntarily. Consequently, their ties with Germany remained strong in every respect.[15]

How very different was the situation of the refugees of the 1930s. As one of them put it: "We were thrown out and that hurt so much." But it was the enormity of the Nazi-crimes committed during the 1940s which, in their eyes, turned Germany into the 'fatherland of barbarism' (Aronsfeld) with which they could not and would not identify. Thus there are strong tendencies among German Jews to dissociate themselves from their country of origin. "I do not feel German at all", remarked an older respondent, "I do not like to be referred to as the 'German Grandma'. I therefore told my daughters to tell their children that I am not German; I was only born in Germany and went to school there." "I don't like being considered German", Mrs F. said, describing as one of her most distressing experiences "filling in my birthplace on forms because I am afraid to be taken for a German. It happens whenever I go abroad and register in a hotel. I hate it; it is most unpleasant." And finally Mrs I.: "I always wanted to dissociate myself from Germany. I asked my mother to speak English, but since she had a strong accent, I asked her not to speak at all on buses etc. It was very traumatic for her. . . . it is not so much antagonism; it annoys me that I am associated with a country I don't identify with and not with the country I want to belong to."

This tension is reflected in respondents' reactions to the question whether they still felt German to some extent. Among the first generation respondents, i.e. those who had felt completely German in Germany, only 3 still felt this (as compared with 6 who feel English) and another 10 feel German "only in little things", "to some extent", "only when it comes to cakes". That means that no more than a quarter of the older respondents still associate themselves with Germany, and not very strongly at that, as against a third who had done so with Britain. This may seem surprising at first sight. But a clue to these figures was given by one respondent who, when the question of identity was raised, replied emphatically: "Definitely British". When I expressed some amazement at this,

The Ambiguities of Ethnic Identification

because he had no English friends whatsoever, this so far soft-spoken respondent exclaimed with unexpected hostility: "What do you expect – German?" As much as the avowed 'English –' or 'Britishness' may reflect a 'natural' alienation from Germany, caused by the passage of time, it certainly also represents a desperate attempt to escape the objectionable link with the German past.

If we look at the second generation, we find a characteristic difference. It has already been mentioned that fewer among them feel unqualifiedly English or British. Interestingly enough, 17 were aware of a strong German element in themselves, of being partly German. That this generation recognizes the German link to a larger extent than the older generation does not necessarily imply a positive attitude towards Germany, though. It more likely reflects this generation's more pronounced disaffection with 'Englishness'.

Mistrust, dislike, hatred – a whole range of negative associations with Germany characterized the predominant attitudes in both generations. Many completely disowned Germany as their 'home' and swore never to set foot on German soil again; Mr G.'s wife (who refused to see me, let alone speak to me) could not even bring herself to change planes at a German airport. This hostility often extends to all things German and it has happened that spouses had arguments over the acquisition of German goods. The reasons for or against the purchase of such goods can be as elaborate and varied as those regarding the observance of Kashrut. Thus one couple proudly showed me their AEG washing machine. But they would never buy a Volkswagen or a Mercedes, they said, because of the association with the 1930s. "But our television set is German", Mrs C. reminded her husband. "Yes, but only because it was on special offer", he replied apologetically. "But otherwise: if prices are equal, we prefer the English product, although, on the other hand, I must admit, we sometimes buy a German appliance regardless, because of the quality." Others buy German cars, but draw the line when it comes to clothes or electrical applicances. One respondent boycotts everything German apart from food, "because I am crazy about German food. But I don't go to the German Food Centre on principle: I don't like to go in there; otherwise I buy German food wherever I can get it." The problem is, however, that it has become more and more difficult to avoid German goods in recent years and, as respondents admitted with a deep sigh, they feel attracted to the style and especially quality of German goods. It also happens that respondents buy German things unwittingly and only discover afterwards, much to their dismay, that these were 'made in Germany'. The extremely principled ones even take them back to the shop and exchange them for something non-German.

Finally, it was the employment of au pair girls which posed another problem. Of course, for some respondents there was no dilemma, because they flatly refused ever to have a German girl in their house. The situation was more difficult for others such as Mrs K., because she "did not get on with any other nationality". Others who wanted German girls because "they are reliable and good" overcame the problem by posing as English and never mentioning the fact of their own German background. Of course, those respondents with less hostile feelings towards Germany displayed different attitudes towards their German au pairs. Some said they had welcomed the opportunity for their children to pick up some German and had allowed their children to visit the au pairs back in Germany. "But I made sure she knew we are Jewish", one respondent added.

The aversion against German products was matched or even exceeded by the dislike of the German people. Most respondents distinguished, in principle, between the younger and the older generation of Germans, although the line sometimes became blurred. Obviously, those Germans who grew up after the war cannot have been Nazis. The refugees' wrath is thus directed primarily against older Germans. Nearly all respondents of all age groups suspect most older Germans of having been Nazis and having been involved in atrocities against the Jews; and this view prevailed, regardless of whether the respondent had good or bad experiences with the non-Jews in Germany before emigration. What made matters worse even now, was that "nobody admits to having been a Nazi. They must all be lying". Or respondents felt that "Germans nowadays don't want to know what has happened" which is no less embittering.

However, not all respondents agreed. "It is disgusting to maintain that all Germans were guilty", declared Mr F. and Mr G. "is strictly against holding all Germans responsible. One should not do unto other people what was done to the Jews, namely condemn them collectively." "But I can't help it", his wife added, although agreeing with her husband in principle, "when I think of older Germans, I see them all in uniform." A few others drew attention to another aspect of the question of guilt: "I think one should be cautious when accusing all Germans", as one respondent put it, "I mean we were lucky in a way to have been Jews under Hitler. What we would have done, had we not been, I am not so sure. I don't think my family would have shown more courage than the other Germans. We might even have been Nazis."

Yet Nazism and antisemitism are not the only negative associations with Germany, although these doubtless lie at the root of other hostile perceptions. Mr T. for example found the Germans "highly unattractive. They lack charm". Mrs B. finds them "rude and impolite". In Mrs B1's view the German character represents a mixture of "sentimentality, servility and brutality". Other comments were: "In most Germans is a kernel of cruelty; in Britain one can touch all animals, but not in Germany, especially not dogs." Mr L. remarked: "I have summed it up often, when I talk about Germans, it is a generalization which is perhaps wrong, but they have no heart, and I fear, it is still very much the case, even with people I got to know professionally, even the younger generation – I often come to that conclusion. There is a lack of compassion in many people in Germany. One does not come across it in Britain . . . I have been to Germany several times, professionally. I have met Germans who come out with horrible stories about the war, about their own misfortune. Only once a man said: 'I feel so sorry for you'. That would be the normal reaction of an English person." Finally Mrs Y., who touched on the same point, but offered a much more subtle analysis: "Every German or Jewish generation since then (the Holocaust) is tainted by something or is characterized by some reactive quality. It does not necessarily mean that I consider those who lived during the Hitler period as worse than the young ones that did not. I think the young German generation is a very messed-up generation which has something to do with their parents' past and their history and how Germans dealt with their past. I think that young Germans might have an irrational fear that they may be affected in some ways by the deeds of their fathers, that there might be something evil in their character as a people, like children fear to get cancer whose parents died of cancer. Some young Germans I met agreed with this (analysis)."

Similar feelings were expressed by quite a number of respondents. But perhaps the most common criticism was that of "materialism". "The Germans are too loud and prosperous. They should have been utterly humiliated after the war, justice should have been done, revenge . . . but instead they are doing extremely well." "They are too rich, too clean, not friendly enough", was another comment.

"The Germans are terribly well off, materialistic, not at all human, but very cultured. Not the type I easily take to", said another respondent. Yet he conceded: 'My sons contradict me. They travel widely through West and East Germany. They say: "Look, Dad, what you tell us about the Germans that is not how they are now." And I must admit that these stereotypes, also of other nations, are really silly. I couldn't uphold any of these arguments rationally."

Indeed, emotions were often more decisive. It is striking on what slender evidence judgments were based. One particular encounter or event sufficed to confirm what was regarded as typical. No doubt the aversion against Germany continues to be deep-seated. It has almost become part of the respondents' life; they cannot do without it anymore. "I feel uncomfortable with Germans", Mrs N. confessed, adding after a pause, "but maybe I am prejudiced; maybe I see what I want to see." This fear of the Germans – understandable as it is, but irrational none the less – became even more apparent in the interview with Mrs P. Having described an unpleasant encounter with a "bureaucratic, heartless German", she continued: "I was really pleased about this incident. It reminded me of the Nazis. The German friends I now have are all so terribly nice that I might begin to like Germany again."

However, it was interesting to observe that different aspects of Germany were affected in different ways by respondents' feelings. The distinction most commonly made was that between Germans as individuals and German society as a whole; this is reflected in the following remark: "I want to trust people and I can't in Germany. Consequently I refuse to go. But I love my German sister-in-law." Such responses must furthermore be set against the feeling for the German landscape.

The widespread aversion against things German hardly ever affected the refugees' love for the German countryside. Many respondents like to take a holiday in Germany. "We absolutely love it", one couple stated. It happened more than once that respondents got quite carried away by their enthusiastic descriptions of the German countryside. But when asked about the inhabitants the mood changed: "The Germans? Oh, never mind the people, I don't care much for them. *Berlin ist mein Berlin*; and I love the countryside, its forests." Or Mr G.: "Whenever I go to Germany, I feel happiest when I am walking in the open country without the people." "I love the Rhineland, I love the warm climate", thus Mrs S. who grew up in that area, "the winters are too cold and too damp in Britain. I am a South German. Each winter I nearly die – but I am tough!" Similar feelings gave Mrs G. the following idea once when she was in Germany: "Send all the Germans to Britain, let them sit in the rain. Send all the English to Germany; we could then live here *gemütlich*. It is so beautiful here."

Yet people did matter. It was mainly through contact with individual Germans that emotions mellowed, although caution was hardly ever completely abandoned. In many cases hatred of Germany has given way to a detached interest, permeated by some of the old ambiguities. The same is true of attitudes towards the Germans as a people. Many ties, even close ones, have been re-established between individuals as will be shown below. This might seem astonishing considering the complicated emotions and reactions on both sides which any encounter between German Jews and non-Jews evokes: painful memories, a heightened sensitivity, suspicion, disgust and not least moral righteousness on the part of the former; feelings of guilt, embarrassment, unease, self-defensive arrogance, egotistical concern with their own fate during the war and tactlessness caused by sheer ignorance about the refugees' fate and feelings on the part of the latter; there is also exaggerated friendliness in an attempt to overcome mistrust and not to give offence. Such reactions tend to be interpreted as 'philosemitism' and as such they are barely more tolerable to many Jews than anti-semitism.

It is not surprising therefore that most refugees of all age groups share Mr R.'s feelings that he is "very uneasy with older Germans. I must first be able to place them". But once the older Germans have 'passed the test', the bonds of friendship can become very close indeed. This is even more true, although not universally, with regard to younger Germans. They tend to be received with more openness and trust.

Where then, do they meet? Many respondents made their first contacts with Germans on holidays abroad, not perhaps the most propitious occasion. As may be expected, some respondents find "Germans in crowds terrible"; "I am repulsed by them, I have nothing in common with them anymore"; "I am pleasantly surprised to meet some quiet Germans." Mrs H. was ambivalent: "The younger Germans I meet on holidays are quite acceptable. It is different with the older Germans. I find it more difficult to make contact with the men; it is better with women. There is some understanding. But there is an arrogance about some of the

Germans, and they are so noisy – but so are other foreigners. Yet somehow it bothers me more. Maybe because the background is the same which makes me more self-conscious. I was brought up to be seen and not heard, but Germans today are so different. It's funny, I seem to identify more with them than with others and that's why they bother me more." Mrs N. felt similarly, but for different reasons: "To meet Germans on holidays is an unpleasant experience for me. I cannot feel comfortable. The younger Germans remind me of my friends I have lost, of those who turned away. So much in the young Germans reminds me of them. And all the disappointment comes back."

Others had more positive experiences. "We get on well with the Germans we meet on holidays. We have had no embarrassing contact so far. We have made many friends. We are not prejudiced. It all depends on the individual." And it also depends on whether the refugees reveal their origin. If they do not wish to, they carry on speaking English. But often they switch to German, when abroad; the crucial moment comes when the German acquaintance marvels at their good knowledge of German. If the refugees are not sure about their German counterpart, they like to play a little game, saying they had a good teacher at school or "you know, there are some good schools in England". Or if they feel more confident or perhaps curious about the German's reaction, they explain who they are. Mrs L. recalled: "I always like to practice my German on holidays. But I admit to being Jewish only when I trust the Germans and think they are O.K. I don't like to say openly that I am Jewish, though. I make it clear indirectly so that the other person can draw his or her own conclusions. It is not out of a feeling of inferiority that I do this. I am embarrassed that one human being could do such a thing to another (as the Nazis did). It is embarrassing being a victim; it creates an embarrassing situation for both parties – oppressor meets victim. I found that many Germans also have a chip on their shoulder in this respect." At which point her (English) husband interrupted: "And yet I am always astonished how well she gets on with Germans; you should see her." "Yes, it is true", Mrs L. continued, "in a strange sort of way I feel more at home with the Germans than with the English."

It is perhaps worthwhile noting that all the respondents who have been quoted more extensively above, belong to the second generation. But there is Mrs C., an older refugee: "We once met a German couple in Switzerland. They were moaning and complaining terribly about the war years, what an awful time it had been for *them*. I did not talk to them, only my husband did. But then another German talked to me and asked me why I was so silent. And I exploded like a bomb. I had never talked to a German before (since emigration). And I told him everything. About our lives, that we were thrown out of Germany, and I wept, but I could not stop, I just talked. He did not say anything. He just listened and looked at me. I felt much better afterwards, as if a stone had been taken off my neck."

Further encounters between respondents and Germans had taken place in Britain: "We always had trainees from Germany in our firm", Mr G. remarked: "I got on extremely well with them. My wife and I still are in contact with some of them." Positive encounters of this kind seem to have been the rule rather than the exception; at least no unpleasant experiences were recorded by respondents. Even Mrs F. who otherwise "still has very bitter feelings towards Germany, had to make an effort to look more leniently at young Germans". She had met them through her work and found that she liked them. She mentioned one young German in particular who "had Berlin written all over his face". When she told him "that I was also from Berlin he just gave me a very charming look, but didn't say anything which I very much appreciated; I felt there was an understanding on his side". Or there was Mr W. who remembered having once met a group of young Germans standing in front of his house talking. "I think it was in the 1960s. Until then, I had avoided all contact with Germans. I didn't want to have anything to do with them. But these young people looked nice. When I heard them speak German, I was mesmerized. Something drew me to them. So I talked to them – in German. After a while I told them that I, too, had come from Germany. We had a very pleasant and interesting conversation. That broke the spell. From then on, I had a better relationship with Germany and the Germans."

Most contacts, especially the more lasting ones, were made in Germany itself. As has been mentioned, quite a number of refugees, to this day, cannot bring themselves to even visit Germany. Many others did go, but the decision was never easy; most went with considerable trepidation and unease which only disappeared after a while or after several trips had been made. Mr N. was "furious" when his father who had emigrated to Africa returned to Germany to settle in an Old People's Home. "I had hoped he would come to

Britain, but he didn't want to. So I had to go and visit him in Germany. And I never wanted to go! Before I went for the first time, I was so upset I had to talk to someone of my Synagogue to calm me down. I was very mixed up. Finally, I went. I took my car. I was there for four or five days and felt very uncomfortable. When I left, I drove off sometime in the morning and when I came round, I was just outside Calais and didn't quite know how I got there. But each time I have been there, it got a little bit better." Another respondent and her husband often drive through Germany: "We feel like strangers. Last year, for the first time, it was nice, it felt natural. We want to go again this year."

This total alienation from what, after all, was once their mother country, developed gradually. It began under Nazi persecution and was reinforced by the separation during the years in Britain. The horrifying revelations about the extent of the Holocaust completed the estrangement. It caused a rift between the German Jews and Germany which became, in many cases, unbridgeable as we have seen.

Yet, other factors, such as time, contributed to the alienation. On the one hand, it was the refugees themselves who, living in a different environment, changed. This was strongly felt by a refugee who wrote, as early as 1946, that he had seen an old, once famous film again, but this time he was greatly disappointed: "I found the diction theatrical, the humour sour, and the acting not artisitic but artificial. How often had we had that experience when we opened a book which we once loved and which seemed to have changed during "the years Between"? Sometimes it is as if these films, books, streets, towns and people we remember existed only in our memory. . . . Not only bombs have transformed the streets and towns which we once loved, but time has changed many other things which had been part of us. We have gone such a long way that the old books, films and people do not seem to reach us any more.'[17]

But Germany had changed too. This was a painful discovery for emigrants like Heinrich Fraenkel who at first saw himself as an exile rather than as refugee. Throughout the 1930s and the war years he had still felt close to Germany and passionately defended the 'good Germans'.[18] But during his early visits to Germany after 1945 he came to realize that 'from an exile's viewpoint matters looked rather less complex than they were. Inevitably we tended to over-simplify things . . . I was yet to learn that not all our heroes were quite so heroic and not all our villains quite so villainous and that the human and material strands of the real pattern were interwoven in a manner far too complex to fit into the simple black and white pattern of an exile's dream world'. Through his repeated contacts with 'German realities' he learnt 'that, much as I still was and for ever would be concerned about its fate, it was no longer my country. The lesson I learned was that I no longer belonged'. But 'it took me five or six years and many trips to Germany to come to the very gradual (and very painful) realization that the return to my homeland was not the home-coming I had visualized for many a year'.[19] It was at this point that he decided to become a British citizen.

As in Fraenkel's case, the detachment from Germany went through a number of stages. This was true for older refugees in particular. In the 1950s, it seems, some of them "played with the idea" of returning, although apparently this is nowadays often perceived as a temporary weakness or 'illness'. "There was a certain crisis when I was offered the position of a judge in Germany", "one has a phase", or there was Mrs S. who was seriously thinking of returning to Germany: "I still had a strong sense of belonging (*Heimatgefühl*) towards Germany. Mainly because of the language. Nobody asks you, where do you come from; but my husband did not want to. He cured me." A few others, although tempted to go in the 1950s, felt "that it was too soon", "emotions were still too raw". Another respondent stated: "I might have thought about it, if a job was offered to me, but my wife and I liked London. If we had gone back, we would have gone to Berlin, but Berlin was too close to the Russians. Berlin was particularly unattractive at the time. And I didn't want to uproot myself and the family again." Finally, he added: "Both of us being Jewish, we felt more secure in Britain." However, the longer they waited and the more rooted they became in Britain, the greater the distance from German society: "In 1950 I still felt at home in Berlin, but in 1960 no longer."

Nevertheless, the majority of respondents said they never seriously thought of returning permanently to Germany. Quite a few among these were men who had been to Germany with the British army at the end of the war and became involved in the denazification procedures, often as interpreters. The sight of devastated Germany was shocking enough. Several went to look for their former home and were upset to find nothing but ruins. It was even worse for respondents to confront defeated Germans whom they found utterly despicable. "I didn't tell anybody that I was German, only on the last day. I couldn't at all identify with those Germans. 'Rather a German at your throat than at your feet', we said. Superman came crawling; I didn't like it. I didn't want anybody to crawl in front of me or tell me stories I knew were not true. I lost my German feeling then." Feelings of revenge – "they deserved what they got"– could only deepen the rift: "I entered Berlin with the first British convoy and felt extremely victorious; nothing sentimental whatsoever. I had not left Germany with great feelings of sympathy, but the defeated Germans were much worse; they were unbearable. It pleased me enormously to see the terrible destruction. I feel good about my feelings of revenge."

Not all shared this attitude. Mr G. thought "it was terrible. We had plenty to eat and the people were starving. We gave the children food". Mr C. even felt "awfully sorry for the Germans because of all the misery. I visited my 'Aryan' friends and relatives. I had nothing whatsoever in common with the English soldiers in my regiment, I felt a complete stranger among them. The officers treated Germany like an Indian colony. I felt much closer to the German population." Even if this was an unusual reaction, for most who came with the British Army, the first encounter was certainly traumatic. One of them even had thoughts of suicide. He never felt at home in Britain and now found it impossible to identify with Germany either. Realizing that, from now on, he would not be truly at home anymore anywhere, he almost despaired. Deeply upset, too, was an older refugee, Fred Uhlmann, who in his autobiography described his return to his home town after the war. He went to the Jewish cemetery to visit his grandmother's grave, where he broke down: 'I wept as I have never wept before and as I hope never to weep again. I was now fifty years old. I wept over my murdered family, my dead friends, my poisoned memories, over the thousands and thousands of murdered Jews and Christians. I wept over Germany. I wept over the ruins of so many beautiful old towns, the background of my youth.'[20]

The destruction of Germany as a homeland for these respondents was thus complete. But it was not the end of their links with the country. Cultural and human ties, although badly shaken, survived and formed the basis of a new relationship, however tenuous.

Childhood has been one significant link which drew the refugees back to Germany. It is because of this though that a number of refugees have refused to go back to Germany or to visit their former home-town. They are afraid the experience would prove to be emotionally too overwhelming for them: "It might stir up all sorts of memories"; "it would be too painful"; "it would break my heart" were some of the reasons given, or "I don't have anybody there anymore"; "I don't want to go to Germany. But I would like to see my birth-place again before I die. I feel a certain longing . . . but no, I don't want to go." Finally, there was Mr W. who has never been back to his home-town, although he is still very fond of it. "I don't want to see what it looks like today. I am sure it is completely different. It was so beautiful before the war. I dream of it and I don't want to destroy my dream. A short time ago, I had a stroke and for three months I went completely blind. But my home-town appeared before my inner eye; that was my greatest comfort during my illness."

Others, who, although afraid of experiencing similar disappointments or bitterness, nevertheless wanted to or had to go to Germany or Austria, but deliberately avoided visiting their home-town. Thus Mr T. regularly takes his holiday in Austria, but avoids Vienna. "I am still too bitter. I would be impatient and bad-tempered." Similarly Mr H. who goes to Germany on business at least once a year. He confessed: "But I don't like to go to familiar places. Too many ghosts would emerge there. I first went to Germany in 1951/52. I was very ill at ease, but this did not last for long. I went to the Cologne Cathedral and heard a man speak *kölsch* and I knew: I am at home here. Oddly enough I had a similar feeling when I went to Jerusalem for the first time. But I don't like to go to my former home-town. Yet the German atmosphere which I am fond of, the German forest, German beer, all sorts of other things – that also exists elsewhere (in that country) and I can enjoy it just as much, if I go to parts of Germany which I do not know."

However, quite a few respondents could not resist the temptation of visiting the place where they grew up. "Germany does not mean anything to me", Mrs I. said, "but I go crazy in Grunewald. There I am, all of a sudden, what I was earlier. When I went for the first time, my heart was beating terribly." A member of the younger (second) generation recently went to Breslau, his birth-place. "Our house was still standing. It gave me a tremendous shock at first. I didn't remember much of the city itself, until I saw it and then I remembered every single house. But I felt numb, numb, numb. I had a feeling of unreality. Nobody spoke German. Therefore I had no feeling of homecoming, only of total, absolute detachment. I had always wanted to go back; I dreamt about Breslau. I had to lay that ghost. I have got it out of my system now – I hope I have." An older refugee had likewise been haunted by a regularly re-appearing dream that he was on the way to his flat in Berlin, but never reached it. He decided he had to go to Berlin and break the spell. He did and, indeed, the dream did not return. Yet, in a way, he did not rediscover his home: "Germany had become a foreign country to me, I discovered. So much had changed. When I see an article on or picture of Berlin, I study them avidly, but it does not mean anything to me anymore."

Most respondents had a "very peculiar feeling" when they first went in search of the place of their childhood and early adulthood. Mrs N. who had been invited by her father, himself an émigré to the United States, to meet him in Germany and visit their former house in Hamburg remembered: "It was very strange. I rang the bell and said: 'We once lived here'. The people were very nice and let me in to have a look round. It didn't look much changed. I was pleased because of this. But my father refused to enter the house. He was too sad." For some this first encounter was more traumatic. Mrs E. who had left as a young girl stated: "I went back to Hamburg for the first time only two years ago. I was shattered by the experience; I was quite unprepared for the violence of my feelings. I went to see our house and went inside. I found how well I had remembered everything. My (English) husband was with me. He was a great help to me in coping with this experience."

It soon became clear why this experience was so important and stirring for many respondents. Persecution and emigration had not allowed them to grow naturally out of one stage of their life cycle into the next. Their life had been seriously disrupted. In effect, their childhood had been completely cut off from the rest of their life. Being furthermore tied up with Germany, it had also taken on some of the negative emotions associated with this country of origin. To go and visit Germany (or Austria) or one's birthplace helped them to accept this part of themselves and to re-integrate their childhood or adolescence into their life. They thus gained an inner security which enabled the refugees finally to come to terms with exile: having found and acknowledged their 'German' childhood, they could accept its loss. It was this deeper meaning which quite a number of respondents' accounts conveyed. Mrs K. was particularly articulate on this point: "My husband and I went back to Berlin in the 1970s for the first time. We had been invited by the

Berlin Senate for a week and we enjoyed it so tremendously that we stayed on. Berlin is home, it is *Heimat*. Our house was bombed out, but many other things were still there such as my school and the Zoo. It was very strange, it did not touch me, and I had thought I would be madly excited. Until I came into the house where I often went as a child. Suddenly my body got out of control. I started to tremble all over – it was like a cartharsis. From that moment on I had found my inner security. I was born in Berlin and that is a fact. As a child, I am German. From that moment it balanced itself out. The insecure feeling of being a stranger (in Britain) has been eradicated by my physical reaction. My childhood was in Berlin. Now I am living abroad and I am doing well here; I will stay here; I function well here. I am now at home here." It was not always as simple as that, she remembered: "I was embarrassed each time someone said: 'You, as a German.'" And I used to think, shall I now tell people the story of my life, shall I say I am not a German; I was a German, but they didn't want me anymore, or what should I say. Very often I said: 'I am Jewish.' 'But what is your nationality?' people would ask. Then I replied: 'Now I am British, but I used to be German, and I launched into a long thing. I felt uncomfortable. The English can't understand. 'Yes, but what do you feel like?' Until I was back in Berlin, I never quite knew how to react. After that I just said: 'I am from Berlin' and nobody asked any more questions. I really am from Berlin. I adore that city. I always did. It is a wonderful, lively, interesting city, which takes nothing too seriously; a fantastic city. And today I don't mind in the slightest saying so anymore. My books are read there, people know who I am. But previously I felt decidedly ill at ease. I didn't want to be identified with the Germans, not at all. Now I feel, I am a German. If they decided that I am not – that does not concern me; that's their business."

It has been pointed out above that Britain had become "home" in a certain sense for most respondents, but not a "homeland". However, accepting the German past, going back to Germany to the familiar places, may provide at least a reflection of the lost *Heimatgefühl*. Thus the L.s have been back to their home-town every year for the last sixteen years. They visit old friends. "We feel English, but when we are over there, some of the old *Lokalpatriotismus* comes back.' Similarly Mr H.: "Naturally, I still feel at home in Germany. There are so many things with which one grew up and one has the illusion as if, all of a sudden, one was much younger. When I go into a German university, I have the feeling, I am still a student myself. One has the illusion that the 50 years in between did not happen. That is probably one of the reasons why I gravitate towards Germany. I know that if I go into a restaurant, I can be sure of getting something which I like to eat. The problem is one of choice, because there is so much I would like to eat. But you can only eat one *Eisbein*. . . . Last year, I went to that region where my family comes from. My sons had asked me to do some research into our family history. I was afraid I would not find anything, I would not be accepted by the local people. But I was very pleased to realize that the H.s were well known. '*Die haben schon immer hier gelebt*', I was told. I was even brought into contact with an old aunt of whose existence I had not known before."

Quite a few respondents still have, or have resumed, contact with old friends of the family or with nannies, cooks or maids whom they visit regularly. All spoke with warm affection of these former members of the household with whom they can now share precious memories from childhood. If nothing else, it often was food, certain scents and language which created a sense of *Heimat*.

Whereas the older refugees rediscovered familiar people and things which bring back the past, some of the younger ones with more diffuse memories, made a discovery on an even deeper level: they discovered themselves, so to speak. "Until three or four years ago I avoided going to Germany", Mr R. explained, "I was very hostile then, I did not buy anything German. But one day I went to Switzerland. I walked through the German part and I was fascinated. It brought back all sorts of memories. I then travelled through Germany and took a tentative look at it. A little later I had to go to Germany to do research. Initially, I felt great anxiety and mistrust. But it disappeared after a few hours. I was fascinated. So many things were familiar, such as food. I recognised the respectability which I had thought was a unique characteristic of my parents. I discovered certain characteristics which I recognized in myself as German. I suddenly realized that my whole upbringing had been German." From then on Mr R. became deeply interested in Germany, personally as well as professionally.

An interesting case is finally that of Mrs S., whose story illustrated in a fascinating way several of the aspects that have emerged so far. She was not born in Germany and is married to an Englishman. One would therefore expect her to be completely estranged from her German background. But this was not so. "I never felt English, but British and this only until recently, when I discovered that I am basically Continental. I have come to terms with that over the past few years. I feel very much more a real person having realized that." The initial impulse for this re-orientation had come through her work in multi-racial education. "I explored backgrounds and cultures and how identities are formed. And I suddenly realized how much I was trying to be something I was not – squeezing myself into something which did not fit." This feeling was re-inforced when only a couple of years ago she went to Germany for the first time in her life. "I felt so much at home. I fitted in immediately, and did so in a way in which I do not in Britain. I discovered that German is still my cultural language. When I was young I preferred to speak English. I never ever spoke German. But I found I could slip into it in a most extraordinary fashion in Germany. It just came; it was really weird. I felt at home with the way people spoke. Even if I did not have the right words, we could understand each other emotionally in a way I still do not feel akin to English people. Although we are speaking the same language, we do not mean the same thing in England. In Germany I may have been using the wrong words, but we meant the same things." 'Even being married to an English husband?' I asked. "Particularly being married to an Englishman", she exclaimed, "my husband's Englishness – not his non-Jewishness – is something I haven't entirely reconciled myself to. It is a difference in outlook." She admitted to not being absolutely sure whether it might not be differences on a personal rather than on a cultural level. But she was inclined to see it in a cultural terms. Being married to an Englishman, she explained, "one realizes how very different one's outlook on life is. He used to criticize me for becoming too emotional, 'don't be so excitable', he used to say. Non-English people tend to talk a lot more with their body; the English, at least those of a certain educational background, rely very heavily on words, on using the precise words, when a shrug or another gesture will say it all. . . . If you think of yourself as something that you are not, you feel that you are constantly failing to be something you should be. But when you realize what you are, it makes it so much easier for both of you, and you can talk over any misunderstandings. We discuss them and come to an agreement." We are now again touching on a problem – the 'Germanness' of the German Jews – which will concern us more directly in the last chapter of this study. For the moment, we are still concerned with Germany and the Germans.

The intensity and absoluteness with which Mrs S. reclaimed her German past and integrated it into her British present, is perhaps rare. Nevertheless, elements of it can be found in other respondents' experiences. Yet to make one's peace with one's past is one thing; to establish a close link with contemporary German society is another. "All my friends in Britain come from the same area in Germany where I have come from", an older respondent remarked, "we have known each other from before emigration. We never talk about politics, as far as Germany is concerned; we have pushed that far away from us; but we do talk about the Germany of our childhood. Our childhood plays a relatively important part in our conversations. It is remarkable how many details one remembers. We don't talk much about contemporary Germany."

Whereas some respondents said they were not at all interested in German affairs and a minority showed themselves "very interested", the majority declared themselves moderately interested in modern Germany, and its political and cultural developments. "When there is an article on Germany, of course, I read it." However, they could not always tell whether this interest could be separated from their general interest in world affairs in which Germany happens to play an important role. However most felt that news concerning Germany struck a chord in them which caused them to pay that much more attention to it. "I am interested because I know more about it than about any other country", Mr F. explained, adding apologetically, "well, you see, I was born there." Quite a few found that their interest in Germany generally has been increasing over the last years; another point which we shall have to come back to in the next chapter.

In spite of this rapprochement and a number of traits which the refugees find familiar, contemporary Germany as a whole continues to be a strange country for many refugees. It contains the Germany of the past, but it is not identical with it. Not every refugee gains access to it as easily as Mrs S. who did not have any problems relating to modern Germany and identifying with it. "I felt nothing (when she went to Berlin) as far as World War II was concerned. I found the Wall much more shattering, because it was an expression of antagonism in today's world. I am more concerned with racism as it is now; it happens everywhere." Mrs K., on the other hand, in spite of her regained positive attitude towards Berlin and her German origin, found it very difficult to extend these emotions to modern Germany: "The Nazi era still is so terrible for me that when

I see a swastika on the TV I run out of the room. I can't get over it; I simply can't. After my visit to Berlin, I was able to put this period into perspective. But it is still very much alive in me. If I now think of Germany, it is like looking through a fog. The country itself is beautiful. But I don't know the people. They are complete strangers, more so than the English. Indirectly, I know a lot about Germany. I read German literature a lot. But otherwise it feels like cotton wool between me and Germany."

In other words, it is the legacies of the past which form an almost impenetrable thicket around modern Germany. The relationship between Austrian refugees and their former homeland is equally disturbed, although allowances were made a bit more readily. Frischauer found some redeeming features: 'It took me fifteen years after the war and more than half a dozen visits to analyze my reactions to Vienna. I feel very much like coming back to my old house, yet it seems rather strange. It is as if it had been occupied by several turbulent tenants, burgled, stripped, half-stripped, half-destroyed and rebuilt. Now it is difficult for me to visualize that I ever lived here. The new housekeeper, too, thinks of me as a stranger.' He also became aware of a barrier between him and his former friends: 'We are separated by the greatest emotional experience of our lives, the war through which we lived on different sides of the fence.' But he continued: 'Inevitably, my heart warmed to Austria again. What I could not forgive a German, did not shock me as deeply where an Austrian was involved. . . . Everything in Austria is mitigated by *Schlamperei*. . . . That Ausrian Nazism had no such redeeming features but was mercilessly and efficiently vicious and cruel, stamped it as an alien importation, "made in Germany".' Even so, he soon left again for England 'where the political air was not contaminated by the poison [of Nazism]. Yet, however happy I was to go back to London, it has not entirely cured me. Vienna, the city of my dreams, is still waiting for me'.[21]

Is there any hope of bridging the gap? Considerable efforts in this direction have undoubtedly been made by official bodies in Germany. Restitution was very important in this respect. Never before had it been offered in the history of the persecution of the Jews. It helped to alleviate the difficult financial situation of the refugees; in particular the older refugees were spared the humiliation of ending their life in poverty; it helped to 'restore (their) badly hit human dignity'.[22] And the refugees have acknowledged it as such.

This is not to say that restitution was never uncontroversial. Some refugees absolutely refused to have anything to do with it; they felt that no money in the world could absolve Germany from the crimes committed during the Third Reich and suspected the Germans of trying literally to pay off their guilt and responsibility.[23] For other refugees, as respondents explained, restitution posed a serious moral dilemma. They shared some of the misgivings of the first group, but needed the money. On the other hand they were afraid of appearing greedy and materialistic. They felt entitled to it, because they had worked hard for it when still in Germany. And yet such arguments did not resolve the dilemma for all of the respondents. "My heart aches on the day I receive my monthly pension from Germany", Mrs C. said. But there was also the father of one respondent for whom, she said, restitution and all the paperwork connected with it, had become the obsession of his old age. It was revenge which drove him on; he wanted to get as much out of the Germans as possible. Nevertheless, most respondents mentioned restitution in a positive way, remarking that they had appreciated it as a gesture of goodwill and that it had softened their hostility. Apparently, bureaucratism remained tolerable. At least, none of the respondents complained having been badly treated. "It was a pleasant experience", remembered Mr M. "I was not treated as someone who was begging for something, but as someone who was entitled to it."

Other attempts at a rapprochement, which were initiated by the Germans, have been either to encourage the refugees to return to Germany by offering them positions, as in the case of the law profession mentioned earlier, or to revive their interest in their home-towns by inviting them for a visit or asking them to contribute to local histories and to the histories of Jewish communities in Germany in particular. Many academics have been offered honorary degrees and were invited to teach at their former universities.

Mention should also be made at this point of the fact that it was not least German–Jewish refugees themselves who played an active role in the process of reconciliation. Their immediate intention was not so much to reconcile the Jews with Germany but rather to mediate between Germany and the rest of the world. German Jews were among the first, after the war, to work for the reconstruction of German society. This was done in various ways. Jella Lepmann, for instance, an important journalist and politician before 1933, went back to Germany with the American occupation authorities as an adviser on youth questions. In 1949 she founded the International

Youth Library which, according too the editor of the TLS helped to lay the foundations for the high standards of German libraries and children's books.[24] Writers and journalists have similarly fulfilled, to this day, an important bridging function as we have seen above. An example from a different field was mentioned in the *AJR Information* only recently. It reported that a well-known authority in medicine 'used restitution monies and his pension as Emeritus Professor in Germany to establish a Foundation for Exchange Lectureships in medical research between Britain and Germany.'[25] Nowadays, we would expect this generous gesture to be widely acclaimed. Yet when memories of the war were still more vivid, such a conciliatory attitude demanded some courage. Not only were there the personal feelings of ambiguity to be overcome which most of the German Jews involved in these actions themselves are likely to have had. Above all, other people, especially many fellow-Jews, were anything but sympathetic. This was Mrs Y.'s experience who has always considered it one of her main tasks to work through her political and journalistic activities for reconciliation. However, when she went to Germany from Israel, where she had first emigrated after she had survived the horrors of the concentration camps, she "needed an alibi" because of the extreme hostility she met when people learnt of her intention to go. After her return she was ostracized by a number of people; even friends refused to shake hands with her. Her reactions to these experiences were very bitter; she felt that after what she had been through, nobody had the moral right to criticize her in this way; what she had hoped to find was respect if not sympathy. Her "refusal to hate and condemn Germany was fairly uncommon among Jews" at that time, during the 1950s, as has been confirmed by our respondents.

The various efforts made by German Jews and Germans alike have not been completely fruitless. But judging from the respondents' feelings, what can at best be generated is a friendly and interested or cautious disposition towards German society on the part of the Jews. It seems that only prolonged and close friendship ties with individuals are able to overcome the deeply ingrained reservations against contemporary Germany. The following examples illustrate how difficult this is – emotionally – for many refugees.

Since institutional and other links offer the chance of meeting individuals, they may be valuable, but not invariably so. Most of those respondents who go to Germany purely on business were found to be the most indifferent; they were barely touched by the encounter with German society. Their situation was not without irony in those cases where they have been sent because of their knowledge of Germany and the German language. It made little difference: "I still find it very strange, although I go a lot to Germany on business. I get on very well with my partners, they are nice, very friendly, very warm; but I am suspicious; they may have been (Nazi-) party members"; another respondent stated: "I go to Germany quite often, but it is purely business. It does not appeal to me emotionally, there are no social contacts."

Yet, even where personal contacts were established, trust still did not follow automatically. Thus a respondent from Vienna went back only recently: "I could not bring myself to go all those years. But then I went and it did me a lot of good. Because there are so many young people there who were terribly nice. If I had not known what nasty people they can be, I would have said how charming the Austrians are."

Mrs F. offers an even more striking example of these inner conflicts. She often goes to Germany "to see relatives or to accompany my husband to meetings of interfaith groups". She reports: "We have never encountered any antisemitism in Germany. And I have some very close friends there, but nevertheless I have a tremendous hang-up with regard to Germany. I once went to a meeting of mixed denominations. And although these were all 'nice' people, otherwise they would not have been there – when I looked at all these 'Aryan' faces, I could have screamed." Even the most intimate relationships with Germans can become complicated because of these "hang-ups". Mrs R., a member of the second generation as the previous respondent, "fell in love with a bloody German" when in Germany for the first time since her emigration. She never wanted to go to Germany and hated all Germans. So much so that when she saw a German flag in London she felt physically sick: "I sat by the curb and cried"; or she got off the bus as soon as she heard German spoken. But in the early 1960s she went to Berlin professionally, because "someone German-speaking was needed. I tried to find the house where we had lived, but it was destroyed. I wanted through Berlin; I didn't know whether it was a dream or reality. I met a German, I fell in love with him, we went dancing. When I looked out of the window and over the city it suddenly struck me that this was Germany, and I am a Jew, and I am back. And this is where I was born – it was all too much for me; and this man who was not a Jew, who was a German.

He poured me some champagne and I said: 'I can't drink champagne with you'. I went to bed with him when he came to visit me in England; the big gesture, you know. Going to bed with a German means to make peace with 6 million Jewish dead. I woke up in the middle of the night and I got out of bed and I thought, I can't go on living. Either I kill him or I kill myself. How can you possibly have slept with a German. I was smoking a cigarette and he woke up and knew exactly what I was thinking. We wrote love letters for a year, but the affair slowly died. On his side there was never anything . . . I still have a thing about going back to Germany. I think I have lately got over having a thing about Germans. I went to Germany in 1975, I felt nothing, it was just business. I met a German couple. We became close friends. We spent a holiday together and they invited me to stay with them in Germany, but I don't want to go yet. Maybe one day I will."

Here we have the whole range of the emotions evoked by the 'German complex', reaching from intense hostility, a personal crisis, to professional detachment and a mellowing of feelings over time and, finally, to a rapprochement through friendship with individual Germans.

Finally, there is Mr N., an older refugee. His – and his wife's – relationship with Germany is much less dramatic and intense than that of the previous respondents. His case is interesting because of the way in which the old and the new Germany are interconnected. Just before we met for the first time Mr N., who is from Munich, had written to one of his old friends there, because "we are both *eingefleischte Royalisten*. He always writes to me on the 12th December because Prince Luitpold was born on 12th March and died on 12 December. This has always been a very nice holiday for us. . . . None of my former friends or business partners have deserted me. In 1948, I went to Germany for the first time, after I had received a letter from my partners urging me to return: '*Komm heim, sei in unserem Bunde der Dritte*'. They offered me back the business, but maybe they were quite glad after all when I said no; just a feeling. I was torn: should I, should I not. But there were still so many with whom one did not want to have anything to do. I have not regretted it, only perhaps from the financial point of view, but I was never particularly interested in money. I have often been in Germany. I have been asked to sit on the board of two firms. My partners helped me a lot when it came to restitution". For nearly 20 years, the N.s had a holiday flat in Switzerland, where they have met many "nice people" from Germany who "gave us German literature to read. We regularly read the *Süddeutsche* [daily paper], mainly the cultural parts. We consider the period between 1938 and 1949 more as a *Sendepause* (intermission). Since then we are in touch again and we always know roughly what things are like over there. One has friends, we ring each other up from time to time". When the N.s go to Munich, they get so many invitations that they cannot accept them all. It thus seemed that the N.s have had nothing but pleasant experiences in Germany. Yet, at this point the conversation took an unexpected turn; the tone changed and became more hesitant: "But when we are in Munich, we are the visitors from London; if we lived there permanently, it would be different. Some people might – one isn't so interesting anymore – our friends are all wealthy, we could not compete with them." And after a pause, Mr N. added: "I feel safe in Germany because of my British passport; I can immediately return to England if I wanted to. People might say something in a restaurant, for instance. But whenever I am over there", Mr N. concluded emphatically, "I absolutely feel as a Bavarian!"

Is caution never completely abandoned by the refugees when they are in Germany? This is probably true for the majority. Close and friendly relations which quite a number of them have maintained or re-established with individual Germans, have helped to mellow feelings over the years, but have failed to dissolve the lack of complete trust entirely. However, a few respondents found to a truly relaxed attitude towards Germans as well as German society.

Mr A. feels perfectly at home when he goes to Germany on his frequent visits: "I have no language problems, the country and the people are familiar. One of my best friends is German. I often visit him in Germany." Another interesting case is that of Mrs V.: "I have no memory of Berlin, but I have been so brought up with names and streets ... I had a feeling of non-strangeness about Berlin. I can't say, I remembered anything, but it felt familiar to me. The food, the typeface of the street signs, the architecture, and, of course, the language. I get the reverse from what I get in England: I talked to people who did not realize who I was and who talked disparagingly about the English. And then I got very stuffy and English and said, I am English etc. Wherever I go people think I belong to that and make remarks about the other half of me. I have been back several times and for longer periods. It is easier now. I don't fight either half. At first, I hardly dared to talk to people. I wanted to ask, what did you do etc. I didn't trust anyone. And now, I am mellowing as time passes; I feel, well, you did your things and I did my things. I have reached a stage where I stop being neurotic about it." Mr G.'s response, who also often goes to Germany, was similar: "Do you want to know my feelings? Appalling – because I have no bad, or anti-feelings at all. It makes me feel guilty. I refuse to be suspicious; I can't ask everybody over 60: 'What did you do?' No, I can't do that. Either I go to Germany and feel perfectly normal about it or I refuse to go to Germany. And I have no intention of refusing to go to Germany." Mr H. has no family connections anymore; he lost many relatives in the concentration camps. "That's why I went back two years ago. . . . But I identify with the Germans." He would have gone back, or considered it, if he had been offered a proper job. "I am afraid, I would fit in awfully well. I like cleanliness, the organization. I even love Switzerland, because it is so antiseptic. I adore efficiency; I think it is marvellous. I love it. It turns me on. It really gives me a tremendous kick. I love things to work. In Germany things do work; here they automatically don't. I don't consider myself a German national." And after a long pause, he suddenly added: "I tell you something. It is silly of me to have secrets from you. I haven't shown anybody else this . . . do you recognize it? It is a German passport. I applied for it. Quite a number of refugees have got it back, for economic reasons mainly, but one doesn't talk about it. I feel safer with a German passport; in case things get worse politically or economically in Britain."

In Mrs I.'s case it was likewise frequent contact with Germans which enabled her "to overcome my anti-German prejudice. Some 20 years ago it was physically difficult for me to cross the German border, it was a physical discomfort. I didn't lose any relatives in the camps, but my husband did. But he was less bitter than me". The I.s are Free Masons and it was Mr I. who initiated contact with German Free Masons. "He got an order from them. I think they were bending over backwards a lot. But through them we met many Germans. We have just come back from Germany. We had a tremendous welcome. Some also come over here and stay with us. Or we rented a flat from one family in Germany for our holidays. We have very good friends among them and I feel completely at home in Germany now through these contacts." She thought that her husband was perhaps even more deeply affected, because he "probably has a longing for a homeland, more so than I have". Mrs

I. never seriously considered going back to Germany, "only jokingly for financial reasons because in my profession I would earn so much more in Germany". Yet, if offered a nice job, preferably for both of them, "I could visualize it, but I would want to retire in Britain. 20 years ago, not under any circumstances could I have contemplated it, but I could now. My husband is even keener than me." Another couple of respondents also belong to the Free Masons and it is again through them that they made "very, very good friends after the war". They regularly travel to Germany to Lodge meetings. "We still see people of our age who my husband grew up with. His father and grandfather were made honorary officers of their old Lodge. . . . naturally we can never forgive for what happened and we will never forget, but we did not want to hate."

Two respondents who had come from East Germany, joined West German refugee organizations after the war. Through these organizations they have rediscovered old friends or made new ones in Germany whom they frequently visit. It seems it is the common fate of emigration which in a curious way unites Jews and non-Jews in these particular cases.

In Mr H.'s case, finally, it simply was human contact with ordinary people which created the bond: "Oh no, the Germans are not strangers to me. I have often talked to people. Also on purpose. People come and sit next to you on a bench or I take a seat next to them; and then you start talking. I have met all sorts of people. I find that I easily make contact with the people and that I have pleasant conversations with them. . . . It would be a lie to say that I have never hated. But I cannot hate limitlessly. Somehow events have long since passed and are mixed with experiences of a different kind which one has had in the meantime. I have encountered a great deal of kindness from many people, people who cared."

What do all these different images of Germany and the Germans add up to? Are they 'true'? No doubt, the majority of the respondents painted rather a gloomy picture, even if it was brightened up by some lighter colours in many cases. Is this picture more reliable than the warmer and friendlier one of the minority presented above? This might well be so. But what seems clear is that these perceptions tell us more about the refugees themselves than about Germany. It was at least to some extent Mr H.'s own kindness and human interest to which people responded. And bitterness or mistrust will equally be reflected and be found confirmed in people's behaviour in Germany. A number of respondents were evidently aware of this themselves. Yet, whatever the basis for these perceptions, they show how far the Jews have distanced themselves from Germany with which they once identified so closely.

This leads to the question of how, in view of the overwhelmingly negative image of Germany, do the Jews of German extraction face the 'German element' in themselves. One might argue that there is no point asking such a question, since relatively few respondents felt "German". However, respondents usually distinguished between Germany in terms of politics and Germany in terms of culture. Whereas, on the whole, they dissociated themselves from the first, nearly all of them were aware that culturally they were still tied to their German background. This is why so many found a number of familiar traits in German life. But more significantly they found it in their own outlook on life, their attitudes of which most of them have become aware not so much in Germany but in Britain, for it is through the contact with the English that their 'Germanness' asserts itself most noticeably. We will therefore return, in the concluding chapter, to the question of a German–Jewish ethnicity in Britain.

7 'Continental' Britons

When talking about the 'Germanness' of the German Jews in Britain, it is important to get the proportions right. The first two chapters of this study were largely devoted to showing the unity of the German–Jewish ethnic identity in which the two component elements had become inseparably blended. The same holds basically true today, although the situation has become complicated through the addition of 'Britishness', on the one hand, and the emotional dissociation and actual detachment from German society, on the other. No wonder many respondents feel "split", "ambivalent", or, "as nothing much", if asked to define their identity in terms of nationality. Yet in terms of ethnicity the large majority of the respondents had no problem of determining their identity: Jewish. And many, especially among the older generation, added that they are 'more aware of their Jewishness in Britain' than they had been in Germany. Since 'Jewishness' as such has become rather a vague term, open to many interpretations, respondents generally felt impelled to qualify the term. Thus it was said: "Not German, but very Jewish, yet not English–Jewish", "Jewish but German–Jewish", "Jewish, but more a refugee", "Jewish, but in a Continental way." Some defined it in religious terms, others more in terms of a 'community of fate'. But what united them and differentiated them from English society was their 'Continentalness': "I like my Continentals best", Mrs J. said with great affection.

PROBLEMS OF IDENTITY

More or less all respondents of the first and second generation agreed that their 'Continentalness' was infused with a strong German element, that culturally they were marked by their German background. This is not, as explained, in contradiction to the dissociation from German society. Nor should one expect the widespread aversion against Germany and the Germans in general to be reflected in equally predominant self-hatred. The overall attitude is, again, one of ambivalence.

Reference as to the character of these 'German' or 'Continental' traits has been made, implicitly or explicitly, at various points in this study. To sum up briefly what respondents appear to have understood by them: a pronounced work ethic, discipline, a sense of duty, order, tidiness, perfectionism as well as an emphasis on the importance of *Bildung* and *Kultur* (general education and 'high culture'); not less important elements include 'excitability' and intimacy and warmth in human relationships. The second set of ethnic traits may seem somewhat contradictory to the first set. In fact, some respondents, especially among the younger ones, tended to distinguish between the 'cold' elements as 'typically' German and the 'warm' ones as 'typically' Jewish. In this way, they were in a position to identify with the Jewish side in them and to dissociate themselves from the German side. Yet it is not difficult to become aware of the common link between these two sets of traits: a relatively high degree of intensity brought to all activities. The same intensity with which the 'Continentals' involve themselves in their work or whatever they do (thus most respondents quite clearly applied the same high standards of professionalism to their hobbies as they had done to their jobs) is also applied in the field of human contact.

On the one hand, respondents were undeniably proud or at least appreciative of their 'German' traits. For is it not due to them that they have succeeded so remarkably well in Britain or in any other country of emigration? Yet, on the other hand, these same traits are seen as a character flaw which ought to be abandoned: "I still feel very Germanic in many ways", Mrs I. remarked, "I have only recently learnt not to worry too much about cleanliness and that it really does not matter too much. I tried to be perfect in all fields, but I have become more relaxed."

Attitudes towards Judaism did not lack ambiguity either, yet positive ones were more common than negative ones. Most of the respondents were involved in German–Jewish group life, more or less closely, as members of one or several of the numerous German–Jewish institutions. In a number of cases, however, the *AJR Information* represented the only – tenuous – link with the community as such. Equally important were non-institutional networks, such as circle of friends and relatives. Among older refugees in particular, it was common practice to seek out old friends from home or find new ones from among those circles "in which one would have moved anyway, had we stayed on in Germany", Mrs W. explained. She continued: "One of my friends actually never got to London; spiritually, she still lives in Berlin, surrounded by all her old friends."

On the other hand, there were also those – a minority among respondents, to be sure – who "felt it was better to stay out of refugee circles", or who "did not want to get caught in the net of German–Jewish refugees". It was for this reason that they had even moved to the provinces or other, 'non-Jewish' parts of London.

Furthest removed and least interested in group life were, generally speaking, the academics and artists among the respondents. This is probably due to the high degree of personal involvement which academics or artists bring to their profession in which job and hobby are often identical. Furthermore, they encounter many like-minded spirits with whom they jointly pursue goals which easily override group differences of an ethnic as well as national character. The international rescue action by academics, as described above, offers an example. Thus sufficient companionship is offered to satisfy the human need of belonging to and identifying with wider groups.[1] Apparently, the 'business community' does not offer the same sense of belonging. This is probably why its members are much more strongly represented in institutions of the ethnic group, as is certainly true in the case of the German Jews in Britain as a whole.[2]

Although less involved institutionally, it does not follow that academics and artists do not, as a rule, identify with the Jewish community. It was found that their self-perception as 'Continentals' in no way differed from that of the other respondents.

The majority of the interviewees explained that their sense of Jewishness and their interest in Judaism, especially in Jewish history, had been awakened or strengthened through the experience of persecution. Thus Mr A., a Rabbi, had taken the decision when still a boy in Germany that pastoral work would be his future profession. "I was told all the time that anything Jewish is bad. I wanted to make something positive out of an evil thing." Most respondents, of course, had a non-professional interest in Judaism. They like to read books or to go to lectures and discussion groups, which occasionally led to remarkable revelations: "I grew up with the guilt feeling that the Jews killed the Christian Jesus and I was somehow also responsible. It was only about 15 years ago (through her participation in a study group) that I realized that Jesus was a Jew!" Or there was Mrs H. who had just been to a lecture on anti-semitism: '. . . and I have always believed the Jews themselves were to blame for the persecutions. But [the speaker] made it quite clear that antisemitism is not their fault. I always thought so. [Indeed she had told me so at an earlier conversation]. I am *so* relieved, *so* glad, it is not like that".

Another indicator of the greater commitment is the interest in Israel. It is well known that Zionism was never very popular with German Jews before 1933. A few were as little concerned about Israel as their parents and grandparents had been. "I am not a convinced – what is the word? – Zionist", Mr F. confessed. But this does not prevent him from giving money to plant trees in Israel. On the whole, however, this attitude did change to considerable degree in the light of the Nazi experience. Some reservations remain to the extent that respondents tended to distinguish between the State of Israel and Israel as a Home of the Jews. Thus quite a few were outrightly critical of or "disappointed by Israeli nationalism", "imperialism" or "anti-Arab racialism" or of Israeli politics in general. Nevertheless, most supported Israel in some way or other, mainly financially or through work in Zionist groups. Feelings towards Israel, on the whole, were mixed; they reflected pride of Jewish achievements; guilt for having failed to support Palestine in the past, and a sense of duty because of this or because "it is a good thing", "Israel is important for Jews", or "one never knows, one might need it one day". Only a small minority described themselves as positively Zionist.

However, there were other elements which had created a bond with Israel: an identification with the nation of Jews, as "the country where Jews have roots"; also of importance were family and friendship ties. The majority of the respondents have been to Israel at least once; some had even lived there for some years. A few were considering retirement in Israel because they wanted to join their children who had recently emigrated from Britain or because of friends and relatives who had settled there in the 1930s. Others felt tempted to go, but were reluctant because of the difficult economic situation in Israel: or they felt to be too European culturally. Most, however, were quite happy just visiting because "one emigration is enough" or because of their dissatisfaction with Israeli politics. One respondent even argued: "There are too many Jews there."

Yet for most, it was exactly this that made Israel attractive: to find themselves among so many Jews which made Israel such a "fantastic" experience for them. "It is a most peculiar feeling that the people there are all Jews and we are not a minority as everywhere else. It is surprising to see Jewish streetsweepers." Another respondent derived a certain satisfaction from the fact that "even criminals are Jews". Another respondent remarked: "I feel I belong to them because we have all been thrown out from somewhere"; "I feel a strong emotional link; I have the feeling as if I know everybody because we are all Jews." Some therefore feel quite at home in Israel, more so in fact, than in Britain; but others did not: "When I went, it was a sort of anti-climax. I had imagined that I would feel more at home than I actually did in spite of my sense of belonging." Yet this feeling was shared by only a minority of respondents.

Without doubt, attitudes towards Judaism either in a general sense or as regards the particular issue of their relationship with Israel, show on the whole a more positive evaluation than of the German element of the cultural heritage. Even so, feelings about the Jewish part of the identity are hardly ever simple and without contradictions, and the effects of these ambiguities can be quite crippling socially. Mrs V, did not like being with English Jews because they were "too religious"; nor with German Jews, if they were "too German"; nor does she associate with English people, apart from three university friends. "I suppose we are a very inward looking family", she commented! Mrs C. represented an even more extreme case. Although this was rarely found among other respondents, her self-perceptions seem worth quoting, because they highlight the complicated feelings which may arise in German-Jewish refugees when confronted with their 'Continentalness'. Mrs C. first described what 'Jewishness' meant to her: "I had a love-hate relationship with Jews for a long time. Half of me thought, how crazy, what does it matter, we are complete strangers. And half of me felt, yes, there is a kinship. To be Jewish for me means warmth, screaming, irritation, and affection, everybody helps each other, a kind of outgoing, unashamed naturalness of human behaviour which I find fascinating, because I can't share it. In my own family every Jewish gesture was considered a crime. But I can see it as a little bit of me being part of it, nonetheless. A little bit of me tries to identify with Jewish warmness; the rest of me does not want it, as too cloying, too claustrophobic." As far as her 'Germanness' is concerned, Mrs C. has not preserved any affection for it whatsoever. On the contrary, for her it has become a sort of devil's mark: 'I hated the idea of being German so much that I said I was Austrian. But I never denied being Jewish." Her hatred for Germany stemmed not so much from the fact "of 6 million dead etc., not consciously at least; but I have never come to terms with the fact that I am a German myself, that part of me is German, part of me is Jewish. Because I hate, to some extent, both the Germans and the Jews. And I am both. I find the mixture unbearable and I am part of that mixture. . . . You have the cringing, arrogant Jew and you have the superior, arrogant, insensitive German and all that is part of me as well. And in any case, if I had not been a Jew I might have made a very good Nazi; how do I know." But it was her 'Germanness' in particular which has created great problems, she believed, for her relationships with her (English) husband. For him it was those "irritating German characteristics which I find very irritating myself: You have to have the last word, you have to be right, you never give up. I used to be good at jobs which needed to be well researched, because I never let go. There is a certain persistence in me which is un-English; absolute perfectionism. But I am not quite as bad as I used to be." And she continued: "I want to change, because I don't like myself. I want to become English. I want to be integrated. I want to be part of the community without any differential, but I know I can never achieve that." And she added quite casually, yet it seems, significantly: "It might have been the same with me had I grown up in Britain. I am sure, it has something to do with my family. Relationships in our family were terribly cold. I was never taught to like others, let alone to respect myself."

Other respondents have alluded to similar feelings, but in this case it becomes particularly clear that it is not the German–Jewishness in itself which makes the ethnic identity problematical, or results in self-hatred in more extreme cases. It may well lead to ambiguity about one's background. Yet how individuals cope with it, whether they are completely thrown off balance, seems to depend largely on their psychological predisposition. Certainly Mrs D. took a very different approach to these problems: "I have had difficulties in the past to accept the Germanness in myself. That was quite a big problem. And I was also aware that the Germanness in myself was quite strong. Subconsciously, I have always been aware of it. I feel quite German in a way. I can't leave things alone. I don't submit easily. I tend to stick my neck out. And then, of course, my work ethic, yes, *das kann man wohl sagen* (you may say so). But I am not always sure, whether my reactions are 'German' or whether it is a question of personal temperament. . . . Sometimes I feel very envious of people who have a homogeneous background and know exactly where they belong. And they have a *Geburtsort*, a place where they grew up; they can go back to where they grew up. And other times, I feel it must be monstrously boring to have all that. This sort of change and conflict and so on which I had . . . was just the right amount to keep things interesting and on the boil."

On the other hand, feelings of identity, as has been repeatedly stressed, are not fixed. Changing circumstances on the personal or socio-political level may affect them in the course of time. Thus we have seen that the hostility towards Germany has mellowed over the last few years. The same applies to the problems of German–Jewish self-perceptions. Quite a number of respondents mentioned that they have become more relaxed over the years as to their 'Continentalness'. Thus Mrs G. "always wanted to become English, to leave the German experience behind. I feel very English, but now I also accept the fact that I am not. I find that people react positively, if they hear about my Continental background. I read a lot in German, I am interested in German literature, though not in Germany as a country. I feel that I am now detached enough from the German experience, and English enough that I can afford to come to terms with the other side in me". Her friendship pattern has equally been affected. Her friends used to be "mainly non-Jewish English, but I have made some very close Jewish friends more recently". She saw this as part of her effort to accept that side of her life which had been suppressed for so long. Mrs G. is married to a Briton. Yet intermarriage in this case has not led to tensions between the spouses, because, as Mrs G. explained, "my husband is very well informed about Continental culture. He has reinforced my own growing interest in my background. I think this is partly the reason why our marriage is very happy".

It may be worth mentioning at this point that some of the 'English' husbands turned out to be of Scottish or Irish descent. This fact and the importance Mrs G. (and a few other respondents in mixed marriages) gave to the cultural closeness between herself and her English husband seem to suggest that intermarriage as such is not necessarily a reliable indicator of 'assimilation'. Even here, ethnicity may assert itself.

ELEMENTS OF 'CONTINENTAL' ETHNICITY

The 'Continentalness' of the German Jews is not restricted to the realm of self-perception. In every day life one also comes across a number of habits and customs easily identifiable as German–Jewish. Yet it is important to distinguish between the unconscious and the conscious, or between primary and secondary expressions of culture.

As to the latter, it has been shown above that cultural activities with an overtly German character were more or less banned or discouraged during the war years or were shunned by the refugees themselves because of their direct association with Germany. The ensuing estrangement from German culture seems to have been permanent in the majority of cases, so it seems, although in this, too, attitudes were found to be changing.

This is particularly marked as regards the German language. Ninety per cent of the interviews with older refugees were conducted in German. "That is the language I speak without an accent", Mr S. remarked. Indeed, the German spoken by the respondents in these cases was perfectly fluent, shaded by distinct local dialects and often interspersed with colourful German colloquialisms and proverbs. It seemed difficult to believe that the speakers had been removed from the German environment for such a long time. They seemed totally at ease in German. However, this impression was deceptive in many cases. Thus the L.s speak German freely at home and in fact were very critical of refugees who did not, but outside in the streets they are careful to speak with a low voice. Some stressed the fact that their German, albeit fluent, is a "dead language"; that it is a language spoken up to the 1930s. But is this true? Surely, the German language has continuously changed in the past. And the refugees' German markedly lacked the Americanisms and sociologisms which have invaded the German language since the 1960s, particularly the German spoken by the younger generation. Otherwise the language has, within this historically rather short period, not changed very markedly. Older forms co-exist with new ones. This probably explains why to a German the refugees' language sounds familiar, whereas the refugees, noticing the changes more clearly, tend to regard their language obsolescent.

Despite their fluency in German, about half of the older respondents prefer to speak English at home. "It appears artificial to us now to speak German between the two of us", the W.s explained. Similarly Mr H. who mentioned that, at various times, he had suggested to his friends (all German–Jewish) to speak German when they are together. "We try, but after 5 minutes we are back to English." A couple of respondents thought it was a "mental block" which prevented them from speaking German at home. A number of others just felt "more at ease" speaking English, even so it was obvious that only few of them mastered the language. Quite a few spoke 'emigranto' or 'Double Dutch', as the mixture of both languages was called, not without expressing some guilt feelings because of it. One respondent tended to speak German (during the interview) when talking about past events and English when describing her present-day life without apparently being aware of this change. A minority detested this mixing of languages. They were very critical of what they considered as "nothing but laziness" on the part of the refugees and made deliberate attempts to keep both languages separate, although it is easy to see why this may be difficult. Thus academics often found it impossible to use German professionally when, for instance, giving lectures in Germany. They felt they lacked familiarity with German scholarly terminology in their field.

At home, the situation might be even more complicated. Elaborate strategies have been developed to adjust to the exigencies of the moment. Thus it was apparently a widespread practice to give up German when the children started school. However, there were elderly parents, aunts or friends who preferred to speak German. Others did not, and consequently one spoke German with some family members, but English with others. The same applies to friends. German also continued to play a significant role as *lingua franca* among refugees. There is a tendency to switch to German whenever relatives or friends from abroad come to visit. Since the children have left home and with increasing age, many respondents have reverted more and more to German. Several cases were reported in which a member of the family had fallen seriously ill or suffered a stroke and completely forgotten his or her English. As a result, communication with the doctors and nurses at the hospital had become almost impossible and a younger member of the family had to be brought in as an interpreter.

This trend on the level of linguistics is reflected in the above mentioned growing interest in German affairs more generally. Nevertheless speaking German and reading it would seem to be two different things. Having been exposed for so long to the English language, many respondents now find written German rather "flowery", "involved" or "too complicated". Hardly any of them read German newspapers regularly, but a few like to do so when abroad. German books are much more widely read. In most cases, however, a clear preference was given for the classics and for the poems and novels familiar from before emigration. "I love to read German literature", remarked Mr L., "I often read poems by Mörike or Eichendorff. That is what we read at school. But we were not all that enthusiastic then. Now I love to read these poems; I don't know why. And I love to hear certain tunes. So much so that it makes me cry, I can't help it. My (German–Jewish) wife always laughs at me at such moments." Many had succeeded in bringing their books out of Germany and can therefore easily go back to them. Quite a few said they had done so more and more in recent years.

The access to post-war German literature, in contrast, is more problematical – practically as well as spiritually. Few bookshops in Britain sell German books. A number of respondents with contacts in Germany are sent more recent publications by these friends. Or they buy German books when in Germany on a visit. But these cases seem to be the exception rather than the rule. The majority of the respondents did not express any particular interest in contemporary literature. An 'innate' conservatism of the elderly may well be partially responsible for this. However, the respondents themselves generally gave as a reason their aversion against modern literary German. It turned out, though, that their knowledge of post-war literature in Germany beyond Heinrich Böll or Günther Grass, was minimal. It is equally plausible therefore that it is the estrangement from contemporary German society which makes refugees shrink back from reading its literature. For it became clear that interest in music, theatre, books and the arts as such were undiminished. Many respondents had just been or intended to go to concerts or exhibitions and talking about books – general literature and history – constituted a part of many interviews.

In other, less problematical areas of cultural expression the German element was much more noticeable. Houses, apartments or gardens were mostly immaculate. And this although most women interviewed disliked the idea of being a *Hausfrau*. The majority were in any case too busy with a job or other activities to be able to devote much time to housework. Nevertheless, standards of cleanliness are high. Many therefore admitted cheating a bit. "I hate cleaning", as one of them said, "but I like the house to be tidy. So I always tidy up. Then at least it looks clean."

The German or 'Continental' atmosphere inside the rooms was striking. This was due not least to the fact that many are furnished with the furniture quite a number of refugees were able to bring out of Germany. More than that: the arrangement of the furniture was equally un-English. In most cases fireplaces were blocked up and hidden behind bookshelves. They were considered 'impractical' or 'too dirty'; central heating was the rule. Certainly the fireplace was not a focal point as it tends to be in English houses. Seating was arranged in the German fashion either in a corner of the room (*Sitzecke*) or around the coffee table with the sofa normally pushed directly against the wall. Even the china was often German; either it had been rescued from Germany or bought more recently. The many plants found in most houses contributed further to the Continental character. Of course, houseplants are also a common feature in English households and have become more so in recent years. Yet here they tend to be dotted around the room. Whereas in German–Jewish houses they are massed together in great abundance, often spilling over onto landings, when respondents lived in apartment blocks. Some complained about the lack of wide windowsills in English houses, commonly found in German houses or flats, and offering such a convenient place for plenty of pot plants.

Even the way people dress is significant in this context. My relevant notes abound with remarks such as *sehr korrekt, sehr gepflegt gekleidet*, i.e. well dressed with a slight air of formality. To wear well-made, high quality clothes is still considered important.[3]

Last but not least it is in eating habits where the German element has perhaps remained most conspicuous. It was mentioned above that even in those cases in which efforts had been made to cut all spiritual links with Germany or Austria, the preference for certain foods was ineradicable. In fact, none among the older respondents had totally given up their German eating habits or at least their preference for them. This was also true of cases where male respondents were married to English partners. They often pointed out that they regretted not being able to eat German food at home and admitted to enjoy it when they visit Germany. They also asked their wives to cook them their favourite dishes from time to time. Some had bought their wives German cookery books.

As far as the majority is concerned, 46 out of 55 of older

respondents had not changed their eating habits at all. This refers to eating a hot meal in the middle of the day and a cold meal in the evening, as is indicated in a little advert in the *AJR Information*: 'Mittagstisch-Pensionär, älterer kultivierter Herr gesucht. Kontinentale Küche'.[4] If it proved impractical to have a hot meal at midday during the week, respondents tended to revert to this pattern at weekends. The timing of the meal is also of significance. Only few have introduced the 5 o'clock tea. Most still ahered to the German habit of having coffee or tea with cake or biscuit at four and supper at seven.

The food itself is, of course, of crucial importance. Respondents still remembered how difficult it was during the early years of emigration to find shops in Britain, even in London, where one could buy Continental food. Fortunately, things have changed in the meantime in this respect. The cooking and seasoning of the food ("a good cook seasons in the kitchen and not at the table"), the regional variations – all this is still clearly German or Austrian. Even the way the fork is held, spoon-fashion, is German and has only rarely changed.

This is not to say that some adjustments to English eating habits have not been made. Eight respondents of the older generation have introduced more English elements, at least temporarily. Thus some found it convenient to prepare a cooked tea for their children as long as they were small. A few got used to an English breakfast. "It took us a long time to learn it", Mrs Ch. remembered, "but we gave it up again. It was too much and too fattening." The C.'s have adopted "what tastes nice" in English cooking, clearly cherishing freedom of choice as one of the advantages of being transplanted into a different cultural environment.

Evidently, the older generation of refugees has hardly been affected by Anglicization in everyday life. One would expect the following generation to have moved further in this direction. As far as language is concerned, this is certainly true. Out of these 67 interviews 56 were conducted in English. Even if some of them may still have had an accent, English clearly was their primary language, even if it cannot be called mother tongue. Only in three households German was the dominant language. But it has not been completely discarded. Only 2 out of 67 respondents had 'unlearned' it. 50 said they were fluent, another seven felt it was 'fairly good' and the rest found it had become rather faulty. Yet German continued to play an important role in certain spheres of life. A few still consider it their "cultural language", whether they use it as dominant language or not. For quite a number it still is – literally – their mother tongue, that is the language they speak with their mothers or with older members or friends of the family. The German terms for mother or grandmother such as *Mutti* or *Omi* have generally been retained. Thus German has partly taken on the character of a special code, conveying intimacy and secrecy. Jokes and certain remarks for which no immediate English pendant exists, are also often expressed in German. One of the most popular uses of German within the family has been that of a secret code when the spouses did not want their children to listen into their conversation – with the ironic result, as we shall see in a moment, that this was exactly how the young ones often picked up their German.

The other main area in which German has proved to be of considerable importance is that of work. In the majority of cases this was not due so much to a conscious choice of German but rather to its being a useful by-product of one's background. Even so, considerable reluctance had sometimes to be overcome to exploit this "natural" advantage. Interestingly enough, with the exception of one respondent in this generation, a professional writer, none of the others had chosen German literature or history as an academic career,[5] although some of the women ended up teaching German against their original intention. English was more commonly chosen as a subject and this in spite of sometimes considerable pressure from well-meaning teachers to study German. "But at that time (in the mid-40s), I felt I just could not bear it. I ruined my career because of it", Mrs L. remarked. Now she finds she uses German a lot, "but only because it makes my work easier. I have to go to the Continent fairly often. And the people with whom I work speak better German than English. I had very strong objections at the beginning but found that I made much more progress by speaking German. I do feel ambivalent, but I am very keen on my work and if I can further my work I am quite happy to speak German. Some of my friends absolutely refuse to speak German which I find rather pointless". Mrs V.'s ambivalence is widely shared by members of her generation, as we have seen, and reflects the fundamental rejection of or aversion against the "German experience". Yet in this context it is interesting to see how cultural elements re-assert themselves, even against the will in pursuing *another* 'Continental' value: the absolute prerogative of achievement. It is because of this that the aversion is overcome. This was even more true in the case of some respondents who taught German. Despite their strong aversion against Germany, they were forced to read German newspapers and modern literature. Involuntarily, they became interested and now have a more positive attitude towards German culture, if not German society as such.

It has been mentioned that the great majority is fluent in German. However, several respondents qualified this statement by adding that their proficiency did not reach beyond the level of "social German" as spoken within the family or with friends. In this generation, respondents were even more aware than the older refugees of lacking a more sophisticated or specialized knowledge with sometimes curious results. On a recent trip to Germany, Mrs X., who works in antiques, went to a specialist to buy some material which she had been unable to find in Britain. But when she tried to explain what she was looking for, she found she was unable to talk about these technical matters in German. She thought the situation was rather embarrassing. Finally, she decided to tell the shop owner that she was not German. "But he would not believe me, because otherwise my German is absolutely fluent, without a trace of a foreign accent. So I got my German friend to help me. In the meantime, I have bought a German book on the subject and have learned the technical terms by now." Mrs I. had a much more unpleasant, or in her words "odd experience". When she once gave a lecture at a German university, she noticed that some students had apparently started to laugh about her accent and some mistakes she may have made, since she was not used to talking about her subject in German. She silenced them by explaining briefly why this was so; that, in fact, she had returned to the city which had previously been the home of her family, several members of which had once been well-known representatives of its academic community. The effect on the students was not lost.

About half of the respondents in the second generation expressed an interest in German culture and said they read German literature from time to time. Again attitudes vary from "in a detached way" to a deeply felt "attachment to" and "love for" German poetry and culture in general. Some would like to read more German but find the written language "too difficult". Thus they reluctantly read German novels in English translations which "is ridiculous". Or it is the growing estrangement from the German experience which made them give up: "I don't read much German anymore. I used to. When I was very unhappy, I tried to read a German book. It gave me some kind of feeling . . . it was, after all, my mother tongue. But I don't find the feeling anymore. It is not as much pleasure as it used to be. It is something I have grown out of in a way." Yet, others found they have taken renewed interest in German literature more recently, following a more general change in perception and self-perception.

If we now look at cultural traits less overtly 'German' in character among the second generation, we discover again a pattern not unlike that predominant among the older generation. Yet some significant divergencies could also be observed. The atmosphere in the houses was less clearly German, probably due to the fact that, some inherited pieces apart, the furniture in most cases did not originate from Germany. On the other hand, the furniture tended to be modern and international, rather than English antique and its arrangement was similarly 'un-English'. Again, in many cases the fireplace was not a focal point. The predilection for houseplants had evidently been transmitted to most respondents of the younger generation. The German element has again been most persistent in eating habits, although there were some significant changes. Some 28 out of 47 still cook completely German-style as regards food, its preparation and mealtimes. Another 17 cook partly German, such as *"aufschnitty* things", the universal dark bread or "what the children like". Yet the other part of their cooking has not been taken up by English cuisine. Only one respondent has adopted it completely and she is married to an Englishman. Male respondents in this generation married to English women also often ask their wives to cook them a German meal; red cabbage seemed particularly popular. Mrs G. "hates" English cooking: she is married to a Briton and so is Mrs J. who has not adopted English cooking either: "We have switched from tea to alcohol." Seven respondents have introduced some elements of English cooking: "The best of both worlds", or some had 'tea' when their children were small or when English friends of their children were visiting. However, 16 respondents have adopted international cuisine, Italian and French in general. This trend is, of course, universal, as is the preference for 'healthy', non-fattening food, also common among respondents. It is interesting, none the less, that the respondents had 'skipped' English cuisine, more or less, and had supplemented their German cooking by other European or international cuisines, not unlike the pattern of furnishing their homes. Despite these changes, the German element has persisted to a considerable degree and it seems clear that eating habits belong to the most deeply ingrained cultural traits that survived all personal and political upheavals.[6]

A more systematic analysis than is possible here would certainly reveal a number of other interesting continuities and discontinuities in the process of cultural behaviour patterns and ethnic identity. Only some of the most salient features have been outlined. Moreover, these have so far been contrasted with English society. Yet it is also, perhaps even more so, *vis-à-vis* the Anglo-Jewish community that German Jews have become aware of their ethnic peculiarities.

ENCOUNTERS WITH ANGLO-JEWRY

Practically none among older respondents and only two among the second generation expressed a sense of belonging to the English–Jewish community. If anything, the link with the non-Jewish English world was felt to be stronger than with the Anglo-Jewish community as a whole. To be sure, leading members of the refugee community did establish some links with Anglo-Jewry on the institutional level. But within the institutions, the two groups tended to keep apart.[7] Even where individuals mix, as in Synagogues for instance, closer contact often did follow but to a much lesser extent than one might have expected. Thus there were only 14 among the respondents of the older generation who had any contact with Anglo-Jews and not more than 3 counted them among their wider circle of friends; only one respondent counted them among her closest friends. With the second generation the picture changes slightly. Here 19 respondents have some contact with Anglo-Jews. Eight of these considered them to be friends, in 3 cases even close friends. We have seen that some 'intermarriage' had taken place in this generation.[8] Nevertheless, the rate of mixing at all levels is well below that of mixing with the non-Jewish English. Even many of those respondents who do mix with English Jews found them "strange" or "different" in some ways, notwithstanding the 'Jewish' warmth in human relationships which so many German Jews miss among the English non-Jews and which quite a number of respondents gave the English Jews credit for. But as it turned out, the perceived differences overrode the similarities.

As the reason most commonly given for the lack of contact between both groups was: "They are completely different, they have a completely different culture"; "we have nothing in common"; "they have a different mentality". When asked in what this difference consisted, among the most common replies were: "German Jews have been more advanced in Western education", "German Jews are more cultured", "better educated – not that we are arrogant", "the English Jews are too materialistic", "they have a different upbringing", "are very conservative", "too loud", and, finally, "too ostentatious".

This sense of separateness was partly based on suspected or experienced hostility on the part of the English Jews. It was the old German-*Ostjuden* conflict which emerged again in the remarks of the respondents. Thus Mrs H. "was very unhappy" when she had to work as a domestic help for an Anglo-Jewish family. "The woman went on and on about how badly Polish Jews had been treated by German Jews." Since Mrs H. was still young, she did not know what it was all about. "I did not know what to say, so I cried." Other respondents likewise talked about encounters with Anglo-Jews which made it clear to them that "they resented our coming"; "we are even worse than the Goyim for them".

This last remark also refers to a further cause of friction, the so-called 'assimilationism' of the German Jew. "They (the English Jews) seem to think it served the German Jews right (to be persecuted by the Nazis), if they behaved like that" (becoming 'assimilated'). These inner Jewish conflicts were sometimes carried over into family relationships where 'intermarriage' had taken place. In-laws from either camp were not always received with open arms by the other side. However, it should be stressed that there were a number of other cases in which contact was described as "very good" from the beginning or having considerably improved after the families had recovered from the initial "shock".

Likewise respondents with more frequent contact with English Jews tended, on the whole, to take a more differentiated and positive view. Thus Mrs I. found them 'most helpful, kind, more imaginative than German Jews". A few respondents were not at all aware of any differences. But more respondents found them "different in some ways, but not all. The common cultural interests are decisive. We have made some very good friends through our work and our Synagogue". So did Mrs A., although she found that "Anglo-Jews do not understand German Jews, because they do not know the Germans". Naturally, the closer or the more prolonged the contact, the more difficult it was for respondents to generalize. Nevertheless, they too, were aware of some differences which, on the whole, confirmed those mentioned by respondents with less contact. Thus what sounds rather prejudiced and "arrogant" may merely indicate an ethnic distinction, subconsciously felt.

There were basically three areas where these differences were most pronounced. One concerned the occupational patterns: German Jews, it was said, gravitated towards professional and academic fields more than do English Jews. This point was particularly stressed by orthodox respondents. "Whereas our boys naturally go on to university after Yeshiva, the Anglo-Jewish boys go into business. They are not very interested in an academic education", it was said. From this derives the second distinction which concerns 'culture'. There was large-scale agreement among respondents that English Jews, generally speaking, are not so keenly interested in intellectual matters: "You never see them at lectures"; nor do they seem to share the German Jews' devotion to the arts and 'culture' generally: "There are no books in their houses; they have loudly-coloured carpets and dining rooms which are not used."

The difference between the two groups became most conspicuous in the sphere of religion. Complaints about German Jews for being "too assimilated", "being more German than Jewish" which respondents had encountered and which were indirectly reflected in German–Jewish criticism of English Jews for living "in a ghetto", being "too Jewish", "too religious" – all have their roots here. But as it turned out, it was not a question of one group being "more religious" or "more orthodox" than the other: it is barely tenable to argue that the English Jews are 'less assimilated' than the German Jews. Similarly, we have seen above that many liberal German Jews take their religion quite seriously and orthodox German Jews are generally described as being radically orthodox, indeed. The differences perceived, in fact, referred to the position of religion within everyday life, its relationship with other spheres of life on the one hand and to a difference in approach to Judaism on the other.

The German Jews "do not fuss about religion in the way the English Jews do"; "they don't get so obsessed with Kashrut", were some of the comments made by respondents. Judaism or Jewishness do not play the same overriding role in the life of German Jews as they appear to do in the life of Anglo-Jews; these aspects are important, but more integrated into other spheres of life. This applies even to orthodox German Jews who may be "fussing" about religion, but who, in general, also consider 'culture' and intellectual education as very important. "The Hassidim are even more orthodox than we are", Mrs E., a member of an extremely orthodox German-Jewish congregation, said, "but they are terribly blinkered, they have no secular education. We do things with more knowledge. We hold more precisely to the letter and are therefore much stricter than the average orthodox English Jews. They get slack because they don't know what they are doing or why they are doing it." Other respondents likewise found English Jews "orthodox in a strangely narrow-minded way" or "too mechanical" in their observation of Jewish rituals which, in fact, impelled some of them to leave their original Synagogue and join one which had a stronger "German" character; a more congenial environment was sought by some respondents for yet another reason: "It is much nicer in our Synagogue, much quieter. The English Jews are so noisy and restless." Clearly, the traditions within Eastern and German Judaism are quite different. And these cultural distinctions in turn reflect a genuine and substantial ethnic differentiation between German and English Jews. In view of this it has to be considered an open question, whether these two groups are ever likely to merge completely. Convergence will doubtless occur, indeed it already does, but whether the core will fundamentally be affected, is less certain. It therefore seems possible that a 'Continental' type of Judaism will survive in Britain.

THE THIRD GENERATION

Some indications as to what form this 'Continental' type might take can be gleaned from interviews with third generation respondents, i.e. those who were born in Britain after the war. Without doubt, the ethnic elements have become even more diffuse in this generation. The issue of ethnicity and ethnic identity is thus highly complex. An in-depth analysis would have to take the English environment into account to a much larger extent than seemed necessary in the case of previous generations. Some fusion of certain English and 'Continental' elements is doubtless taking place. The whole question would merit a full-scale study. In the absence of such an analysis, it seemed nevertheless desirable to present some of the impressions gained from the formal interviews and informal conversations with young 'English Jews of German extraction' and from the information given by second generation respondents about their children. These observations may suggest the direction in which an in-depth analysis might proceed.

When comparing parents' ideas about their children's attitudes towards the German background with the statements which either these children themselves or other respondents of their age group made, a striking discrepancy became apparent: the majority of the parents maintained that their children were not interested in their background, they had become "completely English", they did not want to speak German; such were the comments most frequently heard. Quite a few furthermore felt that their children were ashamed of their 'foreign' parents and especially of their parents' accent. This feeling is apparently widely shared by refugees in general. As was pointed out in the *AJR Information* in 1972, 'parents whose children were born or grew up in this country are often heard to complain that in their case the generation gap is more obvious than elsewhere; that the new generation refuses to listen to their personal histories or is highly critical of their past behaviour, that the young often refuse to speak German or to admit that they understand it, thus obviously widening the gap even more'.[9]

Yet it emerged, when talking to the young people, that these statements were, on the whole, not confirmed by them. Only in one respect did the children's view correspond with that of their parents, and this made clear how the discrepancy occurred in the first place: the majority said not to have discussed the German experience within the family. From this the parents obviously deduced, wrongly as it turned out, that their children did not want to know about it. In many cases this may well have been so. But the discrepancy observed here suggests that indifference or even rejection of their heritage is probably less widespread than parents generally assumed.

More than that: often it was the parents who were reluctant to talk about the past. At least one respondent was quite upset that his daughter studied German history and had gone to visit a former concentration camp in Germany. "Can you explain to me why my daughter wants to know all about it?" he asked in dismay; "I want to forget about it, I want to get away from it as far as possible and now she stirs it all up again." As in this case, there were quite a number of children who were interested in Germany and went across more or less against their parents' wishes. "She wanted to go", said a mother, "but she had to find herself a family, which she did." Some parents feared their child might be exposed to antisemitism (none of them actually did experience it), they might end up with a German boy friend, or girl friend (which did happen) or, if on an exchange, might have to bring home a German boy or girl to stay with the family which was more than some parents thought they could cope with. Mrs C. told her daughter: " 'You can do it [go on an exchange to Germany], but I am not very keen.'" I felt I wouldn't be as sympathetic to a German child as to a French. Therefore I did not want to be put into such a situation, because it is wrong to treat a child like that. Any human being deserves the best you've got to give and if you know you are not going to give your best, you better don't do it in the first place."

The children who went had, on the whole, pleasant encounters with the Germans they met. Kate was "delighted with the contact; I don't always think of the past when I am in their presence. They were educated and fine people". Others, too, made many friends, often close ones. They find Germany "interesting", they "like the standard of living" and "the quality of things". A few even felt "at home" because of a certain familiarity with the food or the language. Anna feels "physically at home in Germany in a way that I don't in England. I find so many people of my shape there. I always buy German clothes when I am there; they fit better and I like the quality".

Andrew sympathized "deeply with the feeling of guilt of many young Germans, that the guilt of the fathers should be inherited upon the children". So did most of the others, especially those who had met young Germans in Israel working in Kibbuzim. "I admire their attitude. A lot of them felt they had paid enough for what has happened in the past. One has to continue with life and has to be positive. They certainly have done their best and, in a little way, tried to make up for what their parents have done in the past." This attitude, shared by all respondents, was summed up by Peter: "Anyone born of my generation has as little guilt for what was done during the Second World War as I have." Of course, most of their parents and grandparents would agree with this – theoretically. On an emotional level however, they find it more difficult to agree. Their children, on the other hand, have not suffered personally; their experiences with Germans differ from those of the older generations. This makes them more open, when they meet Germans, especially members of the younger generation. "I can't bring myself to hate Germans", as Jim put it. This is not to say that German society as such is viewed uncritically. Tony "could live in

Germany, but I find life rather too petty-bourgeois. It is very liberal on the surface but not deep down; I feel it is liberal as long as things work well". It also became apparent that the older the respondents of the third generation, the more similar were their feelings to those which we encountered in interviews with the older refugees: "There is no fondness for Germany in me. When I went I was very conscious that it is the place where it all happened, that Germany is left with the responsibility for a problem which has not yet been solved morally." Another respondent believed that the Germans are "xenophic and brutal". Also some of the suspicion of the older generation of Germans and of the general unease when being in Germany had been transmitted to the younger respondents. This is why Cathy "liked it very much in Germany, but I like Switzerland best. Maybe because it is *like* Germany, but not Germany proper".

However, these attitudes reflect those of a minority. As a whole, this generation sharply distinguished between modern and Nazi Germany. "Of course, you inherit a bit of the resentment", one respondent explained, "but it does not make you feel anti-modern Germany, only strongly anti-Nazi like most people." Some therefore view their parents' inability to distinguish in this way quite critically. Claire thought her mother "really hysterical when we had to drive through Germany. It was only a short bit. And she buys nothing from Germany. I think this really is exaggerated. West Germany, after all, is different from Nazi Germany."

The majority of the third generation respondents enjoy travelling through Germany or living there temporarily, and the younger the more so, unperturbed by the ghosts of the past. At the same time it did not take long to realize that they appreciate Germany as a tourist country, with lots of "nice people" and "pleasant things" to enjoy. The relationship, despite some close friendships with individual Germans, does not go deeper than that; there is no close or special bond. Most of them feel "no particular affinity"; "Germany is a foreign country whose language I happen to know". That it is the home of their parents has not much meaning for them. Richard, for instance, has always been very interested in Germany and thoroughly enjoyed his stay there. But "I would not have gone there to find out about my father's family. I never thought about that. I just like Germany." Others did go because they wanted to see the place where their parents were born or their grandparents had lived. "It is a nice town", Dorothy remembered, "I was aware that my grandparents went for walks in that area. But it did not relate to me." Clearly, Germany has definitely lost its significance as a 'homeland' in the sense minorities tend to see their countries of origin, however mythical this relationship may have become.

However, the detachment from Germany has also led to an emotional detachment from German *history* and from that of Nazi Germany in particular which the parents sometimes find difficult to accept. Nearly all the young respondents considered the events in Nazi Germany as a "thing of the past", "as distant history which does not mean much", as the result of "special circumstances". But if the 1930s are so remote for the young, how can they possibly grasp what these years meant for their parents? In fact, most have difficulties identifying their parents and grandparents with that period of history, "with those people who had to go through it all. It feels, as if it happened to some other people". And this all the more so since the parents were often reticent about their personal experiences. Had Richard's father been more open and explicit, his son might not have developed an interest in Nazi militaria, unwelcome for his father, and greeted him one day with *Heil Hitler* – just for fun!

It was mainly through history books, films and television documentaries that third generation respondents had obtained their information about the Nazi period. Although this probably contributed to its remaining rather abstract, most of them nevertheless came to realize that, somehow, they were more personally affected by the events of the 1930s than other young people. For a few this discovery came as a shock, as in the case of Jane, one of the older respondents in this group, who remembered that her interest grew slowly, as part of her interest in modern history in general. "It never occurred to me that being Jewish and having a German father had anything to do with the gaping hole in the (British) landscape due to bomb damage. I started reading about it. I found it difficult to think that 6 million Jews were 6 million personalities. I suddenly realized these could have been, they were my relatives. It was very distressing. My father never talked about it. I only heard about his family's experiences after his death when people came to sit shiva."

However, most respondents felt their personal involvement less sharply; or rather, they tended to objectify it much more readily than older refugees. They set the Nazi period into the general context of world history. None of them, even those who visit Germany with some misgivings, considered the persecution of the Jews in Germany as a specifically German crime. Parents often have difficulties understanding such an attitude which they are prone to misinterpret as lack of feeling on the part of their children. As a result tensions may well arise within the family. Claire's case is a good illustration in this respect. The "German hang-up" of her parents appeared to be the cause of frictions in her family, simply because she refused to share her parents' very hostile feelings towards Germany. "Because of that, my parents and other people assume I haven't got any [feelings]. That really hurts me." She gave an example: "There was a programme on terrorism on TV recently. The killing of Schleyer was mentioned. My mother said she was glad that Schleyer was killed, because he was a Nazi. I did not agree, for me it was a question of morality. But mother only said: 'You are too young, you don't understand it', which annoyed me immensely." Claire thought that her attitude towards Schleyer, the Nazi, was characteristic for her more neutral attitude towards the whole complex of the holocaust and Nazism. "Of course, it is terrible what happened, but it does not directly affect me, even though my grandparents died in the camps. But I have never known them personally, therefore they do not mean so much to me. The holocaust is just as terrible for me as other events of that kind like the Inquisition. If I were to get upset about everybody who suffers, I would go crazy." She fully agrees with her German pen-friend who thinks that one should get rid of guilt feelings and leave the Nazi period to history. One should not forget what has happened, as Claire stressed, but one should get over it.

Quite a number of the young respondents showed a perhaps amazing degree of understanding for the people in Germany in the 1930s, even for the Nazis. "After all, Hitler promised them such a lot and so convincingly", was Claire's comment. Nevertheless, one was left with the impression that this was primarily a reaction against the parents' whole-scale condemnation rather than anything else. It seemed to have been an effort to restore the balance, not an objective judgment.

But the complexities do not end there. Third generation detachment and most parents' reticence notwithstanding, all of them "always knew about the German background" of their family and most were aware of being culturally influenced by it. Many 'feel a little odd towards Germany'. They do not know how they found out about their German connection, but they cannot "remember a time when we were not conscious of it". "When we were younger, there was the thing of not telling people that our parents are from

Germany, because it was much nearer to the war then. I remember it was a *big secret* when I once told it a friend when we were on holiday. . . . Now it does not matter anymore."

Most of those who have or had grandparents living in Britain considered them – and in particular the grand*mother*[10] – the link with the German background. Not that the grandmothers always accepted the role of transmitting their culture down to the younger generation. We have seen above that some of the older respondents resented being considered the 'German granny'. This attitude was confirmed by some of the third generation respondents who said that their grandmothers never spoke German with them, only with their mothers or older friends. Or it happens that the young mothers of today, realizing the advantage of being able to speak foreign languages and not being fluent in German themselves, would like their mothers to teach their children. But not all grandmothers are happy about this and therefore refuse to do it.

Yet there were many other cases where the grandmothers were less averse to their role of keeping some of the German cultural elements in the family alive. It mainly consisted of speaking German to the little ones and teaching them German nursery rhymes. A number of parents have also been doing this, but it seems to have been primarily the grandmothers who assumed the role as cultural mediators.

If there were no direct influences of this kind, there were enough indirect clues to make the child aware of the German link, whether it was the language spoken among the grown-ups, food, the 'German' friends of the parents; reminiscences about the 'olden days', and last but not least it was 'the family name which frequently needed explanation'.

Language and food were commonly mentioned by respondents as the most conspicuous forms of whatever specific German elements there might still exist. As to the latter, the situation was the same as found in their parents' generation: German cooking was generally preferred to English cuisine, but the trend to international and 'healthy' cuisine was also strong.

The "language link" is more complicated. Practically all respondents stated that they know some German, of having "a smattering", at least of understanding it. Hardly any of them claimed to be fluent, though. Out of 25 of those interviewed 14 had taken up German in school and more would have liked to, but having chosen science they were unable to because of the highly specialized English education system. The reasons given for choosing German and giving it preference over French were familiarity with the language, resentment at not being able fully to understand when the parents talked; or it was just its "usefulness as a language". A number of them now regret not having made greater effort to learn German properly as children. For example, they wish they had not answered in English even in those cases where the parents spoke German to them.

Yet, having parents or grandparents who are native German speakers is not altogether an advantage. Some were glad that their mothers were able to help with homework when they needed it and that they had to chance to practice their German in the family. On the other hand, being fluent themselves, parents sometimes lost patience too quickly (as some of the parents admitted themselves); Jean remembers that "Oma laughs when I speak German because of my accent and the many mistakes I make". Not surprisingly, she does not speak German with "Oma" anymore. Self-consciousness in the face of the parents' fluency clearly had an inhibiting effect on a number of younger respondents. Nevertheless, whatever the level of proficiency, the important fact remains that "German is somewhere in the back of my mind", as Tony put it, who had learned German "very much by feeling. But when I went to Germany, I was amazed how much I understood".

Undoubtedly, interest in the German language is considerable and not only among the young respondents of this study; parents' information on children who were not interviewed, confirmed this impression. This interest does not reflect a deep commitment to German culture, such as one may find among other minorities. But given their parents' ambivalent feelings in this respect, the degree of interest shown by third generation respondents seems quite remarkable. It may even be possible to say that the children are more positive in a way than their parents, as is apparent in the children's assessment of their German cultural background.

Having grown up under completely different political circumstances, there is none of the parents' shame or embarrassment about this part of their heritage. Quite a number of respondents express an interest in the history of the family. True, there are also others such as Liz who finds that her grandmother talks "too much about the past, about life in Germany. It is interesting, but it has no meaning. She shows us her photos and pictures of the past, travel brochures etc. She wants to give them to the family, but we don't want them. I don't want to be burdened with her memories. I have no room for clutter". Yet this attitude does not reflect that of the majority among the respondents.

A remarkable case is that of Peter whose interest in the history of his family was triggered off when he first went to Germany to visit the part where a large part of his family had come from. He visited the houses and the cemeteries and decided to establish the family tree. He has worked at it ever since and has been able to trace the family back for 20 generations to the 15th century. He had found out, among other interesting facts, that one branch of the family had lived in the same house from 1704 to 1933. He even has some valuable historical documents in his possession. His excitement over and enthusiasm for his discoveries was quite infectious and it was easy to feel what it means to him to see himself and his family so firmly rooted in history. He added: "Since I have so few family, I have created a family for myself.'

If Peter's intensive preoccupation with his Continental background may be exceptional, his positive identification with it was basically shared by all respondents. Bob even feels a strange sense of pride for his German background. "I like it when people sit up and say: 'Gosh, really.' It certainly is nothing to feel ashamed about. Germany has a better image today", he explained. Lesley similarly "liked the idea of being of German extraction. It was something different. At school we had to say where parents came from. All the others came from our area. I felt very proud to say: 'From Berlin'. I liked the idea of being different, it was exciting." And finally there is Sarah: "I am quite happy with my German–Jewish background. I do not think I ever resented it. In fact, I was always more impressed with my parents and their friends than with the parents of my Anglo-Jewish friends."

The closeness of their family life was stressed throughout by respondents who often spoke with "admiration", "respect", or "trust" of their parents, even though identification was often stronger with one parent than with the other. Of course, tensions were also mentioned which, in some families, seem to be quite disruptive. The children often explained them by the psychological problems of one or the other parent, caused by the 'German hangup' for which they showed considerable understanding. There was not a single case (among the respondents) where the 'foreignness' of the parents or the family as such was said to have given rise to conflicts or any feelings of alienation on the part of the children from their parents. It certainly contributed to their rootlessness in Britain, of which they are keenly aware, as we shall see in a moment. Yet it has not affected their family life.

This is also true as regards the foreign accent which so worries many of the older refugees. There was only one young respondent who admitted to have been "slightly embarrassed by his grandmother's strange accent" or when she spoke German in front of his friends. None of the others, however, were bothered by it. Most of them, in fact, had never noticed that their parents had any accent at all. It was only "a few years ago that we noticed it". But it did not make any difference whatsoever. Their parents are "perfectly normal", as far as they are concerned. And this matter-of-factness is characteristic of their attitude towards their 'Germanness' in general; as one mother put it: "My children accept their German background. They are neither proud, nor ashamed of it."

If any criticism of their parents was expressed, it was from this position: some wished their parents would feel the same way as they did where the parents had "blotted out" the German experience or become "tearful" whenever talking about Germany. Their children understood perfectly well why their parents reacted like this but some seemed genuinely worried or puzzled that their parents had not yet come to terms with the events of the past. Robert, in fact, regarded his mother's refusal to speak German, her hostility towards Germany in general as a "weakness. She should have more openly accepted her German background. I have great admiration for my father. He was different. He always asserted himself".

Nevertheless, the fact remains that although perceptions of the German background tend to be fairly positive, lacking the parents' ambivalence, its significance as a cultural factor as such is marginal. It is only when it merges with the Jewish element that it continues to be important. As with the older generations, it reinforces the 'Continentalness' of these young English Jews. Most of them were well aware of this themselves.

The question of ethnic identity turned out to be no less complicated among third generation respondents than in the case of their parents. The children may be more secure psychologically, not having suffered the trauma of emigration and persecution. Yet the lack of roots in Britain, which many of them confessed to, was somewhat unexpected. "I regard England as my home, although if I could transplant every member of my family as well as my friends,

I do not think I would mind leaving." This feeling was echoed by most other respondents: "We feel we are here by accident", "I am not sure where I am going to live later on. England might be a possibility", or "out of choice I would still live here, but I could move without too many problems to another country." Germany was never mentioned as a possibility; the United States and Israel were the most popular countries.

The reason generally given for this sense of rootlessness was that "we are different from the English". Or as Andrew put it: "I play the Englishman sometimes, but I don't feel English. Like my father, I feel in a sense that it is my home, and that this is probably where I am going to live, but I do not feel English. I have got a hell of a lot of Englishness in me but I am not English." Or another respondent: "I am not completely English or German. When I am in Germany it gives me great pleasure to pose as an American . . . I think it is a strength being a *Mischling*, a composite of Anglo-Saxon and Teutonic cultures. I can see how the English or the Germans are. But it also has a disadvantage because one does not feel really at home anywhere."

In fact, only two respondents felt "completely English". 'Britishness', on the other hand, was hardly ever mentioned. The differences, where they were perceived, were defined in ways similar to those of the older respondents: "My European upbringing", "cultural barriers", or "difference in mentality". The Jewish factor was regarded as equally important. Thus it was stated: "I am English because I was born in England, but I feel very Jewish as well", "I am English with a Jewish component." The majority felt "positively" or "strongly Jewish". Here, at last, was something like an anchor: "I feel neither German nor completely English. The only thing I definitely know is that I am Jewish".

It was not necessarily hostility to Jews which had given rise to this awareness. Apart from one respondent who has been beaten up a couple of times by gangs of English youths (his scull cap made him clearly recognizable as Jewish), encounters with antisemitism were considered negligible. They were usually restricted to "silly jokes and remarks", "odd remarks" by English non-Jews who "regard me as slightly exotic", "as quite an oddity. They asked funny questions. They expected us to be kosher"; "they lack *Selbstverständlichkeit* when being together with me".

It was primarily on the level of group perceptions that this 'foreignness' is of significance. It does not preclude a high rate of mixing between the groups on an individual level and the establishment of very close friendship ties between English Jews and non-Jews. It is again the 'simultaneousness of closeness and distance' (E. Reichmann) which had also characterized the relationship between Jews and non-Jews in Germany as in most other western societies.

And the same which was true of the Jews in Germany applies in Britain: Englishness and Jewishness were seen by most of the young respondents not as a contradiction, "as people in Israel tried to tell me", Jim remembered. "I am a British Jew or a Jewish English person", Rachel explained similarly. "But there is a duality. Non-Jewish English are more English because they don't have that extra quality. It is something in addition rather than instead of." Nevertheless, it is probably true to say that the Jews in Germany were more deeply rooted in that country than their descendants are in England.

The "extra quality", though called "Jewish", was hardly ever defined in religious terms. "I feel Jewish", said Dorothy, "but it is funny, it is more in a cultural than in a religious sense." If religion as such, in its form of ritual practices, gives rise to controversy, it is between observant and non-observant Jews rather than between Jews and non-Jews. The latter were found by orthodox respondents to be considerably more tolerant of Jewish orthodoxy than non-observant Jews. We thus find the paradoxical situation that Jewishness continues to be generally defined in religious terms and so are the boundaries between Jews and non-Jews. Yet the rifts caused by Judaism and its observance are often much deeper among the Jews themselves than between Jews and non-Jews. This explains the contradiction in the attempts of the young respondents to define what they understood by 'Jewishness'. They tended to stress the importance of religious practices, before they continued: "Being Jewish is being slightly different, sticking together, the slight community feeling you get when you meet another Jew, although it is not always people with the same background we are friendliest with." Most young respondents mentioned the Continental character of their Jewishness more specifically. "I think the difference is a continental–cultural Jewishness and the German–Jewish thing combines those two factors." Yet, trying to explain how these various elements do combine, proved to be quite complicated, as illustrated by the following case. Dorothy and her sister "feel different because of being Jewish, not because of being German. But we are surprised when we meet English Jews, because we think they all come from abroad. Yes, you do distinguish. It means those who have grandparents or parents from abroad. It is amazing how few of our friends have English-born grandparents." Dorothy: "I think, I feel English, just by relation. But I don't know which comes first; the Jewish or the English. It depends who I am with. When I am with English people I feel Jewish, when I am with Jewish people, I feel English." "That is a bit contradictory', her sister interrupted; "I think you feel English, but you are always aware you are Jewish. You never will not be aware of the difference. And I don't know how much that slight difference exists, because it is Jewish or because having continental parents . . . I think it is a bit different, the fact that it's German-Jewish, of not having English grandparents. Although you are not really aware of it . . . I don't know whether the feeling of being Jewish is the fact that you are feeling German-Jewish or just feeling Jewish. It is a bit difficult . . . . one is conscious of not having an English background when you are looking up your family tree and people mention it. I think of things quite objectively as being English, or very British to do something like having tea in the afternoon or certain things, certain foods, cooking . . . there is probably more in our house that is Continental than in houses that are English . . . but we also say: 'We, the English.' It depends on what you are talking about. When it is 'your' country against another country . . . . Even talking about the war, it was 'us' against the Germans. Even for Mum and Dad it is the same."

This Continentalness or Europeanness asserts itself *vis-à-vis* 'English' Jewishness just as strongly as it does *vis-à-vis* non-Jewish Englishness, and in much the same way as it did among the older German Jewish respondents. It is again the approach to Judaism where the differences are most sharply felt. Two cases may serve as illustrations. The first is that of Rachel, with a Liberal–Reform background who married into a family of "extremely orthodox" Anglo-Jews with Hassidic links. She brought up the subject of her marriage when we were discussing the subject of mixed marriages! "In theory I thought it would not matter one way or the other", she began; "in fact, I married into a family of religious maniacs. My in-laws were born and bred in the East End, they never moved or travelled outside. They lived in an exclusively Jewish, devout community, completely closed. My father was horrified, so was I. It was totally outside my experience. My parents were so different:

cosmopolitan, highly educated and articulate, upper-middle class, with a posh private practice in the poshest part of town; their culture was international. That of my in-laws was small-scale. They made a great fuss when Daniel and I got married because the ceremony was in my (Reform) Synagogue. It put me off for life. I absolutely refuse to keep a kosher household. My mother-in-law therefore would not eat in our house, not even from a paper plate. She rarely comes." Rachel, a trained social scientist, stressed the importance of social class which to her primarily accounts for these differences in attitudes. To some extent this is certainly true, but the ethnic factor seems at least just as important, as is best shown by the second case: Kate, coming from a very orthodox home herself, has also married into an orthodox Anglo-Jewish family but of the same social class. Yet the conflicts she is experiencing in her marriage are basically of the same nature as in Rachel's case.

Kate keeps a strictly kosher household. But she differs from her husband as to how and when to relax the rules. "It makes it a bit difficult to eat out with non-orthodox friends. We eat fish, but not meat. It is difficult because one must not forget, when we are invited, to tell people that we do not eat meat. But I feel there is something private, personal about religion, and I find it embarrassing to make it public. You are also conscious of not wanting people to take too much trouble. I would rather sit down and eat quietly what is put in front of me since I am aware what trouble it is for people. We mix a lot and I do not want to make a fuss and draw attention to myself. I am very conscious about it. My husband is less self-conscious. I don't feel it is going to make any difference to my religion in the long run to eat the odd meal here and there. My husband is more upset if he has to eat meat; he makes a great fuss. I find this difficult to take, because he is much more inconsistent. If he was more consistent with his religion, I would respect him far more for these ideas. I am very conscious that in Anglo-Jewry today most people have a very poor Jewish education and my parents had the attitude to give us the best possible education and when we were older we could choose how we wanted to put it into practice. Anglo-Jews observe a superficial ritual. I would be less observant, if my husband would fall in with it in terms of keeping sabbath and eating kosher, but I still feel that however observant or non-observant, one ought to at least have the background educationally before one rejects it so then at least one knows what one is rejecting; whereas most Anglo-Jews reject without knowing much about it. I am therefore pleased that my children get a very good background, a very good Jewish education at school, plus the fact that they get a very good secular education, because if that suffered, I would not send them to a Jewish school." Her 11-year-old daughter wants to be more observant at the moment and is critical of her mother for having dropped certain practices; "but I don't want to be hypocritical and if I don't feel that certain rituals have any significance to me we talk about it, and discuss it and I rather explain to her why. And if she wants to keep it I respect that. I feel it would be much easier to bring one's children up on a strict 'no' as so many English orthodox people do without introducing this element of doubt or questioning. But I just can't do it. And I am not prepared to do it just for the sake of my children. They have to see both sides of the coin and that certain people have different feelings and approaches to religion". Judging from these statements, a fundamental difference in approach to Judaism, that between a philosophical and a more ritualistic one, continues to persist.

The same applies to the old conflict between German Jews and *Ostjuden*, which is perpetuated on both sides. The young 'Germans' are not always received with open arms by their English–Jewish in-laws; nor are the English–Jewish spouses always welcomed by the German-Jewish relatives. Occasionally, the situation is not without irony. Thus one respondent, who is married to an English–Jewish woman, pointed out that there are considerable tensions between the two sets of parents because her parents are *Ostjuden* in the eyes of his parents who had never hidden their feelings. But he was used to problems of this kind, because, as he pointed out, his father's parents had looked down on his mother and her parents, who, although Austrians, had been considered to be *Ostjuden* by the former. "The irony was that my highly cultured maternal grandparents from metropolitan Vienna looked down on my small-town provincial paternal family. And now we have it in our families. It really is ridiculous"; whereupon his wife remarked: "But you are (also) rather snooty sometimes, I must say."

Despite the survival of old animosities, there are indications that a remarkable rapprochement between the two groups has taken place. It seems significant that of the respondents who were married, six had Anglo–Jewish spouses. As regards friendships, one gains the impression that here, too, considerable 'mixing' takes place. To obtain specific information on this matter turned out to be difficult, because ten respondents were quite often unable to say whether their friends' parents were English or German–Jewish. This ignorance in itself seems to indicate that the line between the two groups has become blurred.

Nevertheless, nearly all third generation respondents clearly distinguished between English– and 'Continental'–Jewish, applying the same criteria as those of the first and second generations. These were quite obviously partly transmitted from the parents, but also based on personal experience. Thus, the relationship between both groups is not unlike that between Jews and non-Jews; it is close and distant at the same time. The German Jews draw the lines between them and these two groups according to the pressures of the situation at hand. On some occasions, the bond with fellow-Jews may have to be given priority; at other times it is class and cultural factors which may determine the constellation. "Our community feeling is more ideology than practice", as a young respondent put it. And indeed the German Jews in Britain have undoubtedly preserved, up to now, a distinct group consciousness, but frequently crossed the boundaries without much difficulty. The fairly high intermarriage rate, it is true, alarms the community (as it always has done), but German Jews who do marry out meet with relatively little open resistance on the part of the community.[11] Yet, this should not be interpreted as a contradictory or inconsistent policy. It would be more correct to see it as a combination of continuity and adaptability which has been a traditional characteristic of German–Jewish group life. A distinct ethnic identity has been preserved, yet the boundaries have been kept open. The group has thus risked losing some of its members, but it has also benefitted by receiving influences and ideas from outside.

Conclusions

This study has been concerned with the problem of assimilation and integration of German–Jewish Refugees from Nazism who came to England in the 1930s. It was a three-generational study which also included younger Jews who were born in this country to refugee-parents. It is for the first time that this group has been examined in any great detail and that the life-experiences and perceptions of German Jews in England have been recorded. The empirical material on which the study has been based and which has been presented in previous chapters may therefore be considered as significant in itself. I have pointed to the implications of this material as I went along, and no attempt is made here to summarize the many facets of these life-experiences yet again. However, the chapters raise a number of fundamental questions relating to the position of ethnic minorities in general and Jews in particular in western plural societies which it is worth picking up at this point because they would appear to merit further research.

The empirical data, derived from some 180 interviews, but also from a wide variety of published material, revealed perceptions and behaviour patterns which were difficult to reconcile with received ideas about German-Jewish assimilation. Most historians of the problem whose writings were evaluated in the second chapter, tend to assume that there exists a straight progression from a state of non-assimilation to one of absorption of the German Jews by the majority culture. But on closer inspection this turns out to be a barely tenable assumption which would seem to be the result of the fact that, although German–Jewish assimilation has become a key-concept in Jewish historiography, it has rarely been rigorously scrutinized. An examination of this concept in the light of recent sociological work showed that the process is much more complex than historians have generally thought. As the analysis which introduced the empirical part suggests, assimilation should not be understood as an 'appropriation', by the ethnic group, of the majority culture at the expense of the indigenous culture. Instead it was argued that a *new* ethnicity develops which integrates various elements of *both* cultures in a unique way; in other words, the emergent ethnic culture is not identical with either.

It was further brought out that in plural societies, where members of the various ethnic groups intermingle in every-day life, *overt* cultural differentiations tend to become de-emphasized. It is important therefore to pay particular attention to *covert* cultural elements such as perceptions, life-styles or value systems. This, it was argued, also applies to Judaism which has traditionally been defined in terms of religion. To be sure, religion has contributed to the shaping of Jewish perceptions, but it is not identical with the latter; for it was found that no qualitative differences existed between religious and non-religious Jews as regards ethnic identity and ethnicity.

Whereas the ethnic identity is flexible, ethnicity has proved to be relatively stable, because it is largely rooted in the subconscious or unconscious. This would explain the persistence of ethnic groups, even if exposed to rapid socio-economic change and to various pressures to renounce their cultural peculiarity. From this follows that ethnicity is not the inexplicable residue called upon when other explanations fail, but the recepticle through which other forces and influences are channelled.

The German Jews offer a particularly interesting case in this respect. In spite of considerable pressure in Germany, practically from the emancipation onwards, to 'assimilate' in the sense of becoming absorbed by German society, the Jews – as a group – resisted. Instead, they developed a specific German–Jewish identity which has survived to this day and against great odds. Indeed, it is probably no exaggeration to say that the pressures from within as well as from without the group to denounce and reject that identity were at times enormous. More recently, this pressure has been exerted not so much because of its link with Judaism but because of its association with German culture. Yet, the outcome is no less surprising: however hard quite a few respondents have tried to divest themselves of their native culture and although attitudes towards this whole complex remain ambivalent in many cases, most respondents have at least tacitly accepted the Central European heritage.

It should also have become clear from this study what the most conspicuous characteristics of a German–Jewish ethnicity are or rather are believed to be by the German Jews themselves: a high regard for the work ethic, for conscientiousness, perfectionism, perseverance and a strong urge for '*Kultur*'. Yet, however, pervasive these and other characteristics may be and however distinct German–Jewish culture appears, it is obvious that its constituent elements are not unique, i.e. not completely different from those of other cultures. Rather it is the frequency and evaluation of these elements, their normative force and position within the total set of values and the combination of these various traits which distinguish German–Jewish culture from other cultures. It might be helpful in this context to think in terms of clusters of cultural traits, a notion not unlike the concept of 'race', generally accepted in contemporary science and outlined in the first chapter of this study. There are no qualitative genetic differences among human groups, it was stated; rather it is the frequency, not the absence or presence, of certain blood groups and genes in the various populations which result in their differentiation.

Whereas 'objective' criteria of ethnicity are obviously important, it turned out that in everyday life the subjective, or normative aspect of culture is even more decisive. Whether the actual behaviour of the individuals corresponds with the norm is less relevant. Similarly, certain behaviour patterns are sometimes considered 'typically Jewish' by the Jews themselves even if in fact they are not. The belief in the value of close family ties comes to mind. Yet whether these differences are real or imagined, it is the subjective assumption that they are 'typical' which is important. For the belief that Jews, more likely than other people, share one's expectations and perceptions creates a bond of trust and a feeling of familiarity. Values and norms thus serve to build up a framework for the identification of one's own ethnic group and its differentiation from others and help to categorize an otherwise amorphous mass of people. To be sure, other ties, such as class ties, also exist, but they would seem to be rather weaker. The effects of racism would offer an example here. Although often enough it perverts ethnic traits, it is nevertheless based on cultural differentiations among ethnic groups. If the past is anything to go by, it certainly appears to have proven a far more effective means of generating group solidarity than economic discrimination and exploitation has rallied class interests.

On the other hand, this does not mean that the boundary created by group consciousness is necessarily closed. As the case of the German Jews so well illustrates, trust is often extended to non-

Jews – or *other* Jews, for that matter – but significantly this happens to them as individuals rather than as a group. Nor is it perhaps extended as 'automatically' as to members of one's own group.

Of course, in many ways we are only just beginning to understand the dynamics of group contact in plural societies. This applies also to one aspect of it, the process of assimilation. No doubt, given time our understanding will be more complete. But it will probably always be difficult to arrive at satisfactory generalizations or even at a conclusive theory of assimilation; for, in spite of the surprising persistence of particular cultural traits, this process is inevitably subjected to historical change. Moreover, it also varies from one socio-cultural setting to another. In short, 'the ambiguities of assimilation' extend beyond the specific case of the German–Jewish refugees which has been the topic of this study.

Notes

INTRODUCTION

1. Most studies of Central European Jews in this country focus on internment. Very few adopt a wider perspective and none can be considered to offer a systematic analysis. See Austin Stevens, *The Dispossessed: German Refugees in Britain* (London, 1975); Gerhard Hirschfeld (ed.), *Exil in Grossbritannien: Zur Emigration aus dem nationalsozialistischen Deutschland* (Stuttgart, 1983).
2. Ferdynand Zweig, *The Quest for Fellowship* (London, 1965) p. x; s.a. idem, *Women's Life and Labour* (London, 1952) pp. 11f.
3. C. Wright Mills, *The Sociological Imagination* (Harmondsworth, 1977) p. 69.
4. M. D. Shipman, *The Limitations of Social Research* (London, 1972) p. 19.
5. Unfortunately, Monika Sicharz's third volume of *Jüsdisches Lebeu in Devtsch land: Selbstzeugnisse zur Sozialgeschichte 1918–1945*, (Stuttgart, 1982), appeared too late for this study.
6. Larry D. Nachman, 'The Question of the Jews: a Study in Culture', *Samalgundi*, 44/5, Spring/Summer 1979, pp. 179ff.

CHAPTER 1 CONCEPTS OF ASSIMILATION AND ETHNIC IDENTITY

1. See Benjamin Kaplan, *The Jew and his Family* (Baton Rouge, La. 1967) p. 9.
2. Barnet Litvinoff, *A Peculiar People* (London, 1969).
3. Litvinoff, *Peculiar People*, p. 6. Kurt Lewin, *Resolving Social Conflicts*, (New York, 1948) p. 158.
4. Reprinted in Paul Baxter and Basil Sansom (eds.), *Race and Social Difference*, Selected Readings (Harmondsworth, 1972) p. 68.
5. Phillip V. Tobias, 'The Meaning of Race', ibid., pp. 22f.
6. Ibid., p. 71.
7. Art. 'Ethnic Groups' by H. S. Morris in the *International Encyclopaedia of the Social Sciences*, 1968, vol. 5, p. 167. The term 'group' in this study follows common usage and does not designate a corporate group here. Strictly speaking, the Jews form a category. See ibid., p. 168.
8. Frederick Barth (ed.), *Ethnic Group and Boundaries. The Social Organization of Culture Difference* (Bergen and London, 1970) pp. 9f., 11.
9. W. Lloyd Warner and Leo Srole, *The Social Systems of American Ethnic Groups*.
10. A. L. Epstein, *Ethos and Identity*, (London, 1978) p. x.
11. Nathan Glazer and Daniel P. Moynihan (eds), *Beyond the Melting Pot* (Cambridge, Mass., 1963).

12. Epstein, *Ethos and Identity*, p. x.
13. Glazer and Moynihan (eds.), *Ethnicity. Theory and Experience* (Cambridge, Mass., 1975) pp. 3f.
14. Epstein, *Ethos and Identity*, p. 92.
15. A good example offers the well-known study by Louis Wirth, *The Ghetto* (Chicago and London, 1928).
16. Epstein, *Ethos and Identity*, pp. 109, 111.
17. Glazer and Moynihan (eds), *Ethnicity*, p. 8.
18. Epstein, *Ethos and Identity*, p. 94. See also Harold R. Isaacs, 'Basic Group Identity: The Idols of the Tribe', Glazer and Moynihan (eds.), *Ethnicity*, p. 35.
19. Barth (ed.), *Ethnic Groups*, p. 14.
20. Epstein, *Ethos and Identity*, p. 101.
21. George H. Mead, *On Social Psychology, Selected Papers* (Chicago, 1969) pp. 226ff; Alfred Schutz and Thomas Luckmann, *The Structure of the Life-World* (London, 1974) ch. 4.
22. S. a. Karl Mannheim, *Essays on the Sociology of Knowledge* (London, 1968), p. 298.
23. Barth, *Ethnic Groups*, p. 53; similar: Price, 'The Study of Assimilation', Jackson (ed.), *Migration*, p. 207.
24. Peter Berger et al., *The Homeless Mind. Modernization and Consciousness*, (Penguin, 1977) pp. 62f.
25. Ibid., p. 73.
26. Fred L. Strodtbeck, 'Family Interaction, Values, and Achievement', Sklare (ed.), *American Jews*, pp. 162f.; Robert W. Winch, *Identification and its Familial Determinants*, (Indianapolis 1962), p. 106; Eva Etzioni-Halevy and Zwi Halevy, 'The Jewish Ethic', *JJS*, vol. 19, no. 1, June 1974 *passim*;
27. For a discussion of some of the relevant literature see Jean Millar, *British Management versus German Management* (Westmead, 1979).
28. See e.g. Rudy, *Soziologie des jüdischen Volkes*.
29. Barth (ed.), *Ethnic Groups*, p. 9f.
30. Quoted in Peter Berger and Thomas Luckmann, *The Social Construction of Reality* (Penguin, 1973) p. 20.
31. Epstein, *Ethos and Identity*, p. 101.
32. Ibid., p. 102.
33. For a systematic treatment of the formation of identities see Rinder, 'Polarities in Jewish Identification'.
34. Isaac Deutscher, *The Non-Jewish Jew and other Essays* (London, 1968) p. 50.
35. Martin Buber, *Drei Reden über das Judentum* (Frankfurt, 1916) p. 15.
36. See e.g. Talcott Parsons, 'Some Theoretical Considerations on the Nature and Trends of Change of Ethnicity', Glazer and Moynihan (eds), *Ethnicity*, p. 56.

CHAPTER 2 THE PROCESS OF JEWISH ASSIMILATION IN GERMANY

1. Hermann L. Goldschmidt, *Das Vermächtnis des deutschen Judentums* (Frankfurt, 1965) p. 168.
2. Hans Liebeschütz, 'Judentum und deutsche Umwelt im Zeitalter der

Restauration', Hans Liebeschütz and Arnold Paucker (eds), *Das Judentum in der deutschen Umwelt, 1800–1850* (Tübingen, 1977) p. 2.
3. Jacob Katz, *Emancipation and Assimilation* (Westmead, 1972) p. x.
4. Hermann Grieve, 'On Jewish Self-Identification – Religion and Political Orientation', *LBIYB*, XX, 1975, p. 36; Esra Bennathan, 'Die demographische und wirtschaftliche Struktur der Juden', Werner Mosse and Arnold Paucker (eds.), *Entscheidungsjahr 1932* (Tübingen, 1936) p. 88.
5. Jacob Katz, ibid. For the emancipation s.a. Liebeschütz, Arnold Paucker (ed.), *Das Judentum in der deutschen Umwelt, 1800–1850*; Reinhard Rürup, 'Judenemanzipation und bürgerliche Gesellschaft in Deutschland', R. Rürup, *Emanzipation und Antisemitismus* (Göttingen, 1975) pp. 11–36; Simon Dubnow, *History of the Jews*, vol. V, (New York, 1973); Alex Bein, *Die Judenfrage. Biographie eines Weltproblems*, 2 vols, (Stuttgart, 1980) ch. 5.
6. H. G. Adler, *The Jews in Germany. From the Enlightenment to National Socialism* (Notre Dame, London, 1969) p. 90; Eva Reichmann, *Hostages of Civilization: The Social Sources of National Socialist Anti-Semitism* (Boston, 1951) p. 170.
7. Arno Herzig, 'Das Problem der jüdischen Identität in der deutschen bürgerlichen Gesellschaft', Walter Grab (ed.), *Deutsche Aufklärung und Judenemanzipation,* Jahrbuch des Instituts für deutsche Geschichte, Beiheft 3 (Tel Aviv, 1979–80) p. 261.
8. Sidney M. Bolkosky, *The Distorted Image. German Jewish Perceptions of Germans and Germany, 1918–1935* (New York, Oxford, Amsterdam, 1975) p. 4; s.a. Adler, *Jews in Germany*, p. 5.
9. Dubnow, *History of the Jews*, p. 278.
10. David Bronsen (ed.), *Jews and Germans from 1860 to 1933. The Problematic Symbiosis* (Heidelberg; 1979) p. 5.
11. Gershom Scholem, 'On the Social Psychology of the Jews in Germany: 1900–1933', Bronsen (ed.), *Jews and Germans*, p. 10; s.a. Carl Cohen, 'The Road to Conversion', *LBIYB* VI, 1961, p. 265; Bein, *Die Judenfrage*, p. 199; David Rudavsky, *Emancipation and Adjustment. Contemporary Jewish Religious Movements. Their History and Thought* (New York, 1967) p. 74f; Joseph W. Cohen, 'The Jewish Role in Western Culture', Isaque Graeber and Stenart H. Britt (eds), *Jews in a Gentile World* (New York, 1942) p. 349.
12. Eva Beling, *Die gesellschaftliche Eingliederung der deutschen Einwanderer in Israel*, (Frankfurt, 1967) p. 58.
13. S. e.g. Salon Baron, 'Menace of a new Schism', Michael A. Meyer (ed.), *Ideas of Jewish History*, with an introduction and notes by M. Meyer (New York, 1974) pp. 333f.; Arther Ruppin, *Soziologie der Juden* (Berlin 1930) vol. II, pp. 104ff.
14. Michael R. Marrus, 'European Jewry and the Politics of Assimilation: Assessment and Reassessment', *JMH*, vol. 49, no. 1, March 1977, pp. 92f.
15. Eleonore Sterling, 'Jewish Reaction to Jew-Hatred in the First Half of the Nineteenth Century', *LBIYB*, III, 1958, pp. 103–121; Peter Loewenberg, 'Antisemitismus und jüdischer Selbsthass', *Geschichte und Gesellschaft*, vol. 5, no. 4, 1979, pp. 455–75; Salomon Liptzin, *Germany's Stepchildren* (Cleveland, New York, 1961); Theodor Lessing, *Jüdischer Selbsthass* (Berlin, 1930).
16. Hannah Arendt, *Rahel. Varnhagen. Lebensgeschichte einer deutschen Jüdin aus der Romantik* (München, 1975) p. 210.
17. Marrus, 'European Jewry', pp. 90, 91; Fritz Stern, 'The Burden of Success:

Reflections on German Jewry', Quentin Anderson et al. (ed.), *Art, Politics, and Will. Essays in Honor of Lionel Trilling* (New York, 1977) pp. 142f.; Hans Martin Klinkenberg, 'Zwischen Liberalismus und Nationalismus. Im Zweiten Kaiserreich (1870–1918)', *Monumenta Judaica* (Köln, 1963) pp. 316f.

18. E.g. Scholem in Bronsen (ed.), *Jews and Germans from 1860 to 1933* passim; Stephen Poppel, *Zionism in Germany, 1897–1933: The Shaping of a Jewish Identity* (Philadelphia, 1977) p. 18; Sterling, 'Jewish Reaction to Jew-Hatred', p. 113; Heinz Moshe Graupe, *The Rise of Modern Judaism. An Intellectual History of German Jewry, 1650–1942* (Huntington, New York, 1978) p. 310; Hans-Joachim Schoeps, *Wir deutschen Juden* (Berlin, 1934) pp. 1ff; Joachim Prinz, *Wir Juden* (Berlin, 1934), p. 19.

19. Schoeps, *Wir deutschen Juden*, pp. 29ff; s.a. Goldschmidt, *Das Vermächtnis des deutschen Judentums*, p. 168.

20. Quoted in Marrus, 'European Jewry', p. 91.

21. Peter Pulzer, 'Why was there a Jewish Question in Imperial Germany?' *LBIYB*, XXV, 1980, pp. 140f.

22. Bieber in Bronsen (ed.), *Jews and Germans from 1860 to 1933*, p. 33; s.a. Fritz Stern, *Gold and Iron. Bismarck, Bleichröder, and the Building of the German Empire* (New York, 1977) p. 469; Reichmann, *Hostages of Civilization*, pp. 234f.; Peter Pulzer, *The Rise of Political Anti-Semitism in Germany and Austria* (New York, 1964), passim.

23. For an excellent survey of racism, its roots and effects, see George E. Simpson and Y. Milton Singer, *Racial and Cultural Minorities* (New York, 1972).

24. See e.g. Milton M. Gordon, 'Toward a General Theory of Racial and Ethnic Group Relations', Glazer and Moynihan (eds.), *Ethnicity* pp. 84–110; Robert A. Kann, 'Assimilation and Antisemitism in the German-French Orbit in the 19th and early 20th Centuries', *LBIYB*, XIV, 1969, pp. 94ff.

25. Bieber in Bronsen (ed.), *Jews and Germans from 1860 to 1933*, p. 62.

26. Peter Gay, *Freud, Jews and other Germans. Masters and Victims in Modernist Culture* (New York, 1978), pp. 8, 9f.; s.a. Oscar Handlin, 'Jews in the Culture of Middle Europe', Leo Baeck Memorial Lecture, 7, New York 1974, p. 20.

27. Bolkolsky, *The Distorted Image*, passim.

28. Walter Laqueur, *The Missing Years* (London, 1980) p. 7.

29. Reichmann, *Hostages of Civilization*, p. 19.

30. Jehuda Reinharz, *Promised Land or Fatherland. The Dilemma of the German Jew, 1893–1914* (Ann Arbor, 1975) p. 142.

31. Wanda Kampmann, *Deutsche und Juden. Studien zur Geschichte des deutschen Judentums* (Heidelberg 1963) p. 447; s.a. Lucy Davidowicz, *The War against the Jews, 1933–1945* (New York, 1975) p. 346.

32. Jacob R. Marcus, *The Rise and Destiny of the German Jew* (New York, 1973) p. 5.

33. See e.g. Gordon in Glazer and Moynihan (eds.), *Ethnicity*, passim.

34. Hans-Helmuth Knütter, 'Die Linksparteien', Mosse and Paucker (eds), *Entscheidungsjahr 1932*, pp. 323–45; Donald L. Niewyk, *Anti-Semite and Jews: German Social Democracy Confronts the Problem of Anti-Semitism, 1918–1933*, (Baton Rouge, 1971); Marjorie Lamberti, 'Liberals, Socialists and the Defence against Antisemitism in the Wilhelmine Period', *LBIYB*, XXV, 1980, pp. 147–62; Pulzer, *The Rise of Political Anti-Semitism in Germany and Austria*, passim; Richard Levy, *The Downfall of the Anti-Semitic Political Parties in Imperial Germany* (New Haven, Conn., 1975); Shulamit Angel-Volkov, 'The Social and

Political Function of late 19th Century Anti-Semitism; The Case of the Small Handicraft Masters', Hans-Ulrich Wehler (ed.), *Sozialgeschichte Heute: Festschrift für Hans Rosenberg zum 70. Geburtstag* (Göttingen, 1974), pp. 416–31; Heinz Rosenthal, 'Jews in the Solingen Steel Industry', *LBIYB*, XVII, 1972, pp. 205–23.
35. Laqueur, *Missing Years*, p. 61.
36. S. Adler-Rudel, *Ostjuden in Deutschland, 1880–1940* (Tübingen, 1959); Jack L. Wertheimer, *German Policy and Jewish Politics. The Absorption of East European Jews in Germany, 1868–1914*, Phil Diss. Columbia University, 1978.
37. Laquer, *Missing Years*, p. 40; s.a. Reinharz, *Promised Land or Fatherland*, p. 226.
38. Gay, *Freud, Jews and Other Germans*, pp. 95, 93.
39. George Mosse, *Germans and Jews* (New York, 1970) p. 113.
40. Simpson and Yinger, *Racial and Cultural Minorities*, p. 339.
41. See Reinharz, *Promised Land or Fatherland*, passim; Ismar Schorsch, *Jewish Reactions to German Anti-Semitism, 1870–1940*, (New York, 1972) *passim*.
42. Graupe, *Rise of Modern Judaism*, p. 191.
43. Arthur Ruppin, *Die Juden der Gegenwart* (Berlin, 1918) p. 9.
44. Scholem, in Bronsen (ed.), *Jews and Germans from 1860 to 1933*, pp. 20ff. S.a. idem, *Von Berlin nach Jerusalem*, (Frankfurt, 1977).
45. Dubnow, *History of the Jews*, p. 469; s.a. Alfred Low, *Jews in the Eyes of the Germans. From the Enlightenment to Imperial Germany* (Philadelphia, 1979) p. 412.
46. Simon Dubnow, 'An Essay in the Philosophy of History', in Meyer (ed.), *Ideas of Jewish History*, pp. 253ff.
47. Graupe, *Rise of Modern Judaism*, p. 271.
48. Schorsch, *Jewish Reactions*, p. 10; s.a. Reinharz, *Promised Land*, p. VII; Poppel, *Zionism in Germany*, p. 11.
49. S.a. Ruth L. Pierson, *German Jewish Identity in the Weimer Republic*, Phil. Diss., Yale University 1970, p. 53; Goldmann, *Jude im deutschen Kulturkreis*, pp. 129ff.; Greive, 'Jewish Self-Identification', p. 36.
50. See esp. his *Tradition and Crisis. Jewish Society at the end of the Middle Ages*, (New York, 1961); *Exclusiveness and Tolerance. Studies in Jewish-Gentile Relations in Medieval and Modern Times* (London 1961); *Out of the Ghetto, The Social Background of Jewish Emancipation, 1770–1870* (Cambridge, Mass. 1973): *Emancipation and Assimilation* (Westmead, 1972).
51. Op. cit., *Emancipation and Assimilation*, p. 1.
52. Op. cit., *Out of the Ghetto*, pp. 216, 1ff.; op. cit., *Emancipation and Assimilation*, p. 3.
53. S.a. Selma Stern, *Der Preussische Staat und die Juden*, vol. I, (Tübingen, 1964); Fritz Stern, 'The Integration of Jews in Nineteenth-Century Germany', *LBIYB*, XX, 1975, p. 80; Liebeschütz in Liebeschütz and Paucker (eds.), *Judentum in deutscher Umwelt*, p. 40.
54. S. a. Walter Laqueur, *A History of Zionism* (London, 1972) p. 34.
55. Idem, *Out of the Ghetto*, p. 206.
56. S. a. S. N. Eisenstadt, *The Absorption of Immigrants* (London, 1954), p. 11; an interesting example of absorption are the Chinese Jews. Michael Pollak, *Mandarins, Jews, and Missionaries* (Philadelphia 1980). Donald L. Horowitz, 'Ethic Identity', Glazer and Mogaihan (eds.), *Ethnicity*, pp. 111–76.
57. Laqueur, *Zionism*, p. 34; Goldman, *Jude im deutschen Kulturbereich* p. 111.
58. Cohen in Graeber and Britt (eds.), *Jews in a Gentile World*, p. 350.

59. S. a. Stern, *Gold and Iron*, p. 471.
60. S. a. Stephen Poppel, 'New Views on Jewish Integration in Germany', *Central European History*, vol. IX, no. 1, March 1976, p. 87.
61. Werner Mosse, 'Judaism, Jews and Capitalism – Weber, Sombart and Beyond', *LBIYB*, XXIV; 1979, p. 11f.; Katz, *Out of the Ghetto*, p. 215.
62. Quoted in Laqueur, *Zionism*, p. 8.
63. Marion Kaplan, *The Jewish Feminist Movement in Germany* (Westport, Conn., 1979) p. 19.
64. Rudavsky, *Emancipation and Adjustment*, p. 184; s.a. Moshe Schwarcz, 'Religious Currents and General Culture', *LBIYB*, XVI, 1971, pp. 3–17.
65. Kaplan, *Jewish Feminist Movement*, p. 19; s.a. op. cit., 'German–Jewish, Feminism in the 20th Century', *JSS*, vol. XXXVIII, Winter 1976, no. 1, pp. 39–53; Jacob R. Marcus, *Communal Sick Care in the German Ghetto* (Cincinnati, 1947); Monika Richarz (ed.), *Jüdisches Leben im Deutschland. Selbstzeugnisse zur Sozialgeschichte* 2 vols, (Stuttgart, 1976, 1979).
66. Ismar Elbogen, *Geschichte der Juden in Deutschland*, (Berlin, 1935); idem, *A Century of Jewish Life* (Philadelphia, 1966); Marcus, *German Jew*, passim.
67. Henry Wassermann, *Jews, Bürgertum und Bürgerliche Gesellschaft in a Liberal Era (1840–1880)*, Ph.D. Diss., Hebrew University.
68. Ibid., p. xi (Engl. abstract). Ruppin, *Soziologie der Juden*, vol. II, pp. 232f.; Jacob Toury, *Soziale und Politische Geschichte der Juden in Deutschland 1847–1871* (Düsseldorf, 1977) p. 121.
69. A good example is offered by the Jews of Prague. See Gary B. Cohen, 'Jews in German Society: Prague, 1860–1914', *Central European History*, vol. X, no. 1, March 1977, pp. 43ff. Gustav Mayer makes the same point as regards the relationship between Jews and non-Jews in Hamburg in his *Erinnerungen. Vom Journalisten zum Historiker der deutschen Arbeiterbewegung* (Zürich, Wien, 1949) pp. 10ff.
70. A. Leschnitzer, *Saul und David. Zur Problematik der deutsch-jüdischen Lebensgemeinschaft* (Heidelberg, 1954) p. 79; George Barany, 'Magyar Jew or Jewish Magyar', *Canadian-American Slavic Studies*, vol. 8, nr. 1, Spring 1974, p. 33; Hedwig Wachenheim, *Vom Grossbürgertum zur Sozialdemokratie* (Berlin, 1973) p. 10ff.
71. S. a. Stephen Sharot, *Judaism. A Sociology* (London, 1976) p. 142.
72. Marjorie Lamberti, *Jewish Activism in Imperial Germany: The Struggle for Civil Equality* (New Haven, 1978) p. 184; s.a. Achim von Borries (ed.), *Selbstzeugnisse des deutschen Judentums, 1870–1945* (Frankfurt, 1962) pp. 15, 31f.
73. See e.g. Emile Durkheim and Marcel Mauss, *Primitive Classification* (London, 1970).
74. Max Weber, *Die protestantische Ethik*, I, (Hamburg, 1975) p. 29. Terms like 'tribe' and 'race' were also fairly popular in 19th century-Germany. See Reinhard Rürup, 'Emanzipation und Krise' in Werner Mosse and Arnold Paucker (eds.), *Juden im Wilhelminischen Deutschland, 1890–1914* (Tübingen, 1976) p. 37.
75. F. Rudolf Bienenfeld, *The Religion of the Non-Religious Jews*, (London, 1944) p. 23f.; s. a. Toury, *Soziale und politische Geschichte der Juden*. Similar developments took place in France. See David H. Weinberg, *A Community on Trial. The Jews of Paris in the 1930s* (Chicago, 1977) p. 49.
76. Frank Field, *The Last Days of Mankind. Karl Kraus and his Vienna* (London, 1967)

p. 69; s. a. Isaiah Berlin, 'The Life and Opinion of Moses Hess', in *Against the Current. Essays in the History of Ideas* (London, 1979) p. 222; Graupe, *Rise of Modern Judaism*, p. 113.
77. Mayer, *Erinnerungen*, p. 14.
78. Max Horkheimer, 'Über die deutschen Juden', Vortrag für *Germania Judaica*, (Köln, 1961) p. 13f.
79. Stern, 'Burden of Success', passim; s. a. Werner Mosse, 'Die Juden in Wirstchaft und Gesellschaft', in Mosse and Paucker (eds.), *Juden im Wilhelminischen Deutschland*, p. 83; Goldschmidt, *Vermächtnis des deutschen Judentums*, p. 227.
80. Schwarcz, 'Religious Currents', pp. 7, 13f.; s.a. Hans I. Bach, *Jacob Bernays* (Tübingen, 1974) p. 50; Pinchas E. Rosenblüth, 'Die geistigen und religiosen Strömungen in der deutschen Judenheit', in Mosse and Paucker (eds), *Juden im Wilhelminischen Deutschland*, p. 552.
81. Poppel, *Zionism*, p. 123; s.a. Reinharz, *Fatherland*, p. 223; Pierson, *German Jewish Identity*, pp. 324ff. Max Kreutzberger, 'Bedeutung und Aufgabe deutsch-jüdischer Geschichtsscheibung in unserer Zeit' in Hans Tramer (ed.), *In Zwei Welten. Siegfried Moses zum 75. Geburtstag* (Tel-Aviv, 1964) p. 631.
82. Reinharz, *Fatherland*, p. 231.
83. F. Rudolf Bienenfeld, *The Germans and the Jews* (New York, 1939) p. 131.
84. Katz, *Emancipation and Assimilation*, pp. 221. 256f.
85. From: Memoirs of a Grandmother' quoted in: Alder, *Jews in Germany*, p. 91; s.a. Robert Weltsch, 'Vorbemerkung', in Siegmund Kaznelson (ed.), *Juden im deutschen Kulturbereich* (Berlin, 1959) pp. xviiif.; Deutscher, *Non-Jewish Jew*, p. 48f.
86. Kurt Schubert, *Die Kultur der Juden, Teil II: Judentum im Mittelalter* (Wiesbaden, 1979) p. 16; Jechiel Bin-Nun, *Yiddisch und die deutschen Mundarten* (Tübingen, 1973).
87. Graupe, *Rise of Modern Judaism*, p. 269; Barany, 'Magyar Jew', p. 40. Grete Fischer, *Dienstboten, Brecht und andere. Zeitgenossen in Prag, Berlin, London* (Olten, 1966).
88. S.a. Katz, *Emancipation and Assimilation*, p. 234.
89. Leschnitzer, *Saul und David*, p. 142; Reinharz, *Fatherland*, pp. 195ff.; v. Borries (ed.), *Selbstzeugnisse*, pp. 27ff.; Peter Pulzer, 'Die jüdische Beteiligung an der Politik', in Mosse and Paucker (eds.), *Juden im Wilhelminischen Deutschland*, p. 238; Mosse, 'Juden in Wirtschaft und Gesellschaft', p. 105. For a similar phenomenon among French Jews see Weinberg, *Community On Trial*, p. 218.
90. See e.g. Walter Zwi Bacharach, 'Jews in Confrontation with Racist Antisemitism, 1879–1933', *LBIYB*, XXV, 1980, p. 216; Leschnitzer, *Saul und David*, p. 142.
91. Selma Stern-Täubler, 'The First Generation of Emancipated Jews', *LBIYB*, XV, 1970, p. 39; Hans Liebeschütz, *Von Georg Simmel zu Franz Rosenzweig* (Tübingen, 1970) pp. 1f.
92. Graupe, *Rise of Modern Judaism*, pp. 142ff.
93. Ibid., pp. 240ff; s.a. Moshe Pelli, 'The Beginning of the Epistolary Genre in Hebrew Enlightenment Literature in Germany – The Alleged Affinity between Lettres Persanes and Igrot Meshulam', *LBIYB*, XXIV, 1979, pp. 83–106.
94. This approach is similar to Lucien Goldmann's concept of "genetic structura-

lism". See Raymond Williams, *Problems in Materialism and Culture. Selected Essays* (London, 1980) pp. 22f.
95. Marcus, *German Jew*, p. 224; s.a. Liebeschütz, 'Judentum und deutsche Umwelt', pp. 387f.; Laqueur, *Zionism*, p. 34.
96. Norbert Altenhofer, 'Tradition also Revolution: Gustav Landauer's "gewordenes-werdendes" Judentum', in Bronsen (ed.), *Jews and Germans*, pp. 173f.
97. Gay, *Freud, Jews and other Germans*, pp. 99ff.
98. Ibid., p. 110; s.a. Goldmann, *Jude im deutschen Kulturkreis*, p. 11.
99. Schubert, *Kultur der Juden*, p. 16f.; Adler, *Jews in Germany*, pp. 1ff. s.a. Wolfgang Hamburger, 'The Reaction of Reform Jews to the Nazi Rule', in Herbert Strauss and Kurt R. Grossmann (eds.), *Gegenwart im Rückblick* (Heidelberg, 1970) p. 151; Ernst Schulin and Bernd Martin (eds), *Die Juden als Minderheit in der Geschichte* (München, 1981).

CHAPTER 3 LIFE UNDER THE THREAT OF NAZISM

1. Stefan Zweig, *The World of Yesterday* (London, 1943) p. 13.
2. Reichmann, *Hostages*, p. 53.
3. See e.g. Friedrich Blach, *Die Juden in Deutschland. Von einem jüdischen Deutschen* (Berlin, 1911); Arthur Ruppin, *Memoirs, Diaries, Letters* (London, 1971).
4. Max Born, *Mein Leben* (München, 1975) pp. 12f.
5. See e.g. Eva Ehrenberg, 'The Emigration', transl. from *Sehnsucht-mein geliebtes Kind* (Frankfurt, 1963) p. 1.
6. Margarete Susman, *Ich habe viele Leben gelebt* (Stuttgart, 1964) p. 14.
7. Loewenstein, 'Die innerjüdische Reaktion', Mosse and Paucker (eds), *1932*, passim.
8. Jakob Wassermann, *Mein Weg als Deutscher und Jude* (Berlin, 1921) p. 108.
9. Karl Stern, *The Pillar of Fire* (New York, 1951) pp. 53, 194.
10. Max Gruenewald, 'Critic of German Jewry. Ludwig Feuchtwanger and his Gemeindezeitung', *LBIYB* XVII, 1972, p. 76.
11. Eva Reichmann, *Grösse und Verhängnis deutsch-jüdischer Existenz* (Heidelberg, 1974) pp. 58ff.
12. See e.g. Han Lamm, *Über die innere und äussere Entwicklung des deutschen Judentums im Dritten Reich*, Diss Phil., Erlangen 1951; idem, 'Bemerkungen zur Entwicklung und Wandlung des deutsch-jüdischen Lebensgefühles', Hellmut Diwald (ed.), *Lebendiger Geist. Hans-Joachim Schoeps zum 50. Geburtstag* (Leiden, 1959); Bruno Blau, 'The last days of German Jewry in the Third Reich', *YIVO Annual of Jewish Social Science*, New York, 1953; Hans-Joachim Schoeps (ed.), *Wille und Weg des deutschen Judentums* (Berlin, 1935).
13. See e.g. Scholem, *Von Berlin nach Jerusalem*, passim.
14. Martin Buber, quoted in Ernst Simon, 'Jewish Adult Education in Nazi Germany as Spiritual Resistance', *LBIYB*, I, 1956, p. 69.
15. Stern, *Pillar of Fire*, pp. 158ff.
16. Hermann Sinzheimer, *Gelebt im Paradies* (München, 1953) p. 279.
17. Simon, 'Jewish Adult Education', p. 71, quotation by Martin Buber.
18. Kurt Ball-Kaduri, *Das Leben der Juden in Deutschland im Jahre 1933* (Frankfurt, 1963) p. 27.

19. Quoted in Lamm, *Judentum im Dritten Reich*, p. 105.
20. The figures quoted vary from 70000 in Herbert Freeden, *Vom geistigen Widerstand der deutschen Juden. Ein Kapital jüdischer Selbstbehauptung in den Jahren 1933/1938* (Jerusalem, 1963) p. 14, to 180000 for 1936 in Lamm, *Judentum im Dritten Reich* p. 193.
21. Ibid.
22. See Uwe Dietrich Adam, *Judenpolitik im Dritten Reich*, (Düsseldorf, 1972); Helmut Genschel, *Die Verdrängung der Juden aus der Wirtschaft im Dritten Reich* (Göttingen, 1966).
23. Freeden, *Vom geistigen Widerstand*, p. 14.
24. Ibid., p. 14.
25. Lamm, *Judentum im Dritten Reich*, p. 15; Kaplan, *Jewish Feminist Movement*, p. 90.
26. Hans Gaertner, 'Probleme der jüdischen Schule während der Hitlerjahre', Weltsch, *Deutsches Judentum*, p. 351; s. a. Weltsch, 'Entscheidungsjahr 1932', Mosse and Paucker (eds.), *1932*, pp. 535–62; Loewenstein, ibid.; and below p. 67.
27. Wertheimer, *German Policy and Jewish Politics*, pp. 544.
28. Alder-Rudel, *Ostjuden*, p. 6.
29. Adler-Rudel, *Ostjuden*, p. 6; s. a. Bill Williams, *The Making of Manchester Jewry, 1740–1875*; Irving Howe, *World of Our Fathers. The Journey of the East European Jews to America and the Life They Found and Made* (New York., 1976).
30. Wertheimer, *German Policy and Jewish Politics*, pp. 544.
31. Wertheimer, *German Policy and Jewish Politics*, pp. 546f.
32. Scholem, 'On the Social Psychology of the Jews in Germany', p. 60.
33. Wertheimer, *German Policy and Jewish Politics*, pp. 531f; Adler-Rudel, *Ostjuden*, p. 50; Monika Richarz, *Jüdisches Leben in Deutschland*, Bd. II, *passim*.
34. Max Gruenewald, 'Der Anfang der Reichsvertretung', Robert Weltsch (ed.), *Deutsches Judentum. Aufstieg und Krise. Gestalten, Jdeen, Werke* (Stuttgart, 1963) p. 324.
35. Peter Freimark, 'Language Behaviour and Assimilation – The Situation of the Jews in Northern Germany in the First Half of the Nineteenth Century', *LBIYB*, XXIV, 1979, pp. 157–78; Curt Wormann, 'Kulturelle Probleme und Aufgaben der Juden aus Deutschland in Israel seit 1933', Tramer (ed.), *In zwei Welten*, pp. 292ff.
36. Wertheimer, *German Policy and Jewish Politics*, p. 544.
37. See e.g. Isaac Eisenstein-Barzilay, 'The Background of the Berlin Haskalah', Joseph Blau et.al. (eds), *Essays on Jewish Life and Thought* (New York, 1959); Adler-Rudel, *Ostjuden*, p. 18.
38. Reichmann, *Hostages*, pp. 29ff.
39. Adler-Rudel, *Ostjuden*, p. 26; Bennathan, 'Demographische und wirtschaftliche Struktur', pp. 98ff.
40. S. a. Arthur Koestler, *Arrow in the Blue. An Autobiography* (New York, 1952) pp. 110ff; Wassermann, *Mein Weg*, pp. 107ff.
41. Charles Hannam, *A Boy in your Situation* (London, 1977) p. 58. – Friedrich Blach's admonitions, a generation earlier, the Jews should behave more like the Germans around them, e.g. not use *Jargon* (Yiddish) or 'not gesticulate too wildly' etc., are interesting in that they indicate the considerable extent to which certain Jewish cultural characteristics were still alive in Germany at the

beginning of this century. See idem, *Die Juden in Deutschland*, p. 19ff.
42. Fischer, *Dienstboten*, pp. 73f.
43. Weltsch, 'Entscheidungjahr 1932', p. 560.
44. Loewenstein, 'Die innerjüdische Reaktion', p. 367.
45. Schoeps (ed.), *Wille und Weg*, p. 19.
46. Ibid., p. 19.
47. Reichmann, *Hostages*, p. 171.
48. Stern, *The Pillar*, pp. 154f.
49. Richarz, *Jüdisches Leben*, Bd. II, p. 52.
50. Ruppin, *Juden der Gegenwart*, p. 160.
51. Richarz, *Jüdisches Leben* Bd. II, pp. 16f; Pierson, *German Jewish Identity*, pp. 10ff.
52. Ibid.; Bennathan, 'Demographische und wirtschaftliche Struktur', p. 96.
53. Ruby Jo Reeves Kennedy, 'What has Social Science to say about Intermarriage?', Werner Cahnmann (ed.), *Intermarriage and Jewish Life*, A Symposium (New York, 1963) p. 29.
54. Ibid., p. 28.
55. John Hope Simpson in his *Refugees. A Review of the Situation since September 1938* (London, 1939) p. 29, speaks of about 6000 'Aryan' wives who left their Jewish husbands between 1933-8.
56. Blau, 'The last days', pp. 197ff.
57. Ian Kershaw, 'Antisemitismus und Volksmeinung. Reaktionen auf die Judenverfolgung', Martin Broszat and Elke Fröhlich (eds), *Bayern in der NS-Zeit. Herrschaft und Gesellschaft im Konflikt* (München, 1979) p. 343. These acts continued throughout the war. See e.g. Catherine Klein, *Escape from Berlin* (London, 1944), p. 29; Inge Deutschkron, *Ich trug den gelben Stern* (Köln, 1978) *passim*.
58. Kershaw, 'Antisemitismus', p. 345. See George L. Mosse, 'Die deutsche Rechte und die Juden', Mosse and Paucker (eds), *Entscheidungsjahr 1932*, pp. 183-246, for a critical discussion of this argument.
59. Ibid., pp. 183-246.
60. Reichmann, *Hostages*, pp. 232. s.a. Buber, *Jude und Judentum*, p. 649; Arnold Zweig, *Insulted and Exiled* (London, 1937) p. 5f.
61. See e.g. Adam, *Judenpolitik*; Genschel, *Die Verdrängung*; A. J. Sherman, *Island Refuge. Britain and Refugees from the Third Reich, 1933-1939* (London, 1973); Stephen Leibfried and Florian Tennstadt, *Berufsverbote und Sozialpolitik 1933. Analyse und Materialien* (Bremen, 1979).
62. See e.g. Karl A. Schleunes, *The Twisted Road to Auschwitz: Nazi Policy toward German Jews, 1933-1939* (Champaign, Urbana, 1970); Uwe Dietrich Adam, *Judenpolitik*; Martin Broszat, 'Hitler und die Genesis der Endlosung', *Vierteljahrshefte für Zeitgeschichte* 25 (1977) pp. 739-75.
63. S.a Schoeps, *Wir Deutschen Juden*; Loewenstein, 'Die innerjüdische Reaktion', p. 371.
64. S.a. Werner Rosenstock, 'Exodus 1933-1939. Ein Überblick über die jüdische Auswanderung aus Deutschland', *LBIYB*, I, 1956, Fn. 13.
65. Blau, 'The last days', p. 200; John Hope Simpson, *The Refugee Problem. Report of a Survey* (London, 1939) p. 136 Fn.
66. Rosenstock, 'Exodus', p. 388.
67. Ibid.; s.a. Sherman, *Island Refuge, passim*; Simpson, *Refugees*, Simpson, *Refugee*

Problem; Erich Rosenthal, 'Trends of the Jewish Population in Germany, 1914–1939', *JSS*, 6, 1944, pp. 233–74.

CHAPTER 4 EMIGRATION

1. The same was not necessarily true for obtaining work permits. See Rosenstock, 'Exodus 1933–1939', p. 390; s. a. Sherman, *Island Refuge*, p. 23.
2. Rosenstock, 'Exodus 1933–1939', p. 399; Sherman, *Island Refuge* p. 262.
3. Rosenstock, 'Exodus 1933–1939', p. 404. s. a. Myer Domnitz, *Immigration and Integration* (London, 1957) p. 14.
4. Sherman, *Island Refuge*, p. 227.
5. Ibid., p. 23.
6. Ibid., p. 32; s.a. Herbert Loebl, *Government–Financed Factories and the Establishment of Industries by Refugees in the Special Areas of the North of England, 1937–1961*, M. Phil Diss., University of Durham 1978, p. 89. For British immigration policy in the 1930s, s. a. Bernard Wasserstein, *Britain and the Jews of Europe, 1939–1945* (Oxford, 1979).
7. Sherman, *Island Refuge*, pp. 273, 232.
8. Ibid., pp. 273, 232.
9. Simpson, *Refugees*, pp. 68f.
10. Ph. Schwartz, 'Über die Notgemeinschaft deutscher Wissenschaftler im Ausland', Vortrag, 2. Internationales Symposium zur Erforschung des deutschsprachigen Exils nach 1933, Kopenhagen 17.8.1972.
11. Norman Bentwich, *The Refugees from Germany, April 1933 to December 1935* (London, 1936) pp. 176. ff.
12. Conversation with Miss Simpson, the Society's secretary from its foundation until her recent retirement.
13. Bentwich, *Refugees from Germany*, p. 16.
14. Information from Miss Simpson.
15. Society for the Protection of Science and Learning, *Fifth Report*, Cambridge 1946; it does not state what the proportion of Jews, resp. non-Jews was.
16. Ibid.; as to the migration to the United States see e.g.: Donald Kent, *The Refugee Intellectual* (New York, 1953); Donald Fleming and Bernard Bailyn (eds), *The Intellectual Migration. Europe and America, 1930–1960* (Cambridge, Mass. 1969); H. Stuart Hughes, *The Sea Change. The Migration of Social Thought, 1930–1965* (New York, 1975); W. Rex Crawford (ed.), *The Cultural Migration. The European Scholar in America* (Philadelphia 1953); Helge Pross, *Die deutsche akademische Emigration nach den Vereinigten Staaten, 1933–1941* (Berlin, 1955).
17. See SPSL leaflet, December 1976.
18. Information from Miss Simpson.
19. Hughes, *Sea Change*, p. 38.
20. Information obtained by respondents. Systematic studies of the integration of refugee scholars into British academic and intellectual life are still lacking. The psychological problems mentioned here are based on the American studies, see note 17.
21. Karl Popper, *Unended Quest. An Intellectual Autobiography* (Glasgow 1976) p. 108; s.a. Born, *Mein Leben*, p. 379.

22. See Paul Kecskemeti in his introduction to Mannheim, *Essays on the Sociology of Knowledge*, p. 3; s. a. Hughes, *Sea Change*, p. 31.
23. Popper, *Unended Quest*, pp. 113f.
24. Crawford, *Cultural Migration*, pp. 92f.
25. Hughes, *Sea Change*, p. 29.
26. Born, *Mein Leben*, p. 377; Moritz Bonn, *Wandering Scholar* (London, 1949) p. 359.
27. Hughes, *Sea Change*, pp. 269, 29f.
28. Jacques Vernant, *The Refugee in the Post-War World* (London, 1953) p. 346.
29. Dorothy Frances Buxton, *The Economics of the Refugee Problem* (London n.d. (1939)) p. 21.
30. Stephen K. Westman, *Frauenarzt. Ein Leben unter zwei Flaggen*, (London, 1960) p. 269.
31. Leibfried, *Berufsverbote*, pp. 153 ff.
32. Westman, *Frauenarzt*, p. 266.
33. Norman Bentwich, *Rescue and Achievement of Refugee Scholars* (The Hague 1953) pp. 36f.
34. S.a. Westman, *Frauenarzt*, p. 316.
35. Bentwich, *Rescue and Achievement*, ibid.; *Are Refugees an Asset?* PEP Pamphlets, London, 1944, p. 20.
36. Ibid.; s.a. Jewish Central Information Office, *The Position of Jewish Refugees in England*, London 1945, p. 4, emphasis in the original. The situation of dentists was slightly more favourable, s. Norman Bentwich, *They found Refuge* (London, 1956) p. 53.
37. Westman, *Frauenarzt*, p. 295.
38. A. G. Chloros, and K. H. Neumayer, *Liber Amicorum Ernst J. Cohn, Festschrift für Ernst J. Cohn zum 70. Geburstag* (Heidelberg, 1974) pp. 9f.
39. Recorded for the Imperial War Museum.
40. See above p. 77.
41. Association of Jewish Refugees, *Britain's New Citizens. The Story of the Refugees from Germany and Austria* (London, 1951) p. 44.
42. Bentwich, *Refugees from Germany*, p. 196.
43. Julius Berstl, *Odyssee eines Theatermannes* (Berlin, 1963) p. 87.
44. *AJR Information*, March 1961, p. 10; s.a. John Willett, 'The Emigration and the Arts', typescript, pp. 14f.
45. Paul Tabori (ed.), *The PEN in Exile* (London, 1954) p. 7.
46. Matthias Wegner, *Exil und Literatur. Deutsche Schriftsteller im Ausland, 1933–1945* (Frankfurt, 1967) p. 89.
47. Herbert Friedenthal, 'The Writer's Dilemma', *AJR Information*, May 1946, p. 36.
48. Berstl, *Odyssee*, pp. 178, 187f.
49. Willett, 'Emigration and the Atts', pp. 21f.
50. Ibid., p. 21.
51. Arthur Koestler, *The Invisible Writing* (London, 1954) pp. 426ff.
52. Stern, *Pillar of Fire*, pp. 210f.
53. H. G. Adler, 'Deutsche Exilliteratur in London', *Europäische Ideen*, Heft 45/46, 1979, 29; s.a. Gabriele Tergit, 'Die Exilsituation in England', Mandfred Durzak (ed.), *Die deutsche Exilliteratur 1933–1945* (Stuttgart 1973) p. 135; Klaus Mann, *Der Wendepunkt* (n.p. 1952), pp. 457f.

54. *Die Zeitung*, 3 April 1941, p. 3; PEN Zentrum, *Autobiographien und Bibliographien* (London, 1959) *passim*. In Sweden, by contrast, the exiled writers never gave up German as their literary medium; see Helmut Müssenet, *Exil in Schweden. Politische und Kulturelle Emigration nach 1933* (München, 1973) p. 396.
55. Judith Kerr, 'With borrowed Words', *Times Literary Supplement*, 4 April 1975.
56. Eva Figes, 'The Long Passage to little England', *The Observer*, 11 June 1978.
57. Sinzheimer, *Gelebt im Paradies*, p. 297.
58. Based on information given by several respondents.
59. Judith Kerr, *The Other Way Round* (London, 1975) p. 242.
60. Willett, 'Emigration and the Arts', p. 4; s.a. Hans-Albert Walter, *Deutsche Exilliteratur 1933–1950*, 2. vols. (Neuwied 1974); Mann, *Wendepunkt*, p. 311.
61. Ibid., pp. 457f.
62. Wegner, *Exil und Literatur*, pp. 90f; Erich Stern, *Die Emigration als psychologisches Problem* (Boulogne-sur-Seine, 1937) pp. 41f.
63. *AJR Information*, January 1956, p. 9; s.a. Elisabeth Castonier, *Stürmisch bis heiter. Memoiren einer Aussenseiterin* (München, 1978), pp. 289, 292.
64. S. e.g. the case of the Amadeus Quartet: Daniel Snowman, *The Amadeus Quartet. The Men and the Music* (London, 1981).
65. S.a. Born, *Mein Leben*, p. 364.
66. Berstl, *Odyssee*, p. 187.
67. AJR, *Britain's New Citizens*, p. 56.
68. See below pp. oooff.
69. *AJR Information*, March 1948, p. 5.
70. Willett, 'Emigration and the Arts', p. 16.
71. Fritz Kortner, *Aller Tage Abend* (München, 1959) pp. 428ff.
72. Sherman, *Island Refuge*, *passim*.
73. Loebl, *Government-Financed Factories*, p. 8.
74. AJR, *Britain's New Citizens*, p. 25.
75. Walter Schindler, 'The New Citizens' Contribution to Economic Demands', *AJR Information*, October 1962, p. 17f.
76. Information on the German-Jewish business community is scattered though; the only systematic study of one aspect of it has been undertaken by Loebl, s.note 6.
77. Schindler, 'Contribution to Economic Demands', p. 18.
78. Herbert Loebl, 'Refugee Industries in the Depressed Areas', *AJR Information*, September 1981, p. 2.
79. Schindler, 'Contribution to Economic Demands', p. 17.
80. AJR, *Britain's New Citizen*, p. 31.
81. *Are Refugees an Asset?*, p. 24.
82. *Leicester University Gazette*, 1971.
83. S.a. Schindler, 'Contribution to Economic Demands'; Loebl, *Government-Financed Factories*; Sidney Osborne, *Germany and Her Jews* (London, 1939) pp. 12f.
84. Sherman, *Island Refuge*, passim; Austin Stevens, *The Dispossessed. German Refugees in Britain* (London, 1975) pp. 148ff.
85. Karen Gershon (ed.); *We came as Children. A Collective Autobiography* (London, 1966) p. 22.
86. Herbert A. Strauss, 'Jewish Emigration from Germany – Nazi Policies and Jewish Responses (II)', *LBIYB*, xxvi, 1981, p. 362.

87. See note 85.
88. Bentwich, *They found Refuge*, p. 72; s.a. Margot Pottlitzer, 'What became of Refugee Children?', *AJR Information*, June 1977, p. 10.
89. See e.g. Gabriele Targit, 'How they settled', *Britain's New Citizens*, pp. 61ff.
90. The exception was Shanghai were no visas were required.
91. R. Grüneberg, 'Reflections on re-reading Plato', *AJR Information*, February 1977, p. 3.
92. *Are Refugees an Asset?*, p. 22.
93. Jewish Central Information Office, *Position of Jewish Refugees*, p. 14; Sherman, *Island Refuge*, *passim*.
94. See e.g. Lore Segal, *Other People's Houses*, (New York, 1964).
95. Altogether 14 000 women, accompanied by 1 000 children, arrived as domestics; see Tergit, *Britain's New Citizens*, p. 61.

CHAPTER 5 SEARCH FOR NEW ROOTS

1. *AJR Information*, January 1952, p. 1.
2. Ibid., August, 1946, p. 7; May 1946, p. 6.
3. Ibid., June 1946, p. 45; May 1946, p. 35.
4. Crawford, *The Cultural Migration*, pp. 17f.
5. More recent attitudes towards Britain will be dealt with below.
6. *AJR Information*, April 1948, p. 7.
7. Vivian D. Lipman, 'The Rise of Jewish Suburbia', *Transactions of the Jewish Historical Society of England*, vol. XXI, 1968, pp. 78–103. Howard Brotz, *An Analysis of Social Stratification within Jewish Society in London*, p. 292.
8. Willi Frischauer, *European Commuter* (London, 1964) pp. 128f.
9. See e.g. Adam, *Judenpolitik*, p. 297.
10. Zweig, *The World of Yesterday*, pp. 307ff.
11. Klaus P. Fink 'Victims of political-racial persecution', *Nursing Times*, 22 March 1979, pp. 496–9.
12. Chaim Bermant, *Troubled Eden* (London, 1969) p. 75.
13. Heinrich Fraenkel, *Farewell to Germany* (London, 1959) p. 7.
14. The same applied to the older generation, but to a lesser extent, it seems. See Chapter 6.
15. Segal, *Other People's Houses*, p. 167.
16. *Die Zeitung*, 25 March 1941, p. 3.
17. *AJR Information*, February 1949, p. 5; s.a. Eisenstadt, *Absorption of Immigrants*, p. 7; ibid., *From Generation to Generation: Age Groups and Social Structure* (London, 1956).
18. *AJR Information*, October 1959, p. 10.
19. See above, p. 135.
20. S.a. *AJR Information*, February 1949, p. 5.
21. Morton Weinfeld et. al., 'Long-Term Effects of the Holocaust on Selected Social Attitudes – Behaviors of Survivors: A Cautionary Note', *Social Forces*, vol. 60, no. 1, September 1981, p. 1.
22. Inge Fleischhauer and Hillel Klein, *Über die jüdische Identität. Eine psychohistorische Studie* (Königstein/Ts. 1978) pp. 22f.; s.a. Mayer, *Erinnerungen*, p. 4.
23. S.a. Kenneth Lunn (ed.), *Hosts, Immigrants and Minorities. Historical Responses*

to *Newcomers in British Society 1870–1914* (London, 1980) p. 16.
24. H. B. M. Murphy, 'Practical Measures for Refugee Mental Health in Britain', *The Bulletin of the World Federation for Mental Health*, vol. 4, no. 4, November 1952, p. 5.
25. Bonn, *Wandering Scholar*, p. 358.
26. Alfred Kerr, *Ich kam nach England. Ein Tagebuch aus dem Nachlass*. Ed. by W. Huder and Th. Koebner, (Bonn, 1979) p. 131; s.a. Zweig, *The World of Yesterday*, p. 314.
27. Richard C. Thurlow, 'Satan and Sambo: the Image of the Immigrant in English Racial Populist Thought since the First World War', Lunn (ed.), *Immigrants and Minorities*, p. 42; s.a. Colin Holmes, *Anti-Semitism in British Society, 1876–1939* (London, 1979) *passim*.
28. Fraenkel, *Farewell to Germany*, p. 2; s.a. Ulla Hahn, 'Der Freie Deutsche Kulturbund in Grossbritannien. Eine Skizze seiner Geschichte', Lutz Winckler (ed.), *Antifaschistische Literatur*, vol. 2 (Kronberg/Ts., 1977) p. 149; Hans J. Rehfisch, *In Tyrannos* (London, 1944) *passim*.
29. C. C. Aronsfeld, 'Jewish Enemy Aliens in England during the First World War', *JSS*, vol. 18, no. 4, October 1956, pp. 275–83.
30. Jewish Central Information Office, *Position of Jewish Refugees*, pp. 2f.
31. Eva Figes, *Little Eden. A Child at War* (London, 1978) p. 17.
32. Hannam, *A Boy in your Situation*, p. 201.
33. The Trades Advisory Council, *Annual Reports*, London, 1943–1949, Report 43–4, p. 26.
34. *AJR Information*, September 1943, p. 1.; s.a. Howard Brotz, 'The Position of the Jews in English Society', *JJS*, vol. 1, no. 1, April 1959, pp. 94–113.
35. Trades Advisory Council, *Report 46–47*, pp. 3f.
36. *AJR Information*, July 1946, p. 1; s.a. ibid., April 1946, p. 1.
37. See e.g. Werner Angress, 'Das deutsche Militär und die Juden im Ersten Weltkrieg', *Militärgeschichtliche Mitteilungen*, 1, 1976, 77–146.
38. German Jewish Aid Committee (ed.), *While you are in England. Helpful Information and Guidance for every Refugee* (London, 1939 (?)) pp. 12f (emphasis in text).
39. *AJR Information*, April 1946, p. 31.
40. Ibid., December 1960, p. 9.
41. Ibid., September 1964, p. 1.
42. Ibid., April 1965, p. 1.
43. Ibid., December 1965, p. 1.
44. Ibid., September 1964, p. 1.
45. *Die Zeitung*, 19 March 1941, p. 3.
46. *AJR Information*, May 1947, p. 35.
47. Ibid., January 1960, p. 10.
48. S. a Fischer, *Dienstboten, Brecht* . . . p. 311.
49. Figes, *Little Eden*, p. 19.
50. *AJR Information*, October 1972, p. 1.
51. Gabriele Tergit, 'How they resettled', AJR, *Britain's New Citizens*, p. 63.
52. *AJR Information*, June 1952, p. 7.
53. Ibid., January 1964, p. 1.
54. Ibid., September 1939, p. 1.
55. Ibid., December 1960, p. 9.

56. Ibid., October 1960, p. 16.
57. Ibid., December 1964, p. 14.
58. Ibid., December 1964, p. 14.
59. Hahn, 'Der Freie Deutsche Kulturbund', p. 148.
60. Ibid., p. 137.
61. Ibid., p. 136.
62. Kurt Hiller, *Leben gegen die Zeit*, vol. 1, *Logos* (Hamburg, 1969) pp. 322 ff.; s.a. Hans-Christof Wächter, *Theater im Exil. Socialgeschichte des deutschen Exiltheaters, 1933–45* (München, 1973) pp. 66ff.
63. Freie Deutsche Dichtung, *Und sie bewegt sich doch!* (London, 1943).
64. Lisa Appignanesi, *The Cabaret* (London 1975) p. 168; s.a. Hahn, 'Freier Deutscher Kulturbund', pp. 157ff.
65. *AJR Information*, August 1957, p. 9.
66. Hahn, 'Freier Deutscher Kulturbund', pp. 145f.; Appignanesi, *Cabaret*, p. 168.
67. *AJR Information*, August 1957, p. 9.
68. Appignanesi, *Cabaret*, p. 165.
69. *AJR Information*, August 1957, p. 9.
70. Appignanesi, *Cabaret*, p. 166.
71. *Exiled Theatre* (Laterndl), Box 599 (1), Wiener Library.
72. Ibid.
73. Hilde Mareiner, *"Zeitspiegel". Eine Österreichische Stimme gegen Hitler* (Wien, 1967) p. 10.
74. Ibid.; s.a. Georg Knepler, *Five Years of the Austrian Centre* (London 1944) passim.
75. Hahn, 'Freier Deutscher Kulturbund', p. 166.
76. Club 43, *Zwanzig Jahre Club 1943* (London, 1963); Idem, *25 Jahre Club 1943*, (London 1968); Fischer, *Dienstboten, Brecht* . . . p. 344.
77. J. Rudolf Bienenfeld, 'Die Aufgabe der Jacob Ehrlich Society', Lecture, 22 August, 1942, London.
78. Ibid., pp. 4ff.
79. Ibid., p. 17.
80. Bienenfeld, 'Jacob Ehrlich Society', p. 17.
81. *AJR Information*, October 1962, p. 4 (footnote).
82. Ibid.
83. A smaller German–Jewish organization called Self Aid was founded in 1938. Its first chairman was S. G. Warburg. See *AJR Information*, 18 November, 1963, p. 13.
84. Jewish Central Information Office, *The Position of Jewish Refugees*, pp. 4, 6.
85. *AJR Information*, October 1962, p. 4.
86. Ibid., October 1962, p. 4.
87. Ibid., April 1943, p. 1.
88. Ibid., January 1952, p. 1; July 1946, p. 52.
89. Ibid., March 1973, p. 1.
90. Ibid., October 1962, p. 5.
91. Ibid., October 1972, pp. 2, 1.
92. Ibid., October 1972, pp. 2, 1.
93. See e.g. ibid., April 1950, p. 7; 'Afternoon with Werner Finck'.

94. Ibid., August 1947, p. 62.
95. Ibid., June 1946, p. 43.
96. Ibid., March 1947, p. 22.
97. Ibid., November 1964, p. 1.
98. Ibid., September 1955, p. 3.
99. Ibid., March 1947, p. 19.
100. Ibid., January 1950, p. 2.
101. Ibid., May 1955, p. 3.
102. Ibid., September 1950, p. 5; August 1957, p. 14; April 1963, p. 7.
103. Ibid., October 1962, p. 7.
104. Ibid. The Council of Jews from Germany was set up by the three refugee organizations in Israel, the United States and Great Britain in 1947.
105. *AJR Information*, January 1954, p. 1; s.a. ibid., April 1954, p. 1; ibid., May 1954, p. 1; ibid., April 1956, p. 1.
106. Ibid., February 1947, p. 11.
107. Ibid., August 1947, p.
108. Ibid., March 1950, p. 1.
109. Ibid., June 1954, p. 1.
110. Ibid., October 1962, p. 7.
111. Ibid., July 1955, p. 1.
112. Ibid., July 1955, p. 1.
113. Ibid., September 1964, p. 6.
114. Ibid., May 1948, p. 7.
115. Ibid., October 1948, p.
116. Thanks is due to Mr Peter Johnson, one of the founding members of The Hyphen, who generously provided me with information and material about the group.
117. *AJR Information*, July 1958, p. 1.
118. Ibid., February 1949, p. 5.
119. C. C. Aronsfeld, *Leo Baeck (London) Lodge 1593: The First Thirty Years* (London, 1975) p. 16.
120. *Hyphen News*, February 1950, p. 3.
121. Ibid., p. 4.
122. *AJR Information*, November 1958, p. 11.
123. Ibid.; s.a. ibid., March 1968, p.
124. Ibid., March 1970, p. 1; ibid., March 1979, p. 1.
125. Ibid., July 1960, p. 14.
126. Ibid., November 1953, p. 6.
127. Georg Salzberger, *Our Congregation. The Twenty-fifth Anniversary of the New Liberal Jewish Congregation*, June 1964, p. 4.
128. Ibid., p. 3.
129. Ibid., pp. 15f.
130. Ibid., p. 3.
131. Ibid., p. 17.
132. The same is probably true for the Orthodox congregations of largely German-Jewish membership. However, only few respondents belonged to them. Their statements would suggest such a development. But the numbers involved were not enough to allow for a more detailed picture. A couple of cases among the younger generation will be described in the last chapter.

133. *AJR Information*, May 1962, p. 2.
134. See Salzberger, *Our Congregation*, p. 4.
135. Ibid., p. 13.
136. Bne Briss, *Zum 50jährigen Bestehen des Ordens in Deutschland* (Frankfurt/M. (1933) p. 7; s.a. Aronsfeld, *Leo Baeck (London) Lodge*, p. 6.
137. B'nai B'rith, *Standing Rules and Orders* (London, 1953) (1943-1946) p. 6.
138. Bne Briss, *Zum 50 jährigen Bestehen*, p. 156.
139. Aronsfeld, *Leo Baeck (London) Lodge*, p. 7.
140. Ibid., p. 7.
141. Ibid., p. 7.
142. Ibid., p. 8.
143. Walter Schwab, *B'nai B'rith. Fifty Years of Achievement, 1926-1976* (London, 1976) p. 22.
144. Aronsfeld, *Leo Baeck (London) Lodge*, p. 10.
145. Ibid., p. 16.
146. Bermant, *Troubled Eden*, p. 93.
147. Aronsfeld, *Leo Baeck (London) Lodge*, p. 16f. It is interesting to note, however, that the benefactors of the newly founded Society for Jewish Studies (1948) which was aiming at continuing the tradition of *Wissenschaft des Judentums* were "in the main English Jews". See Ernst, *AJR Information*, July 1948, p. 5.
148. Aronsfeld, *Leo Baeck (London) Lodge*, p. 19.
149. Ibid., p. 8; B'nai B'rith, *Standing Rules and Orders*, p. 7.
150. Interview with Mr Werner Lash, one of the former presidents of the Leo Baeck Lodge.

CHAPTER 6   THE AMBIGUITIES OF ETHNIC IDENTIFICATION

1. Mayer, *Erinnerungen*, p. 373. ('The mother country remains irreplaceable in one's emotional world. The memory of one's home, the places of one's youth and one's mother tongue permanently cling to the notions of *Heimat*').
2. Reichmann, *Grösse und Verhängnis*, p. 160.
3. Jews and Blacks have repeatedly been expelled from Britain. See e.g. Cecil Roth, *A History of the Jews in England* (Oxford, 1964) and James Walvin, *Black and White. The Negro and English Society 1555-1945* (London, 1973).
4. Hans Günther Reissner, 'Die jüdischen Auswanderer', F. Böhm and W. Dirks (eds), *Judentum. Schicksal, Wesen und Gegenwart* (Wiesbaden, 1965) vol. 2, p. 800.
5. *AJR Information*, April 1969, p. 12; ibid., June 1969, p. 16.
6. Ibid., March 1975, p. 1.
7. Brotz, *Social Stratification within Jewish Society*, p. 119.
8. For Britain in general see S. J. Prais and Marlena Schmool, 'Statistics of Jewish Marriages in Great Britain: 1901-1965', *JJS*, vol. IX, no. 2, December 1967. It is difficult to be precise here since, so far, we have only looked at the relationship between German Jews and non-Jewish English. There is another group, however, which has to be considered and that is Anglo-Jewry. Because of the peculiar relationship between German and English Jews, the forms of contact between both groups will be dealt with in a special section below. But at this point it should perhaps be pointed out that whereas none of the older respondents was or is married to an Anglo-Jew, there were 10 among the

second generation. This is an interesting fact in itself and will concern us further below as well. It certainly is also significant with regard to intermarriage but, unfortunately, confuses the issue. Taking the ethnic division between German and English Jews into consideration, one may consider the Anglo-Jews as 'English' in this context. If so, then these 10 spouses would considerably push up the Continental/English intermarriage rate. On the other hand, it might have been the Jewishness which attracted the 'Continental' spouse. Seen from this angle, our 10 spouses would push down the Jewish–non-Jewish intermarriage rate.

9. This constitutes another difference between German Jews and British Jews in general. See Ernest Krausz, 'The Edgware Survey: Occupation and Social Class', *JJS*, vol. 11, no. 1, June 1969. However, Gerald Cromer, *A Comparison of Jewish and Non-Jewish Family Life with Special Reference to Intergenerational Relations*, Ph.D. Thesis, Nottingham, 1973, observed an increase of mixing among the younger generation; ibid., p. 77ff.
10. An incident at a meeting of the Leo Baeck Lodge at which I was present is interesting in this context. An elderly gentleman reported that his granddaughter had told him that her (English) friends at school had maintained that her English showed traces of an accent and that they were able to tell that she came from a family of refugees. Quite a number of Lodge members disputed this most energetically as being impossible in a third generation member. In vain did the gentleman claim to tell the truth. His remark had been provoked by the talk of a speech therapist earlier on that same evening. The reaction of the audience was ambivalent, especially at one point at which the therapist said: 'In an audience like this I need not emphasize that the most difficult sound in English is the "th".' This remark was first greeted with an awkward silence; then a few people started laughing, more joined in until, in the end, general hilarity reigned in the hall.
11. *AJR Information*, January 1970, p. 2.
12. Bermant, *Troubled Eden*, p. 262.
13. See above p. 79ff.
14. Aronsfeld, 'Jewish Enemy Aliens', p. 275.
15. See esp. Werner E. Mosse, Arnold Paucker and Reinhard Rürup (eds), *Revolution and Evolution. 1848 in German-Jewish History* (Tübingen 1981); s.a. C. C. Aronsfeld, 'German Jews in Victorian England', *LBIYB*, VII, 1962, pp. 312–29; idem, 'The German Element', *Jewish Chronicle* (Supplement: Tercentenary of British Jewry) 1956.
16. See e.g. Lamm, 'Bemerkungen zur Entwicklung und Wandlung des deutsch jüdischen Lebensgefühls', Diwald (ed.), *Lebendiger Geist*, p. 234.
17. *AJR Information*, July 1946, p. 52.
18. See above p. 200.
19. Fraenkel, *Farewell to Germany*, pp. 1f.
20. Fred Uhlmann, *The Making of an Englishman* (London, 1960), p. 134.
21. Frischauer, *European Commuter*, pp. 238ff.
22. Reichmann, *Grösse und Verhängnis*, p. 157.
23. Some recent examples of this attitude can be found in the two special issues, 'Germans and Jews', of the *New German Critique*, nos 19, 20, Winter 1980/Spring-Summer 1980.

24. *AJR Information*, December 1979, p. 6.
25. Ibid., November 1980, p. 12.

CHAPTER 7 CONTINENTAL BRITONS

1. In this sense one might consider the academic world as a continuation of the *salons* of the 18th century. For other interpretations see Norman L. Friedman, 'The Problem of the "Runaway Jewish Intellectual": Social Definition and Sociological Perspective', *JSS*, vol. 31, January 1969, pp. 3–19.
2. See above pp. 240ff.
3. In Israel, German Jews have for this reason been nicknamed "Jeckes" (Jecke, der. from German *Jacke*).
4. *AJR Information*, February 1962, p. 10.
5. This is in striking contrast to the United States, where refugees dominate the field of German history and literature.
6. That is probably why food sometimes assumes a highly effective value as a cultural symbol, viz. Afroamerican *soul food* and American Jewish *chicken soup*. S.a. Epstein, *Ethos and Identity*, p. 103.
7. See above pp. 214ff.
8. This was, indeed, the case. Lately the pattern is said to have been changing. See Stephen Aris, *The Jews in Business* (London 1970); D. B. Halpern, *Changes in the Structure of Jewish Industrial and Commercial Life in Britain* (London, 1955); Stephen Sharot, *Judaism* (London, 1976).
9. *AJR Information*, May 1972, p. 1.
10. Female figures in the family apparently play a much greater role during the process of the formation of identity. Fathers or grandfathers were hardly ever mentioned in this context.
11. Very few respondents objected to mixed marriages. Some said they preferred a Jewish partner for their children, but they considered the personality of the non-Jewish partner of primary importance.

Bibliography

Abbreviations
JJS   Jewish Journal of Sociology
JSS   Jewish Social Studies
JMH   Journal of Modern History
CEH   Central European History
LBIYB Leo Baeck Institute Year Book

Adam, Uwe Dietrich, *Judenpolitik im Dritten Reich*, Düsseldorf, 1972.
Adler, H. G., *The Jews in Germany: from the Enlightenment to National Socialism*, Notre Dame, London, 1969.
Adler, H. G., 'Deutsche Exilliteratur in London', *Europäische Ideen*, 45/46, 1979, pp. 29–32.
Adler-Rudel, S., *Ostjuden in Deutschland, 1880–1940*, Tübingen, 1959.
Altenhofer, Norbert, 'Tradition als Revolution: Gustav Landauers "gewordeneswerdendes" Judentum', Bronsen, *Jews and Germans*, pp. 173–208
Angel-Volkov, Shulamit; 'The Social and Political Function of Late 19th-Century Anti-Semitism: the Case of the Small Handicraft Masters', H.-U. Wehler (ed.), *Sozialgeschichte Heute*, pp. 416–31.
Angress, Werner, 'Das deutsche Militär und die Juden im Ersten Weltkrieg', *Militärgeschichtliche Mitteilungen*, 1, 1976, pp. 77–146.
Appignanesi, Lisa, *The Cabaret*, London, 1975.
Are Refugees an Asset?, PEP Pamphlets, London, 1944.
Arendt, Hannah, *Rahel Varnhagen: Lebensgeschichte einer deutschen Jüdin aus der Romantik*, München, 1975.
Aris, Stephen, *The Jews in Business*, London, 1970.
Aronsfeld, C. C., 'German Jews in Victorian England', *LBIYB*, VII, 1962, pp. 312–29.
Aronsfeld, C. C., 'The German Element', *Jewish Chronicle – Supplement*, Tercentenary of British Jewry, London, 1956.
Aronsfeld, C. C., 'Jewish Enemy Aliens in England during the First

World War', *JSS*, 18, Oct. 1956, no. 4, pp. 275–83.
Aronsfeld, C. C., *Leo Baeck (London) Lodge 1593: the First Thirty Years*, London, 1975.
Association of Jewish Refugees, *Britain's New Citizens: the Story of the Refugee from Germany and Austria*, London, 1951.
Association of Jewish Refugees, *Dispersion and Resettlement*, London, 1955.
Bach, Hans I., *Jacob Bernays*, Tübingen, 1974.
Bacharach, Walter Zwi, 'Jews in Confrontation with Racist Antisemitism, 1879–1933', *LBIYB*, xxv, 1980, pp. 197–219.
Ball-Kaduri, Kurt, *Das Leben der Juden in Deutschland im Jahre 1933*, Frankfurt, 1963.
Barany, George, 'Magyar Jew or Jewish Magyar', *Canadian-American Slavic Studies*, 8, no. 1, Spring 1974, pp. 1–44.
Barth Frederick (ed.), *Ethnic Groups and Boundaries: the Social Organization of Culture Difference*, London, 1970.
Baxter, Paul and Basil Sansom (eds), *Race and Social Difference: Selected Readings*, Harmondsworth, 1972.
Bein, Alex, *Die Judenfrage. Biographie eines Weltproblems*, 2 vols, Stuttgart, 1980.
Beling, Eva, *Die gesellschaftliche Eingliederung der deutschen Einwanderer in Israel*, Frankfurt, 1967.
Bennathan, Esra, 'Die demographische und wirtschaftliche Struktur der Juden', Mosse and Paucker (eds), *Entscheidungsjahr 1932*, pp. 87–131.
Ben-Sassoon, H. H. and S. Ettinger (eds), *Jewish Society through the Ages*, London, 1971.
Bentwich, Norman, *The Refugees from Germany. April 1933 to December 1935*, London, 1936.
Bentwich, Norman, *Rescue and Achievement of Refugee Scholars*, The Hague, 1953.
Bentwich, Norman, *They found Refuge*, London, 1956.
Berger, Peter L. and Thomas Luckmann, *The Social Construction of Reality*, Harmondsworth, 1973.
Berger, Peter L. et al., *The Homeless Mind. Modernization and Consciousness*, Harmondsworth, 1977.
Berlin, Isaiah, *Against the Current: Essays in the History of Ideas*, London, 1979.
Bermant, Chaim, *Troubled Eden*, London, 1969.
Berstl, Julius, *Odyssee eines Theatermannes*, Berlin, 1963.
Bieber, Hans-Joachim, 'Anti-Semitism as a Reflection of Social,

Economic and Political Tension in Germany, 1880–1933', Bronsen (ed.), *Jews and Germans*, pp. 33–77.
Bienenfeld, F. Rudolf, *The Germans and the Jews*, New York, 1939.
Bienenfeld, F. Rudolf, 'Die Aufgabe der Jacob Ehrlich Society', Talk delivered 22 August 1942, London.
Bienenfeld, F. Rudolf, *The Religion of the Non-Religious Jews*, London, 1944.
Bin-Nun, Jechiel, *Jiddisch und die deutschen Mundarten*, Tübingen, 1973.
Black, Friedrich, *Die Juden in Deutschland. Von einem jüdischen Deutschen*, Berlin, 1911.
Blau, Bruno, 'The last days of German Jewry in the Third Reich', *YIVO Annual of Jewish Social Science*, New York, 1953, pp. 197–204.
Blau, Bruno, 'On the Frequency of Births in Jewish Marriage', *Conference on Relations*, New York, 1953.
B'nai B'rith, Leo Baeck (London) Lodge, *Standing Rules and Orders*, London, 1953.
Bne Briss, *Zum 50 järigen Bestehen des Ordens in Deutschland*, Frankfurt, 1933.
Böhm, F. and W. Dirks (eds), *Judentum. Schicksal, Wesen und Gegenwart*, Wiesbaden, 1965.
Bolkosky, Sidney M., *The Distorted Image. German Jewish Perceptions of Germans and Germany, 1918–1935*, New York, Oxford, 1975.
Bonn, Moritz J., *Wandering Scholar*, London, 1949.
Born, Max, *Mein Leben*, München, 1975.
Borrie, W. D., *The Cultural Integration* of Immigrants, Paris, 1959.
Borries, Achim von (ed.), *Selbstzeugnisse des deutschen Judentums, 1870–1945*, Frankfurt, 1962.
Bronsen, D. (ed.), *Jews and Germans from 1860 to 1933: The Problematical Symbiosis*, Heidelberg, 1979.
Broszat, Martin and Elke Fröhlich (eds.), *Bayern in der NS-Zeit. Herrschaft und Gesellschaft im Konflikt*, München, 1979.
Broszat, Martin, 'Hitler und die Genesis der Endlösung', *Vierteljahrshefte für Zeitgeschichte*. 25, 1977, pp. 739–75.
Brotz, Howard M., *An Analysis of Social Stratification within Jewish Society in London*, Ph.D. Thesis, London School of Economics, 1951.
Brotz, Howard M., 'The Position of the Jews in English Society', *JJS*, 1, no. 1, April 1959, pp. 94–113.
Buber, Martin, *Drei Reden über das Judentum*, Frankfurt, 1916.

Buber, Martin, *Der Jude und sein Judentum*, Köln, 1963.
Buxton, Dorothy F., *The Economics of the Refugee Problem*, London, 1939.
Cahnmann, Werner J. (ed.), *Intermarriage and Jewish Life. A Symposium*, New York, 1963.
Castonier, Elisabeth, *Stürmisch bis heiter. Memoiren einer Aussenseiterin*, München, 1978.
Club 43, *Zwanzig Jahre Club 1943*, London, 1963.
Cohen, Carl, 'The Road to Conversion', *LBIYB*, VI, 1961, pp. 259–79.
Cohen, Gary B., 'Jews in German Society: Prague, 1860–1914', *Central European History*, X, no. 1, March 1977, pp. 28–54.
Cohen, Hermann, *Deutschtum und Judentum*, Giessen, 1923.
Cohen, Joseph W., 'The Jewish Role in Western Culture', Graeber and Britt (eds), *Jews in Gentile World*, pp. 329–59.
Crawford, W. Rex (ed.), *The Cultural Migration. The European Scholar in America*, Philadelphia, 1953.
Cromer, Gerald, *A Comparison of Jewish and Non-Jewish Family Life with Special Reference to Intergenerational Relations*, Ph.D. Thesis, Nottingham, 1973.
Deutscher, Isaac, *The Non-Jewish Jew and other Essays*, London, 1968.
Deutschkron, Inge, *Ich trug den gelben Stern*, Köln, 1978.
Domnitz, Myer, *Immigration and Integration*, London, 1957.
Dubnow, Simon, *History of the Jews*, vol. V, New York, 1973.
Dubnow, Simon, 'An Essay in the Philosophy of History', Meyer (ed.), *Ideas of Jewish History*.
Durkheim, Emile and Marcel Mauss, *Primitive Classification*, London, 1970.
Durzak, Manfred (ed.), *Die deutsche Exilliteratur 1933–1945*, Stuttgart, 1973.
Ehrenberg, Eva, 'The Emigration', trans. ch. from: *Sehnsucht – mein geliebtes Kind*. Frankfurt, 1963.
Eisenstadt, S. N., *The Absorption of Immigrants*, London, 1954.
Eisenstadt, S. N., *From Generation to Generation: Age Groups and Social Structure* London, 1956.
Eisenstein-Barzilay, Isaac, 'The Background of the Berlin Haskalah' in Joseph Blau et al. (eds), *Essays on Jewish Life and Thought presented in Honour of Salo W. Baron*, New York, 1959.
Elbogen, Ismar, *Geschichte der Juden in Deutschland*, Berlin, 1935.
Elbogen, Ismar, *A Century of Jewish Life*, Philadelphia, 1966.

Epstein, A. L., *Ethos and Identity*, London, 1978.
Etzioni-Halevy, Eva and Zvi Halevy, 'The "Jewish Ethic"', *JJS*, XIX, no. 1, June 1977, pp. 49–66.
Field, Frank, *The Last Days of Mankind: Karl Kraus and his Vienna*, London, New York, 1967.
Figes, Eva, *Little Eden: a Child at War*, London, 1978.
Fink, Klaus P., 'Victims of Political-Racial Persecution', *Nursing Times*, 22 March 1979, pp. 496–99.
Fischer, Grete, *Dienstboten, Brecht und andere Zeitgenossen in Prag, Berlin, London*, Olten and Freiburg, 1966.
Fleischhauer, Inge and Hillel Klein, *Über die jüdische Identität. Eine psychohistorische Studie*, Königstein/Ts., 1978.
Fleming, Donald and Bernard Bailyn (eds.), *The Intellectual Migration: Europe and America, 1930–1960*, Cambridge, Mass., 1969.
Fraenkel, Heinrich, *Farewell to Germany*, London, 1959.
Fraenkel, Josef (ed.), *The Jews of Austria. Essays on their Life, History and Destruction*, London, 1967.
Freeden, Herbert, *Vom geistigen Widerstand der deutschen Juden. Ein Kapitel jüdischer Selbstbehauptung in den Jahren 1933/1938*, Jerusalem 1963.
Freie Deutsche Dichtung, *Und sie bewegt sich doch!*, London, 1943.
Freimark, Peter, 'Language Behaviour and Assimilation – The Situation of the Jews in Northern Germany in the First Half of the Nineteenth Century', *LBIYB*, XXIV, 1979, pp. 157–78.
Friedenthal, Richard, *... und unversehens ist es Abend*, München n.d., (1976).
Friedman, Norman, 'The Problem of the "Runaway Jewish Intellectual": Social Definition and Sociological Perspective', *JSS*, 31, Jan. 1969, pp. 3–19.
Frischauer, Willi, *European Commuter*, London, 1964.
Gans, Herbert, *The Levittowners*, New York, 1967.
Gay, Peter, *Freud, Jews and other Germans: Masters and Victims in Modernist Culture*, New York, 1978.
Genschel, Helmut, *Die Verdrängung der Juden aus der Wirtschaft im Dritten Reich*, Göttingen, 1966.
Gershon, Karen, *We Came as Children: a Collective Autobiography*, London, 1966.
Glazer, Nathan and Daniel P. Noynihan (eds.), *Ethnicity. Theory and Experience*, Cambridge, Mass., 1975.

Glazer, Nathan and Daniel P. Moynihan, *Beyond the Melting Pot*, Cambridge, Mass., 1963.
Goldmann, Felix, *Der Jude im deutschen Kulturkreis*, Berlin, 1930.
Goldschmidt, Herrmann Levi, *Das Vermächtnis des deutschen Judentums*, Frankfurt, 1965.
Gordon, Albert I., *Jews in Transition*, Minneapolis 1949
Gordon, Milton M., *Assimilation in American Life*, New York 1964
Gordon, Milton M., 'Toward a General Theory of Racial and Ethnic Group Relations', Glazer and Moynihan (eds.), *Ethnicity*, pp. 84–110.
Gould, Julius and Shaul Esh (eds), *Jewish Life in Modern Britain*, London, 1964.
Grab, Walter (ed.), *Deutsche Aufklärung und Judenemanzipation: Internationales Symposium, 1979–1980*, Jahrbuch des Instituts für Geschichte Tel Aviv, Beiheft 3.
Graeber, Isacque and Stenart H. Britt (eds), *Jews in a Gentile World*, New York, 1942.
Graupe, Heinz Moshe, *The Rise of Modern Judaism: An Intellectual History of German Jewry 1650–1942*, Huntington, N.Y., 1978.
Greive, Hermann, 'On Jewish Self-Identification, Religion and Political Orientation', *LBIYB*, xx, 1975, pp. 35–46.
Greive, Hermann, 'Zionism and Jewish Orthodoxy', *LBIYB*, xxv, 1980, pp. 173–95.
Gruenewald, Max, 'Der Anfang der Reichsvertretung', Weltsch (ed.), *Deutsches Judentum*.
Gruenewald, Max, 'Critic of German Jewry: Ludwig Feuchtwanger and his Gemeindezeitung', *LBIYB*, xvii, 1972, pp. 75–92
Hahn, Ulla, 'Der Freie Deutsche Kulturbund in Grossbritannien. Eine Skizze seiner Geschichte', Lutz Winckler (ed.), *Antifaschistische Literatur*, vol. 2, Kronberg/Ts. 1977, pp. 131–95.
Halpern, D. B., *Changes in the Structure of Jewish Industrial and Commercial Life in Britain*, London, 1955.
Hamburger, Wolfgang, 'The Reaction of Reform Jews to the Nazi Rule', Strauss and Grossmann (ed.), *Gegenwart im Rückblick*, pp. 150–64.
Handlin, Oscar, 'Jews in the Culture of Middle Europe', The Leo Baeck Memorial Lecture, 7, New York, 1964.
Hannam, Charles, *A Boy in Your Situation*, London, 1977.
Herberg, Will, *Protestant, Catholic, Jew*, London, 1960.

Herzig, Arno, 'Das Problem der jüdischen Identität in der deutschen bürgerlichen Gesellschaft', Grab (ed.), *Deutsche Aufklärung und Judenemanzipation*, pp. 243–64.
Higham, John, *Strangers in the Land: Patterns of American Nativism, 1860–1925*, New York, 1963.
Hiller, Kurt, *Leben gegen die Zeit*, vol. 1, *Logos*, Hamburg, 1969.
Hirschfeld, Gerhard (ed.), *Exil in Grossbritannien. Zur Emigration aus dem nationalsozialistischen Deutschland*, Stuttgart, 1983.
Holmes, Colin, *Anti-Semitism in British Society, 1876–1939*, London, 1979.
Horkheimer, Max, 'Über die deutschen Juden', (talk) Köln, 1961.
Howe, Irving, *World of Our Fathers: the Journey of the East European Jews to America and the Life they Found and Made*, New York, London, 1976.
Hughes, H. Stuart, *The Sea Change: the Migration of Social Thought, 1930–1965*, New York, 1975.
Isaacs, Harol R., 'Basic Group Identity: the Idols of the Tribe', Glazer and Moynihan (eds), *Ethnicity*, pp. 29–52.
Jackson, J. A. (ed.), *Migration*, Cambridge, 1969.
Jewish Central Information Office, *The Position of Jewish Refugees in England*, London, 1945.
Kampmann, Wanda, *Deutsche und Juden. Studien zur Geschichte des deutschen Judentums*, Heidelberg, 1963.
Kann, Robert A., 'Assimilation and Antisemitism in the German-French Orbit in the 19th and early 20th Centuries', *LBIYB*, XIV, 1969, pp. 94–115.
Kaplan, Benjamin, *The Jew and His Family*, Baton Rouge, La., 1967.
Kaplan, Marion, *The Jewish Feminist Movement in Germany*, Westport, Conn., 1979.
Kaplan, Marion, 'German–Jewish Feminism in the 20th Century', *JSS*, XXXVIII, no. 1, Winter 1976, pp. 39–53.
Katz, Jacob, *Tradition and Crisis: Society at the End of the Middle Ages*, New York, 1961.
Katz, Jacob, *Exclusiveness & Tolerance. Studies in Jewish–Gentile Relations in Medieval and Modern Times*. London, 1961.
Katz, Jacob, *Out of the Ghetto: the Social Background of Jewish Emancipation, 1770–1870*, Cambridge, Mass., 1973.
Katz, Jacob, *Emancipation and Assimilation*, Westmead, 1972.
Kaznelson, Siegmund (ed.), *Juden im deutschen Kulturbereich*, Berlin, 1959.

Kennedy, Ruby Jo Reeves, 'What Has Social Science to Say About Intermarriage?', Cahnmann (ed.), *Intermarriage and Jewish Life*, pp. 19-37.
Kent, Donald, *The Refugee Intellectual*, New York, 1953.
Kerr, Alfred, *Ich kam nach England: Ein Tagebuch aus dem Nachlass*, W. Huder and Th. Koebner (eds), Bonn, 1979.
Kerr, Judith, *The Other Way Round*, London, 1975.
Kerr, Judith, *A Small Person Far Away*, London, 1978.
Kerr, Judith, 'With Borrowed Words', *Times Literary Supplement*, 4 April 1975.
Kershaw, Ian, 'Antisemitismus und Volksmeinung. Reaktionen auf die Judenverfolgungen', Broszat and Fröhlich (eds), *Bayern in der NS-Zeit*, pp. 343ff.
Kesten, Hermann, *Ich lebe nicht in der Bundesrepublik*, München, 1964.
Klein, Catherine, *Escape from Berlin*, London, 1944.
Klinkenberg, Hans Martin, 'Zwischen Liberalismus und Nationalismus. Im Zweiten Kaiserreich (1870-1918), *Monumenta Judaica*, Köln, 1963.
Knepler, Georg, *Five Years of the Austrian Centre*, London, 1944.
Knütter, Hans-Helmuth, 'Die Linkspartein', Mosse and Raucker (eds), *Entscheidungsjahr 1932*, pp. 323-45.
Koestler, Arthur, *Arrow in the Blue: an Autobiography*, New York, 1952.
Koestler, Arthur, *The Invisible Writing*, London, 1954.
Kortner, Fritz, *Aller Tage Abend*, München, 1959.
Kramer, Judith and Seymour Leventman, *Children of the Gilded Ghetto: Conflict Resolutions of Three Generations of American Jews*, New Haven, 1961.
Krausz, Ernest, 'Occupation and Social Advancement in Anglo-Jewry', *JJS*, IV, no. 1, June 1962, pp. 82-90.
Krausz, Ernest, *A Sociological Field Study of Jewish Suburban Life in Edgware, 1962-3*, Ph.D. Thesis, University of London, 1965.
Krausz, Ernest, 'The Edgware Survey: Occupation and Social Class', *JJS*, XI, no. 1, June 1969.
Kreutzberger, Max, 'Bedeutung und Aufgabe deutsch-jüdischer Geschichtsschreibung in unserer Zeit', Tramer (ed.), *In zwei Welten*, pp. 627-42.
Lamberti, Marjorie, *Jewish Activism in Imperial Germany. The Struggle for Civil Equality*, New Haven, 1978.
Lamberti, Marjorie, 'Liberals, Socialists and the Defence against

Antisemitism in the Wilhelminian Period', *LBIYB*, xxv, 1980, pp. 147–62.

Lamm, Hans, *Über die innere und äussere Entwicklung des deutschen Judentums im Dritten Reich*, Erlangen, 1951.

Lamm, Hans, 'Bemerkungen zur Entwicklung und Wandlung des deutsch-jüdischen Lebensgefühles', Hellmut Diwald (ed.), *Lebendiger Geist. Hans-Joachim Schoeps zum 50. Geburtstag*, Leiden, Köln, 1959.

Laqueur, Walter, *A History of Zionism*, London, 1972.

Laqueur, Walter, *The Missing Years*, London, 1980.

Leibfried, Stephan and Florian Tennstedt, *Berufsverbote und Sozialpolitik 1933. Analyse und Materialien*, Bremen n.d. (1979).

Leschnitzer, A., *Saul und David. Zur Problematik der deutsch-jüdischen Lebensgemeinschaft*, Heidelberg, 1954.

Lessing, Theodor, *Jüdischer Selbsthass*, Berlin, 1930.

Levy, Richard, *The Downfall of the Anti-Semitic Political Parties in Imperial Germany*, New Haven, Conn., 1975.

Liebeschütz, Hans, *Von Georg Simmel zu Franz Rosenzweig*, Tübingen, 1970 (Schriften des Leo Baeck Instituts).

Liebeschütz, Hans, 'Judentum und deutsche Umwelt im Zeitalter der Restauration', Liebeschütz and Paucker (eds), *Judentum in deutscher Umwelt*, pp. 1–54.

Liebeschütz, Hans und Arnold Paucker (eds), *Das Judentum in der deutschen Umwelt. 1800–1850*, Tübingen, 1977 (Schriften des Leo Baeck Instituts).

Lipman, Vivian D., 'The Rise of Jewish Suburbia', *Transactions of the Jewish Historical Society of England*, vol. XXI, 1968, pp. 78–103.

Liptzin, Solomon, *Germany's Stepchildren*, Cleveland, N. Y., 1961.

Litvinoff, Barnet, *A Peculiar People*, London, 1969.

Loebl, Herbert, *Government-Financed Factories and the Establishment of Industries by Refugees in the Special Areas of the North of England, 1937–1961*, M. Phil. Thesis, University of Durham, 1978.

Loewenberg, Peter, 'Antisemitismus und jüdischer Selbsthass', *Geschichte und Gesellschaft*, 5. Jahrgang, 1979, Heft 4, pp. 455–75.

Loewenstein, Kurt, 'Die innerjüdische Reaktion auf die Krise der deutschen Demokratie', Mosse and Paucker (eds), *Entscheidungsjahr 1932*, pp. 349–404.

Low, Alfred D., *Jews in the Eyes of the Germans. From the Enlightenment to Imperial Germany*, Philadelphia, 1979.

Lunn, Kennth (ed.), *Hosts, Immigrants and Minorities. Historical Responses to Newcomers in British Society 1870–1914*, London, 1980.

Mann, Klaus, *Der Wendepunkt*, n.p. 1952.
Mannheim, Karl, *Essays on Sociology and Social Psychology*, London, 1959.
Mannheim, Karl, *Essays on the Sociology of Knowledge*, ed. by Paul Kecskemeti, London, 1968.
Marcus, Jacob R., *The Rise and Destiny of the German Jew*, New York, 1973.
Marcus, Jacob R., *Communal Sick Care in the German Ghetto*, Cincinnati, 1947.
Mareiner, Hilde, '*Zeitspiegel*': *Eine österreichische Stimme gegen Hitler*, Wien, 1967.
Marrus, Michael R., 'European Jewry and the Politics of Assimilation: Assessment and Reassessment', *JMH*, 49, no. 1, March 1977, pp. 89–109.
Mayer, Gustav, *Erinnerungen: Von Journalisten zum Historiker der deutschen Arbeiterbewegung*, Zürich, Wien, 1949.
Mead, George, *On Social Psychology: Selected Papers*. ed. by and with an introduction by Anselm Strauss, Chicago, London, 1969.
Meyer, Michael A., *The Origins of the Modern Jew*, Detroit, 1967.
Meyer, Michael A., 'Jewish Religious Reform and Wissenschaft des Judentums – The Position of Zunz, Geiger and Frankel', *LBIYB*, XVI, 1971, pp. 19–41.
Meyer, Michael A. (ed.), *Ideas of Jewish History*, ed., with introduction and notes by Michael Meyer, New York, 1974.
Miller, Jean, *British Management Versus German Management: a Comparison of Organisational Effectiveness in West German and UK Factories*, Westmead, 1979.
Mills, C. Wright, *The Sociological Imagination*, Harmondsworth, 1977.
Mosse, George L., 'Die deutsche Rechte und die Juden', Mosse and Paucker (eds), *Entscheidungsjahr 1932*, pp. 183–246.
Mosse, George L., *Germans and Jews*, New York, 1970.
Mosse, Werner and Arnold Paucker (eds), *Juden im Wilhelminischen Deutschland, 1890–1914*, Tübingen, 1976 (Schriften des Leo Baeck Instituts).
Mosse, Warner and Arnold Paucker (eds), *Deutsches Judentum in Krieg und Revolution, 1916–1923*, Tübingen, 1971 (Schriften des Leo Baeck Instituts).
Mosse, Werner and Arnold Paucker (eds), *Entscheidungsjahr 1932. Zur Judenfrage in der Endphase der Weimarer Republik*, Tübingen, 1966 (Schriften des Leo Baeck Instituts).

Mosse, Werner et al., (eds), *Revolution and Evolution. 1848 in German–Jewish History*, Tübingen, 1981 (Schriften des Leo Baeck Instituts).
Mosse, Werner, 'Die Juden in Wirtschaft und Gesellschaft', Mosse and Paucker (eds), *Juden im Wilhelminischen Deutschland*, pp. 57–114.
Mosse, Werner, 'Judaism, Jews and Capitalism – Weber, Sombart and Beyond', *LBIYB*, XXIV, 1979, pp. 3–16.
Müssener, Helmut, *Exil in Schweden: Politische und kulturelle Emigration nach 1933*, München, 1973.
Murphy, H. B. M., 'Practical Measures for Refugee Mental Health in Britain'. *The Bulletin of the World Federation for Mental Health*, 4, no. 4, Nov. 1952.
Nachman, Larry D., 'The Question of the Jews: a Study in Culture', *Samalgundi*, no. 44/45, Spring/Summer 1979, pp. 166–81.
Niewyk, Donald L., *Anti-Semite and Jew. German Social Democracy Confronts the Problem of Anti-Semitism 1918–1933*, Baton Rouge, La., 1971.
Osborne, Sidney, *Germany and her Jews*, London, 1939.
P. E. N. Zentrum, *Autobiographien und Bibliographien*, London, 1959.
Pelli, Moshe, 'The Beginning of the Epistolary Genre in Hebrew Enlightenment Literature in Germany – the Alleged Affinity between "Lettress Persanes" and "Igrot Meshulam",' *LBIYB*, XXIV, 1979, pp. 83–106.
Pierson, Ruth L., *German Jewish Identity in the Weimar Republic*. Ph. D. Thesis, Yale University, 1970.
Pollak, Michael, *Mandarins, Jews, and Missionaries*, Philadelphia, 1980.
Poppel, Stephen, *Zionism in Germany, 1897–1933: the Shaping of a Jewish Identity* Philadelphia, 1977.
Poppel, Stephen, 'New Views on Jewish Integration in Germany', *CEH*, IX, no. 1, March 1976, pp. 86–108.
Popper, Karl, *Unended Quest: an Intellectual Autobiography*, Glasgow, 1976.
Prais, S. J. and Marlena Schmool, 'Statistics of Jewish Marriages in Great Britain: 1901–65', *JJS*, IX, no. 2, Dec. 1967.
Prais, S. J., 'Sample Survey on Jewish Education in London 1972–73', *JJS*, XVI, no. 2, Dec. 1974, pp. 133–54.
Price, Charles, 'The Study of Assimilation', Jackson, *Migration*, pp. 181–237.
Prinz, Joachim, *Wir Juden*, Berlin, 1934.

Pross, Helge, *Die deutsche akademische Emigration nach den Vereinigten Staaten, 1933–1941*, Berlin, 1955.
Pulzer, Peter, *The Rise of Political Anti-Semitism in Germany and Austria*, New York, 1964.
Pulzer, Peter, 'Die jüdische Beteiligung an der Politik', Mosse and Paucker (eds) *Juden im Wilhelminischen Deutschland*, pp. 143–240.
Pulzer, Peter 'Why Was There a Jewish Question in Imperial Germany?', *LBIYB*, xxv, 1980, pp. 133–46.
Redkey, Edwin S., *Black Exodus: Black Nationalist and Back-to-Africa Movements, 1890–1910*, New Haven, Conn., 1969.
Rehfisch, Hans J., *In Tyrannos*, London, 1944.
Reichmann, Eva G., *Hostages of Civilisation: the Social Sources of National Socialist Anti-Semitism*, Boston, 1951.
Reichmann, Eva G., *Grösse und Verhängnis deutsch-jüdischer Existenz*, Heidelberg, 1974.
Reinharz, Jehuda, *Promised Land or Fatherland: the Dilemma of the German Jew, 1893–1914*, Ann Arbor, 1975.
Reissner, Hans Günther, 'Die jüdischen Auswanderer', Böhm and Dirks (eds), *Judentum*, pp. 781–806.
Richarz, Monika (ed.), *Jüdisches Leben in Deutschland. Selbstzeugnisse zur Sozialgeschichte*, vol. I: 1780–1871, vol. II: Im Kaiserreich, Stuttgart 1976, 1979.
Rinder, Irwin D., 'Polarities in Jewish Identification: the Personality of Ideological Extremity', Sklare (ed.), *The Jews*.
Rose, Arnold M., *Sociology. The Study of Human Relations*, New York, 1956.
Rosenblüth, Pinchas E., 'Die geistigen und religiösen Strömungen in der deutschen Judenheit', Mosse and Paucker (eds), *Juden im Wilhelminischen Deutschland*, pp. 549–98.
Rosenstock, Werner, 'Exodus 1933–1939. Ein Überblick über die jüdische Auswanderung aus Deutschland', *LBIYB*, I, 1956, pp. 380–405.
Rosenthal, Erich, 'Trends of the Jewish Population in Germany, 1919–1939', *JSS*, 6, 1944, pp. 233–74.
Rosenthal, Heinz, 'Jews in the Solingen Steel Industry', *LBIYB*, XVII, 1972, pp. 205–23.
Roth, Cecil, *A History of the Jews in England*, Oxford, 1964.
Rudavsky, David, *Emancipation & Adjustment: Contemporary Jewish Religious Movements: Their History and Thought*, New York, 1967.
Rudy, Zwi, *Soziologie des jüdischen Volkes*, Reinbek, 1965.

Rürup, Reinhard, *Emanzipation und Antisemitismus*, Göttingen, 1975.
Rürup, Reinhard, 'Judenemanzipation und bürgerliche Gesellschaft in Deutschland', Rürup, *Emanzipation und Antisemitismus*, pp. 11–36.
Rürup, Reinhard, 'Emanzipation und Krise', Mosse and Paucker (eds), *Juden im Wilhelminischen Deutschland*, pp. 1–56.
Ruppin, Arthur, *Die Juden der Gegenwart*, Berlin, 1918.
Ruppin, Arthur, *Memoirs, Diaries, Letters*, London, 1971.
Ruppin, Arthur, *Soziologie der Juden*, 2 vols, Berlin, 1930.
Segal, Lore, *Other People's Houses*, New York, 1964.
Sharot, Stephen, *Judaism. A Sociology*, Newton Abbot, London, 1976.
Sherman, A. J., *Island Refuge: Britain and Refugees from the Third Reich, 1933–1939*, London, 1973.
Shipman, M. D., *The Limitations of Social Research*, London, 1972.
Simon, Ernst, 'Jewish Adult Education in Nazi Germany as Spiritual Resistance', *LBIYB*, 1, 1956, pp. 68–104.
Simpson, George E. and Y. Milton Yinger, *Racial and Cultural Minorities*, New York, 1972.
Simpson, John Hope, *The Refugee Problem: Report of a Survey*, London, 1939.
Simpson, John Hope, *Refugees: a Review of the Situation since Sept. 1938*, London, 1939.
Sinzheimer, Hermann, *Gelebt im Paradies: Erinnerungen und Begegnungen*, München, 1953.
Sklare, Marshall (ed.), *The Jews: Social Patterns of an American Group*, Glencoi, Ill., 1958.
Snowman, Daniel, *The Amadeus Quartet: the Men and the Music*, London 1981.
Society for the Protection of Science and Learning, Fifth Report, Cambridge, 1946.
Susman, Margarete, *Ich habe viele Leben gelebt*, Stuttgart 1964
Schindler, Walter, 'The New Citizens' Contribution to Economic Demands', *AJR Information*, Oct. 1962, pp. 17ff.
Schleunes, Karl A., *The Twisted Road to Auschwitz: Nazi Policy towards German Jews, 1933–1939*, Champaign, Urbana, 1970.
Schoeps, Hans-Joachim, *Wir deutschen Juden*, Berlin, 1934.
Schoeps, Hans-Joachim (ed.), *Wille und Weg des deutschen Judentums*, Berlin, 1935.
Scholem, Gershom, *Von Berlin nach Jerusalem*, Frankfurt, 1977.
Scholem, Gershom, 'On the Social Psychology of the Jews in

Germany: 1900–1933', Bronson (ed.), *Jews and Germans*, pp. 9–32.
Schorsch, Ismar, *Jewish Reactions to German Anti-Semitism 1870–1940*, New York, 1972.
Schubert, Kurt, *Die Kultur der Juden. Teil II: Judentum im Mittelalter*, Wiesbaden, 1979.
Schulin, Ernst and Bernd Martin (eds), *Die Juden als Minderheit in der Geschichte*, München 1981.
Schutz, Alfred and Thomas Luckmann, *The Structures of the Life-World*, London, 1972.
Schwab, Walter, *B'nai B'rith. 50 Years of Achievement, 1926–1976*, London, 1976.
Schwarcz, Moshe, "Religious Currents and General Culture", *LBIYB*, XVI, 1971, pp. 3–17.
Schwartz, Ph., 'Über die Notgemeinschaft deutscher Wissenschaftler im Ausland', Lecture, 2, Internationales Symposium zur Erforschung des deutschsprachigen Exils nach 1933, Kopenhagen, 1972.
Stearns, Peter and D. J. Walkowitz (eds). *Workers in the Industrial Revolution*, New Brunswick, 1974.
Sterling, Eleonore, 'Jewish Reaction to Jew Hatred in the First Half of the Nineteenth Century', *LBIYB*, III, 1958, pp. 103–21.
Stern, Erich, *Die Emigration als psychologisches Problem*, Boulogne-Sur-Seine, 1937.
Stern, Fritz, 'The Burden of Success: Reflections on German Jewry', Quentin Anderson et al. (eds), *Art, Politics, and Will: Essays in Honor of Lionel Trilling*, New York, 1977.
Stern, Fritz, *Gold and Iron, Bismarck, Bleichröder, and the Building of the German Empire*, New York, 1977.
Stern, Fritz, 'The Integration of Jews in Nineteenth-Century Germany', *LBIYB*, XX, 1975, pp. 79–83.
Stern, Karl, *The Pillar of Fire*, New York, 1951.
Stern-Täubler, Selma, *Der Preussische Staat und die Juden*, Tübingen, 1962 (Schriften des Leo Baeck Instituts).
Stern-Täubler, Selma, 'The First Generation of Emancipated Jews", *LBIYB*, XVI, 1970, pp. 3–40.
Stevens, Austin, *The Dispossessed: German Refugees in Britain*, London, 1975.
Strauss, Herbert A., 'Jewish Emigration from Germany: Nazi Policies and Jewish Responses (II)', *LBIYB*, XXVI, 1981, pp. 343–409.

Strauss, Herbert A. and Kurt R. Grossmann (eds), *Gegenwart im Rückblick*, Heidelberg, 1970.
Strodtbeck, Fred L., 'Family Interaction, Values, and Achievement', Sklare (ed.), *The Jews*.
Tabori, Paul (ed.), *The PEN in Exile*, London, 1954.
Tal, Uriel, *Christians and Jews in Germany: Religion, Politics, and Ideology in the Second Reich, 1870–1914*, Ithaca and London, 1975.
Tau, Max, *Das Land, das ich verlassen musste*, Hamburg, 1961.
Tergit, Gabriele, 'Die Exilsituation in England', Durzak, *Deutsche Exilliteratur*, pp. 135–44.
Thurlow, Richard C., 'Satan and Sambo: the Image of the Immigrant in English Racial Populist Thought Since the First World War', Lunn (ed.), *Immigrants and Minorities*, pp. 39–63.
Tobias, Phillip V., 'The Meaning of Race', Baxter and Sansom (eds), *Race and Social Difference*, pp. 19–43.
Toury, Jacob, *Soziale und politische Geschichte der Juden in Deutschland 1847–1871*, Düsseldorf, 1977.
Trades Advisory Council, Annual Reports, London, 1943–9.
Tramer, Hans (ed.), *In zwei Welten. Siefried Moses zum 75. Geburtstag*, Tel Aviv, 1962.
Uhlmann, Fred, *The Making of an Englishman*, London, 1960.
Vernant, Jacques, *The Refugee in the Post-War World*, London, 1953.
Wachenheim Hedwig, *Vom Grossbürgertum zur Sozialdemokratie*, Berlin, 1973.
Wächter, Hans-Christof, *Theater im Exil: Sozialgeschichte des deutschen Exiltheaters 1933–1945*, München, 1973.
Walter, Hans-Albert, *Deutsche Exilliteratur 1933–1950*, Neuwied, 1972.
Warner, W. Lloyd and Leo Srole, *The Social Systems of American Ethnic Groups*, New Haven, Conn., 1945.
Wassermann, Henry, *Jews, Bürgertum and Bürgerliche Gesellschaft in a Liberal Era (1840–1880)*, Ph.D. Thesis, Hebrew University Jerusalem (English Abstract) 1980.
Wassermann, Jakob, *Mein Weg als Deutscher und Jude*, Berlin, 1921.
Wasserstein, Bernard, *Britain and the Jews of Europe, 1939–1945*, Oxford, 1979.
Wegner, Matthias, *Exil und Literatur. Deutsche Schriftsteller im Ausland, 1933–1945*, Frankfurt, Bonn, 1967.
Weinberg, David H., *A Community on Trial: the Jews of Paris in the 1930s*, Chicago, 1977.

Weltsch, Robert (ed.), *Deutsches Judentum: Aufstieg und Krise, Gestalten, Ideen, Werke*, Stuttgart, 1963.
Weltsch, Robert, 'Entscheidungsjahr 1932', Mosse and Paucker (eds), *Entscheidungsjahr 1932*, pp. 535–62.
Wertheimer, Jack L., *German Policy and Jewish Politics: the Absorption of East European Jews in Germany, 1868–1914*, Ph.D. Thesis Columbia University, 1978.
Westman, Stephan K., *Frauenarzt. Ein Leben unter zwei Flaggen*, London, 1960.
Willett, John, 'The Emigration and the Arts', in Hirschfeld (ed.), *Exil in Grossbritannien*, Stuttgart 1983.
Williams, Bill, *The Making of Manchester Jewry, 1740–1875*, New York, 1976.
Williams, Raymond, *Problems in Materialism and Culture: Selected Essays*, London, 1980.
Winch, Robert W., *Identification and Its Familial Determinants*, New York, 1962.
Wirth, Louis, *The Ghetto*, Chicago, London, 1969.
Wormann, Curt, 'Kulturelle Probleme und Aufgaben der Juden aus Deutschland in Israel seit 1933', Tramer (ed.), *In zwei Welten*, pp. 280–329.
Zweig, Arnold, *Insulted and Exiled*, London, 1937.
Zweig, Ferdynand, *The Quest for Fellowship*, London, 1965.
Zweig, Ferdynand, *Women's Life and Labour*, London, 1952.
Zweig, Stefan, *The World of Yesterday*, London, 1943.

Index

Academic Assistance Council: see Society for the Protection of Science and Learning
Academics, 2, 77ff, 146, 208, 218
Actors, 104, 152
Ahrendt, H., 24, 26
Altenhofer, N., 44
Antisemites, 10, 17, 45, 65, 72, 141, 186
Antisemitism, 24, 25, 26, 27, 28, 29, 30, 38, 47, 48, 50, 53, 60, 61, 62ff, 67ff, 80, 88, 128, 138, 140, 141, 144, 149, 155, 157, 160, 161, 183ff, 190, 193, 195, 210, 235, 244; see also *Antisemites Racism*
Aronsfeld, C. C., 166, 171, 189, 190
Artists, 92ff, 157, 218
Assimilation, 1, 5, 6, 11f, 15, 19f, 21, 22, 23, 25, 26, 31, 32, 34, 35, 36, 38, 39, 40, 41, 45, 55, 58, 83, 98, 101, 134, 137, 145, 146, 147, 148f, 174, 177, 222, 250, 251, 253; see also *Assimilationism*
Assimilationism, 30, 32, 34, 36, 37, 38, 50, 168, 176, 232
Association of Jewish Refugees in Great Britain, 2, 126, 140, 143, 147, 156ff
Association of Jewish Refugee Doctors, 156
Aufbau, 158f.
Austria, 64, 74, 175, 152f, 155, 158, 202, 207
Austrian Centre, 154

Baeck, L., 51, 164, 170
Barth, F., 13, 14
Bavaria, 61
Bentwich, N., 92
Berger, P., 14
Bergner, E., 104

Berlin, 55, 56, 61, 63, 64, 67, 74, 79, 80, 92, 93, 101, 169, 185, 197, 199, 203, 210, 242
Bermant, Ch., 171, 185, 186
Berstl, J., 96f.
Bienenfeld, F. R., 155f
Bing, R., 103
Black immigrants, 187ff
Bloch, M., 95
B'nai B'rith Lodge, 51, 169ff
Bonn, M., 82, 138
Born, M., 47, 82
Breslau, 55, 64, 87
Britain: German–Jewish attitudes towards, 85, 92ff, 97, 100ff, 128, 134, 142f, 148, 154, 155, 173ff, 186, 205, 243f; Jews in, 30, 53, 54, 167, 185, 189, 245
British Medical Association, 83f
Buber, M., 18, 51
Busch, E., 103

Catholics, 28, 46, 64, 184
Central Europe, 1, 18
Chemnitz, 55
Childhood, 99, 135ff, 174, 200ff
Children's Transports, 104, 113ff, 123, 124, 132
Club, 43, 151, 153f
Cohen, H., 43, 45
Cohn, E. J., 87
Communists, 46, 124, 150, 151, 152, 153, 154
Concentration Camps, 72, 88, 124, 130, 131, 133, 142, 170, 209
Conversion, 17, 23, 31, 38, 50
Czechoslovakia, 75, 76

Danzig, 56

Index

Depressed Areas, 106, 107, 110
Deutscher, I., 18
Discrimination, 10, 139, 141, 149, 157, 252
Domestic help, 73, 116, 117, 118f, 115, 116, 117, 118f, 124, 125, 136, 143, 232
Dreyfus affair, 28
Dubnow, S., 32

Eastern Europe, 18, 29, 59
Eating habits, 191, 201, 204, 226f, 230f, 240
Einstein, A., 150
Emancipation: Jewish, 21, 22, 24, 25, 26, 27, 33, 34, 36, 38, 49, 251
Emigration, 48, 55, 57, 59, 63, 66, 67, 73ff, 121ff, 125, 126, 128, 129, 130, 131, 133, 134, 135, 136f, 138, 145, 149, 155, 157, 163, 202
Employment situation, 77, 78, 83ff, 91, 92, 103f, 106ff, 110, 112, 118, 119, 121, 126, 139, 155, 157
Enemy aliens, 139, 144, 145f, 153, 159
English relations, 89, 93, 107, 116ff
Enlightenment, 39, 43
Epstein, A. L., 13, 17
Ethnic culture, see *Ethnicity*
Ethnic group, 1, 2, 5, 12f, 14, 16, 19, 29, 36, 38, 42, 47, 54, 87, 91, 101, 112, 121, 134, 146, 147, 156, 159, 161, 165, 176, 177, 178, 187, 218, 244, 249, 250, 252
Ethnic identity, 13, 16, 18f, 37, 42, 45, 47, 52, 100, 216ff, 221ff, 231, 243ff, 249, 251
Ethnic minority, see *Ethnic group*
Ethnicity, 1, 5, 6, 12ff, 18ff, 36, 45, 54, 223ff, 251f; German–Jewish, 40, 87, 100, 108, 118, 127, 144, 146, 148f, 162f, 164, 166f, 168f, 171, 178ff, 204f, 217, 225ff, 233, 236, 252
Expressionism, 95

Fascism, 28, 150, 155
Feuchtwanger, L., 148, 150
Figes, E., 99, 139, 145
First generation, 3, 52, 59, 61, 62, 64, 66, 123, 133ff, 146f, 174f, 181, 190f, 196f, 199, 202, 204, 207, 211f, 217f, 226f, 240

Four and Twenty Sheep, 151f, 153
Fraenkel, H., 133, 198f
France, 21, 30, 34, 53, 76, 93, 94, 96, 102, 154
Free Austrian Movement, 153, 154, 155
Free German League of Culture (FDKB), 150f, 153, 154
Free Masons, 213, 214
Friendship Club (AJR), 146, 167
Friendship patterns, 58ff, 65, 67, 134, 137, 167, 175, 181, 204, 209, 211, 222, 237, 245, 248
Frischauer, W., 128

Gaertner, H., 53
Gay, P., 27, 29, 42, 44f
German culture, 21, 41, 80f, 95, 97, 102, 134, 145, 147ff, 149, 150, 154, 158f, 163, 207, 216f, 225, 240
German–Jewish Aid Committee, 141, 145, 156
Germanophobia, 139, 145, 149
Germans: non-Jewish, 4, 28, 37, 40, 42, 69ff
Germany: Jewish attitudes towards, 4, 25, 40, 132ff, 147, 151, 154, 179, 189ff, 220f, 235ff; Jews in, 22, 24, 27, 28, 30, 34, 37, 39, 41, 42, 45, 46, 47, 49, 58, 62ff, 72, 107, 119, 127, 135f, 143, 149, 160f, 162, 167, 175, 185, 186, 193, 195; return to, 72, 85f, 90, 91, 93, 99, 105, 122, 123ff, 132, 152, 160f, 174, 199, 208, 209f, 229, 236
Gershon, K., 114
Glazer, N., 12
Glyndebourne Opera, 103
Goethe, J. W. v., 29, 39, 148
Goldschmidt, H. L., 40
Gotfurt, F., 151
Graupe, H. M., 31, 42f
Group of Independent German Authors, 151

Hamburg, 61, 70, 185, 203
Hannam, Ch., 56
Heartfield, J., 151
Hegel, G. W. F., 83
Heidegger, M., 83
Heine, H., 24, 31, 165

Index

Hiller, K., 151
Hirsch, S. R., 40
Hitler, A., 28, 45, 61, 70, 75, 78, 79, 85, 137, 138, 152, 193, 239
Horkheimer, M., 40
Housing, 127, 157, 218
Hughes, St., 82f.
Humanism, 39, 42
Husserl, E., 83
Hyphen, The, 164ff

Identity, 14, 37, 40, 48, 52, 149, 165, 173, 181ff, 190, 204
Immigration policies, 76f, 104, 108, 110, 113, 118, 125
Industrialization, 15
Integration, 23, 25, 35, 40, 47, 83, 146, 165, 171, 250
Intermarriage, 32, 61, 65, 98, 124, 181, 205, 249
Internment, see *Enemy aliens*
Israel, see *Palestine*
Italy, 21, 76

Jacob-Ehrlich-Society, 154ff
Jewishness, 30, 32, 33, 34, 37, 38, 39, 50, 54, 56, 57, 59, 95, 149, 158, 169, 173, 176, 216ff, 252
Jewish Restitution Successor Organization, 162
Jews: 9, 11, 21, 40; Eastern European, 34, 37, 41, 53, 54, 55, 56, 59, 109, 127, 164, 187f, 189, 248; English, 34, 114, 141, 154, 155, 156, 161, 162, 168ff, 178, 189, 231ff, 242, 246ff, 271n; relation with non-Jews, 28, 30, 32, 34, 35, 38, 39, 47, 51, 58, 59, 60, 61, 65ff, 71, 81, 90, 107, 137, 139, 141, 144, 145, 146, 161, 192, 244f
Journalists, 101, 119, 209
Judaism, 17, 18, 23, 24, 30, 31, 32, 33, 35, 37, 38, 39, 40, 43, 45, 50, 51ff, 55, 59, 63, 109, 157, 167f, 169, 217, 220, 233, 245, 246ff, 251 also *Religion*
Jüdischer Kulturbund, 52

Kant, I., 29, 40, 42, 43f
Katz, J., 34, 41, 42
Kerr, A., 101f, 138, 150

Kerr, J., 98f, 101f
Klemperer, O., 106
Kochan, L., 169
Koestler, A., 97
Kokoschka, O., 150
Kokotek, Rabbi, 167, 168, 169
Kortner, F., 105f
Krebs, H., 143f, 144
Kristallnacht, 66, 69, 72ff, 75, 77, 130, 160

Landauer, G., 44
Lang, F., 104
Language, 81f, 85, 92, 96, 97ff, 102, 105, 108, 134f, 137, 145, 147f, 150, 151, 153, 154, 155, 158f, 169, 171, 182f, 192, 204, 205, 210, 223ff, 235, 240f, 243
Laqueur, W., 27, 28
Larsen, E., 151
Lasker-Schüler, E., 44f
Laterndl, 152
Lazarus, M., 43
Legal professions, German–Jewish refugees in, 80, 87ff, 150
Leipzig, 55, 64, 109
Leo Baeck Institutes, 164
Leo Baeck Lodge, 2, 169ff
Lepmann, J., 208f
Lessing, G. E., 39
Lorre, P., 104
Lowenthal, E., 156

Mann, H. and Th., 56, 150
Mannheim, K., 81
Mayer, G., 39, 174
Medical professions, German–Jewish refugees in, 83ff
Melting pot, 11f
Mosse, G., 29
Moynihan, D. P., 12
Murray, G., 150
Musicians, 103ff

National Front, 185, 187, 188
Nationalism, 33, 36, 57, 219
Naturalization, 87
Nazism, 1, 4, 5, 17, 26, 27, 47, 48, 50ff, 58, 63ff, 79, 88, 92, 104, 128, 138, 139,

Index

151, 152, 153, 160, 173, 192, 193, 194, 198, 207, 219, 237, 238, 239
Netherlands, 75
Neumann, F., 122
New Liberal Jewish Congregation, 167ff
Nicolson, H., 93f
Nürnberg Racial Laws (1935), 58

O'Casey, Sean, 150

Palestine, 75, 90, 118, 122, 124, 141, 142, 158, 160, 161, 162, 163, 171, 209, 219, 236, 245
Palmer, L., 104
Panofsky, E., 81
Perception, 13, 16f, 20, 25, 38, 44, 45, 72, 243, 251f
Persecution, 17, 18, 25, 129, 131, 133, 137, 138, 144, 145, 202
Philosemitism, 10, 195
Pioneer Corps, 111, 155
Poland, 28, 55
Popper, K., 80f
Posen (Poznan), 55, 56, 59
Priestley, J. B., 150
Prussia, 55, 56

Race, 9ff, 19, 30
Racism, 17, 26, 28, 103, 140f, 184ff, 189, 206
Rathenau, W., 24, 64
Refugee Liaison Group, 156
Reichmann, E., 27, 47, 49, 55, 70, 245
Reissner, H., 177
Religion, 18, 23, 30ff, 37ff, 43, 45, 52, 109, 167f, 233
Restitution, 89, 90, 112, 127, 158, 207f
Riesser, G., 37
Rosenstock, W., 75
Rosenzweig, F., 51
Ruppin, A., 61
Russia, 28, 102, 154

Schacht, H., 71
Scheler, M., 16
Schiller, F., 29, 39, 41f, 151

Scholem, G., 25, 31, 32, 38
Second generation, 3, 52, 61, 62, 66, 94ff, 98, 123, 133ff, 148, 165, 168f, 175, 181, 190f, 195f, 201ff, 204, 210, 227ff, 234
Seghers, A., 150
Self-hatred, 24, 40, 57, 72, 217, 221
Sherman, A., 76
Silesia, 55
Sinzheimer, A., 100
Social Democrats, 28, 46, 70
Society for the Protection of Science and Learning, 78
Stein, F., 40
Stern, K., 58, 98
Switzerland, 76, 88

Tergit, G., 146
Thank-you Britain Fund, 142f, 144
Theodor-Herzl-Society, 156
Third generation, 3, 234ff
Thompson, E. P., 26
Thorndike, Sybille, 150
Trades Advisory Council, 140f
Translators, 101, 105
Traumato, 67, 68, 84, 90, 109, 114, 123, 124, 126, 129ff, 136f, 138, 145, 150, 200, 202

Uhlmann, F., 150, 151, 200
United States of America, 1, 11, 15, 17, 18, 19, 53, 54, 61, 75, 78, 82f, 101, 102, 105, 110, 113, 117, 122, 123, 124f, 145, 158f, 169, 171, 202

Varnhagen, R., 24
Vienna, 69, 74, 152, 155, 201, 207, 210
Viertel, B., 150

Walter, B., 106
Wassermann, J., 48
Weber, M., 39
Weininger, O., 24
Weltsch, R., 57
Wertheimer, J., 54, 55, 189
Wiener, M., 40

Willett, J., 97, 102
Work ethic, see *Ethnicity, German–Jewish*
World Union of Jewish Students, 160
Writers, 96ff

Xenophobia, see *Germanophobia, Racism*

Yiddish, 42, 54

Zeitspiegel, Der, 153
Zionism, 40, 50, 53, 54, 57, 219f; see also *Nationalism*
Zweig, St., 128f, 138, 150